Creole New Orleans

Creole New Orleans

Race and Americanization

EDITED BY
Arnold R. Hirsch and Joseph Logsdon

Louisiana State University Press
Baton Rouge and London

Louisiana Paperback Edition, 1992
01 00 99 98 97   5 4

Designer: Laura Roubique Gleason
Typeface: Sabon
Typesetter: G & S Typesetters, Inc.

Library of Congress Cataloging-in-Publication Data

Creole New Orleans : race and Americanization / edited by Arnold R.
   Hirsch and Joseph Logsdon.
     p.   cm.
   Includes bibliographical references and index.
   ISBN 0-8071-1708-0 (cloth : permanent paper)
   ISBN 0-8071-1774-9 (pbk. : permanent paper)
     1. Creoles—Louisiana—New Orleans.   2. Afro-Americans—Louisiana—
New Orleans.   3. New Orleans (La.)—Race relations.   I. Hirsch,
Arnold R. (Arnold Richard), 1949–   . II. Logsdon, Joseph.
F379.N59C87   1992
305.8'009763'35—dc20   91-38863
                                                                CIP

The editors are grateful to the editor of *Amerikastudien/American Studies* for
permission to use material from Joseph Logsdon's essay "Americans and Creoles: The
Origins of Black Citizenship in the United States," which appeared in Volume XXXIV
(1989), 187–202.

The map of early French Louisiana in the Introduction to Part I, the maps in Chapter 3,
and the figures in Chapters 2 and 3 are by John I. Snead.

To John Hope Franklin
and Gilbert Osofsky
mentors and friends

Contents

Preface

This work is about the evolution of race relations in a very peculiar city of the United States. Neither of us, the editors of this book, felt prepared by our training or experience to comprehend the unusual patterns we encountered in New Orleans when we first came to the city, and we found no easy way to learn. We were natives of Chicago and initially trained to study that midwestern metropolis. Few of the nation's urban experts, we discovered, had ever tried to place New Orleans within the framework of existing scholarship about American cities. Fortunately, a few notable students of African-American history, particularly John Blassingame, had already taken up the subject in New Orleans and provided some guidance.[1] But no one has significantly extended the scope of his work beyond the two decades, 1860–1880, which he chose to explore.

Since the early twentieth century, when they began studying the modern city, urban specialists have turned to such cities as Chicago, New York, and Boston for their models for measuring social trends or discerning reality in urban America. For the most part, the founders of urban studies were correct in this approach. Urban America as they knew it had been concentrated in a great manufacturing belt that ran from northeastern coastal cities to the midwestern railroad terminals of Chicago, St. Louis, Minneapolis, and Milwaukee. It was no coincidence that in 1890 all but two of the fifteen largest cities lay within that heartland of urban industrial America.[2] As the dominant centers of this vast

1. The only urban biography of New Orleans was published in the 1920s by a former editor of the New Orleans *Times-Picayune:* John S. Kendall, *History of New Orleans* (3 vols.; Chicago, 1922). In addition to John Blassingame's classic work *Black New Orleans, 1860–1880* (Chicago, 1973), see Richard C. Wade, *Slavery in the Cities: The South, 1820–1860* (New York, 1964); Ira Berlin, *Slaves Without Masters: The Free Negro in the Antebellum South* (New York, 1974); and Leonard Curry, *The Free Black in Urban America* (Chicago, 1981).

2. *Twelfth Census, 1900,* vol. I, *Population,* pt. 1, lxix.

industrial region, New York and Chicago also became the chief academic laboratories for the investigation of urban life in the United States.

Of the two largest cities outside of America's great central urban industrial belt, New Orleans has been more neglected by academic inquiry than its fellow misfit, San Francisco. Even if far removed from the center of the nation's industrial nexus, San Francisco developed in a way that better matched the normal patterns of urban America. From its position as the primary Pacific entrepôt, San Francisco moved into both manufacturing and finance and simultaneously sent out a railroad network to draw smaller towns into the major east-west trunk lines that connected it directly to the New York–Chicago axis. New Orleans, however, never became a major industrial city.

More recently, some urban historians have begun to probe the development of southern cities. They have broken from the northern industrial model and taken note of postbellum patterns of race relations in the urban South. Most, however, have chosen to ignore New Orleans or to concentrate on the events of the twentieth century. Some have been daunted by the peculiarities of New Orleans, and others have realized that until the late nineteenth century, the American South had few cities of any comparable size to serve as counterparts to the metropolis on the lower Mississippi.[3]

To understand New Orleans and its peculiar patterns of development, it is not enough to take note of the obvious physical and demographic differences between New Orleans and other American cities. Any city in the United States may lay claim to its own distinctive appearance, geographic setting, and population profile. A serious exploration of New Orleans' peculiarities required research that went beyond comparative census returns, its regional location, or the nature of its economy. We recognized the necessity of delving deeply into the long, divergent history of the creole city.

Like the early settlements along Massachusetts Bay and Chesapeake Bay on the Atlantic coast, New Orleans served as a distinctive cultural entrepôt, where peoples from Europe and Africa initially intertwined their lives and customs with those of the native inhabitants of the New

3. For recent works on southern comparative urban history, see Howard N. Rabinowitz, *Race Relations in the Urban South, 1865–1890* (New York, 1978), and Don H. Doyle, *New Men, New Cities, New South: Atlanta, Nashville, Charleston, Mobile, 1860–1910* (Chapel Hill, 1990).

World. The resulting way of life differed dramatically from the culture that was spawned in the English colonies of North America. New Orleans' creole inhabitants ensured not only that English was not the prevailing language but also that Protestantism was scorned, public education unheralded, and democratic government untried.

Relative isolation as well as divergent experience maintained the differences between Anglo-American settlements and New Orleans. From its founding in 1718 until the early nineteenth century, New Orleans remained far removed from the patterns developed in early Massachusetts or Virginia. Established a century after those seminal English colonies, it remained for the next hundred years an outpost of the French and Spanish empires before Napoleon sold it to the United States with the rest of the Louisiana Purchase in 1803.

Despite the long, separate development of New Orleans, historians have seldom given much attention to this distinctive entranceway to the American experience. We believe that one of the contributions of this book will be to bring the colonial history of New Orleans, the subject of Part I, into clearer view for American historians.

We believe that the postcolonial history of the city deserves similar attention. During most of the nineteenth century, New Orleans remained in counterpoint to the rest of urban America. Newcomers from the South as well as the North recoiled when they encountered the prevailing French language of the city, its dominant Catholicism, its bawdy sensual delights, or its proud free black population—in short, its deeply rooted creole traditions.[4] Its incorporation into the United States posed a profound challenge, the infant republic's first attempt to impose its institutions on a foreign city. That encounter with Americanization is the subject of Part II of this book.

Even though it quickly became Dixie's chief cotton and slave market, New Orleans long remained a strange province in the American South.[5] New influxes of nonsouthern population compounded the peculiarity of its creole past. Until the mid-nineteenth century, a greater number of migrants arrived in the new boomtown from northern states such as New York and Pennsylvania than from the old South. And to

4. The word *creole* is used here, and in most places in this collection, in its eighteenth- and early nineteenth-century sense, that is, meaning indigenous to Louisiana or New Orleans. For later meanings, see Part II of this book.

5. Timothy F. Reilly, "Heterodox New Orleans and the Protestant South," *Louisiana Studies*, XII (Spring, 1973), 533–51.

complicate its social makeup further, more European immigrants than American migrants took up residence in the city before the Civil War.

Such peculiar social and cultural developments make New Orleans a very revealing case study in exploring the ethnic and racial history of the United States. We felt that the most fruitful use of New Orleans as an American counterpoint fell in the area of race relations, the theme of the entire book but the special focus of Part III. We borrowed our conception of historical counterpoint from C. Vann Woodward, who has so often demonstrated the lessons to be learned about race in the United States by probing places and events ignored by dominant scholarship.

In his collection of essays *American Counterpoint: Slavery and Racism in the North-South Dialogue,* Woodward wrote a piece that helped frame the concluding section of this present work. In "The National Decision Against Equality," Woodward traced the struggle initiated by black New Orleanians to reverse the nation's sanctioning of segregation and white supremacy.[6] We, in turn, have tried to place that famous *Plessy* case within an extended treatment of the black community of New Orleans. We have also tried to place the larger experience not so much in a counterpoint, as Woodward had, between the North and South, but rather in a counterpoint between the Franco-African protest tradition of New Orleans and the tragic racial mind-set of Anglo-America.

Historical counterpoint was more the result than the goal of this book. We originally began collecting these essays primarily in hope of gaining a greater understanding about race relations and ethnicity in New Orleans. From the start, we realized that the essays would not tell all one would wish to know about New Orleans. We never expected this collection to be a comprehensive or definitive study of the city. We feel confident, however, that the work of our contributors will help to broaden and revise the history of New Orleans and encourage further scholarly study of the city. Indeed, several of our contributors are already working on more extensive monographs that will flesh out the frameworks fashioned here. We are especially pleased by that result, for New Orleans deserves a better fate than to be relegated to the fringes of American historical awareness.

The intellectual debts that we incurred in assembling this collection of essays about New Orleans are difficult to account and impossible to

6. C. Vann Woodward, *American Counterpoint: Slavery and Racism in the North-South Dialogue* (Boston, 1971), 212–33.

repay. Acknowledgment and thanks are never enough. Both of us have been deeply influenced by the scholarship of John Hope Franklin and Gilbert Osofsky, to whom we have dedicated this book. But neither of us was prepared by our training or experience to comprehend either the city's unusual race relations or its peculiar urban culture.

Before we recognized our common search for understanding and decided upon collaboration in the present project, each of us had called upon our students and colleagues at the University of New Orleans for help. Some of our colleagues, particularly Jerah Johnson, Joseph Tregle, and the now deceased Marcus Christian, had already preceded us in serious study of New Orleans. We have drawn upon their determination to raise new questions. And we learned from them the need to approach the history of the city through the traditions and languages of other cultures. Anglo-American historiography has seldom provided either the tools or the historical perspective to understand New Orleans and south Louisiana. Our pioneering colleagues urged us to draw instead upon scholars who had been trained in French or Caribbean history to discern more about the city's past. These suggestions have added immeasurably to the value of these essays. Most of all we wish to thank the contributors, who responded to our call to produce original essays either by extending their earlier work or by embarking upon a new field of inquiry about New Orleans.

PART I

The French and African Founders

Introduction

The writings of Alexis de Tocqueville provide a good starting point for an explanation of the unusual origins of New Orleans as an American political and cultural entrepôt. When young Tocqueville embarked for the New World in 1831, he had surprisingly few preconceived ideas about what he would see and only a vague notion about what he would report of the United States. One of the many remarkable attributes of the twenty-five-year-old adventurer was that, in addition to writing down his observations carefully in notebooks and letters, he also—almost unconsciously—noted the step-by-step formation of the intellectual conceptions that would make his *Democracy in America*, published four years later, one of the most perceptive analyses of early America ever written.[1]

Like most European visitors of that time, Tocqueville landed in New York City, but after spending six weeks there, he set out with his traveling companion, another French nobleman named Gustave de Beaumont, to seek out some American Indians. His first sight of Indians, however, shocked Tocqueville. The remnants of the once proud Iroquois, lining up at Albany to receive payment for lands they had ceded to the United States, discorded violently with his romantic conceptions about idyllic "noble savages." It set him thinking. Surely, he reasoned,

---

1. *Democracy in America* should be read in its full form rather than in one of the many abridged versions. The best is the Knopf edition, translated by Henry Reeve, revised by Francis Bowen, and edited by Phillips Bradley (2 vols.; New York, 1945). Also see Tocqueville's notebooks, translated by George Lawrence, edited by J. P. Mayer, and published under the title *Journey to America* (New Haven, 1960), and the superb reconstruction of Tocqueville's American journey by George W. Pierson, *Tocqueville and Beaumont in America* (New York, 1938). Dudley C. Lunt published a useful if somewhat abridged version of the latter under the title *Tocqueville in America* (New York, 1959). Pierson's work is particularly useful because he draws from a wide variety of unpublished Tocqueville writings, especially his letters.

these poor creatures in upstate New York were a uniquely sad lot, degraded by the European world that had enveloped them; if he went further west, he would find Indians in their natural environment just as he had always imagined them.

The two Frenchmen took a steamboat across Lake Erie to the Michigan Territory. In Detroit, Tocqueville's awareness that he was at the very rim of European civilization, among Indians, woodsmen, and "half-breeds," tantalized him. He was standing on the site of an old French outpost in the huge North American empire that France had lost to England about sixty years earlier. That the Indians still spoke of the French fondly and of the English fearfully set him to thinking about the heritage of his own people in North America.

This question led to another detour in his travels. Rather than return to New York as they had originally planned, the two curious Frenchmen took another boat through the Great Lakes waterways into eastern Canada. There two observations struck Tocqueville with great force. The first was the size and strength of the French presence in the area. Instead of the sixty thousand or so French-speakers whom he expected to find widely dispersed and thoroughly assimilated into the English-speaking regime, he was stunned to discover more than six hundred thousand French Canadians, tightly grouped, fiercely proud of their French heritage, and in every way "as French as any Frenchman living on the Seine."

He also noted a deep cleavage between them and the English, which made him conclude that the two cultures would not be integrated in the foreseeable future. A second observation struck Tocqueville with almost equal force: in Canada the Indians had not been pushed westward so relentlessly as in the United States; instead, great numbers still lived in eastern Canada, in a mixed settlement pattern, among the Europeans.[2]

As he made his way through New England after returning to the United States, Tocqueville reflected on what he had seen in Canada. While in Boston, he set down some of his first organized thoughts, which would later form the matrix of his great book. His reflections on the terrible plight suffered by Indian populations at the hands of the Anglo-Americans later found their place in a remarkable chapter on the Indians in *Democracy in America*. Tocqueville either chose not to in-

2. See particularly the chapter "Lower Canada: A Lost Empire?" in Pierson, *Tocqueville and Beaumont,* 314–45.

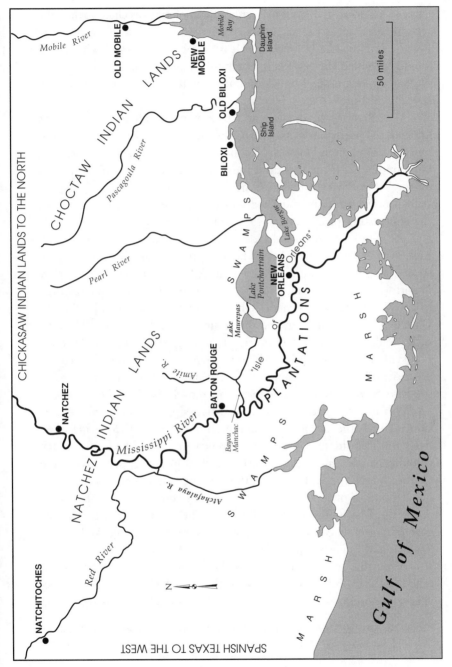

Early French Louisiana

clude in his book or abandoned without completing his chain of thought several other ideas or fragments of ideas that he first noted down in Boston. Among the latter was at least some awareness of what today would be called the problems of ethnically pluralistic societies. Those ideas are perceptible, if only in adumbrated form, scattered through his subsequent notebooks and letters.

From Boston, Tocqueville and Beaumont set off to see America's Old South, particularly its tidewater cities. When they reached Baltimore after a stop in Philadelphia, they encountered black Americans in large numbers for the first time and came face-to-face with another set of Anglo-America's racial attitudes.[3] In part because his experiences with American racism and slavery made Tocqueville think more about the contrasting race relations that he had observed in French Canada and the United States, he decided that he had to see the Mississippi River and New Orleans. Again, he abruptly changed his itinerary. Instead of continuing southward along the Atlantic seaboard, the travelers undertook, in the dead of winter, a grueling overland trek to Pittsburgh to catch a riverboat down the Ohio to reach the Mississippi. But the Ohio began to freeze over, and they found themselves stranded in Kentucky and obliged to travel overland by stagecoach and foot through Louisville and Nashville to Memphis, where they finally reached the great river. Luckily they caught one of the last boats of the season going south to New Orleans, where they landed on New Year's Day, 1832.

With his voyage down the lower Mississippi and his earlier excursion through the Great Lakes and eastern Canada, Tocqueville effectively retraced the span of the vast "French Arch" that had run through colonial North America. The arch stretched in a huge semicircle from Quebec, along the St. Lawrence, through the Great Lakes and the various tributaries of the Ohio, Illinois, and Wisconsin river systems, then down the Mississippi to New Orleans. The outposts along this arch gave France early control of the continent's interior and blocked further Spanish and English expansion.

During his trek through North America—roundabout because it followed the evolution of his thinking about the United States—Tocqueville continued to compare French and English culture. His sojourn in

3. Tocqueville, *Journey to America*, 101–103; Pierson, *Tocqueville and Beaumont*, 625; and Tocqueville, *Democracy in America*, vol. I, chap. 18, "The Three Races that Inhabit . . . the United States," 331–434 of the Knopf edition.

New Orleans encouraged such speculation. His notebooks show that he asked exactly the same questions of New Orleanians that he had asked of Canadians. But he got very different answers. Only twenty-eight years after the end of French rule, instead of the two implacable rivals he had noted in Canada, the same two nationalities in New Orleans appeared to interact more easily, not just with each other but also with numerous smaller ethnic groups.[4]

When Tocqueville observed that "they say that in New Orleans is to be found a mixture of all the nations," his informant, the lawyer Etienne Mazureau, commented: "That is true; you see here a mingling of all races. Not a country in America or Europe but has sent us some representatives. New Orleans is a patch-work of peoples." Tocqueville then probed more deeply: "But in the midst of this confusion what race dominates and gives direction to all the rest?" Mazureau answered: "The French race up to now. It is they who set the tone and shape the *moeurs*."[5] In a conversation with another compatriot, J. F. A. Guillemin, the French consul stationed in New Orleans, Tocqueville got almost the same response about the persistence of French influence in shaping the city's "*moeurs*, customs and habits." When Tocqueville asked about the relationship between the French and Americans in New Orleans, the consul explained that "the French here are not, as in Canada, a vanquished people. On the contrary, they live on a basis of real and complete equality." The French and Americans may, he noted, "criticize each other mutually . . . but at the bottom there is no real enmity."[6]

Behind Tocqueville's inquiries lurked a larger question: What accounted for the markedly different outcomes of the French experience in Canada and in Louisiana? He never found an answer to that question. It was not pertinent to his central subject, the U.S. republic and the inner workings of its civilization.

Tocqueville's unanswered question, however, formed the point of

4. In Pierson, *Tocqueville and Beaumont,* compare pages 314–45 and 619–34; and in Tocqueville, *Journey to America* [the notebooks], compare pages 35–47, 123–24, 136–48, 184–208, 235–36, 240–44, 328–32, 347–74 with pages 71–72, 101–107, 117, 164–65, 178, 236, 240, 378–83.

5. Tocqueville, *Journey to America,* 101–107, 164, 171–73, 383–84. See also Pierson, *Tocqueville and Beaumont,* 625–28.

6. Tocqueville, *Journey to America,* 103–106, 380–83; Pierson, *Tocqueville and Beaumont,* 622–25, 630–32.

A detail from a representation of the plan of New Orleans as it existed around the time of the Louisiana Purchase, with a sketch of the Place d'Armes (now Jackson Square) inset. The growing American suburb of Faubourg Ste. Marie, completed in the 1790s, sits just upriver from the city proper.

departure for Jerah Johnson's analysis of colonial New Orleans, which opens Part I of this collection. Tocqueville used the variant experiences of his French compatriots in Canada and in Louisiana to raise questions relative to his central subject, democracy in America. In his book, he traced many of the origins of the American character through the New England and Chesapeake Bay colonies to the British homeland. American historians had already begun that inquiry and shared their ideas and literature with Tocqueville. But no similar inquiry or literature existed then, or later, for early Louisiana. Jerah Johnson's work is one of the first attempts to explore, in depth, the motives and objectives of the French founders of Louisiana. Much as Tocqueville did, the more Johnson delved into New Orleans' colonial experience, the more he became convinced that differences between the Indian policy of the French and that of the English and Americans furnished an all-important clue to explaining the situation in New Orleans.

Johnson's essay, "Colonial New Orleans: A Fragment of the Eighteenth-Century French Ethos," sets the development in early New Orleans both within the context of the Canadian colonial experience, through which the New Orleans experience was filtered, and within the peculiarly French eighteenth-century ideal of a racially and ethnically assimilated society. In addition to the Canadians, French, Indians, Germans, and Spaniards who made up most of colonial New Orleans' free population, Johnson treats the formation of the city's free black community. In the nineteenth century that group would become the largest concentration of free people of color anywhere in the deep South. And in the twentieth century their descendants would preserve more of the ideal of interracial fraternity than any other group in the city or in the South.

Again, Tocqueville's observations form Johnson's point of departure. Although Tocqueville, and especially his traveling companion Beaumont, found slavery as ruthless in the remnants of French Louisiana as in the Anglo-American South, they also noted the remarkable status and achievements of free black New Orleanians. Like other observers, they recognized that that group's often light complexions denoted intimate contact with Europeans. But the dignified and respectable demeanor of the French-speaking free black population clashed dramatically with the status that both the French and the Anglo-Americans appeared willing to accord them. Both Tocqueville and Beaumont asked their white French-speaking hosts whether they were willing to grant equality to the free blacks. The firm negative replies led Tocqueville to warn them, prophetically: "Then I much fear that they will one day make themselves your ministers."[7]

Most Tocqueville scholars have overlooked the centrality of race in his reflections about American civilization. The division of labor between Tocqueville and Beaumont helped to obscure the full impact that their encounter with racial oppression in America made on both of them. Beaumont took greater note than Tocqueville of the plight of African-Americans because the collaborators decided to divide the report of their observations and judgments. Tocqueville concentrated on democratic institutions and Beaumont on social customs and race relations. The different forms their reports took also resulted in their reaching different audiences.

Beaumont incorporated his views in a curious work, half novel and half sociological treatise, which he published in 1835: *Marie; or, Slavery in the United States.*[8] Beaumont's novel broke new ground in French fiction by focusing on free blacks rather than slaves to expose the depths of racism in American society.

The plight of free blacks in New Orleans and elsewhere in the United States convinced both Tocqueville and Beaumont that emancipation alone would not end racial discrimination. Indeed, burdened by the specter of racism and slavery, Tocqueville and Beaumont, when they returned home, immediately began to promote the French emancipation movement, which reached fruition sixteen years later in the Revolution of 1848. Not only did they appear in the front rank of French abolitionists, but they sought full civil equality for all persons of African ancestry in French territory.[9] As the later essays in this book will make clear, the 1848 French emancipation and enfranchisement program became the enduring model for black creoles in New Orleans.

Gwendolyn Midlo Hall's essay, "The Formation of Afro-Creole Culture," offers a new approach to the early history of Africans in colonial Louisiana. Her ground-breaking work helps explain the origins of the

7. Tocqueville, *Journey to America*, 380.
8. Gustave de Beaumont, *Marie; or, Slavery in the United States*, trans. Barbara Chapman (Stanford, 1958). In addition to the novel, the work contained twelve long appendixes. See particularly the first, "A Note on the Social and Political Condition of the Negro Slaves and of Free People of Color," 189–216.
9. The role of Tocqueville and Beaumont in the French emancipation movement has not been fully treated in any of the many studies about them. For the best treatment in English see Shelby T. McCoy's *The Negro in France* (Lexington, Ky., 1961), 145–58, and his *Negro in the French West Indies* (Lexington, Ky., 1966), 141–59.

unusually accomplished free black community that Tocqueville and Beaumont encountered during their visit to New Orleans. In hitherto unused archival materials in Louisiana and in France, Hall uncovered a series of remarkable facts. She discovered that virtually all slaves brought to Louisiana during the French colonial period came in the twelve years between 1719 and 1731. From the latter date to the end of the French period in the mid-1760s only three hundred or so additional slaves arrived. Moreover, the overwhelming number of slaves in French colonial Louisiana came from a single region of Africa, the Senegal River basin, and brought with them an already formed Bambara culture, a happenstance unique in the annals of New World slavery. Hall also shows how the remarkably cohesive and assertive Africans intertwined themselves with local Indian populations and shaped the habits of both Europeans and the later-arriving non-Bambara slaves.

The essays by Johnson and Hall explain the New Orleans creolization process, that is, the formation, during the colonial period, of the curiously blended Franco-African host culture of the city. Further, they show how that colonial—creole—culture, once formed, was able to resist the attempt of a small Spanish officialdom to make the colony conform to Iberian norms during the forty years Spain held Louisiana. Until the early nineteenth century, New Orleans continued to develop along its French and African creole lines.

These two essays, forming Part I of this collection, thus set the stage for discussion of the immense wave of Anglo-American immigrants that flooded into Louisiana after the 1803 purchase and challenged the very existence of the area's French and African creole culture.

1

Colonial New Orleans: A Fragment of the Eighteenth-Century French Ethos

JERAH JOHNSON

Before Herbert Osgood, George Louis Beer, Charles McLean Andrews, and the other founders of the imperial school began writing around 1900, historians had treated England's thirteen American colonies virtually in isolation, with little or no reference to the British social, intellectual, and imperial complex that was their origin. More recent historians have largely corrected that fault. Historians of France's Louisiana colony, however, have been a long time catching up. Most of them, trained in U.S. or in Latin American history and lacking proficiency in both French language and history, have tended to analyze Louisiana's colonial period either in Anglo-American or Spanish imperial terms. The assumptions and conceptual frameworks they often have applied in their studies have served to obstruct and often to distort their understanding of the area's early and subsequent development. The result has been that all too many such historians have seen Louisiana and New Orleans only as a moral contrast to Anglo-America or have dwelled on Spanish colonial administrative structure and policy.

If, however, one views early Louisiana, and particularly New Orleans, in French colonial terms, as a fragment of the eighteenth-century French ethos, many aspects of its early and later social and ethnic history fall into place.[1] And it follows that central to an understanding of

1. Louis Hartz's brilliant collection of essays *The Founding of New Societies* (New York, 1964) suggested the conceptual framework employed here: a colonial society viewed as a "fragment," *i.e.*, a cross section, of the mother country's society cut out of the

colonial New Orleans is a basic understanding of early modern French social structure and social theory, as well as some appreciation of the adjustments the French had to make when they sought to replicate them in Canada and, a century later, in Louisiana.

When one examines developments in early Louisiana, it must ever be borne in mind that until the very end of the eighteenth century, French society differed fundamentally from England's. Its structure was anything but monolithic. Alexis de Tocqueville in his *Old Regime and the French Revolution*—almost as masterful an analysis of his own country as his *Democracy in America* was of the United States—compared eighteenth-century French society to "those substances . . . in which modern scientists find more and more separate particles." And Alfred Cobban, a recognized authority on the subject, has confirmed Tocqueville's characterization, styling French society of the time "a sum of disunities."[2]

The five-part division of Old Regime society commonly made by historians—old nobility, new nobility, clergy, bourgeoisie, and peasants—is hardly less misleading than the old legal division into the first, second, and third estates. None of these groups functioned as a coherent unit, and each had multiple subdivisions. At least nine major divisions, not counting local and minor ones, have been traced, for example, in the nobility alone. The distinction within the old nobility between court nobles and provincial nobles only begins to tell the story. Similarly, within the new nobility each echelon of officialdom in each locality effectively constituted a separate group, the ministerial families, the intendants, and the members of the parliaments being simply the ones most often mentioned. And though clerics holding high ecclesiastical offices functioned virtually as independent entities each unto himself, the lower clergy, holding variously if minimally endowed curateships and vicarates, tended often to band together locally to protect, defend, and further their common interests.

The third estate encompassed equally numerous and diverse social

---

continuum of its history at a particular point and transplanted overseas, where it grew to maturity, replicating many of the social and attitudinal patterns characteristic of the mother country at the time of the excision.

2. Alexis de Tocqueville, *Old Regime and the French Revolution,* trans. Stuart Gilbert (New York, 1955), 94; Alfred Cobban, "The Decline of Divine-Right Monarchy in France," in *The Old Regime, 1713–63* (Cambridge, Eng., 1957), 236, Vol. VII of *The New Cambridge Modern History,* 14 vols. See also, in the same volume, J. O. Lindsay, "The Social Classes and the Foundations of the States."

groupings. A wealthy group holding titles to municipal offices, mostly hereditary positions, constituted its patriciate. Next came the many guilds and corporations in which membership, also mostly hereditary, ensured special legal standing. Then came the financial class, made up of bankers, financiers, and corporate groups of tax farmers—tax collection supervisors who owned their offices. Lower down the scale various industrial and crafts entrepreneurs, professionals, large and small merchants, and several categories of farm owners and workers found their places individually or in groups. Many if not most towns, cities, provinces, and locales held their own cherished rights and exemptions. Eighteenth-century French society thus contained a multitude of groups, small and large, each functionally a corporate entity with its own particular rights, privileges, prerogatives, duties, obligations, protections, and immunities.[3]

The "disunities," as Cobban called the many corporate groups that made up French society, are easy to grasp. The dynamic of eighteenth-century French society, what Cobban meant by the "sum" of the disunities, is somewhat more difficult to explain. But it is important to understand, for it is what constituted the French social ethos and set it off from that of England. Disunities, remnants of medievalism, plagued early modern European states generally. Individuals moved with a high degree of freedom and security within their corporate group, protected by its rights, but the groups themselves were often at odds with one another. Rivalry, competition, envy, even enmity, were inherent. How to unify the disunities remained a cardinal problem from the Renaissance on, and state builders in different places found different answers.

The English solution, broadly speaking, took the form of imposing norms and forcing conformity to them. The religious settlement was a prime example. Over the course of the sixteenth century, England underwent Protestant reform and its attendant upheavals and achieved a certain repose under the Elizabethan religious compromise. That settle-

3. An astonishingly large volume of work has been done on Old Regime society. The standard work remains Philippe Sagnac, *La Formation de la société française moderne* (Paris, 1945). The finest more recent comprehensive work is Pierre Goubert, *L'Ancien régime* (2 vols.; Paris, 1969–73). Particularly useful also are Elinor G. Barber, *The Bourgeoisie in Eighteenth-Century France* (Princeton, 1955), which focuses on social mobility under the Old Regime; François Olivier-Martin, *L'Organisation corporative de la France d'ancien régime* (Paris, 1938), on the legal rights of French corporate bodies; and Albert Goodwin, ed., *The European Nobility in the Eighteenth Century* (London, 1953), a comparative study.

ment, although severely tested by the Cromwellian aberration of the seventeenth century, not only survived intact but imposed a high degree of conformity, leaving dissenters little choice but colonial immigration. In France, by contrast, Elizabeth's contemporary, Henry IV, took an entirely different tack. He granted toleration, of a typically French sort, to the nearly 10 percent of his subjects who professed Protestantism. His famous Edict of Nantes, a timely adaptation of the medieval practice of bestowing special rights upon corporate groups within the kingdom, guaranteed religious freedom, the right of public worship, not to every individual Protestant but only to designated Protestant groups in geographical enclaves within the kingdom.

Other aspects of English heterogeneity were similarly allowed to drop into obscurity or simply legislated out of existence. Guilds, for example, despite periodic revivals, steadily decayed in England, as Parliament replaced them with national regulations. In France, by contrast, Louis XIV's finance minister, Jean-Baptiste Colbert, revived guilds and increased their number. At the end of the Middle Ages the city of Poitiers had eighteen guilds, but by the eighteenth century it had forty-two. The English social structure, as a consequence of the impulse to homogenize, had by the eighteenth century become much simpler than that of France. But it had also become what Robert R. Palmer, another modern authority on the period, has called "segregationist."[4]

By *segregationist* Palmer meant that by the eighteenth century, English society had become stratified vertically as well as horizontally. First, the English aristocracy consisted not merely of the two hundred or so title-holding nobles but also their untitled close and distant relatives. Adjacent to the nobles stood another hierarchy of rich shipping magnates, mine owners, manufacturers, country gentlemen, and justices of the peace. In the countryside still another hierarchy, made up of those who worked the land, was stratified into freeholders, copyholders, tenants at will, and landless laborers. In addition, urban centers had parallel hierarchies with attorneys, merchants, bankers, and brewers at the top and physicians, surgeons, and publicists lower down. Finally, there

4. Robert R. Palmer, *The Age of Democratic Revolution* (2 vols.; Princeton, 1959), I, 71–74. See also his chapter "Social and Psychological Foundations of the Revolutionary Era," *The American and French Revolutions, 1763–93* (Cambridge, Eng., 1968), 421–47, vol. VIII of *The New Cambridge Modern History*. David Hackett Fisher, *Albion's Seed: Four British Folkways in America* (New York, 1989), has pointed out the cultural diversity of early modern England. But English society was much less pluralistic than premodern France.

was a hierarchy of clergy who, being noncelibate, inclined to perpetuate family-held posts.

Each of these hierarchies remained largely exclusive of the others— segregated, to use Palmer's word. Englishmen could, through marriage, government service, or the influence of money, move upward within their own hierarchy. But lateral movement, interaction with those in another hierarchy, was severely limited.[5]

In contrast, the assimilationist impulse in France offered far greater freedom for individuals to associate not only with members of their own corporate group but, more important, with members of other groups as well. By the eighteenth century, this freedom had become a fundamental characteristic of French society, constituting the sum of disunities Cobban was talking about.

The presence of that assimilationist tendency was no accident. It had been built into the French national ethos during the seventeenth century by Colbert and Louis XIV. Their social engineering program was part and parcel of French mercantilism, which differed significantly from other national mercantile ideologies and practices. Most English mercantilist theory was written by businessmen, usually retired, whereas virtually all French theory came from the pens of intellectuals who had little or no personal entrepreneurial experience. Consequently, English theory was particularistic and practical, focused largely on specifics such as trade regulations and the accumulation of savings that would ensure profits to individuals and private companies. French mercantilist writers tended to be universalistic and philosophical in outlook. They laid down a program they thought applicable to all men in all times. Its focus was much broader, more inclusive, and far more systematic than the English version. It was not without significance, for example, that English New World explorations and colonies were mostly private ventures funded by trading companies, whereas similar French efforts were funded almost exclusively by the crown as extensions of the national enterprise.

When mercantile theorists and administrators talked of "national"

5. Although eighteenth-century English society has not been systematically analyzed as has been French society of the period, useful works include Lewis B. Namier, *The Structure of Politics at the Accession of George III* (2nd ed.; London, 1957); G. P. Judd, *Members of Parliament, 1734–1832* (New Haven, 1955); Mary D. George, *England in Transition* (London, 1931); Gordon Mingay, *English Landed Society in the Eighteenth Century* (London, 1963), and his *The Gentry* (London, 1976); and W. A. Speck, *Stability and Strife in England, 1714–1760* (Cambridge, Mass., 1977).

enterprises and unification, they meant something entirely different from the ideas of nineteenth- and twentieth-century nationalists. Eli Heckscher put it succinctly when he said that for mercantilists the collective entity was not "a nation unified by common race, speech, and customs" but "the state," which is to say, the crown and the territories and populations it governed. In most cases, early modern states included many varied social and ethnic groupings, with which crown authorities, particularly in France, were willing to "deal tolerantly so long as they did not conflict with the interests of the state."[6]

Heckscher opened his long discussion of mercantilism as a "conception of society" with the observation that mercantilism strongly and consistently advocated societal liberty. Few if any slogans, he pointed out, recurred so frequently in mercantilist writing—particularly in the voluminous correspondence of Colbert—as phrases using the words *liberty* and *freedom*. Usually the words occurred in references to freedom of commerce within a country, for mercantilism was fundamentally an economic theory. But mercantilists, particularly the French writers, also increasingly applied *freedom* and *liberty* to the multiple aspects of society as a whole. Colbert, for example, insisted that the social liberties of local merchants' and craftsmen's groups must be protected as a part of their economic freedom and hence their productivity. He staunchly defended religious freedom for Huguenots as well as Jews because he recognized the economic importance of those groups for France. "Toleration," Heckscher summarized, "was the unanimous demand of all theoretical and practical politicians under mercantilism." The "underlying idea of mercantilism," he concluded, was that "people should be taken as they are" and "guided by wise measures in that direction which will enhance the well-being of the state."[7]

The guiding process in French mercantilism was systematic and assimilationist. Because France retained so many old medieval corporate

---

6. Eli F. Heckscher, *Mercantilism*, trans. Mendel Shapiro, ed. E. F. Soderlund (2 vols.; 2nd rev. ed.; London, 1955), II, 14. This work remains the most nearly comprehensive study of the subject.

7. *Ibid.*, 274, 293, and 303. Heckscher's work should be supplemented with articles by Pierre Goubert, Pierre Chaunu, Jean Meuvret, and Emmanuel Le Roy Ladurie, a select list of which appears in Robert Mandrou, *La France au XVIIe et XVIIIe siècles* (Paris, 1967). The overriding concern for "the interests of the state" along with the fact that the crown funded most French overseas ventures led France to keep a much tighter mercantilist grip on her New World colonies than England did on hers, which were private trading company ventures.

groups, its leaders faced special problems in attempting to reconcile the often inherent conflicts among them and to "harmonize the disunities" that made up French society. When possible, crown authorities met the challenge through centralized, direct control. Colbert's revival and nationalization of the old guild structure exemplified that approach, but he quickly found that he could league together relatively few of France's corporate groups under such centralized direction. And anything like the English approach of establishing norms and imposing conformity was out of the question in a realm as large and diverse as France.

Colbert and Louis XIV took recourse to the ancient Roman model. In its Augustan age the tiny city-state of Rome controlled the world less by military might than by making Rome and things Roman so grand, so attractive, and so easily accessible that subject peoples everywhere, though they retained their individual identities and traditions, including their own legal codes, willingly accepted, indeed vied for, participation in the glory of being Roman as well. Colbert and Louis XIV developed a program to make the glory of France such that no subject or group of subjects could resist its lure.

The cultural program encompassed projects designed to bind the crown's subjects together as a people by providing a public culture they could all share. Most famous were the massive building programs—Versailles was the largest single construction project undertaken in Europe since Roman times—and the king's fabled succession of fetes, galas, and carousels, all spectacles that took on the nature of public festivals—Louis XIV's version of Roman circus. Equally effective in creating a public culture, which was what the famous expression *la gloire de France* meant, was the fetish for court-inspired French styles of dress, manners, equipage, and even food. French *haute cuisine,* for example, had its origins in the kitchens at Versailles. More important still was the enormous prestige everywhere accorded the French language, which was rapidly replacing Latin as the international idiom. All the king's subjects could share this prestige, even those in some of the kingdom's remote border provinces where, until recently, French had been spoken hardly at all.[8]

8. Ernest Lavisse, *Histoire de France* (9 vols. in 18 pts.; Paris, 1900–1911), VII, pt. 1, pp. 321–404; VII, pt. 2, pp. 81–184; VIII, pt. 1, pp. 277–388. See especially J. M. Apostolidès, *Le Roi-machine: Spectacle et politique au temps de Louis XIV* (Paris, 1981); and also B. Teyssèdre, *L'Art au siècle de Louis XIV* (Paris, 1967); H. James Jensen, *The Muses Concord: Literature, Music, and the Visual Arts in the Baroque Age* (Bloomington, 1976); and P. Boissonnade, *Colbert, le triomphe de l'étatisme, 1661–1683* (Paris, 1932).

That Louis XIV and Colbert included France's colonies in their assimilationist ethic should not be surprising, for mercantilist theory perceived colonies essentially as fingers of the mother country. But the particular form the assimilationist ideal assumed in France's colonies, the route it took to Louisiana, and the effect it had there are much less well-known.

Within the past decade several scholars, Thomas Fiehrer perhaps chief among them, have suggested that Louisiana's colonial history could best be treated as one part of a circum-Caribbean plantation society.[9] As important as that insight has been, it can be applied most effectively to Louisiana only in the late eighteenth and antebellum nineteenth centuries. Louisiana did not develop a mature plantation economy until planters perfected sugar granulation and introduced cotton during the last decade of the eighteenth century, on the very eve of the U.S. purchase.

Most of colonial Louisiana's history is better understood against its Canadian background. The formative Louisiana colonial experience represented an extension of the French experience in Canada. Few writers have explored the Canadian connection beyond some studies of Louisiana's Acadian language and culture. Compared to the colonial histories of other parts of the United States, few of even the fundamental topics in early Louisiana history have been explored.

Several excellent recent studies of French-Indian relations offer keys to basic French colonial planning in both Canada and Louisiana. The story begins in the council chambers of Versailles, where Colbert and Louis XIV laid down France's Indian policy as part of the overall colonial policy they developed initially for Canada. In essence it was an extension of the social engineering program they developed for France. In Louis Hartz's terms, it represented a transplanted fragment of the ethos of the mother country.

Neither Colbert nor Louis XIV invented the Indian policy. They simply drew together prevailing notions and practices and turned them into state policy. Earlier leaders had given thought to assimilating American natives into French culture, of "making them into Frenchmen" to

---

9. Much of the thinking along these lines jelled at a symposium of historians and social scientists held at Mona, Jamaica, in 1957. The proceedings were edited by Vera Rubin and published as *Caribbean Studies: A Symposium*, reprinted by the University of Washington Press in 1960. Thomas Fiehrer spearheaded the movement among U.S. historians with his journal *Plantation Society in the Americas*, which he founded in 1978.

control them. This notion developed during the late sixteenth century, when France got word, first, of the fierce resistance of the Indians on the banks of the St. Lawrence to Jacques Cartier's attempts to subdue them by force and, later, of the natives' eradication of the colonies France had planted on the Brazil and Florida coasts. It seemed sensible to cultivate the friendship and cooperation of native populations. That idea appeared in its fullest philosophical form in Michel de Montaigne's many admonitions to his fellow Frenchmen that it was their Christian duty to "gently polish" the native Americans into Frenchmen.[10]

By the time France settled Canada at the opening of the seventeenth century, such precepts had found their way into official documents. Canada's first viceroy issued precise instructions to the colony's first patent holders: the settlers were "to seek to lead the nations thereof to the profession of the Christian faith, to civilization of manners, to an ordered life, and to practice and intercourse with the French." As a historian of early Canadian Indian history put it, the French thought the problem of dealing with an inhabited continent "could be solved simply by the peaceful process of assimilation."[11]

Samuel de Champlain, one of the first patent holders in Canada—then called New France—and commandant there until 1627, enthusiastically supported the assimilationist ideal. He envisioned its accomplishment by the combined efforts of the French state and church in civilizing the natives, who, through association with Frenchmen and their language, would "also acquire a French heart and spirit."[12] When he returned to France after founding Quebec, he followed the common practice of bringing several young Indians with him as curiosities for European courts. But he did something new. He left several French boys with the Indians in Canada to learn their languages and ways so they

10. Olive Patricia Dickason, *The Myth of the Savage and the Beginnings of French Colonization in the Americas* (Edmonton, Canada, 1984), offers a good survey of the development of attitudes, and her notes and bibliography are an excellent guide to the scholarly literature. Montaigne's comments are scattered throughout his works, but most are in his essays, "Des coches" and "Des cannibales." Antoine de Montchrétien also spoke of the usefulness of "turning Indians into Frenchmen," in *Traicté de l'oeconomie politique*, ed. Franz Funck-Brentano (Paris, 1889), 269–70 and *passim*, and contrasted French freedom of association with the English lack thereof.

11. Cornelius J. Jaenen, *Friend and Foe: Aspects of French-Amerindian Cultural Contact in the Sixteenth and Seventeenth Centuries* (New York, 1976), 153, 154. This is the best single work on the French assimilationist policy.

12. William L. Grant, ed., *The Voyages of Samuel de Champlain, 1604–1618* (2 vols.; New York, 1917), I, 323.

could act eventually as liaisons between the Indians and the French. When they grew up, those boys became the first of the famous *coureurs-de-bois*.[13]

When Cardinal Richelieu reorganized the colony as a trading company, his 1627 charter specified that "the savages . . . will be deemed and respected to be natural-born Frenchmen, and as such may come to dwell in France when it shall seem good to them," and that they would hold all rights of property and goods that subjects within France held, on an equal footing with them, without the need of any special letters of declaration or naturalization.[14]

The French church immediately responded to the challenge of assimilation. The handful of Recollect missionaries whom Champlain had brought with him to the colony developed a program combining the goals of conversion and assimilation "to make [the Indians] men before we go about to make them Christians."[15] Or as the idea was expressed by one of the more famous of the fathers a few decades later, "Now in order to civilize them it is necessary that the Europeans should mix with them, and that they should live with them, and that they should dwell together."[16]

The work begun by the Recollects was shortly taken up by Jesuits, who, with greater numbers and resources, quickly developed a full-scale assimilation program. Paul Le Jeune, the Jesuit superior in Quebec from

13. Jacques Cartier apparently initiated this practice when he sent two French boys to live with the Iroquois in 1541, but with Champlain it became standard. See Bruce G. Trigger, "The French Presence in Huronia: The Structure of Franco-Huron Relations in the First Half of the Seventeenth Century," *Canadian Historical Review*, XLIX (1968), 107, 118–20; Wilbur R. Jacobs, *Wilderness Politics and Indian Gifts: The Northern Colonial Frontier, 1748–1763* (Lincoln, Neb., 1966); Alfred G. Bailey, *Conflict of European and Eastern Algonkian Cultures, 1504–1700* (Toronto, 1969); and Marcel Trudel, *Beginnings of New France, 1524–1663* (Toronto, 1973), esp. 155–56.

14. Richelieu's *Etablissements de la Compagnie de Canada sous le titre de Nouvelle France,* which he issued on April 29 and May 7, 1627. It was printed in Paris in 1725 by Saugrain and Prault. See also Pierre F. X. Charlevoix, *History and General Description of New France,* trans. John Gilmary (1744; 5 vols.; rpr. Chicago, 1962), II, 31; William J. Eccles, "French Aims and Means in Colonial North America," in *France and North America: Three Hundred Years of Dialogue,* ed. Mathé Allain and Glenn R. Conrad (Lafayette, La., 1973), 59; and R. A. Schermerhorn, *Comparative Ethnic Relations* (New York, 1970), 73–74.

15. Father Gabriel Sagard's *Long Journey to the Country of the Hurons,* ed. George M. Wrong (Toronto, 1939), poignantly expressed the dreams and aspirations of the early missionaries.

16. Louis Hennepin, *A New Discovery of a Vast Country in America* (2 vols.; London, 1698), II, 60.

1632 to 1639, early laid out an ambitious plan. Le Jeune gave first priority to the need for missionaries to learn the native languages by living with the Indians. Second, to "capture the minds" of the Indians, Le Jeune called for sending the children to France for their education or for establishing Indian boarding schools that would rear them *à la française*. The third part of his program established hospitals to provide medical care for the Indians, who were dying in droves from European-derived colds, fevers, tuberculosis, and alcoholism. And the fourth and final step of the program sought to persuade Indians to give up their nomadic life, which violated the regulated, corporative ideal of social organization that the French clerics and officials took for granted. The French wanted to resettle the Indians as farmers among the French, or at very least in all-Indian towns—called republics—adjacent to French settlements.[17]

In the next decade or two the Jesuits as well as other missionaries increasingly expected that the Indians would straightaway accept "right reason" and "right religion," and "with the example of the French which they esteem and respect, inciting them to work, it seems that they will set themselves straight . . . and that they will take their places beside the Frenchmen."[18]

But such early efforts at assimilation remained fragmentary. Only when Colbert took charge of Canada in 1663 did a comprehensive colonial policy begin to develop. If the colony was to prosper, Colbert believed that it had to be properly organized and run, which for him meant organized and run much as France itself was. Stated simply, Colbert's Canadian policy had two mainstays. First, he wanted the colony to remain "compact," its settlements tightly grouped, rather than scattered far and wide in an "expanded Canada." And he wanted to keep its all-important fur trade centered in Quebec and Montreal, where he could control it. This meant that Indians had to bring their pelts to Quebec and Montreal for sale to merchants there, and only a few licensed traders were allowed to travel freely through the hinterlands buying furs. The merchants, organized in the French fashion into corpo-

17. Le Jeune's program is conveniently summarized in Dickason, *Myth of the Savage*, 251–65. Le Jeune wrote year-by-year accounts each entitled *Relation de ce qui s'est passé en la Nouvelle France en l'année* . . . published in Paris from 1633 until 1661.
18. *Les Véritables motifs de messieurs et dames de la Société de Notre Dame de Montréal* (Paris, 1643), 106, a report on their work published by the Company of the Holy Sacrament, the missionary group that settled Montreal.

rate groups, and subject to crown regulations, he could control. Free-roaming Indian traders, he could not.[19]

Second, Colbert formalized the various attempts by preceding generations to assimilate the Indian populations, augmented them with additional ideas and directives of his own, and fashioned them into an official policy. He ordered the French in Canada to "civilize the . . . savages who have embraced Christianity, and dispose them to come and settle them in community with the French, live with them, and bring up their children in their manner and customs . . . in order that, having one law and one master, they may form only one people and one blood."[20]

Colbert was very serious about "one blood." Convinced that a large population was *sine qua non* for a prosperous Canada, and seeing no way to populate the colony without denuding France of a significant portion of its own population, he inaugurated a full-scale policy of intermarriage between settlers and Indians. The idea of mixed marriages had been in the minds of many Canadian leaders since the days of Champlain, and there had been any number of such marriages, almost all between French men and Indian women, as well as even larger numbers of casual, unblessed unions. But Colbert's expanded policy encouraged marriage of French women to Indian men as well, and he set up a fund to provide dowries for women of one race who married men of the other. He believed the dowries would not only bring about more interracial marriages but would also legitimize and stabilize many of the existing illicit unions, for husbands would less readily leave wives who held financial endowments. Moreover, marriage purses would result in more such couples settling down to become farmers, something his colony desperately needed. And they would entice royal troops to marry

19. The best general book on Colbert's Canada is William J. Eccles, *Canada Under Louis XIV, 1663–1701* (Toronto, 1964). S. L. Mims, *Colbert's West India Policy* (New Haven, 1912), is also important for an understanding of his colonial policy, as is H. A. Innis, *The Fur Trade of Canada* (London, 1930). On early Canadian society see Marcel Trudel, *Le Régime seigneurial* (Ottawa, 1956); Allana G. Reid, "The Nature of Quebec Society During the French Regime," *Canadian Historical Association Papers* (Ottawa, 1951); Sigmund Diamond, "An Experiment in Feudalism: French Canada in the 17th Century," *William and Mary Quarterly*, XVIII (1961), 3–34; and Gabriel Debien, *La Société coloniale aux XVIIe et XVIIIe siècles* (2 vols.; Paris, 1953). Colbert did not attempt to create New France as an exact replica of old France; for example, he allowed neither the sale of offices nor the establishment of guilds. See Mathé Allain's instructive "Slave Politics in French Louisiana," *Louisiana History*, XXI (1980), 127–37.

20. From 1666 and 1667 dispatches quoted by Mack Eastman, *Church and State in Early Canada* (Edinburgh, 1915), 114, 117, 119.

and stay in Canada instead of returning home at the end of their tours of duty.[21]

If the relationship that developed between French settlers and Indians in Canada represented a transplantation of the corporate and assimilationist social ideals that prevailed in seventeenth-century France, the segregationist social patterning characteristic of England during the same period was reflected in the very different relationship that developed between settlers and Indians in England's colonies to the south. The striking difference between French-Indian and English-Indian relations is well-known. Gary B. Nash put it succinctly when he noted that the "greater flexibility and willingness" of the French "to accept native culture on its own terms . . . led to a far greater degree of interaction between the cultures in New France than in England's colonies."[22]

The English attitude toward the Indians found expression early. The Virginia Company, in its initial orders to its colonial administrators, limited its instructions on Indian matters to a terse directive: "In all your passages you must have great care not to offend the naturals, if you can eschew it."[23]

The ambiguity inherent in that sentence became characteristic of English Indian policy for over forty years. Though Virginia colonists found the Indians indispensable sources of food and knowledge about survival in the wilderness, they saw little value in trading with them and no worth in using them as a labor force. And after tobacco growing became the economic backbone of the colony, Indians were a nuisance, for

21. Jaenen, *Friend and Foe*, 161–85, and Jean Delanglez, *Frontenac and the Jesuits* (Chicago, 1939), 37–40.

22. Gary B. Nash, *Red, White, and Black: The Peoples of Early America* (Englewood Cliffs, 1974), 106. For examples of comments on the English and French attitudes by both colonial observers and later historians see William K. Boyd, ed., *William Byrd's Histories of the Dividing Line Betwixt Virginia and North Carolina* (Raleigh, 1929), 3–4; Robert Beverley, *The History and Present State of Virginia*, ed. Louis B. Wright (Chapel Hill, 1947), 38–39; Jaenen, *Friend and Foe*, 160; Francis Parkman, *The Conspiracy of Pontiac* (2 vols.; New York, 1908), I, 54–57; Neal Salisbury, *Manitou and Providence: Indians, Europeans, and the Making of New England, 1500–1643* (New York, 1982); A. L. Kroeber, *Cultural and Natural Areas of North America* (Berkeley, 1939), 92; Ruth Benedict, *Patterns of Culture* (Boston, 1934), 11; and James Axtell, *The Invasion Within: The Contest of Cultures in Colonial North America* (New York, 1985). For a notably unsuccessful attempt to disprove such differences in attitudes see chapter 4 of Lewis O. Saum, *The Fur Trade and the Indian* (Seattle, 1965).

23. E. G. R. Taylor, ed., *The Original Writings of Correspondence of the Two Richard Hakluyts*, Hakluyt Society *Publications*, 2nd ser., vol. 77 (London, 1935), 494.

their presence obstructed land development. But when the colonists pushed into Indian lands, the Indians pushed back, and with great force. In response, the English decided that they would rid themselves of the Indian problem and launched into a quarter-century-long campaign of enmity. But the Indians resisted and in 1644 launched an all-out assault on the colonists that convinced the English to change their minds.

Realizing that the goal of total annihilation was impracticable, the English signed a treaty with the Indians that drew a line between Indian and English territory and promised the Indians freedom from molestation as long as they remained in their own area. That 1646 treaty was the forerunner of the reservation system. Henceforth the Virginia policy, adopted quickly by the other English colonies, kept Indians along the periphery of English civilization and discouraged contact with them. As the English colonies needed more land, which they did nearly every generation, they took over adjacent Indian areas and removed the native populations to newly reserved areas in the western hinterlands. The English segregationist policy was bequeathed to, and accepted by, the new American republic at the time of the Revolution and has ever since remained the essence of the U.S. government's Indian policy.[24]

This discussion about the substantive differences between French and English Indian policy is not meant to imply that the French were any more democratic or humanitarian than the English or even that they understood the Indians or their culture any better. Nor is it to say that the French were any less motivated by practical considerations of profit making or power grabbing than the English or any less interested in controlling the Indian populations. Manifestly they were not. When Indians resisted French plans, French authorities were as ready and willing to destroy them as the English. The prolonged and murderous campaigns of the French against the Iroquois in Canada and their annihilation of the entire Natchez Nation in Louisiana made that indisputably clear. Nor can obvious differences in practical dictates be ignored: the sparsity of population in French Canada threatened Indians less than the dense English settlements; and the pressing need for cleared land in most English colonies made resident Indians an obstacle while the fur

24. Nash, *Red, White, and Black,* 46–67, gives a convenient summary of the development of English policy. Axtell, *Invasion Within,* 278 and 304, notes the virtual absence of Indian-European marriages in the English colonies, in contrast to the many in France's colonies. The most famous marriage in Virginia history, that of John Rolfe and Pocahontas, is almost unique.

trade in Canada made them essential. Frontier realities always tempered home government policies.

But in addition to the different demands practical circumstances put on them in the New World, the English and the French colonists held fundamentally different social attitudes harkening back to the fundamentally different conceptions and assumptions about society of the two mother countries. Those social attitudes facilitated French accommodation of the Indians when not precluded by practical realities and made English accommodation of Indians or other nonassimilable groups virtually impossible under any circumstances. In the most notable example, when the English conquered Canada from France in 1763, they immediately imposed a policy that distinctly separated the new dominant English group from the French and Indians and at the same time increasingly separated the two subordinate groups from each other.[25]

But the French assimilationist policy in Canada had developed troubles long before the English conquest. Colbert understood that the assimilation process he envisioned would have to develop slowly and gradually over generations. Colbert's contemporaries on the scene in Canada—the country's first intendant, Jean Talon, its governor, Count Frontenac, and their generation of early administrators—understood this as well. But when Colbert's son Seignelay succeeded him in the Canadian affairs office in 1681 and, upon Colbert's death two years later, in the Ministry of Marine as well, policy directives changed. Unlike his father, who had built the French government bureaucracy from scratch, Seignelay had grown up in the already formed bureaucracy and took it for granted. Consequently, he viewed the still wide gap separating French and Indian cultures in Canada as a sign of failure rather than as a mark of

25. Sociologists and social historians have developed "static" models to portray stratification of plural societies of the English type. See John S. Furnivall, *Netherlands India: A Study of Plural Economy* (London, 1939); his *Colonial Policy and Practice: A Comparative Study of Burma and Netherlands India* (London, 1948); M. G. Smith, *The Plural Society in the British West Indies* (Los Angeles, 1965); and Leo Despres, *Cultural Pluralism and Nationalist Politics in British Guiana* (Chicago, 1967). Also see the sources cited in note 61 below. For a comparison of French and English development in the Caribbean see Arvin Murch, *Black Frenchmen: The Political Integration of the French Antilles* (Cambridge, Mass., 1971). On the defining role of a culture's early years see Harry [Harmannus] Hoetink, "The Cultural Links," in *Africa and the Caribbean*, ed. Margaret E. Crahan and Franklin W. Knight (Baltimore, 1979), 20–40; and, especially, Sidney W. Mintz and Richard Price, *An Anthropological Approach to the Afro-American Past: A Caribbean Perspective* (Philadelphia, 1976).

slow progress. The same attitude tended to prevail among the new generation of colonial administrators that Seignelay sent out to the empire.[26]

The most famous example was Jacques-René de Brisay, Marquis de Denonville, dispatched to Canada as governor in 1685. Within a few months of his arrival, the new governor was sending back reports denouncing the assimilationist policy and pronouncing it a complete failure:

> It was believed for a very long time that domiciling the savages near our habitations was a very great means of teaching those peoples to live like us. . . . I note . . . that the very opposite has taken place because instead of familiarizing them with our ways . . . they have communicated to us the very worst they have and have likewise taken on all that is bad and vicious in us. . . . I could not describe . . . the attraction which our young men feel to this savage way of life which consists of doing nothing, in being restrained by nothing, in pursuing all one's urges, and placing oneself beyond the possibility of correction.[27]

Such comments, however, quoted, as they so often are, out of context, can be misleading. In fact, this is a relatively isolated passage in a series of reports on the state of the colony in general, which, in Denonville's eyes, was total chaos. Sweeping reforms were needed not only in the military and civil administrations but in Canadian society itself. He was particularly disturbed by what he characterized as the debauchery and drunkenness of Canadian youth, who, he said, had no discipline and no respect for authority. Young Canadians had become half savages because, contrary to the policy of keeping the Canadian colony compact, they were allowed to spend most of their time hunting in the wilds or on long, far-off fur-trading expeditions among the Indians. The whole scene struck Denonville, a deeply religious man and a tidy bureaucrat, as appalling.

To correct it, he launched an elaborate program of social and moral

26. See, in addition to the works already cited, William J. Eccles, *Frontenac: The Courtier Governor* (Toronto, 1959), and his *Canadian Frontier, 1534–1760* (New York, 1969); Thomas Chapais, *Jean Talon, Intendant de la Nouvelle France* (Quebec, 1904); Delanglez, *Frontenac and the Jesuits;* J. N. Fauteux, *Essai sur l'industrie au Canada sous le régime français* (2 vols.; Quebec, 1861–65); and Jean Hamelin, *Economie et société en Nouvelle France* (Quebec, 1960).

27. This passage, quoted by writers from Tocqueville on, occurs in a report from Denonville to Seignelay, November 13, 1685, *Public Archives of Canada Microfilm*, Series C11A, Vol. VII, pp. 45–46.

reform. But aside from a provision that opened service in the French navy to the sons of Canadian seigneurs—a provision to which Pierre Le Moyne d'Iberville owed his career—and a training program in iron-working for the sons of Canadian farmers—to which New Orleans ultimately owed its tradition of fine wrought iron—few of Denonville's reforms survived. Within a year or two, Indian troubles and gathering clouds of a new war with England sapped so much of the governor's time and energy that his reform program lapsed.[28]

Moreover, Denonville's replacement in 1689 was none other than Count Frontenac. Again in favor at court and returned to power for a second term as governor of Canada, Frontenac, an old frontiersman at heart, had no stomach for such reforms. He canceled what was left of Denonville's program and in effect reinstated the policies of a generation before. And he held sway in Canada for another nine years until he died in 1698, a month after his former lieutenant, Iberville, had set out from Brest, bound for the mouth of the Mississippi.

Frontenac's second administration gave a new lease on life to the old assimilationist ideals, at least for a time. But they could never be fully put back in place, for Denonville had been right. Canada's French were turning into Indians both in culture and in blood at a far more rapid rate than the Indians were becoming French. So in the 1680s, and particularly the 1690s, the assimilationist ideal declined. But it was a decline, not a demise, and it was very gradual, not, as some writers have suggested, an abrupt about-face in crown policy precipitated by Denonville's memo. Rather, crown priorities were reordered so that the assimilationist ideal was shifted to a secondary level of concern and, remarkably, transferred from Canada to Louisiana.

The reordering of royal priorities came about as a result of the international situation in Europe, specifically the problem of the Spanish inheritance. It had long been clear that the decrepit old Charles II of Spain was going to die without a son to succeed him. Both Louis XIV and the Hapsburg emperor had laid claim to the throne for their families, but nothing was certain. Louis XIV began moving to protect French interests in North America, no matter what happened to Spain's empire. Arrangements for the military security of French Canada and future French imperial prospects thus took precedence over acculturation of the In-

28. Lyse Nantais, "Craftsmen in Quebec," *Canadian Art*, XVIII (July, 1961), 255–62.

dians. In 1698 the crown commissioned Pierre d'Iberville to establish a French base at the mouth of the Mississippi and issued him secret instructions to destroy covertly any English forts or trading posts west of the Alleghenies. The French feared an English move southwestward that could result in the eventual seizure of Spain's rich mines in Mexico. But with a base at the mouth of the Mississippi, France could league together the Indian tribes of the Mississippi Valley and the Great Lakes in a secure alliance. If the Spanish inheritance then went to a French prince, France would be in a position to protect it from English westward aggression; or, if it went to a Hapsburg prince, France herself would be in a position to attack Mexico.

This radical change in France's North American policy brought new and unanticipated problems. The *coureurs-de-bois* immediately took advantage of the new Louisiana outlet, in preference to the Quebec and Montreal markets. Within a few months of Iberville's arrival on the Gulf Coast, Henri de Tonti and twenty-one *coureurs* came down the Mississippi pulling six canoes loaded with beaver pelts for sale. Others followed until soon there were over a hundred. That created a dilemma. The keystone of the crown's Canadian policy had long been concentration of the fur trade in Montreal and Quebec and control of it by means of tight restrictions on the movement of the *coureur* Indian traders. Immediately, Frontenac's successor, the new governor of Canada, Louis-Hector Calliers, wrote to Paris, requesting that post officials in Louisiana be instructed to arrest all fur traders who showed up there and return them perforce to Canada.

As his message passed up through the bureaucracy, an official in the Ministry of Marine appended a note to the dispatch which countered Callier's request with the suggestion that perhaps such men, tough, brave, and knowledgeable of terrain and native ways, could be useful in the new Louisiana settlement. When the dispatch reached the desk of Seignelay's successor in the Ministry of Marine, the Count de Pontchartrain, he scribbled the word "Good" in the margin beside his subordinate's suggestion but stopped short of authorizing the action. A year later, when the same suggestion appeared on another dispatch, Pontchartrain wrote beside it a simple order: "Try it."

Those two short penciled words, William J. Eccles noted, inaugurated a new policy. After forty years, the conception of a compact Canada was abandoned, expansionist dreams won acceptance, and the *coureurs-de-bois* were transformed from renegades and outlaws into agents of French imperialism—and, Eccles might have added, into agents for cultural assimilation in the new colony of Louisiana.[29]

It would be overstating the case to claim that the assimilationist policy was pursued in Louisiana as systematically as it had been in Canada. In spite of striking similarities in the early histories of the two colonies, differences in time and circumstances proved too great for that. Canada was formed in the mid-seventeenth century, Louisiana in the early eighteenth century. And in France, the first half of the eighteenth century was a troubled and unsure time.

Early eighteenth-century economic theory and policy in particular became a murky no-man's land. Mercantilist doctrine, including its colonial ideology, had begun to fall into disrepute, but no new theory had been developed to replace it. François Quesnay and his Physiocrats did not organize their thoughts until midcentury and Adam Smith not until 1776. Consequently, just at the time a shift from the compact colony conception to the idea of a great French defensive arch through North America called for detailed planning and exact administration, crown policy had neither clear focus nor precise direction.

The assimilationist policy furnished a case in point. The king and his ministers never formally or even tacitly canceled or reversed the policy. Colbert's successors at Versailles and Paris, with more overwhelming matters on their minds, simply did not push it, nor did Frontenac's successors in Quebec. After Frontenac's last term, discussions of the policy, except for the issue of Indian marriages, disappeared from the dispatches. Assimilation remained pro forma a crown policy, but its conscious promotion lapsed.

Even so, the parallels between Canada's early history and Louisiana's are striking. Michael Forêt has admirably summarized them by noting that both colonies began as modest endeavors of limited purpose: Canada as a trading post and Louisiana as a frontier garrison. Both commanded great river systems inhabited by Indians divided into rival alliances: the Huron-Iroquois conflict in Canada and the Choctaw-Chickasaw antipathy in Louisiana. Both colonies, frequently neglected by their mother country or cut off completely by European wars, had long, troubled infancies during which they suffered desperately for supplies and reinforcements. Both remained underpopulated, their few

29. Eccles, *Canada Under Louis XIV*, 245–49.

settlers scattered over a vast expanse of territory and always outnumbered by their Indian neighbors; and both almost always were poor. In Forêt's words, there developed in Louisiana "a broad, recognizable pattern of French-Indian relations . . . that derived from earlier French experience in Canada."[30]

The transfer of that experience was direct and quick. It began with Iberville and was continued by his brother Jean-Baptiste de Bienville, both of whom belonged to the core of Canadian assimilationist tradition. They both grew up under the tutelage of *coureurs-de-bois,* roaming their father's vast frontier landholdings and beyond. Iberville matured and began his career under the patronage and guidance of Frontenac and Robert de La Salle, his father's closest friends. Bienville was too young to have known either of them well, but he later imbibed their teaching from his brother. And both developed a respect and appreciation for the Jesuits, probably a legacy from their father, who seems never to have shared La Salle's and Frontenac's antipathy for the order.[31]

Within a few months of his arrival at the mouth of the Mississippi River, Iberville had put in place the basics of his Indian policy. He visited or sent representatives to visit the various Indian tribes, assuring them of French friendship and inviting them, as "sons of the French king," to become "one nation with the French." At the same time, he began negotiations, as his Canadian predecessors had done long before, to settle intertribal wars and effect a general peace among all Indian groups friendly to the French so as to maintain a united front against the English. To seal the bargain he promised a plentiful supply of presents and trade goods. Iberville also laid plans for building forts near Indian towns and for relocating scattered tribes in new settlements adjacent to French installations to bring them into more direct and continuous association with the French. Following a precedent set by Champlain nearly three-quarters of a century before, Iberville, upon taking leave of the Great Sun of the Natchez Nation in March, 1700, and of the Chickasaw chiefs a year later, left several young cabin boys among them to learn their languages and ways.[32]

30. Michael Forêt, "Irresolution and Uncertainty: French Colonial Indian Policy in Louisiana, 1699–1763" (M.A. thesis, University of Southwestern Louisiana, 1982), 5, 29–30.

31. Louis Le Jeune, *Le Chevalier Pierre Le Moyne* (Ottawa, 1937); Guy Frégault, *Iberville le conquérant* (Montreal, 1944).

32. Marcel Giraud, *Histoire de la Louisiane française* (4 vols.; Paris, 1953–74), I, 76–77, or pp. 84–85 of the English translation published by Louisiana State University

Michael Forêt points out that the Indian policy brought by Iberville from Canada remained—with adaptations and alterations dictated by circumstances and with only a brief lapse—in effect throughout the French period of Louisiana's colonial history. Following Iberville, most of Louisiana's governors, as well as the military commandants who administered the colony between governors' terms, held to the policy. The brief ten-year lapse occurred during the time the colony was administered not directly by the crown but by a proprietary company.[33]

The young colony's struggle for survival in the face of epidemic disease, underpopulation, and scant food supplies is well-known. But those problems, particularly food scarcity, led to early adjustments in the Indian policy Louisiana had inherited. For the first several decades the military constituted the preponderant presence in the colony's population. Military personnel were even less prone to settle down and farm than the *coureurs-de-bois*. French and French Canadian commanders alike came as adventurers, men on the move and on the make, out to find gold and silver mines or rich pearl fisheries, or hopeful of enriching themselves through Spanish and Indian trade or as grand, landed seigneurs in the Canadian tradition. The soldiers and sailors under their command were equally footloose. Drawn virtually entirely from urban working classes, not a single one of more than three hundred troops sent to Louisiana before 1720 listed farming as his former occupation. The troops usually spent their lives in barracks, below decks, or in barrooms. That pattern changed little throughout the French period. Of 662 recruits arriving in the 1750s, the last decade France governed the colony, only 94 listed themselves as farmers.[34]

The colonists France sent to "settle and farm" the new area, includ-

---

Press in 1953. See Iberville's journal in Carl A. Brasseaux, ed., *A Comparative View of French Louisiana, 1699 and 1762: The Journey of Pierre Le Moyne d'Iberville and Jean-Blaise d'Abbadie* (Lafayette, La., 1979), and Richebourg G. McWilliams, ed., *Fleur de Lys and Calumet: Being the Pénicaut Narrative of French Adventure in Louisiana* (Baton Rouge, 1953), 28.

33. James T. McGowan, "The Creation of a Slave Society: Louisiana Plantations in the Eighteenth Century" (Ph.D. dissertation, University of Rochester, 1976), explains that the lapse occurred because the proprietary companies were bent on maximizing profits by seizing Indian lands for plantation development. The first chapter of this work was published as "Planters Without Slaves: Origins of a New World Labor System," *Southern Studies*, XVI (Spring, 1971), 5–26. Though marred by several unsupported assertions and some constructions that, in the absence of qualifications and exceptions, seem a bit too pat, McGowan's work offers some important insights.

34. Figures tabulated from Winston De Ville, *Louisiana Troops, 1720–1770* (New Orleans, 1965), and his *Louisiana Recruits, 1752–1758* (New Orleans, 1973).

ing the famous forced immigrants from prisons and workhouses, proved no more suited to the job. The overwhelming number, like the military, came not from agricultural families but from urban artisan and unskilled labor backgrounds. Two-thirds of the settlers recruited for the colony emigrated as craftsmen. Of one group of 624 workers sent to plantations, for example, only 84 had any former experience as farmers.[35]

Even had such an unable population been willing, they largely lacked the opportunity to farm. The simplest food crops had to be planted on a seasonal schedule and took several months to mature, and arrivals of immigrants seldom coincided with the beginning of the growing season. Moreover, fearful of the treacherous sandbars at the mouth of the Mississippi, ships' captains continued even after the founding of New Orleans in 1718 to deposit their cargoes of colonists at French installations on the Gulf Coast, principally at the original 1699 settlement on Biloxi Bay. Adjacent lands, mostly swamps, marshes, dense woodlands, or sandy relict beach soils, proved notably unsuited to farming. Lacking local production and perpetually short of imported foodstuffs, the colony became almost entirely dependent on nearby Indians for sustenance. But what the Indians could supply barely supported the local garrisons, leaving nothing for the new arrivals who flooded in between 1717 and 1722, raising the colony's population from 400 to over 5,400 in a five-year period. Consequently, the newcomers were dispersed, in many cases for long periods, to live with Indian tribes farther inland until a place could be found for them. At times, when food completely ran out, even the military garrison had to abandon the settlements and take refuge for weeks or months among various Indian tribes. That happened at least four times between 1703 and 1710.[36]

To meet the burgeoning demand for food, the Indians, at least the women, who did the farming, brought more and more land under cultivation. But that did not suffice. Indian men, drawn into the French fur trade and alliance system, spent increasing amounts of time trapping and warring. Because systematic destruction of an enemy's fields was

35. Figures tabulated from Glenn R. Conrad, *First Families of Louisiana* (2 vols.; Baton Rouge, 1972). For European background see Jean-Pierre Poussou, "Les Mouvements migratoires en France et à partir de la France de la fin du XVe siècle au debut du XIXe siècle: Approche pour une synthèse," *Annales de démographie historique*, VII (1970), 11–78.

36. Giraud, *Histoire de la Louisiane*, I, 131–32 (142–43 of English translation); and Pierre de Charlevoix, *Journal of a Voyage to North America* (2 vols.; rpr. Ann Arbor, 1966), I, 220–95.

common practice in Indian warfare, Indian agricultural production continued to fall far short of the colony's needs. The prospect of starvation inspired the colonists to encourage their Indian allies to bring in captured Indian women as slaves to grow food for them. Such war captives were plentiful and relatively easy to control, especially after the introduction in 1719 of African slaves, mostly males, whom the Indian women tended to marry. The Indian women proved, as Bienville put it, "very good for cultivating the earth," and by 1722 there were more than 225 such slaves in the colony.[37] The enslavement of Indians in Louisiana—involving almost exclusively women—had no parallel in Canada. But Indian slaves existed in Louisiana, albeit in diminishing numbers, until the end of the colonial period.

The close association of Indians and colonists resulted in considerable intermingling of the two bloods. The *coureurs-de-bois* right away acquired "sleeping dictionaries," and officers, troopers, and traders in outlying districts followed their example. Closer in, the great numbers of female Indian slaves proved too tempting for the mostly male colonists to resist. Governor Antoine de Cadillac complained of local men's infatuation with "Indian women, whom they prefer to French women," upon his arrival in 1713, and a few years later another observer noted that "all except Sieur Blondel and the new arrivals have Indian women as slaves who are always with child or nursing . . . halfbreeds."[38]

In addition to concubinage with Indian slaves, marriages between colonists and Indians flourished. Indian marriages had been at issue since Canadian Governor Denonville raised questions about their workability in 1685. Like so many other policy questions, those relative to such marriages remained either unanswered or unresolved during much of the eighteenth century. Seignelay and his successors in the Ministry of Marine issued various opinions, admonitions, and directives that clearly reflected misgivings about the practice and sometimes the crown's displeasure with it, but all fell short of outlawing it. Those half-answers left it to colonial administrators and clerics to make interpretations, which, depending on circumstances and personal predilections, differed widely. The whole matter continued to be debated in Canada well into the new century.[39]

37. McGowan, "Creation of a Slave Society," 22ff.
38. Quoted *ibid.*, 20–21. The original sources are a letter from Cadillac to Pontchartrain, October 26, 1713, and Minutes of Council, January 2, 1716.
39. See Jaenen, *Friend and Foe*, 162–85; Giraud, *Histoire de la Louisiane*, I, 257–58 (279–80 of English translation); and Charles E. O'Neill, *Church and State in French Colonial Louisiana* (New Haven, 1966), 246–55.

In Louisiana marriages became far more a problem for administrators than they had ever been in Canada. After the first few years, very few French-Indian marriages occurred in the settled areas of eastern Canada; they mostly took place on the wilderness frontier far to the west. But in Louisiana the wilderness was at hand, for the entire colony was frontier. Moreover, the local church, at least for a time, actively promoted such marriages. Louisiana's first presiding cleric, Henri Roulleaux de La Vente, appointed vicar-general of the new colony in 1704 by the bishop of Quebec, not only defended but vociferously advocated French-Indian marriages. In response to critics and opponents he argued forcefully, and all the way to Paris, that "the blood of the savages does no harm to the blood of the French."[40]

La Vente's chief opposition came from Bienville. The Indian policy Iberville had laid out, which Bienville followed, held that Indians living near French settlements on the coast and near the mouth of the Mississippi River should be acculturated—and in 1701 Iberville had advocated Indian marriages for French settlers in those areas. By contrast, Indians living in the interior such as Natchez, though they were to be brought into the French economic system via trade, should be protected from French intrusion so they could maintain themselves as cohesive groups that could serve as protective military buffers between Louisiana and the aggressive English colonists. To that degree Iberville's Indian policy departed from Frontenac's Canadian model. With completion of the French Arch, the expansionists had won their point and no longer stood at odds with the ideal of a compact colony. No settlers were to be allowed in Louisiana's Indian areas except for a limited number of authorized traders and a few priests. Iberville envisioned the latter as his own agents, counseling and conciliating his Indian allies, as well as doing their own work of conversion. Consequently, after Iberville's death in 1706, Bienville began issuing bans against unauthorized residency with Indians and against Indian marriages. In his words, "It is important to bring in all the Frenchmen who are scattered among the Indians and not to authorize them to live as libertines on the pretext that they have wives among them."[41]

After Bienville founded New Orleans in 1718, and particularly after

40. La Vente quoted by O'Neill, *Church and State*, 250. A native of Bayeux in France, La Vente had spent several years on Bourbon Island in the Indian Ocean before coming to Louisiana.

41. Bienville is quoted in McGowan, "Creation of a Slave Society," 18, and O'Neill, *Church and State*, 248. The original source is a letter from Bienville to Pontchartrain, July 28, 1706.

it became the capital four years later, a great many settlers came in, but few of the sort Bienville had in mind. Hardly any of the *coureurs-de-bois* came, but the artisans and craftsmen, who had never adjusted to life on the farm, flooded into the new town. Thus virtually from the beginning, the population of New Orleans was made up primarily of urbanites, a very large number of whom had lived with Indians for prolonged periods. They joined the resident military officers and troops, the Canadians, the Indians, the hundred or so African slaves, and the miscellaneous collection of colonists France was sending in—Rhenish Germans as well as convicted army deserters, smugglers, prostitutes, vagabonds, libertines, and poorhouse inmates. Descriptions of early New Orleans read like Emile Zola's later characterizations of the Paris demimonde, but they are, in fact, descriptions of the uneasy tolerance characteristic of frontier societies everywhere.[42]

The retreat of settlers from the countryside to New Orleans alarmed the plantation owners and the colony's proprietors—the crown had by then turned over Louisiana to a proprietary company, first to that of Antoine Crozat and then to John Law's Company of the Indies. With few hands left, the planters shrilly demanded the importation of African slaves to work their lands. Bienville had foreseen that need and from early on had pushed for their importation. Cargoes of slaves, as distinct from individual slaves brought by owners, began arriving in 1719, but the shipments were few and sporadic until 1723, when the company began sending large numbers of slaves to the colony on a regular schedule. The increased volume, however, gave rise to a new problem.

The company wanted to maximize profits from tobacco culture in Louisiana, but the marshlands along the lower Mississippi and the sandy relict beach soils of the Gulf Coast proved unsuited to that purpose. The best lands for tobacco lay well inland, but those were the cherished fields and hunting grounds of Bienville's Indian allies such as

42. That such heterogeneity was also characteristic of the early stage of development of England's American colonies has been made clear by Bernard Bailyn's recent works *The Peopling of British North America: An Introduction* (New York, 1986) and *Voyages to the West: A Passage in the Peopling of America on the Eve of the Revolution* (New York, 1986) and by Daniel H. Usner, Jr., "Frontier Exchange in the Lower Mississippi Valley: Race Relations and Economic Life in Colonial Louisiana, 1699–1783" (Ph.D. dissertation, Duke University, 1981) and his "American Indians on the Cotton Frontiers: Changing Economic Relations with Citizens in the Mississippi Territory," *Journal of American History*, LXXII (1985), 297–317. The cultural and ethnic heterogeneity of the early English colonies soon gave way to a certain homogeneity, but in New Orleans, for peculiar reasons, it continued.

the Natchez. Though the company urged and finally ordered the establishment of tobacco plantations in those areas, Bienville resisted and steered a course in the opposite direction. He restricted agricultural development to a narrow band on the lower Mississippi, forming a semicircle around New Orleans by making most large land grants only in that area and by awarding those planters most of the incoming slaves, while denying them to those farther inland. This action was counter to company policy, which called for distributing lands lying close to the city to small farmers who could make up a protective militia. By 1722, the midpoint of Bienville's term, not one of the more than seven hundred slaves in the colony had been sent to the upland district; all were on the plantations to the south. Even by the end of 1726, a year after his term ended, 92 percent of all land occupied and cleared for cultivation still lay within the band, and though the number of slaves had greatly increased, 96 percent of them also still lived within the band.[43]

By mid-1725 the company commissioners realized what Bienville was doing, and they fired him, accusing him of favoritism to his friends, the planters within the band to whom he had awarded most land grants and slaves. Etienne de Périer was sent as his replacement. Périer was totally a company man, the only governor of French colonial Louisiana who had no previous New World experience. He quickly expanded agricultural development into the interior, particularly into the rich uplands held by the Natchez. In the face of this encroachment, the Indians' apprehension and resentment mounted. And in 1729, as the result of the particularly egregious actions of a certain Lieutenant Etcheparre (or Chepart), who appropriated a large tract, not of forested area or abandoned farmland, as the French normally did, but of fields the Indians were currently cultivating, the Natchez rebelled and massacred 237 soldiers and settlers. Panicked and angered, the French launched a series of bloody massacres that within three years had annihilated the entire Natchez Nation.[44]

Périer's savaging of the Natchez destabilized the Indian alliance that Iberville and Bienville had spent years building and sent a tremor through

43. McGowan, "Creation of a Slave Society," 72–83. Planters within the band held 850 of the 955 slaves along the Mississippi; 100 or so slaves lived in New Orleans; and 600 were scattered from the Gulf Coast settlements to the Illinois country.

44. Patricia D. Woods, *French-Indian Relations on the Southern Frontier, 1699–1762* (Ann Arbor, 1980), has a great deal of information but must be used with care. See also Charles Wayne Goss, "The French and the Choctaw Indians, 1700–1763" (Ph.D. dissertation, Texas Tech University, 1977).

French officialdom and a shock wave through the faltering Company of the Indies. The company finally gave up on Louisiana and returned the colony to the crown. The crown responded by renaming Bienville as governor.

Bienville's arrival in New Orleans in 1733 marked a milestone in the history of the city and the colony. He began the return of Louisiana, in James McGowan's words, to its "live and let-live" way of life. Charles O'Neill says that Bienville inaugurated the "classical period" of Louisiana's colonial history.[45] Though his phrase is a bit grandiloquent, O'Neill's point is well taken, for it was about that time that the miscellaneously heterogeneous population of Louisiana, or at least of New Orleans, began to jell into a colonial society. The form that society took mirrored much of the structure and many of the qualities that characterized French and Canadian society.

The jelling process was reflected in several ways. For Bienville, settling the Indian problem was paramount, but scarcely less pressing was a problem that had developed with the African slaves, and the two were complexly intertwined. Investigations revealed that a number of African slaves had been involved in key ways with the Natchez revolt. For a decade the slave population and the Indian population had increasingly intermarried. African slaves, mostly males, had taken wives from among the female Indian slave population, and runaway African slaves had often moved into Indian communities or formed mixed Indian-African maroon settlements hidden away in the swamps on the outskirts of New Orleans.[46] Bienville's problem was to make sure that slaves would not again ally with Indians in revolts.

The problem was compounded because Louisiana tobacco and indigo production, despite the company's earlier efforts, was still so profitless that masters often could not afford to feed their slaves, and the persistent food shortage had forced the slave population into closer ties with local Indians. The solution to this two-pronged problem lay in recourse to a policy of viewing each of these two groups as corporate entities. Informal corporate status not only would provide cohesion for

45. McGowan, "Creation of a Slave Society," 110; O'Neill, *Church and State*, 233. A decade after it became the colonial capital, New Orleans still had a population of only around nine hundred.

46. McGowan, "Creation of a Slave Society," 176–78, notes that the shortage of female African slaves accounted for the limited number of mulattoes as well as free people of color in colonial French Louisiana—only 165 of the latter listed in censuses at the end of the French regime, nearly 80 percent of whom were mulattoes. See below, note 79.

each group, but it would make both easier to control. At the same time, such a policy would allow members of each group, as individuals, the freedom to associate with individuals from other sectors of the population, which was necessary for the economic prosperity, indeed, the survival of the colony.

Bienville and his successors as governor, Pierre de Rigaud de Vaudreuil and Louis Billouart de Kerlérec, attempted to solve the Indian half of the problem by trying to restore peace between Indian tribes, reconstructing a French alliance system with friendly tribes such as the Choctaws, and checking and reducing the power and influence of unfriendly tribes such as the Chickasaws. Simultaneously the governor successfully detached one tribe after another from the English trade network into which they had been drawn and reattached them to the French colonial economy. The latter accomplishment was particularly impressive because the English offered a greater quantity of trade goods of better quality, on a much more regular schedule, and at considerably lower prices than the French. The French succeeded largely because, in contrast to the English, they did not encroach on the Indians' lands, rupture their societies, or push them farther and farther afield. While they held the Louisiana colony, the French generally kept settlers out of Indian territories and preserved individual Indian societies. Those living near New Orleans or near French outposts up the Mississippi and Red rivers and along the Gulf Coast increasingly participated in local town market economies. Each day they brought into town and sold baskets, medicinal herbs, firewood, and foodstuffs, including sassafras leaves and root bark used for making the filé powder still famous today in the flavoring of New Orleans gumbo.[47]

New Orleans' earliest, as well as its last, all-Indian market was held in an open area called the Place Bretonne at the conjunction of what are now Esplanade Avenue, Bayou Road, and Dorgenois, Bell, and DeSoto streets. It lasted, with gradually dwindling numbers of Indians after 1809 (when the opening of Faubourg St. John separated it from Bayou St. John, which had been the main route the Indians followed into town), until the construction on that spot of the LeBreton Market build-

47. See, for example, Woods, *French-Indian Relations,* 116–18, 121, 153–58, and 164, on Indian trade and her concluding comments on the differences between French and English Indian policy, 171–73. John G. Clark, *New Orleans, 1718–1812: An Economic History* (Baton Rouge, 1970), and Nancy M. Surrey, *The Commerce of Louisiana During the French Regime, 1699–1763* (New York, 1916), are basic for an overview, and Usner's "Frontier Exchange" provides a detailed analysis of Indian trade.

ing in 1867. Small groups of Indians still continued to sell goods there as well as in other parts of the city. Indeed, the marked Indian presence in New Orleans throughout the nineteenth century contrasted so sharply with the general absence of Indians from other U.S. cities east of the Mississippi that almost all visitors who wrote accounts of their travels remarked on it.

In the 1880s, at the time of the New Orleans Cotton Centennial, fifteen to twenty Choctaw women, their features showing the signs of generations of intermarriage between Indians and Africans, spread their wares in the French Market on Wednesdays and in the Place d'Armes on Saturdays, as some continued to do, more and more irregularly, into the 1920s, when they finally vanished. Indians disappeared from sight in New Orleans not because they died out or moved away but because, in the words of an 1880s observer, they "melted away into mulattoes." The Indians became New Orleanians by gradually blending into the city's African community. An overwhelming number of black families in New Orleans today have in their genealogies several not very remote Indian ancestors.[48]

As to the slaves, McGowan says, "Employing the Catholic Church, the Court system of the Superior Council, and the military administrators in distant posts, the [Bienville] regime forged a social consciousness premised upon assimilation of the African population as members of the community with social rights and defined limits to their subjugation to their masters."[49] And he convincingly argues that official recognition and encouragement of such things as slave baptisms, godparenting, marriages, family units, protections for slave women against rape, and

48. Robert A. Sauder, "The Origin and Spread of the Public Market System in New Orleans," *Louisiana History,* XXII (Summer, 1981), 281–97; John Chase, *Frenchmen, Desire, Good Children and Other Streets of New Orleans* (2nd ed.; New Orleans, 1960); New Orleans *Times,* June 6, 1867; James S. Zacharie, *New Orleans Guide: With Descriptions of Routes to New Orleans, Sights of the City Arranged Alphabetically, and Other Information* (New Orleans, 1885), 102. Grace King and John R. Ficklen, *A History of Louisiana* (New York, 1897), 165; Helen Pitkin Schertz, *A Walk Through French Town in Old New Orleans* (New Orleans, 1920), 31; Lyle Saxon, ed., *New Orleans City Guide* (New York, 1938), 101. Quotations are from *Historical Sketch Book and Guide to New Orleans and Environs* (New York, 1885), 169, 258–63. A telling 1885 photograph of the Indian vendors in the French Market is in the New Orleans Museum of Art's collection of stereographs from the Cotton Centennial Exposition.

49. McGowan, "Creation of a Slave Society," 120. Briefly during the late 1720s and early 1730s a few black students were schooled by the Ursuline nuns. See Jean Delanglez, *The French Jesuits in Lower Louisiana, 1700–1763* (Washington, D.C., 1935), 136.

respect for slave holidays were designed to define the social rights of slaves as a group.

Although the second article of the 1724 Code Noir required all masters to instruct their slaves in the Catholic faith and have them baptized, slaveholders more often than not ignored the obligation. But between 1731 and 1733, St. Louis Church in New Orleans registered 425 slave baptisms and began more or less regularly administering the sacraments to slaves, most often in groups. Masters and mistresses also began more commonly to stand as godparents for slaves, and slaves themselves, once catechized, increasingly stood as godparents for members of their own community. Though Bienville had some of his own slaves married by clergy, most planters apparently did not, for records of such ceremonies are rare.[50]

Recognition of slave families, as called for in article forty-three of the code, seems to have been generally accorded and respected. Succession and foreclosure inventories began to list slave families as units with a value assigned to the whole family, including children under age fourteen. The 56 percent male to 44 percent female imbalance that prevailed in the slave community throughout the French period produced sexual tensions that made practical and wise the enforcement of article eight of the code, which prohibited forcing slave women to take mates.[51]

Even planters who were still solvent after capital supplies were cut off following the 1731 collapse of the Company of the Indies faced a bleak future. Many banked on expansion of their slave forces to bring them economic recovery, but the complications following the collapse of the company also cut off slave imports. Between 1731 and the end of the French period only two shipments totaling not more than 330 slaves reached the colony. The planters immediately saw the enormous advantages recognition of slave families and maintenance of protections for slave women could bring them. A stable slave society and slave families offered the only possibilities for an increased slave labor force.

50. For the text of the Code Noir see *Louisiana Historical Society Publications*, no. 4 (1908), 75–90, or Newton D. Mereness, *Travels in the American Colonies* (New York, 1916), 17–92. On slave baptisms see O'Neill, *Church and State*, 270, and McGowan, "Creation of a Slave Society," 121–35.

51. Even in New Orleans, which had 176 adult slaves in 1732, the heavy labor requirements of a frontier town outweighed the need for domestic service and kept the male-female balance in the 1740s at 58:42, the reverse of the pattern that developed in the antebellum American decades (McGowan, "Creation of a Slave Society," 126–35).

Similarly, harder-pressed planters, who could no longer afford to care for or even feed their slaves, saw the advantages inherent in article five of the code, which exempted slaves from forced labor on Sundays and religious holidays. On those free days slaves could visit away from their plantations, hire themselves out for pay, work their own garden plots, hunt, fish, trap, or gather fruits, nuts, firewood, and pot ashes, and take the products of their labor into town and sell them. Because no work was required of slaves on their free days, masters expected slaves to provide for themselves on those days. Within a short time it became customary also to give slaves Saturday afternoons off and to assign them plots of land on which to grow their own food and barns and bins in which to store it. In effect, slaves became a self-supporting group, participating in the New Orleans market economy.[52] By the end of the French period slaves regularly held a Sunday market on the edge of the city at the end of Orleans Street. After the Spanish built Fort St. Ferdinand on the site a short time later, the slaves' market continued at the foot of the fort's gorge, on the esplanade that ran just inside the city's walls. And after the Americans pulled the fort down in 1804, slaves held their market on the resulting open space designated Place du Cirque, known during the antebellum decades as Congo Square.[53]

Besides the Indians and Africans, the only other identifiable ethnic group in the French–French Canadian society of New Orleans was a handful of Germans. The Indian unrest following the Natchez war caused a few German farmers to abandon the countryside for safety in New Orleans. And in the 1740s, a prosperous time for planters but a bad one for small farmers, still more came to the city. Those Rhenish, Palatine, Alsatian, and Swiss Germans, expert farmers brought in by the Company of the Indies during the 1720s and settled along the Mississippi north of New Orleans on the "German Coast," had proved the single most important factor in saving the colony from starvation during that critical decade.[54] In the city, they became workmen and tavern

52. *Ibid.*, 135–45, and especially the account of a remarkable court case late in the Spanish period involving slave "rights" to free days (pp. 183–93). Laura Porteus, "Civil Procedures in 1774—Loppinot's Case," *Louisiana Historical Quarterly*, XII (1929), 49–120, provides a translation of the proceedings.

53. Jerah Johnson, "New Orleans's Congo Square: An Urban Setting for Early Afro-American Culture Formation," *Louisiana History*, XXXII (Spring, 1991), 117–57.

54. John Hanno Deiler, *The Settlement of the German Coast of Louisiana and the Creoles of German Descent* (Philadelphia, 1909), 119–28; Helmut Blume, *Die Entwicklung der Kulturlandschaft des Missippideltas in kolonialer Zeit* (Kiel, 1956), 61–62.

keepers and settled among some of the two hundred or so Swiss-German mercenaries that the company and the crown maintained in the colony, some of whom stayed on after their enlistments ended. But they were too few to achieve a lasting identity. Most of the German-speakers who remained on their farms as well as those in the city were Catholics, and they rapidly assimilated by intermarriage with their French neighbors. Most German names came to be pronounced in the French fashion—Lutz is still pronounced Luetz—some spelled in French orthography—Verlay for Wehrle—and some literally translated—Zweig became LaBranche.[55]

But even as the early Germans were losing their identity, another group in the city was developing an identity, or at least a corporate self-conception. This group consisted of members of the Superior Council, which was the equivalent of the largely hereditary caste of judicial bureaucrats, the members of the *parlements,* in the mother country. Jerry A. Micelle has shown in his study of what he called the "metamorphosis" of the Superior Council that by the latter decades of the French period the members of the council not only constituted the colony's chief judicial body, a function sanctioned by royal edicts dating from 1712 and 1716, but did a good deal more besides. Though the crown explicitly directed that the council "must not take part directly or indirectly in what concerns the government and the general administration of the colony," the council evolved into a legislative body as well, issuing com-

---

Newer works such as Giraud, *Histoire de la Louisiane française,* III, 277–83, and IV, 154–57, and Reinhart Kondert, "Germans in Louisiana: The Colonial Experience, 1720–1803," *Yearbook of German-American Studies,* XVI (1981), 59–66, correct Deiler's inflated figures.

55. Recent genealogical work used in conjunction with the increasing number of published baptismal, marriage, and funeral records form virtually a new source for Louisiana's social history. Newer family genealogies are fuller and more accurate than older works such as Grace King's *Creole Families of New Orleans* (New York, 1921) and Herman de B. Seebold's *Old Louisiana Plantation Homes and Family Trees* (2 vols.; New Orleans, 1941). For German Coast families Jack Belson's edition of Deiler's *Settlement of the German Coast* (Baltimore, 1969), to which Belson has added a valuable introduction on sources, remains prime. For New Orleans, as well as the German Coast, Earl C. Woods and Charles E. Nolan, eds., *Sacramental Records of the Roman Catholic Church of the Archdiocese of New Orleans, 1718–1750* (New Orleans, 1987), is basic, though its usefulness to historians is severely restricted by its alphabetical rather than chronological arrangement. Local genealogical journals such as the *New Orleans Genesis* and *Le Voyageur* are valuable. O'Neill, *Church and State,* 258–72, comments on the Germans who were Protestants, as does Glenn R. Conrad, "Alsatian Immigration to Louisiana, 1753–1759," *New Orleans Genesis,* XIV (1975), 221–26.

mercial, slave, property, and licensing regulations. Moreover, it was able to force the colony's *commissaire-ordonnateur*, the king's resident personal agent, to respect the formality of issuing his directives under the authority of the council.[56]

Indeed, it was the members of the Superior Council who led the protest against the crown's cession of the colony to Spain in 1763 and the open revolt against the first Spanish governor in 1768. The council sent a score or more letters and petitions to the king and his ministers expressing concern that the cession eroded the customary corporate rights and privileges of the judiciary—its "liberties," in the eighteenth-century French understanding of the term.[57]

Micelle explains that the members of the Superior Council evolved this conception of themselves because in the remote colony "customary and traditional practices were far stronger than royal decrees," and "when the laws did not fit the circumstances, custom prevailed." In the absence of close supervision, the council was able "gradually to accumulate routine administrative functions," and "when the laws could not be enforced . . . medieval government functioned in the New World as it had in the Old."[58]

The stabilizing of colonial New Orleans society is also reflected in an often told story of Bienville's successor, the Marquis de Vaudreuil. When he came to town in 1743, the "Grand Marquis," the son of a former governor of Canada, was horrified, as his earlier predecessor Governor Cadillac had been, at the rowdiness of the colony's population. Like Cadillac, he resolved to civilize the people. The local populace greeted Vaudreuil's exacting decrees of 1750–51 with none of the outraged derision that had forced Cadillac to abandon his earlier attempt to legislate social graces. Instead, they responded with a respect and an appreciation reflecting a new maturity.[59] New Orleans residents soon vied for invitations to Vaudreuil's elegant dinner parties and anxiously

56. Jerry A. Micelle, "From Law Court to Local Government: Metamorphosis of the Superior Council of French Louisiana," *Louisiana History*, IX (1968), 85–107.

57. *Ibid.*; see also Hans W. Baade, "Marriage Contracts in French and Spanish Louisiana: A Study in 'Notarial' Jurisprudence," *Tulane Law Review*, LIII (December, 1979), 34. The most recent addition to the historiography of the 1768 revolt is Carl A. Brasseaux's *Denis-Nicolas Foucault and the New Orleans Rebellion of 1768* (Ruston, La., 1987).

58. Micelle, "From Law Court to Local Government," and Baade, "Marriage Contracts in French and Spanish Louisiana," 32–40.

59. McGowan, "Creation of a Slave Society," 145–55, discusses the articles of the code that pertained to slaves.

awaited assignments to a place in the formal and ceremonial little court with which the new governor surrounded himself. They looked willingly to the governor to set the city's social pace, its tone and style. During the brief three and a half decades that separated Vaudreuil and Cadillac, New Orleans had come into being and its society had become typical of colonial enclaves everywhere, a tiny would-be microcosm of the home country's society, a colonial fragment.[60]

The structure that New Orleans' society assumed, in imitation of the motherland's, is best visualized in what social scientists and social historians call reticulated models. Such models are designed to show that individuals belonging to different cultural groups are so enmeshed in an overall stratification system or a shared common culture that the subcultures of the several groups blur or erode in favor of the pervasive shared culture, which assumes its form by drawing elements from the various subcultures. Reticulated models require two-plane diagrams: one plane representing the overall stratification or shared culture, the second representing the various subcultures superimposed upon the first. Such diagrams show the members of most cultural or ethnic groups distributed through the full range of the general stratification or common culture and a few groups—in New Orleans, slaves on one extreme and members of the Superior Council on the other—distributed only through the lower or the upper ranges.[61]

Thus it was that by the middle of the eighteenth century, New Orleans had become, at least in its social structure, a peculiarly French city, or more precisely, a peculiarly eighteenth-century French colonial city. And it was that city, along with the rest of the colony, that Spain took over following the collapse of France's North American empire at the close of the Seven Years' War in 1763. Throughout the nearly forty years that Spain held it, New Orleans remained a colonial French city. It never became Spanish in a cultural sense, and it would still be a colonial French city when the United States took over in 1803.

60. At the end of the French period New Orleans had only 3,190 people, of whom 1,288 were slaves and 99 were free people of color. See Jacqueline Voorhies, *Some Late Eighteenth Century Louisianians: Census Records, 1758–1796* (Lafayette, La., 1973).

61. For examples of such reticulated models see Despres, *Cultural Pluralism and Nationalist Politics in British Guiana*, 19. Harmannus Hoetink, *Slavery and Race Relations in the Americas* (New York, 1973) and his *Two Variants in Caribbean Race Relations: A Contribution to the Sociology of Segmented Societies* (New York, 1964) are also instructive on the point, as is Emerich K. Francis, *Interethnic Relations* (New York, 1976). G. Carter Bentley's *Studies in Ethnicity and Nationality: An Annotated Bibliography* (Seattle, 1978) is a basic guide to such studies.

Had Spain gotten New Orleans earlier, or had the city's ancestry been other than French, or had Spain been able to flood it with Spanish colonists, the story might have been different. But as it was, the Spanish who came to New Orleans found themselves far more changed by the city than they were ever able to change it. Like other groups who had and would come in, they became New Orleanians.

Numerically, the Spanish presence in New Orleans was minimal, limited largely to administrative personnel, who constituted an essentially military presence. The military nature of the Spanish administration is not surprising, for during the time she held Louisiana, Spain was moving toward reorganizing her empire along the lines laid out in the massive administrative and commercial reforms developed by the enlightened despot Carlos III, who had just come to the Spanish throne in 1759. A major goal of the reorganization was to protect the productive heart of Spain's American empire—Mexico and Peru and, increasingly, the Rio de la Plata basin and Cuba—by militarizing the administrations of the outlying frontier provinces, among them the newly acquired Louisiana.[62] The staff of the military administration consisted of the governor, twelve district military commandants, a few score army officers, and a modest force of troops—an average for the period of only about eight hundred men.[63]

Neither the governor nor the district commandants had civilian staffs to speak of. Spain, knowing, in the words of Jack D. L. Holmes, that she had to "populate Louisiana or lose it," recruited great numbers of miscellaneous colonists.[64] Louisiana's population increased sixfold

62. Aspects of the reorganization of the Spanish empire may be found in Allan J. Kuethe, *Military Reform and Society in New Granada* (Gainesville, Fla., 1978) and "The Development of the Cuban Military as a Socio-Political Elite, 1763–1783," *Hispanic American Historical Review,* LXI (1981), 695–704. For a general but informative view see John Lynch, "The Iberian States and the Italian States, 1763–1793," in *The American and French Revolutions, 1763–93,* 360–78, Vol. VIII of *The New Cambridge Modern History;* and R. A. Humphreys, "The Development of the American Communities Outside British Rule," *ibid.,* 398–406. Spanish plans for organizing Louisiana are outlined in the latter pages of John Preston Moore's *Revolt in Louisiana: The Spanish Occupation, 1766–1770* (Baton Rouge, 1976); and J. A. Robertson, ed., *Louisiana Under France, Spain, and the United States* (2 vols.; Cleveland, 1971).

63. In the early decades the number averaged five to six hundred and in the later decades a thousand to thirteen hundred. In times of crisis, which occurred, on average, every three years, the force was built up, only to be reduced when the crisis passed. See Jack D. L. Holmes, *Honor and Fidelity: The Louisiana Infantry Regiment and the Louisiana Militia Companies, 1766–1821* (Birmingham, Ala., 1965).

64. Jack D. L. Holmes, *Gayoso: The Life of a Spanish Governor in the Mississippi Valley, 1789–1799* (Baton Rouge, 1965), 24.

during the Spanish period and that of New Orleans nearly tripled, but few of the newcomers were Spanish, and most of those few who were Spanish scattered into outlying districts of the colony. As a result, their presence had little effect. District law courts, for example, continued to be drawn virtually entirely from long-resident French creole families. Even in New Orleans, which, as the capital, had the largest contingent of administrators and troops, the story was the same. The Cabildo, which replaced the Superior Council as the colony's high court and the city's chief administrative agency, became a completely venal institution, in line with Spanish law and administrative practice. Rich French creole planters who had residences in or near the city purchased and held most of its seats throughout the period.[65]

Even the military was surprisingly un-Spanish. Of the 226 officers and sergeants in the colony in 1793 for whom we have full service records, slightly less than half came from Spain. A few of the others came from elsewhere in Europe: 5 from Italy, 4 from Germany, 2 from Portugal, 2 from Ireland, and, notably, 15 from France. The remaining 88 were born in Louisiana: 85 in New Orleans and 3 in the districts.[66]

Some of the eighty-eight locally born Spanish infantry officers had Spanish parents, for a handful of officers and a few troops brought wives with them to the colony, but most were issues of marriages between Spaniards and local French creoles. Four of the eight Spanish governors who served in Louisiana, for example, married local brides. Such marriages were not always between Spanish men and local women, for daughters of Spanish officers and troops sometimes married local men.[67]

Marriages into the local population by the Spanish military were far fewer than one might expect. Military personnel had to secure official permission to marry, and any officer exercising judicial authority, which included not only governors but also district commandants, was inter-

65. John E. Harkins, "The Neglected Phase of Louisiana's Colonial History: The New Orleans Cabildo, 1769–1803" (Ph.D. dissertation, Memphis State University, 1976).

66. Holmes, *Gayoso*, 168. Figures adjusted to the 226 officers and sergeants whose records appear in Holmes, *Honor and Fidelity*. Virginia R. Dominguez, *White by Definition: Social Classification in Creole Louisiana* (New Brunswick, N.J., 1986), 109, gives a tabulation of French and Spanish officers in the infantry in 1793 and 1803 that parallels the above figures.

67. Holmes, *Gayoso*, 27, 30–31, 121–24, 278. Records of the period show few of the children of Spanish fathers and French mothers attaching their mothers' maiden names to their fathers' surnames in the Spanish fashion, as in *Otero y Dubreuily*, but far more cases of the children of French fathers and Spanish mothers doing so, as in *Dubreuily y Otero*, which indicates that women generally controlled the naming process.

dicted by Spanish imperial regulations from marrying into any family living in his district. Exceptions required special and difficult-to-come-by permission.[68] More important, most of the military, being mobile professional soldiers, chose bachelorhood. Something like 67 percent of Spanish officers over twenty years of age remained unmarried. And judging from the New Orleans post hospital records, which rank venereal diseases along with fever and dysentery as the most frequent ailments, probably the overwhelming majority of troops, who came from an even more diverse assortment of non-Spanish ethnic backgrounds and served on five-year enlistments, remained single. Thus Spaniards in New Orleans were not only limited in number, but their marriages into the local population were even more limited.[69]

But that did not mean that Spanish crown authorities had no interest in Hispanicizing the new colony. They did, and they tried. They decreed Spanish as the official language, and all official documents and court records, including notarial acts such as wills and contracts, were normally drafted in that language, at least in New Orleans. In the districts, however, Spanish was almost never used, even in official documents and communications to the governor. In official documents and on census rolls, French first names were translated into Spanish and surnames often were spelled in the Spanish fashion. In his youth Bernard Philippe Xavier de Marigny de Mandeville, the future "Grand Creole," appeared on the record as Bernardo Felipe Javier de Marigni de Mandevil. But, of course, he never called himself anything but Bernard, nor was he called anything but that by anyone else, save his masters at the Spanish school who were trying to teach him the new language.[70]

68. Richard Konetzke, "La Prohibitión de casarse los oidores o sus hijos é hijas con naturales del distrito de la Audiencia," in *Homenaje a Don José Mariá de la Peña y Cámara* (Madrid, 1969), 105–20. See Jack D. L. Holmes, "Do It! Don't Do It!: Spanish Laws on Sex and Marriage," in *Louisiana's Legal Heritage*, ed. Edward Haas (New Orleans, 1983), 14–42.

69. The percentage tabulated from the service records compiled by Holmes, *Honor and Fidelity*, 89–258; see also *ibid.*, 75–77 for a description of the troops. The service records usually give place of birth, but in the absence of such information, one can judge ethnic origin only by surnames, a tricky procedure that has to be employed with great care. Many surnames that may appear to be Spanish—Suarez, Perez, Miranda, Suelo, Como, Cenas, and Valle, for example—were French. Conversely, a few Gallic-sounding names, such as Bouligny, were Spanish.

70. Carondelet was still complaining in 1796, after nearly thirty years of Spanish rule, that his district commandants sent reports in "a foreign language," for they could find no local Spanish-speaking secretaries (Baade, "Marriage Contracts in French and Spanish Louisiana," 58). Sometimes the task of transliterating names taxed the phonetic

The only groups within the creole population to adopt Spanish-form names in everyday usage were those who held government positions that required it, such as notaries. Jean Baptiste Garic, *Greffier* during the French period became Juan Bautista Garic, *Escribano* under the Spanish. One of his successors in office, Pedro Pedesclaux, *Escribano,* remained such through the last Spanish-language entry he made in his notary book on November 30, 1803, which mentioned the change of sovereignty from Spain back to France. In his very next entry, in French and dated by the French revolutionary calendar as "the eleventh of *Frimaire* of the Year Twelve of the Republic, or December 22, 1803," two days after the United States formally took possession of Louisiana, he became again Pierre Pedesclaux, *Greffier.* A few pages later he changed the word after his name to "*Notaire,*" though he never felt obliged to change the language of his entries to English.[71]

Within two years of finally quelling the explosive local resistance to Spanish rule in 1769, royal authorities developed a plan for increasing knowledge and use of the Castilian language in the colony by opening a Spanish-language school. A year later, in 1772, they sent four teachers, four crates containing 236 volumes for a library, and six crates holding 3,183 textbooks for the students and opened the school. Though in the beginning it offered some elementary instruction, it became essentially a *colegio,* or high school–level military academy, which students entered between the ages of twelve and fifteen and stayed in normally for four years. It operated until the American purchase. It got off to a slow start in large part for lack of Spanish-speaking students of the right age, but over the thirty-one years of its history, even though as few as half a dozen students attended some years, it normally had thirty to forty cadets enrolled and graduated eight to ten a year, not an unimpressive record, given the time and circumstances. The difficulty of finding enough Spanish-speaking students almost immediately forced the school to begin offering instruction in French, which it continued to do.[72] The bi-

ingenuity of the record keepers: Clouard to Cluaatre; Grivois to Gribaun; Benoit to Venua; Guidry to Lledri; and Alexis Breaux to Aleccibro.

71. On the notaries see *ibid.,* 11, 52–54. Vain attempts to introduce Spanish-speaking priests and the Spanish language into church services are described in John W. Caughey, *Bernardo de Galvez in Louisiana, 1776–1783* (Gretna, La., 1972), 45–47, and Roger Baudier, *The Catholic Church in Louisiana* (New Orleans, 1931).

72. David K. Bjork, "Documents Relating to the Establishment of Schools in Louisiana, 1771," *Mississippi Valley Historical Review,* XI (1925), 561–69. Caughey, *Bernardo de Galvez,* 47, calls the school "another fruitless effort to make Spanish the Louisi-

lingual policy of the school reflected its mixed student body. It was never, as has been reputed, a preserve for Spanish officers' sons. About 55 percent of the cadets were sons of French-creole families; 42 percent came from Spanish families; and 3 percent were Irish or Anglos.[73]

Architecture provided Spain's greatest opportunity for leaving a visible mark on New Orleans. Two great fires all but obliterated the town during the Spanish period. One in 1788 burned four-fifths of the buildings to the ground, and another in 1794 destroyed one-fifth of the city. The new city that arose—one of tile-roofed, masonry and stucco buildings, each sited adjoining or nearly adjoining its neighbor, and all abutting the sidewalks—looked substantially different from the earlier French town, which held mostly shingle-roofed, board-walled houses sited well back from the street and apart from one another, each surrounded with ample open spaces for gardens, orchards, chicken yards, and stables. But the many erroneous statements in the historical literature on New Orleans to the contrary notwithstanding, the city that took shape during the Spanish period was not Spanish in architectural form, style, or design.

It is understandable that visitors to the city—few if any of whom were more astute architectural observers than most tourists today—knowing they were in a Spanish colony, or former Spanish colony, hearing a bit of Spanish spoken in the streets, and not knowing that stucco, roofing tile, patios, and wrought iron were not exclusively Spanish architectural features but common to many parts of France as well, would have reported that they saw "Spanish" buildings.[74] It is also understandable, if much more regrettable, that historians, often untrained in architectural analysis, have uncritically incorporated the early travelers' observations into their own works.

New Orleans architectural historian Samuel Wilson's nearly fifty years of research has failed to reveal a single Spanish architect working

---

ana French." See also Holmes, *Gayoso*, 127–29, 209, his *Honor and Fidelity*, 77, and Baudier, *Catholic Church in Louisiana*, 217.

73. Tabulated from the service records of infantry and militia officers who had attended the school. The records are appended to Holmes, *Honor and Fidelity*. See also Charles E. A. Gayarré, *The Spanish Domination* (4th ed.; New Orleans, 1903), 204–206, Vol. III of his *History of Louisiana*, 4 vols.

74. The first permanent building—as distinct from makeshift structures and dwellings—built in New Orleans, the administrative offices of the Company of the Indies, hence the capitol building of the colony, had wrought iron grillwork covering the transom of its main entrance. See Samuel Wilson, Jr., *Bienville's New Orleans: A French Colonial Capital, 1718–1768* (New Orleans, 1968), 17–18.

in the city at any time during the entire forty years of the Spanish period. He learned instead, that the architects of the period were a coterie of French creole designers plus a few resident Anglo-Americans such as Robert Jones. Moreover, they worked within the maritime-French and French-Canadian architectural tradition, enriched with a few elements from the Anglo-American design stream. The new city—which forms today's French Quarter—represented a continuum of New Orleans French colonial architectural development, translating the old city from wood to masonry and placing its components closer together to accommodate the growing population within the physical strictures of the available high ground inside the protective walls of the town.[75]

Even though forty years of Spanish ownership failed to make Louisiana or New Orleans Spanish in culture, language, or architecture, Spain did leave marks on the colony. Spanish surnames and place names still dot the city and the state and the Mississippi and Alabama Gulf coasts, and a few Spanish words such as *picayune* and *perdido* still color New Orleans nomenclature if not its speech. Louisiana in general, and New Orleans in particular, benefited from Spanish governance and judicial administration, and many elements of Spanish law stand today alongside French elements in Louisiana's civil code. And several celebrated items from the catalog of New Orleans cuisine derived from Spanish dishes, jambalaya from Spain's paella for instance.[76]

The two most important other ethnic groups during the Spanish period were refugees from the revolutions on the Caribbean French island of Saint Domingue, who soon came to be called the "foreign French" by New Orleans creoles, and Anglo-Americans, who increasingly immigrated to Louisiana from British-ruled Florida and from the United States. The major accommodation both groups would have to make would be not to the Spanish authorities, who required little of incoming settlers beyond a pledge of loyalty to the Spanish crown, observance of

75. Samuel Wilson, Jr., has shared the results of his research in countless lectures both in the classrooms of Tulane University's School of Architecture and in public forums. Some of his lectures are on videotape in the collection of the Audio-Visual Center of the University of New Orleans. In particular, see his "Gulf Coast Architecture" in *Spain and Her Rivals on the Gulf Coast,* ed. Ernest F. Dibble and Earle W. Newton (Pensacola, 1971), 123–24.

76. There is considerable literature and debate on the origins of Louisiana's Civil Code. See Joseph M. Sweeney, "Tournament of Scholars over the Sources of the Civil Code of 1808," *Tulane Law Review,* XLVI (1971–72), 585–603, and the notes to Warren M. Billings, "Louisiana Legal History and Its Sources: Needs, Opportunities and Approaches," in *Louisiana's Legal Heritage,* ed. Haas, 189–202.

Spain's trade laws, and outward conformity to the Catholic church, but to the local French creoles. At the end of the Spanish period there were only about two hundred foreign French in New Orleans and a like number of resident Anglo-Americans. In any given week, the city also hosted a considerably larger number of transient Anglo entrepreneurs and agents, riverboatmen and barge hands, and ships' officers and crewmen associated with the ever-increasing flow of trade goods coming down the Mississippi, some for sale locally and, increasingly, for transshipment from New Orleans' port.[77] But the wave of both groups' immigration crested after the American purchase. Hence their story belongs not to Louisiana's colonial period but to its early antebellum American decades.

By contrast, it was during the Spanish period that Louisiana's free people of color achieved sufficient numbers and a political importance that enabled them to mature into a community.[78] Natural increase, but more important, the greater ease with which manumission could be accomplished under Spanish administration and the influx of free blacks from Saint Domingue, raised the 165 or more free people of color in the colony at the end of the French period to almost 1,500 by the end of the Spanish period.[79] For most of the period more than half of the free

77. These estimates are drawn from a comparison of varying figures given by Antonio Acosta Rodriguez, *La Publacion de Luisiana Española, 1763–1803* (Madrid, 1979), 227–81; Berquin Duvallon, *Travels in Louisiana and the Floridas in the Year 1802*, trans. John Davis (New York, 1806), 48 (this source should be used with care because the translator used much of his own information); John Gurley, one of the early U.S. land registrars, to Gideon Granger, July 14, 1804, cited in Dominguez, *White by Definition*, 110; John Graham to James Madison, January 2, 1806, cited in Charles E. A. Gayarré, *The American Domination* (4th ed.; New Orleans, 1903), 123–24, Vol. IV of his *History of Louisiana;* Gabriel Debien and René Le Gardeur, "Les Colons de Saint-Domingue réfugiés à la Louisiane (1792–1804)," *Revue de Louisiane/Louisiana Review,* X (1981), 132; Vincent Nolte, *Fifty Years in Both Hemispheres: or, Reminiscence of a Merchant's Life* (New York, 1854), 86; George Dargo, *Jefferson's Louisiana: Politics and the Clash of Legal Traditions* (Cambridge, Mass., 1975), 9–11, 180–81; and *New Orleans in 1805: A Dictionary and a Census* (New Orleans, 1936). For some of the complexities of using Spanish censuses see Jack D. L. Holmes, "A New Look at Spanish-Louisiana Census Accounts," *Louisiana History,* XXI (1980), 77–86. The large number of transient English-speakers much in evidence in the commercial quarter of the city probably led several contemporary observers to overestimate the number of Anglo-American residents. See Dominguez, *White by Definition*, 110.

78. The terms *free people of color* and *free blacks* are, for convenience, used interchangeably here, though colonial records distinguished, as later U.S. census takers did, between blacks and mulattoes.

79. After 1770, Spanish law provided slaves virtually automatic rights of emancipation by self-purchase and no longer required, as French law had, registration, *i.e.,* ap-

people of color lived not in New Orleans but on small farms or as tenants outside of town. In 1785, for example, nearly three-quarters of the way through the Spanish period, 563 free people of color lived in New Orleans and 612 lived in the districts. But about that time the balance began to shift, probably because of increased opportunities in a growing New Orleans. By 1803 the overwhelming number lived in the city, close to 1,200 of the 1,500 or so.[80]

Because of their unique social and legal standing, midway between the free and the slave sectors of the population and recognized as such in law, the free people of color developed the most nearly complete corporate status of any of the several such groups in colonial Louisiana society. Acutely conscious of their legal rights and their group's interests as well as the tenuous and fragile nature of their position, they tended to act with an exceptionally high degree of cohesiveness. At the same time, individual members of the group freely associated with the European colonials, the African slaves, and the Indians, both free and slave. Work, service, trade, and *plaçage,* the developing institution of formalized mistress-keeping, brought them into close contact with the European community, while close cultural and family bonds tied them to both the slave and Indian communities. Except for recently arrived islanders, there were few free people of color who did not have relatives, often immediate family members, among the African slaves and not infrequently among the Indians.[81]

---

proval, of manumission by the Cabildo. The number of free people of color either at the end of the French period or at the end of the Spanish and the opening of the American period cannot be fixed exactly, but the 165 usually cited for the end of the French period is almost certainly a considerable undercount. See Gwendolyn Midlo Hall, *Africans in Colonial Louisiana: The Development of Afro-Creole Culture in the Eighteenth Century* (Baton Rouge, 1992), chap. VIII. For a useful, if debatable, table of New Orleans' population of color from 1721 to 1970 see Dominguez, *White by Definition,* 116–17. At the time of the American purchase New Orleans had about 8,050 people, of whom 2,775 were slaves and 1,335 free people of color, according to Berquin Duvallon's figures.

80. Henry E. Sterkx, *The Free Negro in Ante-Bellum Louisiana* (Rutherford, N.J., 1972), 85; McGowan, "Creation of a Slave Society," 196–99, 200–202, 205–207. Construction jobs in the rebuilding of New Orleans after the disastrous fire of 1788 may have attracted large numbers of free people of color to the city.

81. The literature on Louisiana's colonial free people of color is large, but much of it is marred by conceptions and assumptions carried over from studies of free blacks in Anglo-America. See Ira Berlin, *Slaves Without Masters: The Free Negro in the Antebellum South* (New York, 1974), 108–32; Gary B. Mills, *The Forgotten People: Cane River Creoles of Color* (Baton Rouge, 1977); Mary J. Woods, *Marginality and Identity: A Closed Creole Family Through Ten Generations* (Baton Rouge, 1972); Hans W. Baade,

Political circumstances, moreover, provided an unusual opportunity for the free people of color. Among the many problems faced by the Spanish governing authorities in the colony, two that assumed paramount importance involved the planters and the slaves. First, the Spanish authorities were continually troubled over the independent and testy stance assumed by the colony's creole planters, who, along with the other members of the Superior Council, had organized and led the worrisome and embarrassingly effective mass resistance to the coming of Spanish rule in 1768–69. Second, harsh treatment of slaves, who formed a majority of the colony's population, by the creole planters made the Spanish authorities increasingly anxious about possible slave revolts. That anxiety turned to alarm after the French revolutionary government freed all slaves on France's Caribbean islands in 1794 and began spreading "dread republican doctrines" in Louisiana.

The overall Spanish imperial policy of militarizing the administrations in frontier provinces had largely neutralized the planters by stripping them of policing powers over local populations, including the free people of color. Convinced that unduly harsh treatment engendered slave revolts, but unable to persuade the planters of their argument, Louisiana's Spanish governors began to interpose themselves and the local administration as guarantors of slaves' rights as specified in Spanish law, particularly the rights to reasonable treatment and self-purchase. The effect was further to isolate the planters by driving a wedge between them and their slaves, provoking the planters to heightened resentment and recalcitrance.

Fearful of an explosion, the Spanish determined to keep close watch on the planters lest they develop plans for action. At the same time, having shouldered the burden of policing the population—including slaves as well as an increasing number of runaways, who often moved in with Indians or formed troublesome maroon settlements in the swamps outside the city—the Spanish lacked reliable manpower to secure the colony. They found the answer in the free people of color.

The French had used black troops, both slave and free, since the 1730 Natchez uprising and continued to do so throughout the time they

---

"The Law of Slavery in Spanish Louisiana, 1769–1803," in *Louisiana's Legal Heritage*, ed. Haas, 19–42; Laura Foner, "The Free People of Color in Louisiana and St. Domingue: A Comparative Portrait of Two Three-Caste Slave Societies," *Journal of Social History*, III (1970), 406–30; and Donald E. Everett, "Free Persons of Color in Colonial Louisiana," *Louisiana History*, VII (1966), 21–50, though the latter has to be used with care.

held the colony, but only in small numbers and on rare occasions. The Spanish used blacks in greater numbers, and during the campaigns against the British in the American revolutionary war, formalized the practice by organizing a free black militia composed of two companies, each with its own officers. After the war the Spanish authorities kept the militia unit intact and used it to police slaves, pursue runaways, attack maroon infestations, and, in the 1790s, when fear of "republicanism" and possible attacks from the United States and France sent near panic through the local administration, to man the forts and city walls of New Orleans—an action that the local population regarded more as a threat than a protection.[82]

Many other members of the free black community, recognizing the enormous advantages government protection and patronage would bring not only to free people of color generally but to their brothers and sisters still in bondage as well, made the best of a bad bargain and supplied Spanish authorities with information gleaned from their daily contacts with planters, slaves, and Indians.[83]

But the precariously balanced alliance between free blacks and Spanish authorities tipped in 1795, never again to right itself. In the spring of that year the district military commandant at Point Coupée, Don Guillermo DuParc, uncovered plans for a sizable slave revolt. News of the near catastrophe, in which some Indians and not a few free people of color were implicated, coupled with the almost simultaneous discovery in New Orleans of a "French revolutionary republican plot" to topple the Spanish regime and the rumored presence of a French fleet in the Gulf, plunged the colony into pandemonium. The unholy alliance with the free people of color crumbled, leaving the governor, the Baron de Carondelet, no choice but to join forces with the planters and restore policing authority to them. Together they laid the colony under a regime of counterterror. They hanged twenty-three slave conspirators, deported some thirty-five more, reinstituted rigid slave control and discipline, and, after the discovery of another planned slave uprising just a

<hr />

82. Sterkx, *Free Negro*, 26–28, 73–79; Roland C. McConnell, "Louisiana's Black Military History, 1729–1865," in *Louisiana's Black Heritage*, ed. Macdonald, Kemp, and Haas, 32–62; McConnell, *Negro Troops of Antebellum Louisiana: A History of the Battalion of Free Men of Color* (Baton Rouge, 1968), and Jack D. L. Holmes, "The Role of Blacks in Spanish Alabama: The Mobile District, 1780–1813," *Alabama Historical Quarterly*, XXXVII (1975), 5–18.

83. Sterkx noted the untenable position in which the Spanish authorities placed the free people of color (*Free Negro*, 79–87), and McGowan elaborated it, making it the matrix of the latter part of his "Creation of a Slave Society," 296–401.

year later, banned the importation of any more slaves from the West Indies.[84]

In the crackdown, the free people of color suffered renewed scrutiny and control. On June 1, 1795, Carondelet ordered that all authorities, including the planters who had been made syndics or local justices of the peace, should "observe that all free people of color labor either in the field, or at some trade within their district, and shall send the indolent and vagabonds to the commandant of the post, who shall fix them at the capital, where they shall be employed upon the king's buildings, and other public works."[85]

The great scare of the mid-1790s passed and the authorities lifted the harsh repressions and restored legal protections to slaves and "liberties" to the free people of color, but things never really settled down. Spain's last three colonial governors served only brief terms of two years each, followed by a very active and ambitious twenty-one-day period of renewed French administration before it turned over authority to the United States. Carondelet's successor reopened the slave trade in 1797 and then closed it; his successor opened it again in 1800, but the next governor closed it again in 1803. The simultaneous and dramatic shift to an economy based on trade with the United States and the rise of a prospering merchant class in New Orleans only added to the disorder that characterized the last six years of Louisiana's colonial history.

The free people of color survived with their liberties and property intact, but at the cost of new suspicions and jealousies. It is not surprising that, a few years later, the free people of color, those with the most to lose, would be among the first groups to demand recognition of their unique status from the new American authorities. Nor is it surprising that those authorities would view New Orleans' free people of color as a peculiar and dangerous problem that had to be dealt with as soon as possible. And when they attempted to deal with it, they did so not in the assimilationist mode that had characterized the whole of New Orleans' and Louisiana's colonial history, but in the Anglo-American mode of exclusion.

Like the Spanish before them, however, the incoming Anglo-Americans soon found that they could not easily superimpose their culture

84. McGowan, "Creation of a Slave Society," 269–401. See also Jack D. L. Holmes, "The Abortive Slave Revolt at Pointe Coupee, Louisiana, 1795," *Louisiana History*, XI (1970), 341–62.

85. Quoted by Everett, "Free Persons of Color in Colonial Louisiana," 49.

and institutions on the city. The city's hundred-year history as a fragment of the eighteenth-century French ethos proved too strong. In New
Orleans the seventeenth- and eighteenth-century French assimilationist
ethos finally achieved its apotheosis. Although it would be overstating
the case to conclude that the assimilationist attitude in New Orleans
caused, in the sense of forced, the remarkable cultural meld that has
characterized the city's history, the existence of such a social attitude
permitted and facilitated that meld. In that sense and to that degree, in
New Orleans at least, Champlain's two-hundred-year-old dream of
making a new France in the New World became a reality.

2

The Formation of Afro-Creole Culture

GWENDOLYN MIDLO HALL

The essential patterns of New Orleans culture took shape early and remained apparent throughout the city's history. When Louisiana became part of the United States in 1803, newcomers had to adjust to the existing culture. The African imprint was formidable and constant throughout the eighteenth century. Slave culture in Louisiana should not be treated in isolation, as if it were sealed off from the rest of society and the world. Culture is a dynamic process. The definition of culture as socially acquired knowledge, as "what people have to learn as distinct from their biological heritage . . . whatever it is one has to know or believe in order to operate in a manner acceptable to its members,"[1] is far too static. Eric R. Wolf's definition of culture as "a series of processes that construct, reconstruct, and dismantle cultural materials, in response to identifiable determinants,"[2] is closer to the mark. In the Americas, new cultures were formed through intense and often violent contacts among peoples of varied nations, races, classes, languages, and traditions. The Europeans in this equation were far from omnipotent. It is wrong to assume that an all-powerful, static national culture and society was brought over by the European colonizers into which non-

1. W. H. Goodenough, "Cultural Anthropology and Linguistics," in *Report on the Seventh Annual Round Table Meeting on Linguistics and Language*, ed. P. L. Garvin (Washington, D.C., 1957), quoted in R. A. Hudson, *Sociolinguistics* (Cambridge, Eng., 1980), 74.
2. Eric R. Wolf, *Europe and the People Without History* (Berkeley, 1982), 387.

Europeans were more or less socialized and acculturated.[3] Cultural influences intensely interpenetrated the extremely varied population of the Americas. Like the native Americans and the Africans, Europeans were acculturated by the people and the world they encountered. This chapter will focus on some of the many-faceted historical reasons why New Orleans remains, in spirit, the most African city in the United States.

During the last two decades, American historians have begun to pay serious attention to the crucial formative period of slavery, race relations, and slave culture in the English Atlantic colonies. Beginning with Peter Wood's study of colonial South Carolina, slavery, race relations, and culture formation have been treated in the context of time, place, and circumstance. Ira Berlin has criticized historical scholarship since World War II for focusing on the mature phase of slavery in the antebellum South, promoting an essentially static vision. Berlin discussed the development of slavery in three regions during the seventeenth and eighteenth centuries—the North, the Chesapeake, and the Carolina and Georgia low country—identifying varying patterns of the slave trade, proportions of whites and blacks, and the labor demands of particular export crops as crucial factors shaping the formation of the particular slave culture of each region.[4]

If recent historical scholarship has been slow to appreciate the importance of the early colonial period for the development of varying patterns of Afro-American culture in different regions of Anglophone United States, the problem has been compounded for the very distinctive slave culture that developed in Louisiana during the eighteenth century. The Afro-creole slave culture of Louisiana, firmly established by the time the United States purchased the Louisiana Territory in 1803, has not been given the attention it deserves. This culture was based on a separate language community with its own folkloric, musical, religious, and historical tradition. Unlike the Gullah dialect, which survived in the isolated Sea Islands off the coast of South Carolina and Georgia, the Louisiana creole language, created by slaves brought directly from Africa between 1719 and 1731, survived widely in southern Louisiana un-

3. For an influential contrary view, see Louis Hartz, *The Founding of New Societies: Studies in the History of the United States, Latin America, South Africa, and Australia* (New York, 1964).

4. Peter H. Wood, *Black Majority: Negroes in Colonial South Carolina from 1670 Through the Stono Rebellion* (New York, 1974); Ira Berlin, "Time, Space, and the Evolution of Afro-American Society on British Mainland North America," *American Historical Review*, LXXXVI (1980), 44–78.

til World War II and is still spoken by tens of thousands of people, white as well as black, in some parts of the state. A cultural revival of artistic expression in the Louisiana creole language is currently taking place.[5]

Certainly, the Afro-creole culture of New Orleans has had a significant impact not only on blacks of Louisiana and Afro-American culture in the United States but on American culture in general. New Orleans was the commercial center from which the slave system expanded into the Southwest during the nineteenth century. Slaves imported through New Orleans from the Atlantic Coast encountered and were partially socialized by an established, self-conscious, self-confident Afro-creole slave community. The largest slave plantations of the antebellum South were in Louisiana. Slave participation in the Civil War began and was most extensive in Louisiana. The bitterest battles of Reconstruction, as well as the first mass migrations north after its end, occurred in Louisiana.[6] Afro-creole folklore, religion, and music, most notably jazz, spread up the Mississippi Valley into Memphis, Chicago, New York, Los Angeles, and, ultimately, the world.

Throughout the Americas, the word *creole* has been redefined over time for social reasons and has many meanings. It derives from the Portuguese word *crioulo,* meaning a slave of African descent born in the New World. Thereafter, it was extended to include Europeans born in the New World, now the only meaning of the word in Portugal.[7] In Spanish and French colonies, including eighteenth-century Louisiana, the term *creole* was used to distinguish American-born from African-born slaves; all first-generation slaves born in America and their descendants were designated creoles. The meaning of the word changed during the Latin American struggles for independence in the late eighteenth and early nineteenth centuries. The Latin American elite born in the Americas was called the creole elite and was accused of being incapable of self-rule in part because of its racially mixed heritage. Rejecting this heritage, the creole elite of Latin America redefined the word *creole* to mean people of exclusively European descent born in the Americas. Since creole lan-

---

5. Ingrid Neumann, *Le Créole de Breaux Bridge, Louisiane: Etude morphosyntaxique* (Hamburg, 1985), 40–43, 43n. For an example of the language revival see *Chicory Review,* I (1988), 1.

6. Joe Gray Taylor, *Louisiana Reconstructed, 1863–1877* (Baton Rouge, 1974); Nell Painter, *The Exodusters: Black Migration to Kansas Following Reconstruction* (New York, 1977); William Gillette, *Retreat from Reconstruction, 1869–1877* (Baton Rouge, 1979).

7. John Holm, *Pidgins and Creoles: Theory and Structure* (2 vols.; Cambridge, Eng., 1988), I, 9.

guages did not exist in Ibero-America, this redefinition was less complicated than in the non-Hispanic Caribbean and in Louisiana.

New Orleans under French rule was a permeable frontier village with a small, often dwindling white population whose survival depended on maintaining good relations with France's Indian allies, mainly the Choctaws, and the labor and military skills of its African and Afrocreole slaves. France's British rivals on the Atlantic Coast kept up constant pressure on this sparsely populated strategic colony through the Chickasaw Indians and, at times, by successfully infiltrating the Choctaw Indians, using better and cheaper trade goods as a lure.[8] The greatest strength of these mainly Canadian and French settlers was their openness to people of other races and cultures. This attitude was surely the main reason for their survival in such a dangerous and inhospitable land.

Although we normally think of African slaves as a culturally and linguistically divided population and the European colonizers as powerful and homogeneous, the whites of French Louisiana were far from a coherent, self-conscious class of slaveowners. Louisiana was founded mainly by Canadians, along with some Frenchmen and some pirates from the Caribbean. The first census, dating from December, 1699, lists five officers (among whom at least two were Canadians), five petty officers, four sailors, nineteen Canadians, thirteen pirates, ten laborers, six cabin boys, and twenty soldiers stationed at Biloxi. The German population, survivors of settlers brought in by John Law, became a very significant and stable element of the European population. By 1724, sixty households of Germans were established in villages located above New Orleans, living in relative isolation and, at least initially, holding very few slaves.

Social and cultural conflict among the whites was intense. French bureaucrats looked down on and felt threatened by the flexible and adaptable Canadian *coureurs-du-bois*. A few members of the military-bureaucratic elite that ruled Louisiana held large concentrations of slaves. Bienville, his relatives, and his Canadian favorites lived in luxury in fancy houses, with many slaves obtained through ill-gotten gain, while most of the white population went hungry and naked.[9] Most of the French-speaking colonists owned no slaves or only a few.

8. Gary B. Nash, *Red, White, and Black: The Peoples of Early America* (Englewood Cliffs, 1974); Patricia Dillon Woods, *French-Indian Relations on the Southern Frontier, 1699–1762* (Ann Arbor, 1980).

9. La Chaise to Commissaires de la Compagnie, September 6, 1723, in C13 7, fol. 7, Archives Nationales, Paris, hereafter cited as AN.

Louisiana had a legitimate reputation as a land of disease, famine, and political and military exploitation. It was difficult, to say the least, to obtain voluntary colonists in France. During 1717 and 1718, prisoners who had been condemned to the galleys had their sentences commuted and were sent to Louisiana to work for three years, after which time they were to get part of the land they had cleared and cultivated. The prisoners were brought to the port under heavy guard and chained aboard the ships. At the same time, the names of soldiers who had deserted, vagabonds, and persons without means were placed on lists to be deported to Louisiana. Some had been arrested for acts of violence, murder, debauchery, and drunkenness, but they were mostly beggars and vagabonds from Paris and the French provinces.

By 1719, deportation to Louisiana was considered a convenient way of getting rid of troublesome neighbors or family members. Some families asked that incorrigible sons, daughters, nieces, and nephews be deported. Persons from all social milieus were denounced for their conduct, and police inquiries were held. The following were typical comments in police files: "Here is a true subject for Louisiana" and "A very bad subject who deserves . . . to be among those who are destined for the new colonies."

A special police force received head taxes for each victim apprehended. The police roamed around Paris and the provinces grabbing people for profit, often based on false accusations. Bloody collisions took place in Paris between these police brigades and the population. Kidnappings, fights between police and potential victims, and riots erupted in the streets. Prisoners in Paris awaiting deportation to Louisiana rioted. On January 1, 1720, the prison of St. Martin-des-Champs held 107 prisoners destined for Louisiana. Fifty men and women forced the doors, wounded two guards, and fled. Because of these disorders, on May 9, 1720, the king forbade further forced deportations to Louisiana.[10] In addition to the forced immigrants and indentured servants, there were French and Swiss soldiers in the colony who had been sent by force and were treated, in some respects, worse than slaves or indentured servants. Soldiers were tortured and executed for the most trivial reasons. The normal punishment meted out to Swiss soldiers was to be sawed in half.[11]

10. Marcel Giraud, *Histoire de la Louisiane française* (4 vols.; Paris, 1953–74), III, 252–76.
11. Jean-Bernard Bossu, *Travels in the Interior of North America, 1751–1762,* trans. Seymour Feiler (Norman, Okla., 1962), ix–xii, 178–83.

Both biology and ecology led to the creation of a permeable society and culture. Cypress swamps surrounded the city, creating an excellent refuge for runaways who knew how to survive by hunting and fishing. There were many more men than women among whites as well as blacks. Race mixture was common and widely accepted. New Orleans was a seaport and a city of deserters. The city's early history involved a struggle for survival on the most elementary level. Desperation transcended race and status, and diverse peoples cooperated in their efforts to escape the colony. Indian and African slaves, deportees from France, including women sent against their will, Swiss and French soldiers, and indentured workers (*engagés*) fled in all directions. In 1720, fifteen people were accused of plotting to desert to the English by going beyond the Choctaw lands in a conspiracy of the damned that transcended race, sex, age, and nationality. The accused included an eighteen-year-old Indian slave, a fifteen-year-old runaway African slave, a French sergeant of the troops, a twenty-eight-year-old Swiss soldier, and a twenty-seven-year-old French woman who had been sent to Louisiana by force and married against her will. In 1745, a runaway slave who had been gone for a year was seen frequently around New Orleans, but no one apprehended him.[12]

Slaves escaped by sea, as the following tauntingly defiant slave song explains:

> O Zenéral Florido!
> C'est vrai yé pas ca-pab' pren moin!
> Yen a ein counan si la mer.
> C'est vrai yé pas ca-pab' pren moin!
>
> Oh General Florido!
> It's true they cannot catch me!
> There is a schooner out at sea.
> It's true they cannot catch me![13]

Slaves and soldiers continued to cooperate in escaping during the 1730s and 1740s. Havana was a favorite destination. In October, 1739, five soldiers of the guardhouse seized a dugout moored at the mouth of Bayou St. Jean and "abducted" six slaves, Nègres and Négresses, be-

---

12. Testimony before Louisiana Superior Council, May 31, 1720, January 16, 1741, and March 15, 1745, Records of the Superior Council of Louisiana, Louisiana Historical Center of the Louisiana State Museum, New Orleans (hereafter cited as RSC LHC).

13. The song was among those collected by George Washington Cable during the late nineteenth century from creole former slaves. There were several attorneys general in Louisiana named Fleuriau throughout the eighteenth century.

longing to Tixerant, officer of marine troops in New Orleans, and his partner Aufrère. They were pursued but escaped. The dugout they escaped in was later found splashed with blood, and a decomposed corpse lay on the shore. It appears that this was not a case of slaves being abducted against their will but of cooperation between slaves and soldiers to escape from the colony. Almost a decade later, two fugitive Nègres brought back from Havana supplied the first news of these slaves. They were well established in Havana. No master was mentioned. One of the "abducted" slaves named Suquoy lived in a cabin near the port in a place called Mouraille. He was a vendor, perhaps a shopkeeper. Suquoy had been married in the church in Mobile to a woman named Susanna and had a daughter in New Orleans. But he had two more wives in Havana, one named Catherine, who lived with him, and another named Juana, who was his neighbor. Another of these "abducted" slaves was the Négresse Marie, a creole of Mobile. She had been married in Havana and had given birth to two children there, although she was already married to a man named François, who still lived in New Orleans. Another Négresse named Babet was married to a carpenter named André, and they lived on Campeche Street. These witnesses identified other slaves "abducted" from Bayou St. Jean in 1739 who were alive, well, and apparently free in Havana. One of them was seen five years later in Havana. Witnesses identified a considerable number of slaves of various masters who had disappeared from Louisiana and were living as free persons in Havana.[14] During its early decades, then, New Orleans was a town with loose, flexible race relations and a mobile population that took advantage of the communications networks radiating from the port city to undermine the hierarchical ideals of the French colonial empire.

The crucial position of the Indians during these early decades provided a vital avenue of escape for African slaves and their descendants. From the earliest years, Africans and Indians escaped together. Indians were the first group enslaved in significant numbers, and they led the way. As increasing numbers of Africans arrived during the 1720s, African and Indian slaves, sometimes owned by the same masters and sharing the same fate, ran off together, stealing food, supplies, arms,

14. October 16, 1739, Heloise H. Cruzat, trans., Records of the Superior Council of Louisiana, *Louisiana Historical Quarterly*, VII (1924), 497 (hereafter cited as RSC LHQ); November 7, 1739, RSC LHQ, VII (July, 1924), 506, and September 1, 1744, RSC LHQ, XIII (January, 1930), 156; Declaration by Fugitive Negroes Manuel and Juan Belonging to Mr. de Benac, March 22, 1748, RSC LHQ, XIX (April, 1936), 503.

and ammunition from their masters before they left and raiding the settlers for supplies as needed. In 1726, the attorney general complained about large bands of escaped Indian slaves who had long been hanging out around the city. Their masters were "thus deprived of their arms as well as their slaves, putting their lives at risk." This official was "convinced that they are planning a severe blow against us." He urged that they be hunted down by other Indians and executed in accordance with the Code Noir of 1724. In 1727, an Indian slave who had escaped and been recaptured revealed the existence of a settlement named des Natanapallé where there were fifteen other fugitive slaves, both African and Indian. They were armed with eleven guns and ammunition with which they expected to defend themselves if attacked.[15]

Documents surviving from the 1730s and 1740s record the departure of Indian and African slaves, often together, to seek refuge among Indian tribes. They were often Indian-African couples. A Indian named Chicacha enticed away two adolescent African slave girls.[16] A plantation inventory lists an African slave named Thomas who "ran away to the Choctaw."[17] In 1748, Indian and African slaves, including mixed African-Indian couples, led their fellow slaves to a pro-British faction among the Choctaws.[18] The lower river settlements had become a haven for "a large, tightly knit and highly efficient band of maroon [runaway] raiders, composed of fugitives from plantations as far north as Pointe Coupée and as far south as Gentilly."[19]

French New Orleans, then, was far from a stable society controlled by a culturally and socially cohesive white elite ruling a dominated, fractionalized, and culturally obliterated slave population. The patterns of the slave trade to both French and Spanish Louisiana as well as the socially chaotic conditions prevailing in the colony contributed to an unusually cohesive and heavily Africanized slave culture—arguably the most Africanized slave culture in the United States. The proportion of

15. Testimony before Louisiana Superior Council, August 17, 1726, March 31, 1727, RSC LHC.
16. *Ibid.*, October 1, 1745.
17. Heloise H. Cruzat, "Documents Concerning Slaves of Chaouachas Plantation, 1737–38," Inventory of January 24, 1738, RSC LHQ, VIII (October, 1925), 594–646.
18. Interrogation of Joseph, François, and their Negro and Indian accomplices, slaves, defendants, and accused, May 18–26, 1748, in Cruzat, "Records Superior Council," RSC LHQ, XIX (July, 1936), 768–71.
19. Carl A. Brasseaux, "The Administration of Slave Regulations in French Louisiana, 1724–1766," *Louisiana History*, XXI (1980), 139–58.

FIGURE 1.   Slave and Free Population of French Louisiana, 1721–1763

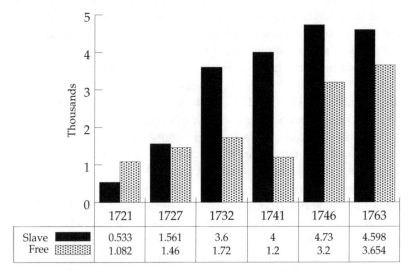

	1721	1727	1732	1741	1746	1763
Slave ████	0.533	1.561	3.6	4	4.73	4.598
Free ▒▒▒▒	1.082	1.46	1.72	1.2	3.2	3.654

SOURCES: Charles R. Maduell, *The Census Tables for the French Colony of Louisiana from 1699 Through 1732* (Baltimore, 1972); Mémoire sur la colonie de la Louisiane (around 1740), C13C 1, 384, Archives Nationales, Paris; Mémoire sur l'état de la Colonie de la Louisiane en 1746, C13A 30, 244–57, Archives Nationales; Antonio Acosta Rodríguez, *La población de Luisiana española, 1763–1803* (Madrid, 1979), 31, 110. The 1763 census covers territory only from the mouth of the Mississippi River through Pointe Coupee.

blacks to whites in the French settlements in the lower Mississippi Valley rose sharply after 1721, just three years after the founding of New Orleans. The last general census under French rule, which was taken in 1731–1732, clearly shows the resulting impact on the colony's population. After the Natchez uprising of 1729, the black population survived by natural increase but the white population declined because of out-migration, mortality, and almost complete absence of immigration. By 1731 the Africans outnumbered the whites in lower Louisiana by more than two to one (see Figure 1). But their cultural impact was more than a simple result of numbers.

Almost all the slaves brought to Louisiana under French rule came directly from Africa and arrived within a twelve-year period following the founding of New Orleans. Very few slaves were brought to French Louisiana after 1731. Unlike the formative contingent of slaves brought to the English Atlantic Coast colonies, who came from the British West

Indies and constituted a relatively small minority,[20] the formative contingent of slaves brought to Louisiana came directly from Africa and quickly became a substantial majority. Except for those who were uncontrollable, export of slaves from the French islands to Louisiana was, in practice, prohibited.[21] There was only a handful of black slaves in Louisiana before the first slave-trading ship arrived from Africa in 1719, the year after New Orleans was founded. Between 1719 and 1731, twenty-two of the twenty-three slave-trading ships that came from Africa while France ruled Louisiana arrived. Between June, 1719, and January, 1731, sixteen slave-trading ships arrived in Louisiana from the Senegal region. Six ships came from Juda (Whydah, a slave-trading post on the Gulf of Benin near Dahomey) and one from Cabinde (Angola) during the same period. The slave trade from Senegal intensified after 1725. Between February, 1726, and January, 1731, twelve slave ships from Senegal landed 3,259 slaves at Balize at the mouth of the Mississippi River. During the same period, one ship from Juda landed 464 slaves at the same port (See Figure 2). The only other slave-trading ship that came from Africa to Louisiana while the colony was under French rule arrived in 1743 and was from Senegal.

The African nations represented among the slaves as well as the patterns of introducing them into New Orleans contrast sharply with those of Anglophone United States. The African slaves brought to the Chesapeake during the eighteenth century came mainly from the 'Bight of Biafra and were heavily Ibo, Ibibio, Efkin, and Moko, with a significant minority from Angola.[22] Between 1735 and 1740, 70 percent of the Africans brought to South Carolina came from Angola.[23] Between 1717 and 1767, 22 percent came from Angola and only 5 percent from Gambia, although these figures are uncertain because the origin of 61 percent of the slaves was listed simply as "Africa," with 8 percent from "Guinea."[24] Margaret Washington Creel concludes that Senegambia and the Windward Coast provided 61 percent of the slaves entering Charleston from Africa for almost forty years (1749–1787) and that

20. Allan Kulikoff, *Tobacco and Slaves: The Development of Southern Cultures in the Chesapeake, 1680–1800* (Chapel Hill, 1986), 319; Wood, *Black Majority*, 20–21.
21. For example, Hurson au Ministre, Martinique, September, 1752, in F3 90, fols. 70–71, AN.
22. Kulikoff, *Tobacco and Slaves*, 321.
23. Wood, *Black Majority*, 335.
24. Daniel C. Littlefield, *Rice and Slaves: Ethnicity and the Slave Trade in Colonial South Carolina* (Baton Rouge, 1981), 111.

FIGURE 2. Slaves Landed in Louisiana by French Slave Trade: Numbers and Origins

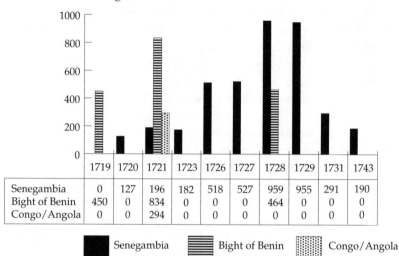

	1719	1720	1721	1723	1726	1727	1728	1729	1731	1743
Senegambia	0	127	196	182	518	527	959	955	291	190
Bight of Benin	450	0	834	0	0	0	464	0	0	0
Congo/Angola	0	0	294	0	0	0	0	0	0	0

■ Senegambia   ▤ Bight of Benin   ▦ Congo/Angola

n= 5,980

SOURCE: Calculated from Jean Mettas, *Autres Ports* (Paris, 1984), Vol. II of Mettas, *Répertoire des expéditions négrières françaises au XVIIIième siècle*, ed. Serge and Michelle Daget.

the proportion coming from Angola dropped to 11.1 percent. Slaves coming from Angola rose to 37.7 percent between 1804 and 1807, with those coming from the Windward Coast rising to 28.6 percent, and those from Senegambia dropping to 7.5 percent. Slaves from the Gold Coast remained a substantial minority, fluctuating between 13.3 and 17.2 percent between 1749 and 1807. Almost none came from the Bight of Benin.[25]

Two-thirds of the slaves brought to Louisiana under French rule came from Senegambia, and they included a strong and influential contingent of Bambara. The French slave trade to Louisiana focused on Senegambia and specifically Bambara because in 1720, the Company of the Indies was given administrative control and a trade monopoly in both Louisiana and Senegambia. The Senegal concession was the only place on the African coast where the company held exclusive trading

25. Margaret Washington Creel, *"A Peculiar People": Slave Religion and Community-Culture Among the Gullahs* (New York, 1988), Appendix A, 329–34.

rights. Elsewhere, it sold private permits to engage in the slave trade.[26] The English had taken Cabinda, and the English and the Portuguese dominated the entire coast of Angola. The French had little hope of trading in Angola except with great difficulty. Although the Company of the Indies had a trading post at Juda (Gulf of Benin), there it competed with all the nations of Europe. The Portuguese were taking the upper hand at Juda. The kings of Ardres (Allada or Porto Novo)[27] were hostile to the Europeans and interrupting trade. The slave trade at Juda was becoming uncertain and unprofitable.[28]

Between 1726 and 1731, almost all the slave-trading voyages organized by the Company of the Indies went to Louisiana. Thirteen slave ships landed there during these years. All but one of them left from Senegambia, which was the source of two-thirds of the slaves brought to French Louisiana, 3,947 out of 5,987. The last ship, arriving in 1743, also came from Senegambia. The most important kingdoms of Senegambia maintained a tight control over which peoples could be enslaved and sold to the Europeans. It seems that during the 1720s, neither the Foul (Fulbe)[29] nor the Mandinga sold their own people or allowed others to sell them. The Bambara (Bamana) enjoyed no such protection during the 1720s. Those sent to Louisiana were mainly captives taken during the wars arising out of the founding and consolidation of the Segu Bambara Empire established by Marmari Kulubali. The Bambara were the preponderant nation among the formative contingent of slaves sent to Louisiana, and slaves coming from Senegambia continued to be prominent throughout the eighteenth century (see Table 1). Linguistic as well as historical evidence has established that the Louisiana creole language was created by these early slaves and was not imported from the French islands.[30] This language became a vital part of the identity, not only of Afro-creoles, but of many whites of all classes.

26. Pierre Pluchon, *La Route des esclaves: Négriers et bois d'ébène au XVIIIieme siècle* (Paris, 1980), 24.

27. Pierre Verger, *Flux et reflux de la traite des nègres entre le Golfe de Bénin et Bahia de Todos os Santos* (Paris, 1968), 693.

28. Mémoire sur le Senegal, Approuvé par St. R(obert), October 16, 1723, C6 10, AN.

29. Philip D. Curtin, *Economic Change in Precolonial Africa: Senegambia in the Era of the Slave Trade* (2 vols.; Madison, 1975), I, 183.

30. Ingrid Neumann, "Bemerkungen zur Genese des Kreolischen von Louisiana und seiner historischen Relation zum Kreolischen von Haiti," in Norbert Boretsky, Werner Enninger, and Thomas Stolz, eds., *Akten des Essener Kolloquiums über "Kreolsprachen und Sprachkontakte"* (26 vols.; Bochum, 1985), Vol. I.

TABLE 1. Origins and Numbers of Slaves Brought to Louisiana from
Africa, 1719–1743

Place of Origin	Year Landed	Number of Slaves
Juda (Whydah):		
L'Aurore	1719	200
Le Duc du Maine	1719	250
L'Afriquain	1720	182
Le Duc du Maine	1721	349
Le Fortuné	1721	303
La Diane	1728	464
Total 1,749		
Cabinde:		
La Nérèide	1721	294
Total 294		
Senegal/Goree:		
Le Ruby	1720	127
Le Maréchal d'Estrees	1721	196
L'Expédition	1723	88
Le Courrier de Bourbon	1723	87
L'Aurore	1726	290
La Mutine	1726	228
L'Annibal	1727	261 (average)
Le Prince de Conti	1727	300
Le Duc de Noaille	1728	237
Le Vénus	1728	341
La Flore	1728	356
La Galathée	1729	273
La Vénus	1729	363
Le Duc de Bourbon	1729	319
Le St. Louis	1731	291
Le St. Ursin	1743	190
Total 3,947		

Grand total: 5,989

SOURCE: Jean Mettas, *Répertoire des expéditions négrières françaises au XVIIIième
siècle*, ed. Serge Daget and Michelle Daget (2 vols.; Paris, 1978, 1984), Vol. II.

Documents from the early colonial period indicate a preponderance of Bambara slaves. In 1731, there was a conspiracy involving four hundred Bambara slaves in French settlements throughout Louisiana.[31] In surviving Louisiana court records involving slaves accused of crimes between 1728 and 1752, eighteen slaves identified themselves as Bambara, one as Sango, two as "Sénégal" (which meant Wolof in Louisiana),[32] one as Biefada (from Upper Guinea), three as Samba, one as Fonda (probably Fon), and one as Fulbe. The sample is small but well distributed in time.[33]

One court case illustrates the defiant attitude among the Bambara in Louisiana as well as the solidarity among them. Biron, a Bambara slave who arrived on the ship *Aurore*, had run away several times. When he was making another attempt to escape, his master fired several shots into the air and then aimed his gun at him and threatened to shoot him. Biron grabbed the gun while his master was trying to have him shackled. The gun broke during the struggle. Biron was brought before the court, and the attorney general charged that his acts were a rebellion against his master, "all the more punishable from the fact that the number of blacks is increasing in this colony, and that one would not be in safety on the distant plantations." Samba Bambara, who later led a conspiracy of the Bambara slaves to take over Louisiana, was appointed interpreter in Biron's case and reported that the accused stated he was trying to prevent his master from shooting him and did not intend to attack his master with the gun. Biron was sentenced to be whipped at the foot of the gallows by the public executioner, warned not to run away again under threat of greater punishment, and returned to his master.[34]

When the slave trade from Senegal intensified between 1726 and 1729, the Company of the Indies, which ruled Louisiana between 1720 and 1731, was attempting to establish a prosperous tobacco colony at the Natchez settlement, the present site of Natchez, Mississippi. Many of the newly arrived Africans were sent to Natchez. They played a promi-

31. Diron D'Artaguette to unknown, Mobile, June 24, 1731, F3 24, fols. 427–28; Diron D'Artaguette to Controleur Général, Fort Conde de la Mobile, August 20, 1731, C13A 13, fol. 155, AN.

32. Le Page du Pratz wrote, "Among all the Nègres whom I have known, the senegal, who are called among themselves Wolofs (*Djolaufs*), are of the purest blood" (*Histoire de la Louisiane* [3 vols.; Paris, 1758], I, 344).

33. Heloise H. Cruzat, "Trial and Sentence of Biron, Runaway Negro Slave, Before the Superior Council of Louisiana, 1728," RSC LHQ, VIII (1925), 23–27.

34. *Ibid.*

nent role when the Natchez Indians rose up against the French and wiped out their settlement at Natchez on November 28, 1729. At the time of the uprising, the settlement consisted of 200 French men, 82 French women, 150 French children, and 280 black slaves.[35] Before they revolted, the Natchez assured themselves of the support of several blacks, including those of the White Earth concession and two of their *commandeurs* (slave foremen), who told the other blacks that they would be free if they supported the Natchez. Slaves who refused to support the Natchez were threatened with being sold to the Chickasaws along with the French women and children.[36]

Some of the Africans at Natchez remained loyal to the French. Three blacks escaped after the revolt, arriving in New Orleans on December 3, 1729. They informed Governor Etienne de Périer that they had seen the heads of the French officers and employees lined up opposite the heads of the French settlers.[37] It was reported that the Natchez spared as many French women as possible during the massacre, and the surviving French women and children had several black men and women with them, perhaps loyal domestics. They were all kept in two houses where they were carefully watched.[38]

The French military position was desperate. French settlers, voyageurs, and priests were being killed throughout the colony. Governor Périer wrote to the Ministry of Colonies, "The French are being killed everywhere without being able to help each other, because we are in as much danger and have as much to fear by assembling together as by remaining at our posts." Panic seized the French settlers of New Orleans. To reassure them and to create conflicts between Africans and Indians, Governor Périer had a contingent of blacks destroy the Chaouchas, a small Indian nation below New Orleans. He wrote, "If I wanted to use our blacks I would have destroyed all the little nations who are not at all useful to us and who can, on the contrary, push our blacks to revolt, as we have seen from the example of the Natchez." Hesitating to arm more

---

35. For a study of the economic aspects of the Natchez revolt of 1729, see James T. McGowan, "Creation of a Slave Society: Louisiana Plantations in the Eighteenth Century" (Ph.D. dissertation, University of Rochester, 1976), 43–96. The population figures are given in Diron D'Artaguette to unknown, La Louisiane, March 20, 1730, F3 24, fols. 188–89, AN.

36. Rélation du Massacre des Natchez arrivé le 28 novembre, 1729, New Orleans, March 18, 1730, Périer to minister, F3 24, fols. 170–72, AN.

37. Périer to minister, New Orleans, March 18, 1730, C13A 12, fol. 41, AN.

38. Diron to minister, Mobile, February 9, 1730, C13A 12, fols. 362–65, AN.

blacks, Périer resorted to arming the few French remaining in New Orleans.[39]

The French and the Choctaws attacked Natchez, the main village of the Natchez Indians, on January 27, 1730. Fifty to one hundred blacks and fifty-four French women were recaptured by the Choctaws.[40] Those blacks who were not captured fought alongside the Natchez, preventing the Choctaws from taking their powder and giving the Natchez enough time to enter the two forts. The blacks were decisive in preventing the total defeat of the Natchez. The French and their Choctaw allies had not expected to have to fight the blacks as well as the Natchez. Fifteen blacks were armed by the French and accompanied their expedition against the Natchez. Governor Périer wrote that they "behaved with surprising valor. If these soldiers were not so expensive and so necessary to the colony, it would be better to use them than our soldiers who seem made especially for Louisiana, they are so bad."[41] They were given their freedom, and a black militia was organized.[42]

Some of the black slaves who sided with or were taken by the Natchez were recaptured by the French. Three of the most active black leaders who sided with the Natchez were turned over to the Choctaws and "burned alive with a degree of cruelty which has inspired all the Negroes with a new horror of the Savages, but which will have a beneficial effect in securing the safety of the Colony."[43]

Alibamon Mingo, the Choctaw chief, drove a hard bargain for the return of some fifty black slaves his tribe had recaptured from the Natchez, but some of them were eventually returned. Many of the Africans held by the Natchez and the Choctaws belonged to the Company of the Indies, and they were eventually returned to the company's estate in New Orleans. These returned and recaptured Africans formed the nucleus of African conspiracies in New Orleans, in alliance with Indian nations, to overthrow French rule.[44] Some of the Africans who had lived

39. Périer to minister, New Orleans, March 18, 1730, C13A 12, fols. 37–41, AN.

40. Périer to minister, New Orleans, March 18, 1730, C13A 12, fol. 43, AN, Paris, reports one hundred blacks and fifty-four French women retaken, one hundred Natchez killed, and fifteen to twenty taken prisoner. Diron to minister, Mobile, February 9, 1730, C13A 12, fol. 366, reports about fifty blacks retaken in the same battle.

41. Périer to minister, New Orleans, March 18, 1730, C13A 12, fol. 43, AN.

42. Cruzat, "Records Superior Council," May 13, 1730, RSC LHQ, IV (1921), 524.

43. Reuben Gold Thwaites, ed., *The Jesuit Relations and Allied Documents* (73 vols.; Cleveland, 1900), LXVII, 199.

44. Régis du Roulet to Périer, March 16, 1731, C13A 13, fols. 189–90, AN.

among the Natchez and the Choctaws maintained ties with Indian nations that wanted to drive out the French. Many of these slaves were
Bambara belonging to the Company of the Indies, and upon their return, they plotted with the Indians to overthrow the French.

During the winter of 1730–1731, Périer ordered a French officer living with the Choctaws to organize a party of three hundred men to cut
a wedge between the Natchez and the Chickasaws, but this maneuver
failed. Then he ordered the officer to enlist the Choctaws to declare war
against the Chickasaws to help them hold out until more aid from France
arrived, but his plans were foiled when the Natchez and the Chickasaws
made overtures to the Illinois, the Arkansas, part of the Miamis, and the
black slaves in the French settlements. The Indians sent a black to New
Orleans to tell the blacks there that they would be free and would have
everything they could wish for with the English, who would take good
care of them. Governor Périer wrote: "This black was a Bambara of a
nation which the others do not understand. He recruited all the blacks
of his nation."[45]

The uprising was scheduled to take place on June 24, 1731, but the
conspirators were not ready, and it was put off until June 29. In the interim, the French found out about the plan. All the whites from Pointe
Coupée to Balize were to be massacred. The Bambara had joined to free
themselves and take possession of the country by this revolt. The blacks
in the colony who were not of the Bambara nation were to serve them as
slaves.[46] It was reported that four hundred Bambara slaves were involved in this conspiracy. The officials did not wish to investigate thoroughly because of the damage that would be caused to slaveowners if
they lost their slaves.[47]

Périer questioned a black woman who was a domestic slave in New
Orleans. She had joined the conspiracy and was told that there was a
plan to take the church of New Orleans when everyone was at the parish mass and set fire to several houses in the city to disperse those who
had not been taken in the church. According to Périer, the conspiracy
was proven. Several conspirators were killed by breaking them on the

45. Périer to minister, December 10, 1731, C13A 13, fols. 63–64, AN.
46. Beauchamp, major at Mobile, to minister, Fort Conde de la Mobile, November
5, 1731, C13A 13, fol. 200, AN.
47. Diron d'Artaguette to unknown, Mobile, June 24, 1731, F3 24, fols. 427–28;
Diron d'Artaguette to controller general, Fort Conde de la Mobile, August 20, 1731,
C13A 13, fol. 155, AN.

wheel, and one woman who was involved in the affair was hanged.[48] The owners of the executed slaves sought compensation by being given slaves belonging to the Company of the Indies.[49]

Périer later expressed doubt about whether the conspiracy had actually existed but stated that if it was indeed real, it could be explained by the revolt of the Indians whom the slaves saw massacring the French every day and the small number of troops whom they knew to be in the country. He was sure that the colony would be lost if the Indian nations and the black slaves united but concluded that "happily there has always been a great aversion between them which has been much increased by the war, and we take great care to maintain it." He urged that the slaveowners rid themselves entirely of the "blacks who had lived for a long time among the Natchez who had taken them from the French and among the Choctaw who retook them from the Natchez. They were not at all badly treated by the one or the other, and they have returned with a spirit of laziness, independence and insolence." [50]

The comptroller for the Company of the Indies complained that the Choctaws held the blacks they had recaptured from the Natchez for eighteen months and that the governor had made a big mistake by putting them among the blacks of the company. These returned prisoners let the other blacks know about the freedom they enjoyed among the Indians, going hunting and cultivating the land only when they felt like it. As a result, they plotted to revolt and assassinate the French. The revolt would have succeeded if the plot had not been revealed by an indiscreet black woman who told a friend that she would be named Madame Périer and by a black who, in anger, threatened to make war against the French. All the principal leaders of the conspiracy were to take the places and the names of the commanders and majors, captains, officers, and storehouse guards. Instead, they were tried and found guilty. To prevent a revolt among the other Bambara seeking to avoid execution of their leaders, all the settlers had to be armed.[51]

---

48. Périer to minister, December 10, 1731, C13A 13, fols. 63–64, AN. The number of conspirators reported executed varies between five and twelve.

49. Salmon to minister, New Orleans, January 19, 1732, C13A 15, fol. 29, AN.

50. "Mouvements des Savages de la Louisiane depuis la prise du fort des Natchez par M. de Périer sur la fin de janvier 1731," July 21 and 28, 1731, C13A 13, fol. 87, AN.

51. "Mémoire de Raymond Amyalt, Sieur d'Auseville, conseilleur au Conseil Superieur de la Louisiane, commissaire aux comptes de la Compagnie des Indes," New Orleans, January 20, 1732, C13A 14, fol. 273, AN.

Le Page du Pratz was director of the Company of the Indies, and his version of this conspiracy focuses on Samba Bambara, his first *commandeur* and interpreter before the Superior Council in cases involving Bambara slaves, as leader of the conspiracy. His second *commandeur* was also involved. Du Pratz described this plot as "a betrayal from people of whom one had no distrust whatsoever. The Nègres planned to get rid of all the French and establish themselves in their place, taking over the Capital and all we owned." In his history of Louisiana, Le Page du Pratz wrote that he had overheard the conspirators urging that they wait for the return of a courier they had sent to the Illinois Indians before beginning their revolt. Du Pratz learned that Samba Bambara had been enslaved and sent to Louisiana for conspiring against the French in Senegal and had organized another revolt on the slave ship that brought him to Louisiana. After being confronted with Le Page du Pratz's memoir about him, Samba Bambara was quoted as saying, in Louisiana creole, "Ah! M. le Page li diable li sabai tout" (Mr. Le Page is a devil who knows everything). This quotation dates from 1731 and is one of the earliest recorded examples of any creole language.[52]

A few months later it was reported that the black slaves were planning another revolt to take place during the midnight mass on Christmas of 1731. A simultaneous revolt was to erupt at Balize but was discovered by Tizel Pilott. He had been sitting down smoking behind the slave cabins when he heard the *commandeur* going from cabin to cabin telling the blacks not to sleep and to be ready when the clock struck. This *commandeur* was arrested and brought to New Orleans.[53]

The extant documents leave little doubt that there was a large Bambara contingent among the Africans who cooperated with the Natchez in their revolt against the French settlement and that they continued to maintain ties with the Indian nations opposed to the French after they were retaken from the Natchez and the Choctaws and returned to the estate of the Company of the Indies. The French authorities were indeed walking a thin line between Africans and Indians, creating enmity between the two groups but trying to avoid excessive military dependence on either. Africans were used for military purposes in increasing numbers during the long-drawn-out, costly, and largely unsuccessful wars

52. Le Page du Pratz, *Histoire de la Louisiane*, III, 304–17.
53. "Mémoire de Raymond Amyalt, Sieur d'Auseville, conseilleur au Conseil Supérieur de Louisiane, commissare aux comptes de la Compagnie des Indes," January 20, 1732, C13A 14, fol. 273, AN.

against the Chickasaws. In April, 1736, a contingent of 140 Africans, both slave and free, were enlisted for service in the Chickasaw War. The slaves were promised freedom for risking their lives. During the same month, another company of 45 armed blacks led by free black officers was formed. In 1739, Bienville was commanding 270 blacks, including 50 free blacks.[54]

Unlike the British Atlantic colonies, which became heavily populated by whites and Africans during the eighteenth century, the intrusive population, both white and black, was sparse, especially under French rule. Under these circumstances, Africans and Indians prevailed in many of the most crucial aspects of life. White control was relatively feeble. The weakness of the dwindling French population, especially after the Natchez uprising, and the heavy reliance on slaves for skilled labor as well as for defense and warfare in this vast frontier region enhanced the bargaining power and self-confidence of the slaves.

In 1746, there were about three thousand black men, women, and children in New Orleans and only eight hundred white male settlers and nearly as many white women and children.[55] Most of the black slaves in New Orleans were apparently highly skilled. In 1743, Bienville reported that Joseph Dubreuil, the contractor of the king's works, had trained blacks in all trades and employed very few French workmen.[56] By 1746, Dubreuil was listed as the richest settler in New Orleans, "owning 500 blacks, men, women, and children, whom he employs mainly on the public works of the King."[57] His plantations were industrial as well as agricultural units, achieving near self-sufficiency.[58] In 1748, three of his slaves were arrested and imprisoned, accused of theft. Dubreuil complained bitterly in a petition to the Superior Council that his sawmill and blacksmith shop were closed, suspending his cabinetmaking, and he was much in need of his surgeon to dress the wounds and take care of

54. Roland C. McConnell, *Negro Troops of Antebellum Louisiana: A History of the Battalion of Free Men of Color* (Baton Rouge, 1968), 11–13.

55. Mémoire sur l'état de la Colonie de la Louisiane en 1746," C13A 30, fols. 244–57, AN. For a summary of the population estimate, settlement by settlement, see fol. 256, *ibid.*

56. Bienville to Maurepas, February 4, 1743, in Dunbar Rowland and Albert G. Sanders, eds., *Mississippi Provincial Archives, 1704–1743* (3 vols.; Jackson, Miss., 1927–32), III, 779.

57. Mémoire sur l'état de la Colonie de la Louisiane en 1746," C13A 30, fols. 246–48, AN.

58. John G. Clark, *New Orleans, 1718–1812: An Economic History* (Baton Rouge, 1970), 52.

the sick. He insisted that his slaves were innocent and demanded their immediate return. One of Dubreuil's slaves, an eighteen-year-old creole named Louis, when asked his trade, replied that he was a surgeon, that his master had had him go to the king's hospital to learn surgery.[59] Other documents from eighteenth-century Louisiana reveal that slaves were heavily relied on to cure the sick.

The openness of New Orleans society was greatly enhanced by the ecology of the city and its surrounding cypress swamps and luxuriant waterways. The maroon communities of escaped African and Indian slaves that began during the first half of the eighteenth century evolved into permanent settlements under Spanish rule. By the 1780s, a stable community almost entirely made up of creole slaves had created maroon villages in the swamps surrounding the city. The ecology of the land made it possible for slaves to live on their own while maintaining close ties with those who remained with their masters. Plantations were measured in arpents along the Mississippi River and larger bayous, their lands trailing back from these waterways an undeterminable distance into the impenetrable cypress swamp, the *siprière*. The cypress industry grew in economic importance under Spanish rule. To develop the Louisiana economy, Spain required that sugar from the Spanish Caribbean and Gulf of Mexico ports be carried in boxes made of Louisiana cypress. Slaves toiled in the *siprière*, cutting and hauling the logs almost entirely on their own. Few whites were eager to follow them into the swamp. Each plantation had its trackless *siprière*, where slaves from various estates met, worked together, learned how to survive on their own, and eventually escaped in large numbers. The spirit of the slaves is well expressed in the following song about Moluron, a folk hero, a "nègre maron" (fugitive slave), who feared nothing. He ran away many times although he was always caught and brought back to his master. The song about Moluron was frequently sung openly toward the end of the Civil War, when the slaves were sure of freedom.

> Moluron! Hé! Moluron! Hé!
> C'est pas 'jordi mo dans moune.
> Si yé fait ben avec moin, mo resté.
> Si yé fait mo mal, m'a-chap-pé.

59. Cruzat, "Records Superior Council," June 9, 1748, RSC LHQ, XIX (1936), 1091–94.

Moluron! Hé! Moluron! Hé!
I wasn't born yesterday.
If you treat me well, I'll stay.
If you treat me bad, I'll escape.[60]

The slaves surrounded and infiltrated the French settlements with a network extending through New Orleans, the countryside, and into the *ciprière*. Although to some extent these maroon settlements in Louisiana were similar to others throughout the Americas, Louisiana maroons were different in several respects. There was a high proportion of women as well as some children among the runaways. Small settlements of maroons, called *pasajes* of various plantations, were located in the cypress swamps that surrounded the settled areas all along the Mississippi River and the larger bayous. But the swamps surrounding New Orleans, especially to the south and east, where small bayous led into Lake Borgne and the Rigolets and thence to coastal trading centers along the Gulf of Mexico, became the organizing center of these maroon communities. They were the refuge of families rather than single men. They were populated almost entirely by Louisiana creole slaves, although by the 1780s large numbers of African slaves had been imported into the colony. The maroons were well supplied with guns and ammunition to hunt for food as well as to defend themselves against raids organized by the slaveowners and the colonial militia for the purpose of recapturing them and destroying their settlements. The greatest threat they posed was to the planters' control over slaves who had not run away.

A very high level of cooperation existed between maroons and slaves both on plantations and in the city. The maroons did not seek to withdraw from the economy of New Orleans but actively engaged in trade in the city. They cut and sold squared cypress logs to white sawmill owners and cypress troughs and tubs for processing indigo. They made and sold baskets and sifters from willow reeds. They fished, trapped birds, collected berries, and grew corn, sweet potatoes, and squash, as described in a creole slave song:

Little ones without father, little ones without mother,
What do you do to earn money?
The river we cross for wild berries to search;

60. Irène Thérèse Whitfield, *Louisiana French Folk Songs* (Baton Rouge, 1939), 140–42.

We follow the bayou a'fishing for perch
and that's how we earn money.

Little ones without father, little ones without mother,
What do you do to earn money?
Palmetto we dig from the swamp's bristling stores
And sell its stout roots for scrubbing the floors;
And that's how we earn money.

Little ones without father, little ones without mother,
What do you do to earn money?
For making tea we collect sassafras,
For making ink, we collect pokeberries,
And that's how we earn money.

Little ones without father, little ones without mother,
What do you do to earn money?
We go to the woods cancos berries to fetch,
And in our trap cages the birds we catch,
And that's how we earn money.

Little ones without father, little ones without mother,
What do you do to earn money?
At evening we visit Mom'selle Maroto,
In St. Ann's Street to gamble at keno,
And that's how we earn money.[61]

From these maroon communities emerged a charismatic and symbolic leader known by his contemporaries as St. Malo. Known as Juan Malo when he was a D'Arensbourg slave, he became widely known among the slaves and maroons of the colony. *Malo* means bad in Spanish. It could also derive from the name of the French port St. Malo. But *malo* means shame in Bambara and refers to the charismatic leader who defies the social order, giving him the capacity to act when social conventions paralyze others. In accordance with their concepts of balance, duality, and the unity of opposites, the Bambara provide an honored place for both the conformist and the innovator. The Bambara language

61. George Washington Cable, *Creoles and Cajuns: Stories of Old Louisiana*, ed. Arlin Turner (New York, 1959), 410–11. I have altered Cable's translation from "How do you keep body and soul together?" to the literal meaning, "What do you do to earn money?" *L'a zanc* means money, derived from *l'argent* in French, in the original Louisiana creole version of the song. Cable was under the false impression that the creole slaves did not operate in a money economy and therefore changed the literal meaning of the song to conform to his mistaken impression.

has words for both principles. The term *badenya*, literally mother-childness, which is also the term for the family compound, represents order, stability, and social conformity centered around obligations to home, village, and kin. Yet the community recognizes that it cannot survive without the innovator: the individual who breaks social bonds. The principle of innovation is called *fadenya*, literally father-childness. Mande youth learn that their culture lavishes esteem and adulation on its rebels. Heroic poems are sung continually in the Mande world.

Charles Bird explains that the Bambara term *malo* means "shame" and is attached to the Mande hero because he is shameless and thus capable of acting when social conventions paralyze others.[62] Did St. Malo's name mean *sans malo* (in French and Bambara, "without shame") for the Mande hero? This is an unprovable but plausible explanation.

St. Malo established his headquarters and a centralized refuge for maroons in the deep swamps near New Orleans, unifying the network of maroon communities surrounding the white settlements. St. Malo and his followers controlled the swamps below New Orleans between the Mississippi River and Lake Pontchartrain. Runaway slaves were attracted to his villages from the various maroon settlements behind the plantations. One of these villages, located to the east of New Orleans, was called Chef Menteur, meaning Chief Liar. According to Charles Gayarré, Chef Menteur was named for a Choctaw chief exiled from the tribe for lying, who retired there with his family and a few adherents.[63]

St. Malo's most famous settlement, however, was Ville Gaillarde. *Gaillard* means strong, healthy, free, adept, and clever. Ville Gaillarde was located in St. Bernard Parish along Bayou Terre aux Boeufs. In 1784, Governor Miró described it as a rich, well-populated village established in a strategic location, which could be defended by five hundred men against any number of attackers. The area was, according to Miró, a "most propitious land for the maintenance of human life because of sweet potatoes, because of the great abundance of forest products, of much fish and shellfish, and very abundant game." One of Miró's spies reported that when St. Malo had last returned to Ville Gaillarde, he buried his ax in the first tree he encountered, saying, "Woe to the

62. Charles S. Bird and Martha B. Kendall, "The Mande Hero," in *Explorations in African Systems of Thought*, ed. Ivan Karp and Charles S. Bird (Bloomington, 1980), 13–26.

63. Gayarré, *History of Louisiana*, I, 351.

first white who passes this boundary" ("Malheur au blanc qui passera ces bornes"), to which his companions gave a shout of approbation.[64]

The slaves often fled in family groups. Testimony of recaptured slaves revealed one family consisting of mother, stepfather, son, daughter-in-law, daughter, and a small child, all belonging to the same master, who had fled to St. Malo's village, Ville Gaillarde. Another family consisted of husband, wife, wife's daughter, and son. Husband and son were leaders of the maroons. For both of these families, flight was precipitated when the master punished the wife.[65]

The strength of the family ties among Afro-creoles, slave and free, black and mixed-blood, was recognized by the officials of the Cabildo of New Orleans. Their experience with the militia of free blacks and mixed-bloods made them reluctant to use these militia units against the maroons. Both free blacks and mixed-bloods, including members of the militia, not only engaged in commerce with the maroons "but even favor them and supply them all they need for their defense." The Spanish officials also discovered from "criminals whom we have apprehended that most of the maroons are creoles of this province" whose kinship networks extended into New Orleans and other settlements, and their family ties were so strong and their kinship groupings so numerous that free blacks and coloreds were afraid that the relatives of the maroons they might capture or kill would seek vengeance and retaliate against them. Thus the expeditions by the free black and mixed-blood militia had proved to be useless.[66]

A powerful family network united maroons and plantation slaves, including free blacks and mixed-bloods, most of whom, it was claimed, actively aided the maroons, or at least feared them and their relatives enough that they were unlikely to pursue the maroons. This is another example of permeability of the society, which contradicts the idea that there was deep conflict and hostility between the slave and emancipated black and mixed-blood population or between mixed-blood and black. This permeability extended to relations among peoples of all races,

64. Miró to Galvez, July 31, 1784, A.G.I., Papeles de Cuba 3A, Document 638; Miró to Espeleta, July 1, 1784, Cuba 3A, Document 639, Archivo Général de Indias, Seville.

65. Laura L. Porteus, "Index to Spanish Judicial Records," March 1, December 23, 1783, August 7, October 25, November 10, 1784, *LHQ*, XX (July, 1937), 840–65.

66. Acts and Deliberations of the Cabildo of New Orleans, June 4, 1784, II, 215–17, Spanish Transcription, Louisiana Division, New Orleans Public Library.

classes, and nationalities in New Orleans, producing a culturally open and profoundly Africanized milieu.

The final campaign that captured St. Malo and his companions required two hundred soldiers to guard the exits of the bayous leading into Lake Borgne as well as the path to Chef Menteur and the Rigolets. St. Malo was caught after he was wounded by a shot fired from afar.[67] He was remembered by Afro-creoles of Louisiana well into the nineteenth century as a symbol of freedom and defiance.

Shortly after slavery was abolished, the following magnificent dirge for St. Malo was collected from an old former slave woman in St. Bernard Parish, where Ville Gaillarde was located:

> Alas, young men, come make lament,
> For poor St. Malo in distress!
> They chased, they hunted him with dogs,
> They fired a rifle at him.
> They dragged him from the cypress swamp.
> His arms they tied behind his back.
> They tied his hands in front of him.
> They tied him to a horse's tail.
> They dragged him up into the town.
> Before those grand Cabildo men.
> They charged that he had made a plot
> To cut the throats of all the whites.
> They asked him who his comrades were.
> Poor St. Malo said not a word!
> The judge his sentence read to him,
> And then they raised the gallows tree.
> They drew the horse—the cart moved off
> And left St. Malo hanging there.
> The sun was up an hour high
> When on the levee he was hung.
> They left his body swinging there
> For carrion crows to feed upon.[68]

The Afro-creole culture of New Orleans was strongly re-Africanized after Spain took over the colony in 1766. The only existing study of na-

---

67. Report of Governor Esteban Miró to his Excellency Conde de Galvez, New Orleans, July 31, 1784, Legajo 2556, fols. 542–49, Archivo Général de Indias, Seville. Microfilm copy in Historic New Orleans Collection, C 84-44-L.

68. Cable, *Creoles and Cajuns*, 418–19.

tions of origin of Louisiana slaves under Spanish rule is my own data base on the slave population of the Pointe Coupée post. Such a study would probably be less productive for New Orleans because the Spanish notaries working there paid little attention to the nations of origin of the slaves. Of 2,453 slaves whose place of birth was listed in documents from the Pointe Coupée post dating between 1771 and 1802, only six came from the French West Indies. Three were from Saint Domingue, two from Martinique, and one from "Des Isles." Some English-speaking slaves were brought in by loyalist refugees from the American Revolution, but evidence points toward the eventual socialization of them and their offspring into the Afro-creole language and culture everywhere but in the Natchez region. At Pointe Coupée, almost all the Anglo slaves had accompanied Dr. Benjamin Farar, a master from South Carolina, and after Farar's death, many of them as well as their offspring were absorbed by the Poydras estate, where Louisiana creole was spoken.[69] A Spanish royal order of December 1, 1788, encouraged immigrants from the United States, promising religious freedom, free land, and citizenship. But the results were unimpressive. Very few Americans chose to immigrate to Spanish Louisiana.[70] The movement of Anglo slaves into Louisiana before 1803 as well as the population growth rate among creole slaves of Louisiana seems to have been exaggerated, leading to a sharp underestimation of the numbers and influence of African slaves in Spanish Louisiana.[71] The slave population barely held its own under French rule, according to Antonio Acosta Rodriguez, increasing very slowly and, at times, having a negative growth rate between 1789 and 1803.[72] The slave population in Spanish Louisiana began to grow because of a massive re-Africanization beginning in the 1770s. At the Pointe Coupée post, the vast majority of adult slaves were Africans (see Figure 4). The early Africanization of the culture of New Orleans under French rule was reinforced by a massive re-Africanization under Spanish rule.

69. See Gwendolyn Midlo Hall, *Africans in Colonial Louisiana: The Development of Afro-Creole Culture in the Eighteenth Century* (Baton Rouge, 1992), 275–313.

70. Arthur P. Whitaker, *The Spanish-American Frontier, 1783–1795* (1927; rpr. Gloucester, Mass., 1962), 103–107, 157–62.

71. Allan Kulikoff, "Uprooted Peoples: Black Migrants in the Age of the American Revolution, 1790–1820," in *Slavery and Freedom in the Age of the American Revolution,* ed. Ira Berlin and Ronald Hoffman (Charlottesville, 1983), 149, 168–71.

72. Antonio Acosta Rodríguez, *La Población de luisiana española (1763–1803)* (Madrid, 1979), 272.

FIGURE 3. Percent of Slaves at Pointe Coupée from Major Regions of
Africa, 1782–1802, in Five-Year Moving Averages

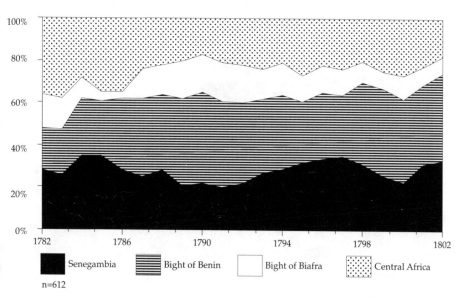

n=612

SOURCE: Calculated from Pointe Coupée Notarial Records, 1771–1802. There are
no extant records for 1772–77 and 1780–81.

The large numbers of English-speaking slaves who began to arrive
through New Orleans after Louisiana was absorbed by the United
States did not enter a cultural vacuum. The formative slave culture of
the Mississippi Valley and the Gulf Coast was creole. This tightly knit,
self-confident, self-reliant language community survived, deeply influ-
encing the peoples of all races and languages who lived among them.
Founded on the openness and permeability that existed throughout the
eighteenth century, the culture of New Orleans remains heavily African
in flavor. During the French period, creole slave children grew up in
tightly knit families. Many of them, no doubt, knew their African parents and grandparents. When a massive re-Africanization of the slave
population began during the 1770s, a substantial minority of these
slaves newly arriving from Africa came from Senegambia. Slaves coming
from the Bight of Benin, including Fond, Mina, Ado, Chamba, and
Yoruba, were the largest group (see Figure 3). Slaves from the Bight of
Benin probably account for the emergence of voodoo in Louisiana,
which was reinforced by the massive immigration of Haitians in 1809.

FIGURE 4.   Creole and African Slaves by Age and Sex, Pointe Coupée,
1771–1802

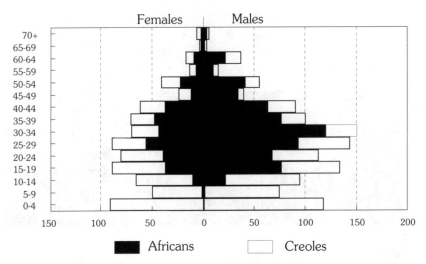

SOURCE: See Figure 3.

The terms *ounga* and *gri-gri,* meaning harmful charm, have been widely used in New Orleans by speakers of English as well as by creoles. It is possible but far from certain that these terms were brought by slaves from Saint Domingue, where they are also used. Some elements of voodoo no doubt originated in Haiti (Saint Domingue) and were brought to Louisiana by immigrants from that former French colony, where voodoo is the primary popular religion, but the folk religion of New Orleans has its roots in the eighteenth century. The massive migration of Haitians to New Orleans did not take place until 1809, when large numbers of Haitian refugees, including white creoles, free coloreds, and their slaves, were expelled from Cuba in reaction to Napoleon's invasion of Spain.[73] The term *gri-gri* appears in New Orleans court records as early as 1773. *Zinzin,* meaning amulet of support or power in Louisiana creole, is a Bambara word with the same meaning.[74] Whites in New Orleans also practiced voodoo, further evidence of the enormous im-

73. See Paul Lachance, "The 1809 Immigration of St. Domingue Refugees to New Orleans: Reception, Integration, and Impact," *Louisiana History,* XXIX (1988), 109–41.

pact of Afro-creole folk religion on the creolized culture of New Orleans.[75]

Although slaves from various African nations created new language communities in Louisiana based on their native tongues, the African slaves gradually learned Louisiana creole, and their children were socialized into the Afro-creole language and culture. A coherent, functional, well-integrated slave culture emerged in New Orleans and has proved to be remarkably resilient and influential. The openness and interracialism of the frontier society in which this distinctive culture was born has been remarkably influential among peoples of all classes, colors, and nations. Its creativity, intelligence, biting wit, joyfulness, musicality, poetic strain, and reverence for beauty make this culture inherently attractive. But what is most important is its powerful universalist trend. Senegambia had long been a crossroads of the world where peoples and cultures were amalgamated in the crucible of warfare and the rise and fall of far-flung trading empires. An essential feature of the cultural materials brought from Senegambia as well as from other parts of Africa was a willingness to add and incorporate useful aspects of new cultures encountered. This attitude was highly functional in a dangerous and chaotic world. New Orleans became another crossroads, where the river, the bayous, and the sea were open roads, where various nations ruled but the folk continued to reign. They turned inhospitable swamplands into a refuge for the independent, the defiant, and the creative "unimportant" people who tore down barriers of language and culture among peoples throughout the world and continue to sing to them of joy and the triumph of the human spirit through the sounds of jazz.

74. Viviana Paques, *Les Bambara* (Paris, 1954), 94; Marcus Bruce Christian, "Manuscript for a Black History of Louisiana," in Archives and Manuscripts Department, Earl K. Long Library, University of New Orleans.

75. Henry C. Castellanos, *New Orleans as It Was: Episodes of Louisiana Life* (1895; rpr. Baton Rouge, 1978), 90–101.

PART II

The American Challenge

Introduction

The massive migration of white Americans to New Orleans during the nineteenth century represented more than just the addition of another immigrant strain to the city's rapidly growing population. These people were intent upon seizing control of the city and directing its destiny. Although they eventually succeeded, their takeover was neither easy nor ever complete. Indeed, the long contest between the creoles and the Americans proved a major force in shaping the unusual character of New Orleans.

Long ago, local historians turned the dramatic tale of the creole-American struggle into one of the great legends of New Orleans. In doing so, however, they have piled up myths and frequently distorted the nature of both the American migrants and the creole natives. No scholar has done more than Joseph Tregle to unravel the entangled story and to provide a clear, revised account of the interaction between the two groups.

Tregle began his reexamination of nineteenth-century New Orleans many years ago. In his Ph.D. dissertation, "Louisiana in the Age of Jackson," done under the tutelage of Roy Nichols, one of the nation's most meticulous political historians, Tregle sorted out the first several decades of political intrigue in the city and state. His careful combing of voluminous government records, numerous newspapers, and many scattered holdings of personal papers led him to discard the earlier stereotypes of the creoles as cultured aristocrats and the Americans as uncouth backwoodsmen. Somewhat later, in his now classic study in the *Journal of Southern History*, "Early New Orleans Society: A Reappraisal," he noted that the majority of antebellum Americans came to New Orleans not from the southern frontier but from the northeastern seaboard. Their impressive education, capital resources, and business acumen enabled these newcomers to take control rather quickly of the city's mercantile economy and to launch a massive expansion of the city's wealth and population. The creole businessmen were no match for the Yankee entrepreneurs.[1]

Gaining political control, however, proved much more difficult for the Americans. Although the Americans had far greater experience with democratic government, the creoles retained superior voting strength in Louisiana until the 1830s. To compensate for their limited educational and political experience, the creoles recruited their political leaders from among the better-educated French immigrants, who continued to come to New Orleans in large numbers.

Paul Lachance's essay "The Foreign French" provides one of the first thorough examinations of the French who came to Louisiana after the American purchase in 1803. These immigrants, coming in the wake of dramatic upheavals during the Napoleonic era, provided not only crucial skilled, literate, and experienced reinforcement of the local creole elite, but also shored up French and Franco-African society in New Orleans from top to bottom.

Literally wedding themselves to and preserving the city's creole base for a generation after the American takeover, these Gallic immigrants made certain that the obliteration of French influence that followed the Yankee invasions of Detroit, Chicago, St. Louis, and other French colonial settlements in the Mississippi Valley was not replicated at the foot of the great French Arch in North America.[2] Lachance's pioneering essay documents the persistence of a culture that for many decades made New Orleans' early American migrants strangers in their own land.

Tregle's earlier work showed how the French-speaking voters managed to keep control of state and city government even after they lost their numerical dominance in Louisiana. Through a manipulation of constitutional devices and legislative gerrymandering, they maintained control of state government until the mid-1840s. The resulting political impasse forced the frustrated American leaders in New Orleans to take

1. Joseph G. Tregle, Jr., "Early New Orleans Society: A Reappraisal," *Journal of Southern History*, XVIII (February, 1952), 21–36.
2. Malcolm J. Rohrbach, *The Trans-Appalachian Frontier: People, Societies, and Institutions, 1775–1850* (Belmont, Calif., 1990), 105–13. For a more detailed view of the quick American takeover of Chicago and Detroit, see the essays by Jacqueline Peterson, "'Wild' Chicago: The Formation and Destruction of a Multiracial Community on the Midwestern Frontier, 1816–1837," and by Melvin G. Holli, "French Detroit: The Clash of Feudal and Yankee Values," in *The Ethnic Frontier*, ed. Melvin G. Holli and Peter d'A. Jones (Grand Rapids, Mich., 1977), 25–95.

recourse to a device unprecedented in the history of American cities. Adapting the Parisian model of city government, the Americans joined with the creoles in dividing New Orleans into three separate munici- palities, each virtually autonomous and each based on the largely sepa- rate residential enclaves of Americans and creoles.[3]

This unusual division lasted for more than a decade and a half, from 1836 to 1852. In his essay "Creoles and Americans," Professor Tregle uses manuscript census returns and newspaper accounts to demonstrate that, although the ethnic boundaries of the municipalities were never as sharply drawn as earlier historians have suggested, the new political ar- rangement flowed from the creole-American clash and helped tempo- rarily to still the violent passions between the ethnic rivals. Each of the three municipalities, two downtown dominated by French-creoles and one uptown controlled by Anglo-Americans, had its own council to draft ordinances and its own municipal court system to enforce the often disparate regulations. Each conducted official business in its own language, and each tried to perpetuate its culture and language through its own public school system.

Shortly after the Americans persuaded Horace Mann to send a Mas- sachusetts educator to set up their school system, the creole munici- palities looked for models in continental Europe. Eventually they de- signed a unique set of bilingual schools that taught some subjects in French and others in English. Graduates of the schools were expected to become fluent in both languages. Scores of the girls who finished the secondary curriculum returned to teach elementary pupils in both En- glish and French.[4]

Even after the Americans used their dominance in the state legis- lature to reconsolidate the city in 1852, the creoles managed to hang on to their independent school systems, despite strong pressure to merge them with those of the Americans. When, in the mid-1850s, a furious spate of Know-Nothing nativism engulfed New Orleans and prompted moves in the state legislature to unite the school districts, the creoles responded with a revealing public protest. On one hand, they expressed delight with their citizenship in the United States. They wanted to be

3. Joseph G. Tregle, Jr., "Political Reinforcement of Ethnic Dominance in Louisiana, 1812–1845," in *The Americanization of the Gulf Coast, 1803–1850,* ed. Lucius F. Ellsworth (Pensacola, 1972), 78–87.

4. Robert C. Reinders, "New England Influence on the Formation of Public Schools in New Orleans," *Journal of Southern History,* XXX (May, 1964), 181–95.

The three semiautonomous municipalities of New Orleans and the suburb of Lafayette are shown as they existed under the city charter of 1836. The numerals on the map refer to the wards within the three municipalities. In 1852 the city was reconsolidated, with Lafayette included.

Courtesy the Historic New Orleans Collection Museum/Research Center, Acc. No. 1952.29

EXPLANATIONS
Municipality boundary lines
Ward
Fire Limits
Elevation of the City above the Sea 8½ Feet
½ Mile distance Circles rising from Canal St

"one people, entirely separated from other nationalities and bound together by a community of feelings and interests." On the other hand, they insisted that American nationality should allow for diversity, particularly for their French language. They envisioned that its survival would help shape something new in New Orleans—an open, shared culture that reflected the city's unique experience in the United States: "We hope that this language will never be suffered to die out amongst us; that from the two main elements of our population, in the crucible of American institutions, there will spring a people with original characteristics."[5]

But the creole vision was never to be realized. As Tregle notes, several developments helped the Americans batter down creole resistance. First, the Americans found new allies among the waves of European immigrants that came to New Orleans from nations other than France, particularly from Ireland and Germany. Before the Civil War, New Orleans ranked second only to New York as the nation's leading port of immigration. Located at the mouth of the Mississippi River, it offered immigrants the easiest gateway to the opportunities found in the North American interior and became what one scholar called the nation's "backdoor to the land of plenty."[6]

Most of the half-million immigrants entering New Orleans before 1860 hastened well beyond the slave states of the South, but tens of thousands remained in the city. Before the Civil War, the French, Germans, and Irish dominated the flow of immigration into the city. But even after the 1860s, when New Orleans slipped to a lesser role as an immigrant port, a steady stream of Spaniards, Latin Americans, Greeks, Dalmatians, Chinese, Filipinos, and particularly Italians continued to settle in the city.[7] The numbers and diversity of these newcomers helped both to shape New Orleans into one of the world's leading commercial centers and, at the same time, to keep it a bizarre and cosmopolitan outpost in the American South.

5. *Memorial*, a printed poster pasted into the Minutes of the Board of Directors of the Public Schools of District Two, February 2, 1856, in Orleans Parish School Board Collection, Earl K. Long Library, University of New Orleans.

6. Fredrick Marcel Spletstoser, "Backdoor to the Land of Plenty: New Orleans as an Immigrant Port, 1820–1860" (2 vols.; Ph.D. dissertation, Louisiana State University, 1978).

7. Joseph Logsdon, "Immigration Through the Port of New Orleans," in *Forgotten Doors: The Other Ports of Entry to the United States*, ed. Mark Stolarik (Philadelphia, 1988), 105–24.

TABLE 1. Nationality and Linguistic Survey of Students
in School District Two, 1852 and 1853

Birthplace	1852	1853	Mother Tongue	1852	1853
Louisiana	1,408	1,712	French	1,288	1,122
Other U.S.	307	236	English	968	1,109
France	232	255	German	141	446
Germany	184	246	Spanish	42	44
Ireland	162	173	Italian	40	27
Spain	49	16			
Italy	44	19			
Great Britain	11	60			
Mexico	7	6			
West Indies	4	21			
Others	9	4			
Totals	2,417	2,748			

SOURCE: Minutes of the Board of Directors of the Public Schools for the Second District of New Orleans, May 17, 1852, December 19, 1853, in Orleans Parish School Board Collection, Earl K. Long Library, University of New Orleans.

Many of the immigrants drew solace from the well-rooted Catholic church in New Orleans and adopted creole habits of cuisine and festivity, but they showed little interest in learning the French language. Leaders within the creole municipalities resisted the bilingual instructional programs set up by the French-speaking educators. And by the 1850s, surveys made clear that the creoles and their foreign French allies had become a minority even within their own residential districts (see Table 1).

The increasing use of the English language in New Orleans does not alone account for the sudden decline of creole resistance to the process of Americanization. In the conclusion of his essay, Tregle notes that the passions of sectional and racial conflict in Louisiana played a much more important role in bringing an accommodation between the two host populations. Tregle's exploration of the creole-American theme beyond the antebellum period reveals that Union military occupation in the Civil War not only halted separate, French-based instruction in the city's public schools but, more important, pushed the white creoles into full acceptance of the racial outlook of their fellow white southerners.

When tracing the evolution of the word *creole*, Tregle shows how white creoles began to divorce themselves from their historical association with black creoles by attempting to deny use of the traditionally broad designation to anyone of African ancestry. Tregle is correct in his suspicion that the ensuing semantic debate displayed its antebellum roots when Americans accused some of their creole rivals of having mixed racial ancestry. In 1854, for example, such charges succeeded in removing from elected office George Pandely, the son-in-law of Alexander Dimitry, one of the city's leading creole spokesmen. Tregle clearly demonstrates, however, that the new usage of the word *creole* emerged only during the Reconstruction era when the struggle for white supremacy brought about a fundamental and lasting political rapprochement between all white conservatives, regardless of their antebellum ancestry. For white New Orleanians—creole, American, and immigrant—color proved to be the most effective force for assimilation.

The white creoles' fervent embrace of the Anglo-Americans' racial mores was doubly ironic. It was ironic, first, as an act of self-denial. Turning their backs on much of their own history, they rejected in the rush to whiteness the historic closeness, indeed, interconnectedness, of the white and black creole communities, particularly in those downtown municipalities that enjoyed a large degree of freedom from American administrators down to the 1850s. Second, the antebellum ethnic, cultural, and political divisions among whites provided the space within which New Orleans' unique community of free people of color could flourish. The attempt to hijack the *creole* label for exclusive white use not only furnished evidence of the white creoles' Americanization but also meant that, to the extent New Orleans' creole character survived at all, it did so primarily among nonwhites.

The creole-American split detailed by Lachance and Tregle had its counterpart in black New Orleans, and the dualism produced an extraordinary racial environment in the city in the nineteenth century. The vast majority of New Orleans' very large and mostly Catholic free colored community lived in three of the wards that stretched across the two downtown creole municipalities, while the entire uptown American sector held less than 12 percent of the free black population. As Leonard Curry's exhaustive survey of free blacks in urban America revealed, the New Orleans free colored community had other unusual features. According to Curry's examination of the nation's fifteen largest cities, only in New Orleans were as many as 5 percent of the free people of color

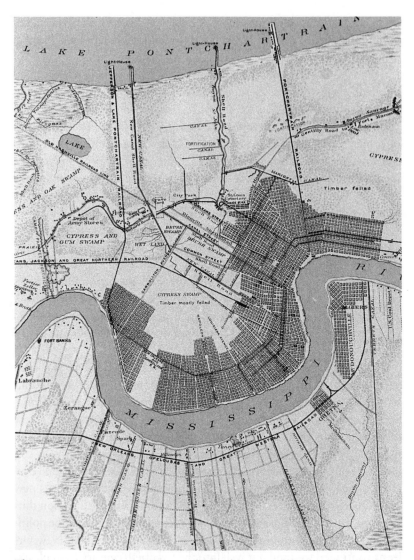

This is a portion of an 1863 map drawn for General Nathaniel P. Banks by Chief Topographical Engineer Henry L. Abbot. It shows how the populated areas of New Orleans remained confined to the higher ground along the Mississippi River. The densely settled neighborhoods forced various racial and ethnic groups into close association.

Courtesy the Historic New Orleans Collection Museum/Research Center, Acc. No. 1974.25.18.122

engaged in professional occupations, and that high total was achieved despite the virtual absence of black Protestant ministers, a category that provided 30 percent of the professionals in the other cities.

Moreover, the number of free persons of color in New Orleans listing their occupations as clerk accounted for 70 percent of such listings in all the cities combined. New Orleans had more entrepreneurs than any of the other cities surveyed and engaged 62 percent of its free men of color as artisans. The nearly $2.5 million in real estate held by New Orleans' free black community in 1850 represented nearly 60 percent of the total property held by free black inhabitants of the cities examined and was fifty times as great as the holdings reported in Boston. The wealth of the New Orleans community was not merely a function of its size. In 1850, the free black population of Baltimore was more than two and a half times the size of its New Orleans counterpart but managed to accumulate property worth only 5.5 percent of the holdings of free black New Orleanians. Overall, some 650 free people of color owned land in New Orleans, while only three other cities had as many as 100, and none had over 200. In sum, New Orleans' unusual colonial and early national development had fostered a racial order unique in the United States.[8]

Tregle's analysis moves beyond the antebellum era to set the stage for the study of race relations discussed in Part III. If American notions of the color line proved totally acceptable to most white creoles, those notions produced contradictory reactions among black creoles in New Orleans. Some emulated the color consciousness of the whites, but many of the city's Franco-Africans fiercely held to their identities as creoles and sought out new French models to fuel their continuing and ever more radical protests against racial discrimination. In the form of a new and stubborn social activism, creole resistance to Americanization thus survived long into the postwar era, producing some of the major political and legal confrontations in American history. As a result, New Orleans continued to stand out well into the twentieth century as a cultural and social counterpoint to other cities in both the North and the South.

8. Leonard P. Curry, *The Free Black in Urban America, 1800–1850: The Shadow of the Dream* (Chicago, 1981), 22–26, 29, 39–44.

3

The Foreign French

PAUL F. LACHANCE

Antebellum New Orleans struck contemporaries and continues to strike historians as *sui generis* in the ethnic composition of its population. It had a full-fledged three-caste racial system: whites, free persons of color, and slaves. The language divide cut across the racial cleavages. During his first residence in New Orleans in 1806 and 1807, the merchant Vincent Nolte estimated that three-fifths of the inhabitants were French and the remainder Spanish, American, and German. He may have underestimated the French majority. According to an 1806 census, the city contained approximately 2,500 white adult males, of whom only 230 were Spaniards and 350 were men "whose language is not French, or Spanish . . . [including] *all* the Americans."[1] The resist-

A Social Sciences and Humanities Research Council of Canada Leave Fellowship supported this study.

1. Laura Foner, "The Free People of Color in Louisiana and St. Domingue: A Comparative Portrait of Two Three-Caste Societies," *Journal of Social History*, III (1970), 406, 423–30; Thomas Fiehrer, "The African Presence in Colonial Louisiana: An Essay on the Continuity of Caribbean Culture," in *Louisiana's Black Heritage*, ed. Robert R. Macdonald, John R. Kemp, and Edward F. Haas (New Orleans, 1979), 19–25; Vincent Nolte, *Fifty Years in Both Hemispheres; or, Reminiscences of the Life of a Former Merchant*, trans. from German (1854; rpr. Freeport, N.Y., 1972), 86; "Recensement général du Territoire d'Orléans au 1er de janvier 1807," item 1, in Joseph Dubreuil de Villars Papers, William R. Perkins Library, Duke University, Durham, N.C.; Secretary John Graham to Secretary of State James Madison, January 2, 1806, quoted in Charles Gayarré, *The American Domination* (New Orleans, 1885), 123–24, Vol. IV of his *History of Louisiana*, 4 vols.

ance of this predominantly Gallic population to Americanization is a major theme in the history of early nineteenth-century New Orleans.

The Anglo-French conflict has long been represented as a bipolar struggle for dominance between Americans arriving from the East and French-speaking natives of Louisiana, or creoles. Now, however, it is usually recognized that a third group—the "foreign French"—was also involved. The term is a literal translation of *français étrangers,* or *français de dehors,* which in antebellum New Orleans meant immigrants whose first language was French.[2] In his influential revisionist interpretation of early New Orleans society, Joseph Tregle, Jr., says this group was the true rival of the Anglo-Americans. Creoles, he argues, were handicapped by limited education, middling wealth, and a provincial life-style. They would have been no match for the aggressive, acquisitive Americans, but the "political tutelage and leadership" of talented French immigrants enabled them for several decades to resist Americanization and maintain a dominant position in New Orleans and the state.[3]

Despite Tregle's clear distinction between creoles and the foreign French, his characterization of them has not yet been verified by systematic quantitative analysis. In this chapter I have used census data, city directories, church records, marriage contracts, and municipal registers to draw a collective portrait of the foreign French. First, I identify the three major subgroups of French-speaking immigrants, white and non-white Saint Domingue refugees and the European French, telling when they arrived and the circumstances of their migration. Then I estimate the size of these groups relative to creoles and non-French elements of the population and show where they fit in the socioeconomic structure.

This analysis reveals the presence of foreign-born Frenchmen and Frenchwomen in all ranks of the social hierarchy, whether measured by race, wealth, literacy, or occupational status. It also calls attention to the institutional completeness of the Gallic community at the outset of

2. A good source for expressions used by the foreign French to distinguish themselves from creoles is the correspondence of Jean Boze, a Saint Domingue refugee who settled and died in New Orleans, with Henri de Ste. Gême, a refugee who returned to France after the Battle of New Orleans. The correspondence covers the years 1818 to 1839 and is in the Henri de Ste. Gême papers, MSS. 100, Historic New Orleans Collection (hereafter HNOC), New Orleans.

3. Joseph Tregle, Jr., "Early New Orleans Society: A Reappraisal," *Journal of Southern History,* XVIII (1952), 20–36; Tregle, "Political Reinforcement of Ethnic Dominance in Louisiana, 1812–1845," in *The Americanization of the Gulf Coast, 1803–1850,* ed. Lucius Ellsworth (Pensacola, 1972), 78–87.

the nineteenth century. This perspective shows that not only the minority of French-speaking immigrants who successfully made their way into the elite but also the majority who remained artisans and petty proprietors contributed to the persistence of a French-speaking culture in New Orleans after the Louisiana Purchase.

The Refugees from Saint Domingue

Located in the western part of the island of Hispaniola, Saint Domingue was the richest and most populated French colony in the eighteenth century. Between 1791 and 1804, black revolutionaries won control of the colony and renamed it Haiti. It became the first independent nation of former slaves in the Americas. The majority of the refugees from the Haitian Revolution in the 1790s went to the United States. The most spectacular exodus occurred on June 23, 1793, when ten thousand civilians and soldiers, literally pushed into the sea by slave rebels descending from the hills on Cap Français, sailed on three hundred ships for Baltimore, Norfolk, and other ports on the Atlantic seaboard. In the summer of 1798, Jamaica received a large contingent of refugees. Two thousand French collaborators retreated with the British expeditionary force that had occupied more than one-third of the colony at their invitation since 1793. The last and largest of the mass departures took place in 1803. With the defeat of the army sent by Napoleon to restore French authority, practically all the remaining whites, many free persons of color, and some slaves, altogether thirty thousand individuals, fled to neighboring Cuba.[4]

4. An insightful essay on Saint Domingue and the revolution with special reference to Louisiana is Thomas Fiehrer, "Saint-Domingue/Haiti: Louisiana's Caribbean Connection," *Louisiana History*, XXX (1989), 419–37. The Haitian Revolution is recounted in the classic histories of T. Lothrop Stoddard, *The French Revolution in San Domingo* (Boston, 1914), and of C. L. R. James, *The Black Jacobins: Toussaint L'Ouverture and the San Domingo Revolution* (2d ed.; New York, 1963). An overall view of refugee movements resulting from the revolution is in John Baur, "International Repercussions of the Haitian Revolution," *Americas*, XXVI (1970), 394–418. Saint Domingue refugees on the Atlantic Coast figure prominently in Frances Childs, *French Refugee Life in the United States, 1790–1800* (Baltimore, 1940). All histories of the Haitian Revolution describe the events of June 21–23, 1793. See, for example, H. Castonnet des Fosses, *La Perte d'une colonie: La Révolution de Saint-Domingue* (Paris, 1893), 130. For Jamaica see David Geggus, *Slavery, War, and Revolution: The British Occupation of Saint Domingue, 1793–1798* (Oxford, 1982), 271–72, 314; Philip Wright and Gabriel Debien, "Les colons de Saint-Domingue passés à la Jamaïque (1792–1835)," *Bulletin de la société historique de la Guadeloupe*, XXVI (1975), 70. The migration to Cuba is described in

Many refugees from Saint Domingue subsequently settled in New Orleans. During the 1790s individual refugees filtered into Spanish Louisiana from the East Coast of the United States. Jacques-François Pitot, for example, naturalized as an American citizen in Philadelphia, moved to New Orleans in August, 1796, where he anglicized his name to "James" and became a prominent merchant, mayor, and judge. Two other refugees arriving in the Spanish period, Louis Duclot and Jean-Baptiste Lesueur-Fontaine, launched the first newspaper in New Orleans, *Le Moniteur de la Louisiane*. Louis Guillaume Du Bourg, born in Cap Français and educated in France, would later be named bishop of the Diocese of Louisiana. These first refugees, though few in number, were among the most famous to end up in New Orleans.[5]

Several boatloads of refugees expelled by the British from Jamaica arrived in 1803 and 1804. One of them, Louise Davezac de Castera, married Edward Livingston, then an attorney already embroiled in New Orleans politics, in 1805. Her brother Auguste Davezac became Livingston's ally and eventually followed him into the Jackson camp. Another Jamaican refugee, the future poet and professor Tullius Saint-Céran, was born in Kingston in August, 1802. Saint Domingue refugees straggled in over the next few years, including Louis Moreau Lislet, a native of Cap Français, who arrived in New Orleans by way of Cuba in 1805. Along with James Brown, he compiled and prepared the 1808 digest of the Civil Code that was to serve henceforward as the basis of Louisiana law.[6]

The last and largest wave of Saint Domingue refugees reached New

---

Gabriel Debien, "Les Colons de Saint-Domingue réfugiés à Cuba, 1793–1815," *Revista de Indias*, XIII (1953), 559–605, XIV (1954), 11–36; and in Alain Yacou, "L'Émigration à Cuba des colons français de Saint-Domingue au cours de la Révolution" (Doctoral dissertation, University of Bordeaux, 1975).

5. Henry Clement Pitot, *James Pitot (1761–1831): A Documentary Study* (New Orleans, 1968), 33–37; Edward Larocque Tinker, *Les Écrits de langue française en Louisiane au XIXe siècle: Essais biographiques et bibliographiques* (1923; rpr. Geneva, 1975), 147; Samuel J. Marino, "Early French-Language Newspapers in New Orleans," *Louisiana History*, VII (1966), 310–11; Roger Baudier, *The Catholic Church in Louisiana* (New Orleans, 1939), 264.

6. Gabriel Debien and René LeGardeur, "Les colons de Saint-Domingue réfugiés à la Louisiane (1792–1804)," *Revue de Louisiane/Louisiana Review*, X (Winter, 1981), 119; Joseph Tregle, "Louisiana in the Age of Jackson: A Study in Egopolitics" (Ph.D. dissertation, University of Pennsylvania, 1954), 199–203; René R. Nicaud, "The French Colonists from St. Domingue and, in Particular, Louis Moreau Lislet," *Louisiana Bar Journal*, XX (March, 1973), 291–93.

Orleans in 1809. When Cuba deported many of the French colonials who had settled there six years earlier, Louisiana was the preferred destination of those leaving from the ports of Baracoa and Santiago de Cuba. According to a special report made by the mayor of New Orleans, 9,059 Saint Domingue refugees from Cuba arrived between May, 1809, and January, 1810. Additional arrivals in the first months of 1810 pushed the total to more than 10,000. By comparison, only several hundred refugees arrived in the last decade of Spanish rule and roughly a thousand at the time of the Louisiana Purchase.[7] All three castes were well represented in the influx of 1809: 2,731 whites, 3,102 free persons of color, and 3,226 slaves.

The *Courrier de la Louisiane,* sympathetic to the plight of the white refugees, characterized them as "for the most part rich planters driven from their property in Saint Domingue by a bloody revolution, who carried to Cuba the debris of their fortune, their industry, and their activity." Despite the stimulus they provided to sugar and coffee production in Cuba, they became the scapegoats of the backlash (*contre-coup*) to the Spanish revolution, that is, the refusal of Spanish colonies to accept Joseph Bonaparte as king of Spain. Obliged "to search again a friendly shore where they might finally rest," they were said to be attracted to Louisiana by its language, climate, and type of agriculture. The newspaper called the slaves accompanying the refugees "faithful servants who preferred all the horrors of exile and poverty to the idea of separation from their masters."[8]

As a plea for a hospitable reception for these people, the image conveyed in the editorial in the *Courrier* served an obvious function. Portraying the refugees as "unhappy" and "innocent" victims of war and revolution evoked humanitarian sentiments. Noting the contribution of French planters to economic progress in Cuba suggested their potential utility to Louisiana. Insisting on the parallels in culture and language between Saint Domingue and Louisiana counteracted the xenophobia of creoles toward refugees arriving earlier. Description of the slaves who accompanied the refugees from Cuba as "faithful servants" mitigated

7. Rapport du maire de la Nouvelle-Orléans au Gouverneur Claiborne, January 18, 1810, in *Moniteur de la Louisiane,* January 27, 1810. Debien and LeGardeur, "Colons de Saint-Domingue réfugiés à la Louisiane," 132, estimate one hundred arrivals between 1791 and 1797, two hundred between 1797 and 1802, and more than a thousand in 1803–1804, adding that it is impossible to determine how many of these people settled permanently in New Orleans.

8. "Aux Louisianais," *Courrier de la Louisiane,* May 22, 1809.

deeply entrenched fears that blacks from the French Caribbean were carriers of revolution.[9]

The documentary value of the image is less certain. It ignored the large free colored component of the refugee population and stereotyped the slaves. Calling the refugees hapless victims of revolution was a half-truth. Although they migrated under constraint, their own actions helped precipitate their departure first from Saint Domingue and then from Cuba. In Saint Domingue, they had sided with the expeditionary force sent by Napoleon to pacify the island and restore slavery by means as brutal as the tactics of counterinsurgency of the twentieth century.[10] It is not surprising that when Charles Victor Emmanuel Leclerc's army was defeated, collaborators should have found their lives and property in jeopardy. In Cuba, the refugees proposed to Napoleon the creation of a new French colony in Oriente province, where many of them had settled.[11] Thus Cuban authorities had reason to suspect their loyalty. Finally, one might question how strong was the attraction of Louisiana's language and economy if the refugees first sought refuge in Cuba and left only under order of expulsion.

It is easier to point out distortions in contemporary accounts of the refugees than to cut through the rhetoric surrounding their arrival and provide an objective appraisal of the reasons they came to New Orleans. Suffice it to say that the events that deprived revolutionary France of her colonies in the Caribbean produced a floating population of former colonials, white and nonwhite, many of whom eventually made their way to Louisiana when the fortunes of war made them *persona non grata* in British and Spanish colonies. Those who migrated from Cuba in 1809 chose Louisiana in part because of the limited number of alternative refuges available at that late date in the Napoleonic Wars, the relative proximity of New Orleans in sailing time from eastern

9. Berquin Duvallon, *Vue de la colonie espagnole du Mississippi ou des provinces de Louisiane et Floride occidentale, en l'année 1802, par un observateur résident sur les lieux* (Paris, 1803), 226; Paul Alliot, "Réflexions historiques et politiques sur la Louisiane," in *Louisiana Under the Rule of Spain, France and the United States, 1785–1807,* ed. James A. Robertson (2 vols.; Cleveland, 1911), I, 66–68; Paul Lachance, "The Politics of Fear: French Louisianians and the Slave Trade, 1786–1809," *Plantation Society in the Americas,* I (June, 1979), 167–69.

10. For example, the drowning en masse of captured insurgents and the use of dogs especially trained to chase and attack blacks. See James, *Black Jacobins,* 359.

11. Report of General Turreau, June, 1807, cited in Debien, "Colons de Saint-Domingue réfugiés à Cuba," XIII, 590–91; Alexandre Joseph Lambert, "Quelques idées sur l'isle Espagnole de Cuba" (1807), CC 9B 27, Archives Nationales, Paris.

Cuba, the hope that the ban on importation of foreign slaves into the United States as of 1808 might not be enforced in territorial Louisiana, and the presence there of refugees who had arrived over the preceding decade. Refugees involved in privateering in Cuba needed only to transfer their base of operations to Barataria.[12]

Despite the organization of two relief committees, one for whites and another for free persons of color, and various initiatives to aid the refugees, they were not universally welcomed. William C. C. Claiborne, the governor of the Territory of Orleans, reported to the secretary of state in Washington, "The native americans, and the English part of our society . . . (with some few exceptions) appear to be prejudiced against these Strangers, and express great dissatisfaction that an Asylum in this territory was afforded them." When Congress voted not to apply the 1808 ban on importation of foreign slaves to slaves belonging to the refugees from Cuba, it also made an exception to the Non-Intercourse Act then in effect and authorized a French ship to enter the port of New Orleans and take on refugees wishing to depart for France or a French colony.[13]

Some refugees undoubtedly left then or later, but a large number

12. In 1809, France had lost all of its Caribbean colonies except Guadeloupe, which would fall to the British in February, 1810. War with England ruled out British colonies as possible refuges. Like Cuba, other Spanish colonies were in revolt against Napoleon. The United States consul in Santiago de Cuba reported that most of the French inhabitants banished from Cuba looked to the United States "as the only one capable of affording them a safe and peaceful asylum," the only difficulty being the law prohibiting the introduction of foreign slaves into its territories. See Maurice Rogers to Robert Smith, April 22, 1809, Despatches from U.S. Consuls in Santiago de Cuba, 1799–1806, microfilm T-55, roll 1, in National Archives, Washington, D.C. See also Letter of James Wilkinson to a deputation of French subjects, Havana, April 2, 1809, in Luis Perez, "French Refugees to New Orleans in 1809," *Publications of the Southern History Association*, IX (1905), 297; Claiborne to Robert Smith, May 20, 1809, in Dunbar Rowland, ed., *Official Letter Books of W. C. C. Claiborne, 1801–1816* (6 vols.; Jackson, Miss., 1917), IV, 363–64. French privateers sailing out of Cuba operated, like the Baratarians, under Guadeloupe commissions. See Stanley Faye, "Privateers of Guadeloupe and Their Establishment in Barataria," *Louisiana Historical Quarterly*, XXIII (1940), 431–33.

13. See *Moniteur de la Louisiane*, June 7, 1809, for the text of the motion of the Municipal Council forming a welfare committee to help white refugees from Cuba; *ibid.*, June 24, 1809, on the voluntary subscription to aid refugees who were free persons of color. Newspapers allowed refugees in search of employment to advertise their talents free of charge. Newspapers also contain advertisements of land and employment addressed specifically to the refugees. See, for example, *Courrier de la Louisiane*, June 5, 12, 1809. Claiborne to Robert Smith, July 29, 1809, in Rowland, ed., *Letter Books of Claiborne*, IV, 392; "House Debate on Emigrants from Cuba," June 28, 1809, *Annals of Congress*, 11th Cong., 463.

stayed in the city. Pierre Lambert, a coffee planter in Cuba, put up three-fifths of the capital to open a pharmacy shortly after his arrival in New Orleans, helped found the Collège d'Orléans, and eventually became one of the city's leading physicians. Jean Augustin, a planter in Saint Domingue before fleeing to Cuba, took up a new career in New Orleans as professor at the Collège d'Orléans. His son Jean-Baptiste Donatien Augustin, born in Port-au-Prince in 1802 and thus only a youngster when his family arrived in New Orleans, studied and practiced law and was active in local politics, holding such posts as secretary to the municipal council, sheriff, district judge, and brigadier general in the Louisiana Legion.[14]

Some families that fled directly from Cuba to New Orleans were joined over time by relatives who had entered the United States through other ports. The Canonge family, for example, fled to Philadelphia from Cuba. One son remained in Philadelphia, another moved to New York, and the four other children and their mother settled in New Orleans. After studying law in Philadelphia, Jean-François Canonge was admitted to the bar in New Orleans, served as clerk in the Louisiana legislature, and was appointed to the bench of the Criminal District Court.[15]

Quantitative evidence of the decision of many refugees to settle permanently in New Orleans is to be found in the marriage records of St. Louis Cathedral and the Ursulines Chapel, the churches in which almost all marriages involving French-speakers were celebrated up to 1840.[16]

14. Advertisements in the *Moniteur*, November 15, 1809–February 24, 1810, reveal that space was still available on the eve of the departure of the ship dispatched to New Orleans to transport refugees to Bordeaux. Lambert Family Papers (1798–1862), box 1, folders 3, 4, 23, Louisiana Collection, Howard-Tilton Library, Tulane University, New Orleans; Augustin-Wogan-Labranche Family Papers (1803–1923), Howard-Tilton Library, Tulane University; Stanley Arthur and George Huchet de Kernion, *Old Families of Louisiana* (1931; rpr. Baton Rouge, 1971), 49–51.

15. Arthur and Kernion, *Old Families of Louisiana*, 137–40. Other refugees from Saint Domingue who settled in New Orleans are mentioned in Alfred Hunt, *Haiti's Influence on Antebellum America: Slumbering Volcano in the Caribbean* (Baton Rouge, 1988), 53ff.

16. Data base on the origin of spouses named in the following registers from Catholic churches in New Orleans, 1790–1839: St. Louis Cathedral, Archives of the Archdiocese of New Orleans, Books II (1784–1806), III (1806–21), IV (1821–30), V (1830–34), VI (1834–37), and VII (1838–40) of marriages of whites, and Books I (1777–1830), II (1830–35), and III (1835–39) of marriages of Negroes and mulattoes; Ursulines Chapel and the Church of St. Mary, Books I (1805–37) and II (1837–40) of marriages of whites; St. Mary's Italian Church, the nonwhite register for 1805–80; and the marriage index for St. Patrick's Church (1833–62), in the New Orleans Public Library, City Archives. Use was made of a translation of Book II of the white registers of St. Louis Cathedral: Alice Forsyth,

The number of white spouses born in Saint Domingue or Cuba of refugee parents increased from 2 in the 1790s to 63 in the 1800s and 258 in
the decade following the mass migration from Cuba before declining to
173 in the 1820s and 59 in the 1830s. The number of nonwhite refugees
marrying in New Orleans jumped from 6 in the 1790s and 7 in the 1800s
to 63 from 1810 to 1819, 147 in the 1820s, and 127 in the 1830s.[17]

Natives of Saint Domingue who were married in New Orleans came
from throughout the colony. One-third of the whites gave as their birthplace a parish in the Department of the South, slightly over one-third
cited a parish in the Department of the North, and just under one-
third cited a parish in the Department of the West (Map 1). Jurisdictions
containing the four largest ports in Saint Domingue—Port-au-Prince,
Jérémie, Le Cap (Cap Français), and Port-de-Paix (Môle St. Nicholas)—
furnished more refugees than did rural parishes. When the slaves rose
up in the Saint Domingue countryside, white families fled their plantations for the relative safety of coastal cities, where the children were
born who appeared twenty to thirty years later in New Orleans marriage registers. The urban birthplace of the refugees is a first indication of
the presence in the refugee population of a sizable *petit blanc* element.[18]

By comparison, almost two-thirds of the free persons of color from
Saint Domingue who married in New Orleans were born in the Department of the West. Only 22 percent were born in the Department of the
North and 15 percent in the Department of the South (Map 2). This
proportion corresponds roughly to the geographical distribution of free
persons of color in Saint Domingue. On the eve of the revolution,
43 percent lived in the west, 32 percent in the north, and 25 percent in
the south.[19]

The marriage records also reflect the size of the Saint Domingue
subgroups relative to the foreign French of other origins. Over the pe-

---

ed., *Louisiana Marriages: I, A Collection of Marriage Records from the St. Louis Cathedral
in New Orleans During the Spanish Regime and the Early American Period, 1784–1806*
(New Orleans, 1977). This data base is described and analyzed at length in my "Intermarriage and French Cultural Persistence in Late Spanish and Early American New Orleans,"
Histoire Sociale—Social History, XV (1982), 47–81.

17. Paul Lachance, "The 1809 Immigration of Saint-Domingue Refugees to New
Orleans: Reception, Integration and Impact," *Louisiana History*, XXIX (1988), 126.

18. James, *Black Jacobins*, 33, includes in the category of "small whites" in the
towns, "the small lawyers, the notaries, the clerks, the artisans, the grocers."

19. Robert Stein, "The Free Men of Colour and the Revolution in Saint-Domingue,
1789–1792," *Histoire Sociale—Social History*, XIV (1981), 12.

MAP 1. Regional Origins of White Saint Domingue Refugees Marrying in New Orleans, 1790–1839

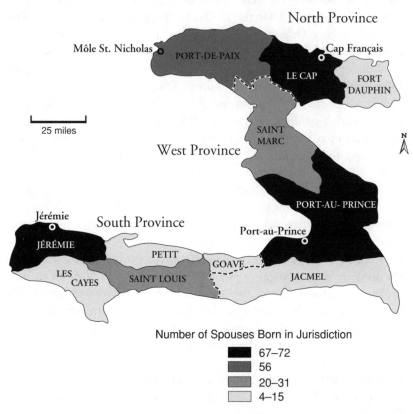

Number of Spouses Born in Jurisdiction

- 67–72
- 56
- 20–31
- 4–15

SOURCES: Marriages listed in registers of St. Louis Cathedral and the Ursulines Chapel, 1790–1839, Archives of the Archdiocese of New Orleans; "Liste des paroisses de Saint-Domingue en 1789," d'après Barbé-Marbois, Etat des finances de Saint-Domingue, cited by Blanche Maurel, *Les cahiers de doléances de la colonie de Saint-Domingue* (Paris, 1933), 345.

riod from 1790 to 1840, almost all foreign-born French-speaking free persons of color were born in Saint Domingue or in Cuba of Saint Domingue parents. By contrast, only 30 percent of white French-speaking immigrant spouses were natives of Saint Domingue or Cuba. Less than 3 percent were born in other French colonies in the Caribbean or in French Canada. That leaves approximately two-thirds who were natives

MAP 2. Regional Origins of Free Persons of Color Born in Saint Domingue and Marrying in New Orleans, 1790–1839

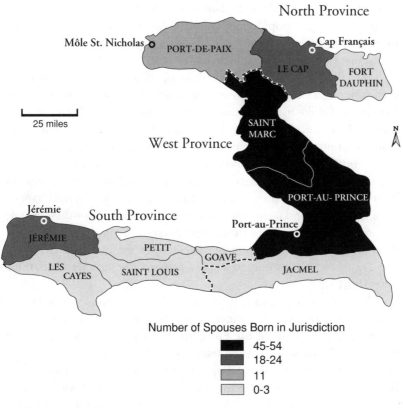

of France, Belgium, and the French-speaking cantons of Switzerland. Together, they make up the third and numerically most important component of the foreign French population.

The European French

Some of the immigrants born in France were refugees from the Saint Domingue revolution. For example, Louisiana's fifth governor, Pierre Derbigny, born into the French nobility in Laon, a town near Lille,

France, is said to have fled the French Revolution for Saint Domingue, escaping in turn from there to Pittsburgh in 1792, where he married the daughter of an important French family of the Illinois country. After visiting Havana, he finally settled in Louisiana in 1797.[20] Nevertheless, within the refugee population, colonials born in France were distinct from natives of Saint Domingue. Like the native-born population of Louisiana, the latter were called creoles.

Over the whole of the antebellum period, most of the European French immigrated to New Orleans without ever having set foot in Saint Domingue. Unlike natives of that colony, spouses born in France did not become less numerous in the 1830s, reflecting a stream of migration that was continuously replenished at its source. Until 1832, according to the *Annual Reports on Immigration to the United States,* fewer than one thousand French immigrants per year passed through the port of New Orleans. From then until the Civil War, annual arrivals ranged from three thousand to over seven thousand. Only some of these people stayed in New Orleans, but they were enough to make the French the third largest immigrant group in the city after the Irish and Germans. The census of 1850 enumerated 7,522 natives of France. By 1860, there were 10,515.[21]

The marriage registers provide an impression of the areas of France from which emigration to Louisiana was heaviest (Map 3). From 1790 to 1830, three-fourths of the European French were born in the west and south: 24 percent in Aquitaine, where the port of Bordeaux is located; 28 percent in other Atlantic regions from Poitou-Charentes to Normandy; and 25 percent in the southern regions of the Midi-Pyrénées, Langeudoc, Provence–Côte d'Azur, and Rhône-Alpes. In the eighteenth century, the west and south of France had provided comparable proportions of the immigrants to Saint Domingue.[22] New Orleans seems to have been the beneficiary of a redirection of this current of French migration to the Caribbean after the loss of Saint Domingue.

20. Arthur and Kernion, *Old Families of Louisiana,* 342; Joseph Tregle, Jr., "The Governors of Louisiana: Pierre Auguste Charles Bourguinon Derbigny, 1828–1829," *Louisiana History,* XXII (1981), 298.

21. Alan Conway, "New Orleans as a Port of Immigration" (Master's thesis, University College, London, 1949), 48; J. D. B. De Bow, comp., *Statistical View of the United States* (1854; rpr. New York, 1970), 399; *Eighth Census, 1860,* I, 615. In addition, 49 free persons of color are listed as born in France.

22. Jacques Houdaille, "Quelques données sur la population de Saint-Domingue au XVIIIe siècle: Etude démographique," *Population,* XXVIII (1973), 863.

MAP 3. Regional Origins of French Immigrants Marrying in New Orleans, 1790–1829

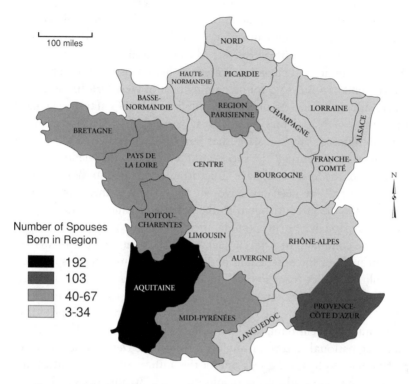

SOURCES: Marriages listed in registers of St. Louis Cathedral and the Ursulines Chapel, 1790–1829, Archives of the Archdiocese of New Orleans.

NOTE: The map excludes European French marrying in the 1830s, when the number of spouses born in Alsace and Lorraine rose sharply.

The European French came to New Orleans for diverse reasons. Some were exiles from the revolutions punctuating French history from 1789 on, among them royalists such as Louis Philippe Joseph de Roffignac, whose godparents were the Duke and Duchess of Orleans, the parents of the future French monarch sharing Roffignac's first two names. Roffignac arrived in Louisiana in 1800, and he served for ten years in the legislature, was a colonel in the Louisiana Legion and director of the State Bank of Louisiana, and several times was elected mayor of New Orleans before returning to France in 1828. From the other side of the barricades, the regicide Joseph Lakanal also made his way to New Orleans, where, on the recommendation of Edward Livingston, he was named president of the Collège d'Orléans.[23]

The *coup d'état* of Napoleon Bonaparte sent a second collection of French exiles to New Orleans: first, individuals at odds with his regime, the two most famous being Etienne Mazureau and General Jean Joseph Amable Humbert; then, after Waterloo, his partisans. One of them, Pierre-Benjamin Buisson, found employment in New Orleans as an engineer and architect. As director of public works in Lafayette, he gave the names of Napoleon's battles to its streets. By 1810 Bonapartists were so numerous in Louisiana that James Brown perceived a threat to American sovereignty: "The success of the British in the Islands and the struggles of the Spaniards, have concentrated the forces of Bonaparte in this Territory." He need not have worried. Many of these former soldiers of Napoleon contributed to the defense of American sovereignty over Louisiana when they fought their last battle against the British under the command of Andrew Jackson in the winter of 1814–1815.[24]

Throughout the antebellum period New Orleans served as a haven for political exiles from France. To escape two years in prison for an attack on church and state, Pierre Soulé fled Restoration France in 1825. In New Orleans, he was admitted to the bar, named as president of the Improvement Bank, and bankrupted by the Panic of 1837 before attaining national stature through a career in the Democratic party. As ambassador to Spain, he was one of the authors of the Ostend Manifesto. In the aftermath of the revolutions of 1830 and 1848 in France, still more exiles arrived in New Orleans, among them the writers Louis Dufau, Eugène Dumez, and Jean-Sylvain Gentil.[25]

23. Henry C. Castellanos, *New Orleans as It Was: Episodes of Louisiana Life* (1895; rpr. Baton Rouge, 1978), 14–27, 69–70.

24. On Mazureau, consult Tinker, *Ecrits de langue française*, 344–50; on Humbert, Castellanos, *New Orleans as It Was*, 28–51; on Buisson, Inès Murat, *Napoléon et le rêve américain* (Paris, 1976), 94 (translated into English by Frances Frenaye as *Napoleon and the American Dream* [Baton Rouge, 1981]). James Brown to Henry Clay, February 26, 1810, in "Letters of James Brown to Henry Clay, 1804–1835," ed. James Podgett, *Louisiana Historical Quarterly*, XXIV (October, 1941), 931. The ethnic composition of the Uniformed Battalion of Orleans Volunteers is described in Powell Casey, *Louisiana in the War of 1812* (Baton Rouge, 1963), 30–32.

25. Tinker, *Ecrits de langue française*, 434–51, 148, 155, 246. Tinker's comprehensive bio-bibliography of French-language writers in nineteenth-century Louisiana, updated by Auguste Viatte, "Complément à la bibliographie louisianaise d'Edward Laroque Tinker," *Revue de Louisiane/Louisiana Review*, III (1974), 12–57, lists 124 foreign French writers, at least 39 of whom were political exiles.

These political exiles are reputed to have been freethinkers and atheists. If so, their influence was counterbalanced by the clergy, another small but important element of the European French. By 1854, the Archdiocese of New Orleans contained forty parishes, eighteen of them in the city itself, served by seventy-seven priests. A seminary to train Louisiana-born clergy was not founded until 1858. Until then, most of the priests came as missionaries from Europe. Not until the twentieth century did a native American become archbishop of New Orleans. The first bishop appointed after the Louisiana Purchase, Louis Guillaume Du Bourg, was a Saint Domingue refugee. His successors in the antebellum period were Leo Raymond de Neckère, born in Belgium, and Antoine Blanc, born in France. The tradition continued after the Civil War. Francis Janssens was born in Holland, but the other four bishops of New Orleans from 1861 to 1906 were French-born.[26]

Most immigrants from France probably came in search of adventure, fortune, or a combination of the two. In a travel account published in 1828, Karl Postl wrote: "The emigrant French are numerous in New Orleans. Among them are many very respectable merchants, some lawyers, physicians, &c., the greater part, however, consists of adventurers, hair-dressers, dancing-masters, performers, musicians, and the like."[27] The diverse backgrounds of French-speaking immigrants were important in shaping the social role they played in the Gallic community of New Orleans. Before exploring that area, however, it is necessary to measure their demographic impact: how much they added to the size of the Gallic population relative to Anglo-Americans and non-French-speaking immigrants.

The Demographic Impact of the Foreign French

For the period before the federal census of 1850, the first to contain a question on nativity, the size of the foreign French population of New Orleans must be estimated from other sources. Entries in the marriage registers of Catholic churches in New Orleans gave birthplaces. Assuming that up to 1840 almost all Louisiana-born Catholic spouses were

26. Liliane Crété, *La Vie quotidienne en Louisiane, 1815–1830* (Paris, 1978), 227; Baudier, *Catholic Church in Louisiana*, 376; Leonard Huber and Samuel Wilson, Jr., *The Basilica on Jackson Square: The History of the St. Louis Cathedral and Its Predecessors, 1727–1965* (New Orleans, 1965), 46–56.

27. Charles Sealsfield (Karl Anton Postl), *The Americans as They Are; Described in a Tour Through the Valley of the Mississippi* (London, 1828), 174.

French-speaking, as were those born in a French-speaking country or colony, the proportion from each group can serve as an indicator of the relative importance of creoles and the foreign French in the Gallic community. Additionally, the rate of increase in the number of spouses of French origin in the marriage registers, that is, of creoles and immigrants combined, makes possible an estimate of the extent to which the Gallic community kept pace with the growth of the city as a whole.

Separate marriage registers were kept for whites and free persons of color. In addition to forbidding whites to marry free persons of color, the Civil Code prohibited free persons of color from marrying slaves.[28] Although it did allow slaves to marry other slaves with the consent of their masters and on the understanding that such marriages had none of the usual civil effects,[29] only 7 of more than 900 marriages recorded in nonwhite registers between 1810 and 1839 involved slaves.

The proportion of French-speaking white spouses who were foreign-born increased from 23 percent in 1800 to 53 percent in 1810 and 51 percent in 1820, then dropped to 43 percent in 1830.[30] Allowing for over-representation of immigrants in the age groups from which most spouses were drawn, it is still likely that the foreign French made up at least one-third of the white component of the Gallic community in the first decades of American rule.

The marriage registers for free persons of color reflect the presence of many immigrants in that caste as well. Some were African-born. In the 1790s, 17 percent of nonwhite spouses were born in Africa, but the proportion of those of African origin declined in each subsequent decade until, in the 1830s, they represented less than 2 percent of free persons of color marrying in New Orleans. Saint Domingue refugees furnished about 5 percent of all nonwhite Catholic spouses from 1790 to 1810, then 23 percent from 1810 to 1819, 32 percent in the 1820s, and 15 percent in the 1830s.[31] Over the half-century from 1790 to 1840, one-fourth of the nonwhite French-speaking spouses were foreign-born, fewer than among their white counterparts; but the proportion of the foreign French of both races was greatest from 1810 to 1830 and for the same reason—the influx of Saint Domingue refugees in 1809.

28. Joseph Dainow, ed., *Compiled Edition of the Civil Code of Louisiana* (17 vols.; St. Paul, 1973), XVI, 55. The statute was Article 8 of the 1808 Digest of the Civil Code and Article 95 of the 1825 Louisiana Civil Code.
29. Article 182 of the 1835 Louisiana Civil Code.
30. Lachance, "Intermarriage and French Cultural Persistence," Appendix Ia, 78.
31. *Ibid.*, 69.

Most slaves in New Orleans were also French-speaking at the outset of American rule in 1803. Two newspaper advertisements from 1809 provide a glimpse of the range of their linguistic capabilities. At one end of the scale, knowledge of French was rudimentary. A runaway slave belonging to a Saint Domingue refugee was described as a pregnant, parrot-toed, thirty-six-year-old Negro woman, branded "Malard" on her breast, who "speaks bad French." At the other extreme, some slaves were fluent in several languages, for example, the cook described in the *Moniteur de la Louisiane* as an "excellent . . . pastry-maker in the English and French manner, speaking the two languages, sober and well-behaved." An advertisement from 1812 suggests assimilation into the Gallic community of non-French slaves imported during the territorial period: "For sale, An American Negro, in this Country seven or eight years ago, about thirty four years old, speaking a little French, very good cook, pastry-cook, very clever, and being useful to a printing office." The proportion of slaves in New Orleans who spoke French was augmented by the 3,226 slaves accompanying the refugees of 1809.[32] Several of the distinctive features of New Orleans slave culture—the dances in Congo Square, the creolized French dialect, the practice of voodoo—reflect the influence of slaves from the French Caribbean on their peers.

The significance of the numerical reinforcement of the slave, free colored, and white components of the Gallic community by the foreign French can be appreciated when it is set against the population growth of the city as a whole and its changing racial composition (Figure 1). The addition of white French immigrants to the white creole population enabled French-speakers to remain a majority of the white population until almost 1830. If a substantial proportion of free persons of color and slaves had not also spoken French, however, the Gallic community would have become a minority of the total population as early as 1820.[33]

Slaves were probably the first caste to cease to be predominantly

32. *Courrier de la Louisiane*, June 26, 1809; *Moniteur de la Louisiane*, February 11, 1809, July 11, 1812; Mayor's report on refugees arriving in 1809, *ibid.*, January 27, 1810. The number of Saint Domingue slaves was greater than the increase in the slave population of Orleans Parish, which rose from 8,378 in 1806 to 10,824 in 1810, according to the census of January 1, 1807, in Villars Papers, and *Third Census, 1810: Population*, 82.

33. The rates of increase of the two nonwhite castes from 1810 to 1820 were barely more than 2 percent per annum, that is, within the range of possible natural increase, so it is likely that they remained predominantly French into the 1820s.

FIGURE 1.   Racial Composition and Size of Subgroups of the White Gallic
Community, New Orleans, 1810–1860

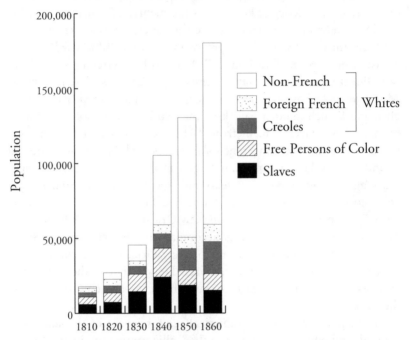

SOURCES: The number of whites, free persons of color, and slaves and the total population are based on aggregate returns in *Third Census, 1810: Population*, 82; *Fourth Census, 1820: Population*, 81; *Fifth Census, 1830: Population*, 104–105; *Sixth Census, 1840: Population*, 256; *Seventh Census, 1850: Population*, 474; *Eighth Census, 1860: Population*, 195. The total population is that of urban areas of the parish of Orleans up to 1830 and of Orleans and Jefferson parishes from 1830 on. The number of foreign French in 1850 is taken from J. D. B. De Bow, comp., *Statistical View of the United States* (1854; rpr. New York, 1970), 399; and in 1860 from *Eighth Census, 1860: Population*, 615. Otherwise, the sizes of the white Gallic population and its components have been estimated from the rate of increase of spouses in the marriage registers of St. Louis Cathedral and the Ursulines Chapel.

French. Between 1820 and 1830 they doubled in number from 7,355 to 14,440, mostly because of domestic imports at the end of the decade. In a letter written in March, 1830, a Saint Domingue refugee living in New Orleans reported that so many American slaves were being imported "that they will soon be more numerous than creoles and foreign slaves both in the country and in the city. Only house servants of American birth are to be seen in every home." In January, 1831, he wrote that over the two preceding years more than twenty thousand slaves had been introduced into the state and complained that "everywhere one only hears English spoken, for in every house there are a number of old servants who have become fluent in this idiom."[34] One can imagine the inconvenience to unilingual French-speaking masters of household slaves conversing in a language they did not understand. By providing such masters with an incentive to learn English, slaves may well have contributed to their Americanization.

The linguistic turning point for the white population of New Orleans occurred in the decade of the 1830s, when it tripled from 20,110 to 61,131, with Irish and German immigrants accounting for the larger part of the increase. In the last two years of the decade, creoles and the foreign French together made up only one-third of the white Catholic spouses in the city.[35] By 1840, they may have slipped to less than one-fourth of the total white population, including Protestants as well as Catholics.

According to the federal censuses, the number of free persons of color in New Orleans grew from 11,607 in 1830 to 19,376 in 1840. An increase of this magnitude cannot be accounted for by natural increase alone. It implies substantial migration. Since most free persons of color migrating to New Orleans after 1809 were born in other states, their arrival necessarily decreased the proportion of the caste whose first language was French. It is possible, however, that the 1840 census over-enumerated free persons of color.[36] To the extent that their actual number was lower, immigration in the 1830s was less important, perhaps even limited enough for free persons of color to have remained preponderantly French-speaking as late as 1840, or longer than a majority of whites and slaves continued to speak French.

The Gallic community became further marginalized in the last two

34. Boze to Ste. Gême, March 10, 1830, January 28, 1831, HNOC.

35. *Sixth Census, 1840: Population*, 256; John Frederick Nau, *The German People of New Orleans, 1850–1900* (Leiden, 1958), 4–5; Earl Niehaus, *The Irish in New Orleans, 1800–1860* (New York, 1970), 23–26; Lachance, "Intermarriage and French Cultural Persistence," 56–57.

36. In the "Register of Free Colored Persons Entitled to Remain in the State," (Mayor's Office, Vol. I [1840–57], City Archives, New Orleans Public Library), 60 of those who were born in another state arrived in New Orleans between 1810 and 1819 and 152 from 1820 to 1825, compared with 97 Saint Domingue refugees, almost all of whom arrived before 1810. See also De Bow, *Statistical View*, 62n, 192n.

decades of the antebellum period. More immigrants from France re-
sided in New Orleans in 1860 than ever before, but they were far outnumbered by Irish and German immigrants. Furthermore, only 10,237
free persons of color were enumerated in 1850 and 11,133 in 1860.
Depending on the degree of overstatement in the 1840 census, out-
migration in the 1840s equaled in-migration in the 1830s. Even if all
free persons of color who remained in the city spoke French, their decline to 6 percent of the total population in 1860 limited their capacity
to add to the numerical mass of French-speakers.[37] The French-speaking
population did not keep up with the dramatic growth of New Orleans
in the last antebellum decades. Only in the first two or three decades of
the nineteenth century, when French was the dominant language in the
city, was the place of the foreign French within the Gallic community of
major importance.

A Social and Economic Profile of the Foreign French

The revisionist interpretation of Anglo-French conflict in antebellum
New Orleans assigns a leadership role to the foreign French. The jurists
Louis Moreau Lislet and Etienne Mazureau and the politician and dip-
lomat Pierre Soulé played such roles. As Joseph Tregle observes, those
men would have been outstanding in any community. This perspective,
however, takes in only part of the foreign French population. A more
comprehensive view is afforded by marriage contracts signed in New
Orleans between 1804 and 1819. The information they yield on wealth,
literacy, and occupations provides a basis for a collective portrait of the
foreign French.[38]

Like wills and probate records used to establish the characteristics

37. On the linguistic character of free persons of color around 1860, see David C.
Rankin, "The Impact of the Civil War on the Free Colored Community of New Orleans,"
Perspectives in American History, XI (1977–78), 380–87.

38. Tregle, "Early New Orleans Society," 31. The marriage contracts are located in
the Notarial Archives, Civil District Court, New Orleans, where they are bound with
other acts in the books of the following notary publics: Narcissus Broutin (1804–19),
Christoval de Armas (1815–19), Michel de Armas (1809–19), Stephen de Quinones
(1805–16), Marc Lafitte (1810–19), Hugues Lavergne (1819), John Lynd (1805–19),
Pierre Pedesclaux (1804–16), Phillippe Pedesclaux (1817–19), Carlisle Pollock (1817–19),
and Benedicte van Pradelles (1806–1808). Specific contracts will be identified by the
names of the groom and bride and the date of the contract with the notary's name in pa-
rentheses. Most, but not all, of the contracts have been listed and indexed in Charles R.
Maduell, Jr., comp., *New Orleans Marriage Contracts, 1804–1820* (New Orleans,
1977).

of preindustrial populations, marriage contracts capture individuals at a particular point in their life cycle and are selective.[39] It is probable that the fortunes of many immigrants on the eve of marriage were greater than at the moment of arrival in Louisiana and less than they would accumulate over their lifetimes. Unsuccessful immigrants were less likely than successful ones to find a partner in New Orleans' competitive marriage market, let alone have marriage contracts drawn up. Nevertheless, individuals from all ranks of the free population had recourse to contracts, and these contracts help to reveal the socioeconomic status of the foreign French relative to other groups in New Orleans.

The average wealth declared by males in marriage contracts was $7,688, while for females it was $3,683. With assets at marriage averaging $7,663, European Frenchmen were close to the mean for all bridegrooms. European French brides, whose dowries averaged only $2,931, were below the norm for their gender. White Saint Domingue refugees brought less wealth into their marriages than did the European French, but their average declarations—$3,136 for males and $2,450 for females—were greater than those of nonwhite refugees—$1,116 and $2,010 respectively. Louisiana-born free men of color declared on average $2,161 and Louisiana-born free women of color $941. By comparison, the average fortunes at marriage of white creole males and females, $10,309 and $4,810, were well above average, and the average declarations of Anglo-Americans—$20,413 for males, $9,691 for females—were double those of creoles. Their average assets at marriage indicate that white French-speaking immigrants formed a middle group between Anglo-Americans and creoles above them and free persons of color below them.

There was a wide range in the levels of wealth within groups.[40] The foreign French are found at all economic ranks. Laurent Millaudon, a native of Avignon, was in the richest percentile of bridegrooms. He had $327,000 in assets diversified in international commerce, shipping, banking, and a plantation in Plaquemines Parish, against $253,000 in debts, for a net worth of $74,000. An example of a middle-level fortune is the $7,000 declared by Toussaint Brias, a shopkeeper born in Cambray, France, whose property consisted of part of a lot near the river with a

---

39. For a succinct discussion of methodological issues involved in analysis of marriage contracts, wills, and inventories, see J. Dennis Willigan and Katherine A. Lynch, *Sources and Methods of Historical Demography* (New York, 1982), 133–59.

40. The standard deviations are up to two times greater than the average declarations of groups.

house built on pilings, originally purchased for $6,000, plus $1,000 in merchandise in his store. Further down the scale appear Julien Renoy, whose $1,500 represented the profit he had made on his father's gift of $1,000 when he emigrated from Bordeaux; Pierre Robin, the son of a ship captain from Nantes who rose to the position of master surgeon in Cayes, Saint Domingue, but whose possessions in New Orleans were limited to surgical tools and books valued at 150 piasters and 100 piasters in cash; and François Gevrier, a Swiss carpenter who declared the "tools of his trade and other household effects" worth 200 piasters.[41] Seventeen husbands declared in their contracts that they brought no property into their marriages. The distance separating a destitute Saint Domingue refugee or an artisan with only the tools of his trade from the affluent merchant Millaudon is a measure of how unequally property was distributed among the foreign French.

The ability of the foreign French to sign their marriage contracts affords a second measure of their social standing. The erudition of immigrant lawyers and the active role of individuals born in France and Saint Domingue in the theater and in journalism have produced the impression that the foreign French were better educated than creoles. Indeed, the latter have a reputation for illiteracy that dates back to observations made by French and American officials around the time of the Louisiana Purchase. The "State of Wretched Ignorance" of the *ancienne population* was one of the arguments Governor Claiborne used to rationalize the delay in granting Louisiana statehood and self-government.[42]

The marriage contracts do not support this stereotype of creole illiteracy. Rather, they indicate that by contemporary standards, literacy was high in New Orleans. Excepting free persons of color, over one-third

41. Marriage contracts of Laurent Millaudon and Marie Marthe Elmire Montreuil, November 24, 1818 (Marc Lafitte, notary); Toussaint Brias and Catherine Jean Glaudé, November 3, 1818 (Christoval de Armas, notary); Julien Jubel Renoy and Josephine Delery, April 20, 1818 (Michel de Armas, notary); Pierre Jean-Baptiste Robin and Marie Ursule Chalabruey, April 25, 1817 (Narcissus Broutin, notary); François Gevrier and Marie Frere, April 28, 1807 (Narcissus Broutin, notary).

42. On foreign French journalists, in addition to Marino, "Early French-Language Newspapers," see John Kendall, "The Foreign Language Press of New Orleans," *Louisiana Historical Quarterly*, XII (1929), 363–80. On key personalities in the theater, see René LeGardeur, *The First New Orleans Theatre, 1792–1803* (New Orleans, 1963). For contemporary observations see Pierre Clément de Laussat, *Memoirs of My Life*, trans. Agnes-Josephine Pastwa (Baton Rouge, 1978), 68; William Claiborne to Thomas Jefferson, September 29, 1803, in Clarence Edwin Carter, ed., *The Territorial Papers of the United States* (26 vols.; Washington, D.C., 1934–62), IX, 60; "Queries respecting Louisiana, with the Answers" (in the hand of Daniel Clark), n.d., 1803, *ibid.*, 38; Claiborne to

of whom had to make a mark in lieu of a signature, well over 90 percent of parties to these contracts signed their names.[43] Anglo-Americans were the only universally literate group to sign contracts in New Orleans, but well over 90 percent of white signers of other origins were also literate. The second highest signature rate for men belonged to creoles. The absence of significant differences in literacy rates among white males raises doubts as to whether the level of education among urban creoles was inferior.[44] White females from the Americas, whether born in Louisiana or in other states and territories of the United States or in the colony of Saint Domingue, were also more than 90 percent literate. By contrast, only 79 percent of European French brides were able to sign their contracts.[45]

One should be careful not to read too much into these findings. Illiteracy was almost certainly more widespread among residents of New Orleans who married without marriage contracts. Still, it is clear that in education as in wealth, judging from the below average literacy of brides born in France, the foreign French in the aggregate did not measure up to the standard set by creoles.

The occupations of contract signers provide a third basis for comparing the social standing of ethnic groups (Figure 2). The foreign French were more active in the mercantile and professional sectors than were the creoles. Roughly one-third of both the European French and white refugees born in Saint Domingue were merchants, bankers, clerks in counting houses, accountants, doctors, lawyers, and schoolteachers, whereas only one-sixth of the white creoles were merchants or professionals. Even more striking, almost half of the foreign French, but only one-fifth of the white creoles, were in other trades in the service sector, the most common occupational titles here being shopkeeper, trader,

---

Jefferson, August 30, 1804, *ibid.,* 288. Claiborne acknowledged that in "New Orleans and its vicinity, the Society may be considered as tolerably well informed."

43. According to Kenneth Lockridge, the signature rate in the wills of New England males at the end of the eighteenth century was similar and was above rates in Pennsylvania and Virginia and equaled in Europe only in Sweden and Scotland (*Literacy in Colonial New England: An Inquiry into the Social Context of Literacy in the Early Modern West* [New York, 1974], 77, 99).

44. Contracts were signed by 96.5 percent of creole and European French bridegrooms and 93.7 percent of Saint Domingue bridegrooms but by only 64.7 percent of free men of color.

45. All Anglo-American brides signed, as did 94.3 percent of creole and 94.9 percent of Saint Domingue brides. With a signature rate of 79 percent, European French brides fell midway between other white females and free women of color, 58.3 percent of whom signed.

FIGURE 2.   Distribution of Occupations of Bridegrooms by Ethnic Group,
New Orleans, 1804–1819

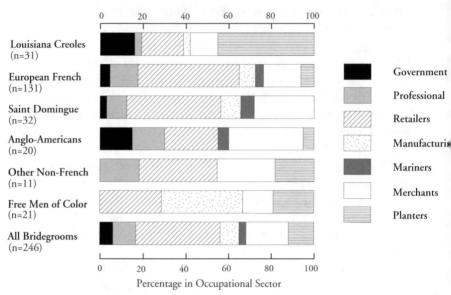

SOURCES: Marriage contracts in New Orleans Notarial Archives (see note 38);
Thomas H. Whitney, comp., *New Orleans Directory, and Louisiana and Mississippi Al-
manac for the Year 1811* (New Orleans, 1810). The occupations of 153 males are ascer-
tainable in the marriage contracts. The 97 other cases have been identified through linkage with the 1811 directory and John Adems Paxton, comp., *The New Orleans Directory
and Register* (New Orleans, 1822). The scheme of classification is adapted from Jacob
Price, "Economic Function and the Growth of American Port Towns in the Eighteenth
Century," *Perspectives in American History*, VIII (1974), 177–84.

baker, and carpenter. Less than 10 percent of all the white groups were in
the manufacturing sector, in contrast to 38 percent of free men of color.

Conversely, the foreign French were much less likely than Louisiana-
born bridegrooms to belong to the planter class. Only 6 percent of the
European French and none of the Saint Domingue refugees were planters, compared to almost half of white creole grooms. Some of the refugees referred in their contracts to plantations and slaves left behind in
Saint Domingue, but they filled a different niche in the social structure
of New Orleans. In August, 1809, the mayor observed that among the
two-thirds of the white adult males who practiced some trade, several
"who once possessed estates, or belonged to wealthy families in the Is-

land of St. Domingo, now follow the occupations of Cabinet Makers, Turners, bakers, Glaziers, upholsterers."[46]

The average wealth of spouses in different occupational sectors points to a definite hierarchy in which planters shared the top rank with merchants. The fortunes at marriage of merchants and individuals playing an ancillary role in maritime commerce averaged $19,226, but planters were just below them with average declarations of $13,737. No other general occupational category surpassed the $10,000 level. Professionals came closest with average declarations of $9,562. In the middle were retailers and government officials with average declarations of $6,336 and $4,899 respectively. The bottom rank was composed of artisans and mariners whose declarations averaged $2,679.[47] Almost two-thirds of the foreign French practiced trades in the middle and lower ranks of this hierarchy.

The primary social cleavage in New Orleans was racial. Whether foreign- or native-born, free persons of color were at the bottom of the social ladder. French-speaking white immigrant spouses differed from their Louisiana counterparts in their lower average wealth and the larger proportion of males in middle- and low-level occupational ranks. In literacy, there was no substantial difference between foreign French and creole males. Both were highly literate. European French females, however, were less apt to be able to sign their marriage contracts than creole brides.

Equally important was the presence of the foreign French in all sectors of the urban social structure except the rentier-planter class. Although on average less wealthy than creoles, a few French immigrants did amass considerable fortunes and become part of the economic elite; almost as large a proportion of the European French were among the richest tenth of bridegrooms as creoles (Figure 3). The reason for the difference in average wealth between the two groups was that there were fewer creoles among the poorest 30 percent of spouses rather than more creoles in the richest deciles. French immigrants were distributed evenly

---

46. James Mather to Claiborne, August 9, 1809, in Rowland, ed., *Letter Books of Claiborne,* IV, 405.

47. These averages are based on the 190 cases in which the occupation of the bridegroom was either mentioned in the marriage contract or given in the 1811 or 1822 directory for New Orleans and whose assets were described in the marriage contract. Such was the case for 41 merchants, 27 planters, 16 professionals, 45 retailers, 11 government officials, 45 artisans, some in the service and others in the industrial sector, and 5 mariners.

FIGURE 3.   Distribution of Wealth of Bridegrooms by Ethnic Group, New
            Orleans, 1804–1819

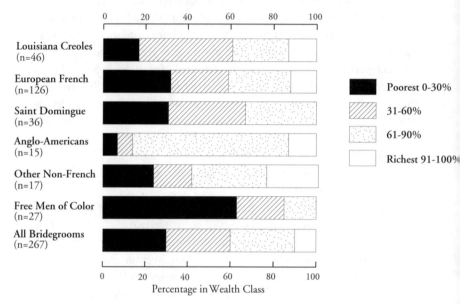

SOURCE: Marriage contracts in New Orleans Notarial Archives (see note 38).

through all economic ranks, including the poorest 30 percent, in which
creoles were underrepresented.

   The contribution of the foreign French to a viable Gallic community
in New Orleans in the initial decades of American domination can be
more accurately described against this background. On one hand, their
fortunes at marriage and occupational characteristics differed suffi-
ciently from those of creoles to suggest distinct social identities. On the
other, the presence of the foreign French at all economic ranks and the
complementary roles of the foreign French and creoles in the urban
economy afforded a basis for mutually advantageous interaction.

The Role of the Foreign French
in the Gallic Community

Intermarriage is a revealing indicator of interaction between ethnic
groups. The frequency of marriage between ethnic groups generally corresponds to the frequency of other, less binding forms of social contact.

The same article of the Civil Code that prohibited free persons from marrying slaves also banned marriages between whites and free persons of color, reflecting the strength of racial barriers in Louisiana society.[48] Social relations between whites and nonwhites were limited, even within the creole and Saint Domingue subgroups, not to mention the Gallic community as a whole. By contrast, men and women of the same caste were free to marry each other regardless of birthplace or language. The proportion of the foreign French who married French-speakers reveals the extent to which they became part of the Gallic community in New Orleans; and the proportion who married creoles reveals the level of interaction between subgroups of the community.

Between 1790 and 1840, most of the foreign French who married in the city took French-speaking spouses. Among the European French and white Saint Domingue refugees, over 90 percent of the grooms and 80 percent of the brides married another French-speaker. Among nonwhite Saint Domingue refugees, an even higher proportion did so. Only 1 percent of the grooms and 6 percent of the brides married outside the Gallic community. Clearly, most of the foreign French remained in the Gallic community, even those who married Anglo-Americans. Since children tend to learn their mother's language first, and more French females than males took non-French spouses, Anglo-French marriages may have produced more replacements for the Gallic community than for the American.

Within racial boundaries, there was considerable intermarriage between the foreign French and creoles. Over half of the foreign-born bridegrooms of both races took Louisiana-born wives. Intermarriage between foreign French brides and creole men was much rarer, in part because fewer females than males immigrated from Europe, but also owing to the preference of creole grooms for creole brides. Over 90 percent of Louisiana-born males married endogamously, in striking contrast to their sisters, more than half of whom married exogamously.

The occupational differences between the foreign French and creoles meant that intermarriage between wealthier members of the two groups linked the planter class with the mercantile community. Although 45 percent of white creole males whose occupations have been determined were planters, only 13 percent of the creole brides took husbands

---

48. David Heer, "Intermarriage," in *Harvard Encyclopedia of American Ethnic Groups*, ed. Stephan Thernstrom (Cambridge, Mass., 1980), 513–14; Dainow, *Compiled Edition of the Civil Code of Louisiana*, XVI, 55.

in this category. By comparison, 33 percent of creole women married merchants, who represented 19 percent of all potential bridegrooms, and 70 percent of their husbands in this sector were born in France or Saint Domingue.

The fortunes involved in endogamous and exogamous marriages reveal how creole families profited from marrying their daughters to foreigners. Only for Louisiana-born spouses was the average wealth of both parties in endogamous unions high enough to reflect some unions between the sons and daughters of a social elite. Creole women who married creole men put up dowries of an average of $6,910, while their husbands declared property amounting on average to $9,948; but when creole women married immigrants, they obtained with dowries worth less ($4,110) husbands worth more ($11,794). Matching their daughters with the wealthiest foreigners was a strategy by which the creole elite turned to its economic and political advantage the aspiration of upwardly mobile immigrants to form links with the socially dominant planter class.[49]

This strategy did not exclude creole marriages to wealthy and politically prominent Anglo-Americans. On the contrary, for example, Eléonore Destrehan took as her husband the Scottish merchant Stephen Henderson, who had assets of $242,000 and debts of only $66,300, and the de la Ronde family agreed to the alliance of one daughter to Maunsel White, an Irish merchant worth $20,000, and of another to Thomas Cunningham, an officer in the United States Navy. Less frequent were alliances involving creole bridegrooms and Anglo-American brides, but they include the marriage of the richest creole planter, Bernard Marigny, to Mary Jones, the daughter of Evan Jones, one of the most important American merchants to settle in New Orleans during the Spanish period.[50]

Each of these examples involves a prominent creole family,[51] indi-

49. Creole grooms acquired richer brides with less property when they married within their group. They were, among all grooms, the most prone to endogamous marriages.

50. Marriage contracts of Stephen Henderson and Eléonore Destrehan, October 19, 1816 (Michel de Armas, notary); Maunsel White and Celeste Elisabeth de la Ronde, April 22, 1812 (Narcissus Broutin, notary); Thomas Cunningham and Josephine de la Ronde, December 22, 1817 (Phillippe Pedesclaux, substituting for Narcissus Broutin, notary); Bernard Xavier de Marigny de Mandeville and Mary Jones, May 19, 1804 (Pierre Pedesclaux, notary).

51. Arthur and Kernion, *Old Families of Louisiana*, 316–20, 394–400, 414–16.

cating a need to qualify insistence on Anglo-French conflict, at least in the first decades of American rule. What one glimpses instead is a characteristic strategy of colonial elites—marriage of their daughters to representatives of the metropolitan center sent to the colony. Creoles had pursued this strategy of co-optation vis-à-vis high Spanish officials, so it is not surprising that they should have continued it with respect to Americans after the Louisiana Purchase. In light of the openness of the creole elite to intermarriage with foreigners, the importance of the foreign French lies in part in the competition they offered to Anglo-Americans in the marriage market. In their absence, the integration of the creole and American elites would undoubtedly have proceeded more rapidly, to the detriment of the Gallic community.[52]

The behavior of elites, however, is only part of the story. Most of the marriage contracts were drawn up for men and women from the middle and lower economic and occupational ranks. They, too, considered property when choosing a spouse. An example is the contract of Pascal Hoffmann, from the Rhineland, and Eugénie Grand, born in Nantes, a young widow with two daughters. Hoffmann's declaration of $500 consisted of a cart, three horses, and some household furnishings. The bride brought into the marriage a new house in the faubourg Ste. Marie worth $1,500, a female slave evaluated at $500, and furniture worth $600. Her modest assets still multiplied fivefold the property to be administered by her husband and presumably improved his social status by making him a slaveholder and *propriétaire*. Eugénie Grand gained a husband whose regular employment as a carter promised greater security than her assets of $2,600 would have afforded. In other contracts between people below the elite level, Saint Domingue refugees pooled their limited resources or promised to add property left behind in Saint Domingue "when order and peace permit";[53] husbands took over the workshop or store belonging to the bride from a previous marriage; and spouses with little or nothing to bring to the marriage referred to inheritance rights.

52. According to Robert Reinders, *End of an Era: New Orleans, 1850–1860* (New Orleans, 1964), 9–13, there was frequent intermarriage between prominent creole and American families in the last decade before the Civil War. From a list of fifty-five such marriages, he argues that creoles and wealthy Americans "merged to form the main economic and social components of what was the upper class in the 1850's."

53. Marriage contracts of Pascal Hoffman and Eugénie Grand, June 4, 1810 (John Lynd, notary), and Etienne Rousset and Elisabeth Stainer, January 27, 1807 (Pierre Pedesclaux, notary).

If elite marriages are defined as those in which either party was among the richest 10 percent of his or her sex, 17 percent of the European French and 8 percent of Saint Domingue refugees made matches at this level. That confirms the presence in New Orleans of outstanding individual French-speaking immigrants. The marriage contracts give the impression that upward mobility was achieved by the most talented of the foreign French. This talented fraction, however, should not exclude from our vision the large majority of French-speaking immigrants who advanced less far in the social hierarchy.

To do so would be to slight the importance, first, of the demographic effect of the foreign French in the first decades of American domination, and second, of their contribution to the institutional completeness of the Gallic community. As late as 1835 a visitor to New Orleans observed, "As we approached the market, French stores began to predominate, till one could readily imagine himself, aided by the sound of the French language, French faces and French goods on all sides, to be traversing a street in Havre or Marseilles."[54] Without the foreign French, free persons of color as well as whites, who became artisans, shopkeepers, and café owners, this island of French culture would no longer have existed in 1835. Use of the French language would already have retreated to the private circle of the family. The persistence of a Gallic community in New Orleans for over three decades after the Louisiana Purchase was in large part owing to its reinforcement by racially and socially heterogeneous French-speaking immigrants.

54. Joseph Ingraham, *The South-West by a Yankee* (2 vols.; New York, 1835), I, 101.

4

Creoles and Americans

JOSEPH G. TREGLE, JR.

When the October, 1873, issue of *Scribner's Monthly* introduced the American public to "'Sieur George," George Washington
Cable's first portrayal of creole life in Louisiana, there was little reason
to suspect that appearance of this gentle story of the baleful consequences of addiction to gambling marked the beginning of a controversy soon to make its author the "most cordially hated little man in
New Orleans."[1]

Nonetheless, in succeeding years Cable's depiction of the original
Louisianians and their descendants in such works as *Old Creole Days*
(1879) and *The Grandissimes* (1880) so infuriated those about whom
he wrote that a veritable flood of abuse and damnation swirled around
him in newspapers, pamphlets, and public meetings. Even the venerable
priest-poet Adrien Rouquette vilified his character in such scurrilous
and vulgar denunciation that friends in the North actually feared for his
safety.[2]

The volatility of creole sensibilities central to the uproar traced back
to the beginnings of a cultural conflict already old when Cable first appeared in print, its pivot the inevitable question which had loomed im-

1. Elizabeth Robins Pennell, *The Life and Letters of Joseph Pennell* (2 vols.; Boston,
1929), I, 57.
2. [Adrien Rouquette], *Critical Dialogue Between Aboo and Caboo on a New
Book; or, A Grandissime Ascension* (New Orleans, 1880); R. W. Gilder to George W.
Cable, January 13, 1881, in George W. Cable Papers, Tulane University Library, New
Orleans.

mediately upon acquisition of Louisiana by the United States in 1803—who was to rule in this community now jointly occupied by indigenous Latin inhabitants and hoards of parvenu Anglo-American migrants from a world of vastly different mores and traditions? By the 1840s the newcomers would enjoy a clear ascendancy, dominant in a society whose tensions had produced within it clearly understood adjustments and adaptations between the two competing loyalties. But this finely articulated arrangement shattered upon the shoals of civil war and reconstruction, destroying the pattern of certitudes which had prevailed in antebellum days. The tumult set off by Cable's writings erupted with such violence because they appeared at the very moment of radical transformation in long-established ethnic and racial conventions within the New Orleans community, challenging emerging new concepts of identity and producing confusion in altered relationships which in many ways continues to confound our understanding. The resultant exacerbating fear and resentment drove creole passions to formulation of a hardened orthodoxy in which to enfold what they perceived as their endangered heritage, creating what has become, in effect, a veritable creole mythology. A continuing dissenting tradition in the community of those descended from racially mixed antebellum free people of color has indeed survived, but in such insularity and with such lack of supposed expert sanction as to present only a negligible alternative to the established dogma.

This almost mystical set of beliefs has become so deeply entrenched in New Orleans folklore, and indeed even in the state's judicial pronouncements, that to challenge it is to court ridicule and recrimination. But no appreciation of the true complexity of the city's history is possible without a clarification of how the myth came to be and how it does violence to the past.

The end of the nineteenth century saw the essential postulates of the faith firmly in place. At their very core stands the explication of *creole* itself, rigid, absolute, and closed to any gradation of meaning: it holds that the word can never be used except to designate a native Louisianian of pure white blood descended from those French and Spanish pioneers who came directly from Europe to colonize the New World. Thus even Acadians, or cajuns, are rigorously excluded, having arrived in the colony not straight from the Continent but by way of Canada.[3]

---

3. Albert Fossier, *New Orleans: The Glamour Period, 1800–1840* (New Orleans, 1957), 266; Edward Laroque Tinker, *Toucoutou* (New York, 1928), 8; Jules O. Daigle, *A*

The core race purity of the definition receives magnified confirmation in the specific insistence that no black or person of mixed blood can or ever could have been correctly termed a *creole*, no matter his parentage, place of birth, language, or cultural orientation. To accommodate the inescapable fact that some persons of color have been and indeed still are called creoles, the myth maintains that such error in usage stems from the pre–Civil War association of members of this class with the true creole population, giving them identity as "creole negroes" in much the same way that one refers to "creole tomatoes" or "creole cattle," signifying origin in Louisiana soil. Orthodoxy makes clear, however, that in this adaptation *creole* serves only as an adjective, in no way implying admission of blacks into the group itself, though there is some grudging willingness to accept *creole of color* as a permissible designation for mixed-race offspring or descendants of legitimate creoles, seemingly in the belief that the phrase has some natural physical unity that makes separation into its component parts an impossibility and thus preserves the noun *creole* for whites alone.[4]

The word derives from the Spanish *criollo*, the myth maintains, an invention of the conquistadors designed to distinguish the progeny of European whites in New World colonies from native aborigines and the European-born. Transfer of Louisiana to the Spanish crown in 1763 allegedly brought the term to the banks of the Mississippi, providing thereby a name for the population finally joined to the American Union in 1803.[5]

Passing over for the moment the chronological inaccuracy of the foregoing thesis, currency of the term *creole* in Spanish Louisiana is beyond dispute, but the more significant truth rests in the reality that creole identity actually figured very little in the community's concerns during the whole of Louisiana's colonial experience. It was the clash between original Louisianians and migrant Anglo-Americans after the Louisiana

---

Dictionary of the Cajun Language (Ann Arbor, 1984), xi; Lewis W. Newton, *The Americanization of French Louisiana* (New York, 1980), 9.

4. Tinker, *Toucoutou*, 7; Lafcadio Hearn, "Los Criollos," in *Occidental Gleanings* (2 vols.; New York, 1925), I, 197–200; Charles B. Rousseve, *The Negro in Louisiana* (New Orleans, 1937), 24.

5. Even supposedly definitive authorities on word usage have given ambiguous and contradictory accounts of the origin and meaning of the term, as in the 1869 and 1929 editions of the French *Larousse*. W. H. Coleman, *Historical Sketch Book and Guide to New Orleans and Environs* (New York, 1885), 16, and Herbert Asbury, *The French Quarter* (New York, 1938), 92, add to the confusion by indicating, as Asbury would have it, that *creole* was "unknown in Louisiana during the French occupation."

Purchase which for the first time made place of birth a critical issue and gave the *creole* label its crucial significance. That it took so long for a mature creolism to develop in Louisiana reveals much about the area's colonial relationship to both France and Spain. Sheer primitive dependence of the society and its constant exposure to foreign threat made any native challenge to European control virtually unthinkable during the French dominion. Nor was there to be any appreciable drawing of ethnic distinctions against the dons after 1763. For though it is certainly true that the cession to Spain resulted in more dramatic and violent opposition from Louisianians than anything attendant upon their assumption into the Union, that earlier crisis produced few of the ethnic polarities so starkly highlighted in the aftermath of the events of 1803. Like France, Spain was monarchic, her culture Latin, grounded in Roman law and Catholicism. Most important, perhaps, an archaic economy and declining population ruled out any serious effort to channel ponderable numbers of her own people into the newly acquired colony. In everything but the formalities of sovereignty, Louisiana after the transfer of 1763 continued essentially French. Divisions among the population remained blunted, therefore, pitting no special "native" or "creole" particularity against this paucity of intruders.[6]

The events of 1803 provided no such soft edges. Now the new partners in the community derived from a democratic republic, children of English common law and the language of Shakespeare, heirs of the Protestant Reformation. In almost every conceivable way they represented a tradition utterly unknown to the indigenous population. And unlike the Spaniards, they came in ever-growing numbers, vigorous, assertive, demanding, often boisterous and domineering. There could be no escaping awareness that they represented a deadly threat to the way of life of the original inhabitants or that their presence made conflict for control of the community an inevitability.

The drama of that factional clash not only produced the actual historic stimulus to a vigorous Louisiana "creolism" but also in due time provided creators of the creole myth a perfect context in which to project both the inflexible definition of their protagonists and a detailed delineation of their qualities and character as well. In the process they would manage to fashion yet a second myth, that of the crudity and vulgarity of the newcomers to the region, for how better to magnify the

6. Arthur P. Whitaker, ed., *Documents Relating to the Commercial Policy of Spain in the Floridas, with Incidental References to Louisiana* (Deland, Fla., 1931), *passim.*

supposed superior attributes of the "creole" than to balance them against imputed inferiorities in his foil, the "American"?

Of all the polarities possible in such an apposition, none has been put to more frequent use than that which poses "aristocrat" against "plebeian." In the veins of the creole, the myth assures us, ran the blood of those intrepid servants of the Bourbons who had planted the French lily along the banks of the Mississippi as nobles of the robe or as young cadets in the military service of the crown, mingled perhaps with that of courtiers who had come as officers in the retinues of later Spanish governors. This "race of proud and arrogant men," we are told, produced "the aristocracy of the region" through most of the nineteenth century, maintaining family circles renowned for haughty exclusivity as well as cultural refinement and worldly sophistication, the whole invigorated and sustained by fierce conceit of ancestry and a "chivalry" which gave its inheritors certainty of their superiority over lesser breeds of men. Illustrative of the nonsensical extremes to which this claim of empyrean ascendancy might be pushed, a late nineteenth-century tale centers on a creole whose "birth" gave him the right "to treat some of the kings and queens of Europe as if they belonged to a pack of playing cards."[7]

How reasonable, then, the determination of the mythical creole to stand aloof from the Americans, generally depicted either as brutal and swinish "Kaintucks" storming from their river flatboats and barges to carouse in the waterfront dives of the city, or as crabbed skinflint Yankee tradesmen cold to the joys of the theater and ballroom as well as to more shadowy pleasures of life. Shutters and doors supposedly slammed shut to the newcomers as if they were bearers of the plague, with none so cloistered as young creole womanhood. Rejected by the "fierce pride" of "creole aristocrats" incapable of mingling with river bullies or common shopkeepers, the Americans are pictured as having been forced to look elsewhere than in the established creole neighborhoods for a place to live and work, settling finally in the raw Faubourg Ste. Marie upriver from the original city. Separating these two antagonistic clusters of hostile populations, we are told, ran the broad expanse of Canal Street, a virtual *cordon sanitaire* between warring camps. So disdainful

7. See, for example, the letter of Henry St. Paul to the Mobile *Register*, July 6, 1884; Alfred Mercier, *L'Habitation Saint-Ybars*, ed. Reginald Hamil (Manchester, N.H., n.d.), 1; Council on the Development of French in Louisiana, *The CODOFIL French Program* (Lafayette, La., 1975), 1; Roger Baudier, "The Creoles of Old New Orleans" (Typescript in Tulane University Library, New Orleans), 1–3; Wingrove Bathon, "A Creole Courtship," *Cosmopolitan*, XXIV (April, 1898), 652–55.

of the barbarous aliens were these polished creoles, it is said, that they seldom if ever condescended to set foot in the despised American enclave, while only the bravest of Yankees would be so bold as to venture across the dividing line.[8]

Creole life as thus portrayed stands as an idyll of spacious contentment, suffused with a sensitivity to the best part of man's nature, which takes rank in the mythology only slightly below the hallmark of "aristocratic chivalry." It is peopled by men and women of an incredibly honed politeness, which yet has room for a lighthearted exuberance of manners marked by "gracious intellectualism, spontaneous and fecund spirit, subtle, delicate and penetrating refinement," and "an exquisite suavité, delicious perfume, and particular cachet" in "all things of the spirit." The generic creole male of this fantasy moves in a world devoted to the theater and opera, occupying himself with thoroughbred horses, dueling foils, and the pleasures of both dining and gaming tables, eschewing in his patrician self-esteem all employment which might require removal of his jacket or the use of his hands. Women of the demi-paradise shine as paragons of gentility, style, and grace, matrons ruling as arbiters of all the nuances of polite society, demoiselles reigning as cameos of beauty and flirtatious charm. Small wonder that it could be said of them, "The people of New Orleans were looked upon, even by the French, as the most cultured people in the world."[9]

Regrettably, this by-now hallowed vision of creole society violates the past in two fundamental respects: it demonstrably affirms error as historical fact, and it so exaggerates some verities of creole society as to create a caricature rather than a faithful portrait of its subjects. The myth's exclusive "pure white, French or Spanish descent" definition of *creole*, for example, loses all credence in the voluminous evidence of contrary usage in the historical record of New Orleans itself, as well as in that extending over long periods of time in widely separated regions of the New World. This possibility of variant meanings seemingly eludes a mentality that conceives the term as possessed of a Platonic quiddity impervious to alteration by mere mortals. But no such orientation can

8. David Kirby, *Grace King* (Boston, 1980), 96; Auguste Viatte, *Histoire litteraire de l'Amérique Française, des origines à 1950* (Quebec, 1954), 221; Ernest G. Vetter, *Fabulous Frenchtown* (Washington, D.C., 1955), 61.

9. Helen Hulse Cruzat, "L'Influence de la France sur le tempérament louisianais," *Comptes Rendus de l'Athénée Louisianais,* July, 1915, pp. 80–92, hereinafter cited as *Comptes Rendus;* comments of Bussiere Rouen, *ibid.,* January–May, 1926, pp. 6–7; Pierre Paul Ebeyer, *Paramours of the Creoles* (New Orleans, 1944), 32.

change the fact that *creole* has meant a variety of things to a variety of different societies, a simple reflection of the reality that language represents a consensus of the people who create it.

It is for the historian to demonstrate how a particular term was generally used in a particular time and place, and with respect to *creole* the record is clearer than later controversy would lead one to expect. Garcilaso de la Vega, "The Inca," writing in the early 1600s, tells us: "The name was invented by the Negroes. . . . They use it to mean a Negro born in the Indies, and they devised it to distinguish those who come from this side and were born in Guinea from those born in the New World. . . . The Spanish have copied them by introducing this word to describe those born in the New World, and in this way both Spaniards and Guinea Negroes are called *criollo* if they are born in the New World." Recent scholarship has determined that this Spanish adoption of black usage dates from the 1560s, before which time the "word creole applied . . . exclusively to Negroes." Later practice in the Spanish empire seems to have been variable, with most South American creoles eventually fixing on purity of white blood as a mark of their kind, while in other areas, particularly the Caribbean islands, the distinction continued to apply to all those indigenous to the region regardless of race.[10]

In the French colony of Saint Domingue during the seventeenth and eighteenth centuries, *creole* meant simply native-born, again without reference to color, and it was this tradition which took root in colonial Louisiana as early as the beginning of French settlement at Mobile. Long before the transfer to Spain, Iberville and Bienville referred to *creoles* as a matter of course in their communication with royal officials, and church functionaries regularly so described native parishioners in registering births, marriages, and deaths among their flock. Spanish officials, for their part, identified native Louisiana slaves as *criollos*, while bondsmen themselves in the late eighteenth-century colony separated their numbers into those who were creoles and those who were not.[11]

10. Garcilaso de la Vega, *Royal Commentaries of the Incas* (2 vols.; Austin, 1966), I, 606–607; James Lockhart, *Spanish Peru, 1532–1560* (Madison, 1968), 175; Salvador de Madariaga, *The Rise of the Spanish American Empire* (New York, 1947), 21–22.

11. Edward Braithewaite, *Development of Creole Society in Jamaica, 1770–1820* (Oxford, 1971), xv; Pierre de Vaissiere, *Saint-Domingue: La Société et la vie créoles sous l'Ancien Régime (1629–1789)* (Paris, 1909), vii; Charles Gayarré, *Address . . . to Graduates of the Centenary College* (New Orleans, 1852), 5; Peter J. Hamilton, *Colonial Mobile* (New York, 1898), 68, 146, 169, 187; Gerald L. St. Martin and Mathe Allain, "A Slave Trial in Colonial Natchitoches [1770]," *Louisiana History*, XXVII (Winter, 1987), 58, 76.

One of the effects of the Louisiana Purchase, ironically, in light of the eventual myth, was its reinforcement of this color-blind identification of creole with native-born, a consequence of the indigenous population's serious cultural limitations in its contest of strength with the incoming Americans. Fully aware of their deficiencies, the original inhabitants sensed that their most persuasive claim to precedence lay in the proposition that those born to the region had priority rights within it, a natural endowment flowing from those primal attachments which bind men to the place of their birth. What had been lacking in the relationship with their Spanish masters, the need to establish a primacy of native identity against the newcomer, was thus present full-blown after 1803. Origin in the soil became, therefore, the very essence of the concept *creole,* precisely because it gave the older residents the most profound warrant of the right not to be dispossessed in their own land.

But the very stress on the inherent claims of the naked criterion of birth made it illogical to discriminate against those equally indigenous who differed from the majority only by reason of parentage sprung from other than French or Spanish ancestry. It followed inescapably that creole identity must then be extended even to those of Yankee, German, Irish, or Italian descent, so long as they had drawn first breath in Louisiana. Indeed, the very simplicity of the concept allowed for little if any confusion in its application. Acadians, therefore, such as Alexander Mouton or Paul O. Hebert, native Louisianians no less than A. B. Roman of St. James or Bernard Marigny of New Orleans, claimed place as creoles without question, while foreign-born such as the Frenchmen Pierre Derbigny and Etienne Mazureau, or the San Domingan Louis Moreau Lislet, despite their impeccable Gallic credentials, remained always outside the creole circle.[12]

Nothing in any of this involved the slightest need to exclude black or colored natives from membership in the creole community, where they remained, as countless references in newspapers, correspondence, and judicial records certify, for the whole of the antebellum period. The

12. New Orleans *Louisiana Advertiser,* July 24, 1823. All subsequent newspaper references are to New Orleans publications. Virginia Dominguez, *White by Definition* (New Brunswick, 1986), maintains incorrectly (pp. 102–103, 113) that immigrants from Haiti and Saint Domingue carried their creole identity with them into Louisiana and that such foreign French leaders as Pierre Derbigny and Nicholas Girod were counted as creole public officials. Equally in error is Liliane Creté, *Daily Life in Louisiana, 1815–1830* (Baton Rouge, 1979), who claims (p. 69) that "little by little, the term [creole] came to designate the entire French-speaking population of Louisiana."

phrase *creole of color* must be recognized, therefore, as a favorite of more recent times, seized upon to support post–Civil War theories of distinction based on race, the term being essentially foreign to antebellum usage. Cable himself, oddly enough, once argued that the title *creole* was "adopted by, not conceded to, the natives of European-African or Creole-African blood, and is still so used among themselves." But it should be clear that slaves and free persons of color never enjoyed power to mandate the language or habits of white men in prewar years, certainly not to the extent of dictating how they themselves should be labeled in court proceedings or newspaper reports, which time and time again routinely identified them by the unmodified noun *creole*.[13]

Such usage, indeed, fitted easily into the structure of the state's antebellum society. Despite deep-seated fear of possible slave insurrection or general race war, especially after the mid-1830s, the community felt not even minimal concern that nonwhites might contest for political or social position. If ever there was such, pre–Civil War Louisiana constituted a white man's dominion, every political, judicial, and police power cemented immovably in the ruling race. Within such a society, legal definition as white gave practically impenetrable protection from black or colored challenge. As a consequence, antebellum New Orleanians perceived no danger from common acceptance of blacks and whites under the creole rubric, no risk that such definitional partnership might diminish the social status or prerogative of the dominant class. These were too tightly woven into the very fabric of the state. One simply does not find, therefore, any antebellum insistence in Louisiana on pure whiteness as a condition for acceptance as a creole, there being not the slightest possibility that local birth might be thought to confer political or social status upon the black or colored man. To be sure, white creoles troubled over the common impression abroad that *creole* always implied mixed or Negro blood, and though they often feigned unconcerned amusement at the error, they were diligent in warning against it. This explains, no doubt, why during pre–Civil War years it is only in travel accounts that one finds any reference to creoles as pure white, testimony to a

13. Unusual circumstances requiring stress on specific identity occasionally mandated antebellum use of *creole of color*, as when a free Negro wrote to Governor Claiborne to warn that "certain Creoles of color in the City of New Orleans" were plotting insurrection to return Louisiana to Spain. See Clarence E. Carter, ed., *The Territorial Papers of the United States* (26 vols.; Washington, D.C., 1934–62), IX (Orleans), 575; George W. Cable, "New Orleans," in *Report on the Social Statistics of the Cities, Tenth Census*, comp. George E. Waring, Jr. (Washington, D.C., 1887), XIX, pt. II, 218.

probably overzealous instruction by hosts mindful of the usual foreign misconception on this point. Even in the travel literature, however, other observers of greater discernment provide counterbalancing testimony, and the internal domestic evidence overwhelmingly repudiates the race purity criterion.[14]

Despite the sure knowledge that no rational member of the community would ever impute civic or political rights to a free man of color, or confuse an "American" with one of Latin descent, the original inhabitants of New Orleans could not ignore the fact that the term *creole* did indeed legitimately apply to any such persons native to the state. Early on in the ethnic disputes wracking the city, therefore, they devised a more exclusive term to designate those white residents whose attachment to Louisiana extended back into colonial times and whose ancestry derived almost certainly from French or Spanish progenitors. They called themselves the *ancienne population,* employing a phrase in which stress on the factor of time might also justify the group's determination to remain masters of their native soil, a position challenged now not only by the Americans but by yet another newly arrived faction, the "foreign French." Refugees from the convulsions of the revolutionary and Napoleonic eras, these last had come from the Continent, their political affinities ranging from royalist to Jacobin, or from Caribbean homes such as Saint Domingue or Cuba, wanderers fleeing political persecution, slave insurrection, and economic ruination. Determined not to set out again on their journeys, they counted in their ranks many men of superb ability and training, deferential neither to creole nor Yankee.

Although it was easy in these continuing disputes to employ *American* or *French* in any number of variations, the phrase *ancienne population* soon proved cumbersome and unwieldy, especially in its unsuitability as an adjectival modifier. Simple practicality, therefore, dictated use of the handier *creole* in its place, for though the native-born of American stock did indeed have equal claim to the designation, they stood for the moment far removed from adulthood and thus did not figure as part of the public equation. Such practice offended them little if at all, even upon attainment of their majority. Proud as they might be of their status as natives in a community of such diverse origins, it was for them in no way the fundamental concern which it had become for their

14. *Louisiana Courier,* April 3, June 11, 24, 1828; *Louisiana Advertiser,* July 25, 1823; *Picayune,* September 8, 1844. Even the rabidly racist *La Rénaissance Louisianais,* June 1, 1862, speaks of "les familles créoles blanches."

Gallic counterparts. Their deeper sense of belonging inhered in American identification, tying them as it did to the expansive Anglo-Saxon
stock of the great majority of the national population. They knew no
fear of cultural annihilation, while their security as members of a dominant group not dependent on any claim to Louisiana nativity made the
creole name something pleasant, perhaps, but never critical or definitive. As for blacks or colored, the rigid conventions of the society made
racial confusion in the use of the term nonexistent.[15]

Out of this set of relationships there consequently emerged a consensus in early nineteenth-century New Orleans as to what meaning should
be derived from any particular use of *creole*. To state simply that a person was "a creole" meant that he was native to the state, whether white
or black, free or slave, Gallic or Yankee. Reference to "the creoles" implied equation with the *ancienne population,* the indigenous Latin inhabitants. The simple plural form of the term might embrace all native-
born, as in the statement "creoles are acclimated against yellow fever,"
unless the context of the comment obviously ruled out slaves or free persons of color. If one wished to give more precise ethnic dimension to an
individual, there was always the possibility adopted by the New Orleans
Picayune, which referred to then ex-Governor A. B. Roman as "a creole
proper—that is, of French origin." [16]

For several decades after 1803 the history of New Orleans and Louisiana centered largely in vigorous battle among Latin creoles, Americans, and foreign French for control of the society, each group determined to mold the whole to its particular design. Issues dividing the
factions ran so deep that those involved in the contest not unreasonably
thought of themselves as engaged in struggle for the very soul of the
community. Aside from its intrinsic importance, the clash does much to
highlight the distinguishing characteristics of each of the contending
groups, providing particular insight into the fantasy-world nature of the
creole myth. Whatever the illusions of that tradition, for example, the
actual historical record fails to reveal any imperious, worldly-wise,
proud and disdainful "aristocrats" among the indigenous New Orleans
population at the time of the Louisiana Purchase, revealing instead a

---

15. *Harper's Magazine,* XV (September, 1857), 565–66; Barbara Bodichon, *An
American Diary, 1857–58,* ed. Joseph B. Reed (London, 1972), 92; C. D. Arfwedson,
The United States and Canada in 1832, 1833, and 1834 (2 vols.; London, 1834), II, 58.

16. For a fuller discussion of these points see Joseph G. Tregle, Jr., "Early New Orleans Society: A Reappraisal," *Journal of Southern History,* XVIII (February, 1952),
21–36.

people almost pitifully ill-equipped for the struggle against those outsiders vying for control of their homeland. It could hardly have been otherwise, given their history as a colonial backwash of French and Spanish imperialism throughout the eighteenth century. Illiteracy was rampant among them, to the extent that it is recorded that street signs were unknown in New Orleans at the turn of the century, there being so few inhabitants able to decipher them. Daniel Clark, former American consul in the city, reported to Secretary of State James Madison in 1803 that in the new territory there "are no Colleges, & but one Public School. . . . There are a few private children's schools, [but] not above half the inhabitants can read or write the French, & not two hundred in the whole country with correctness—in general their Knowledge extends little further." In gloomy confirmation, Claiborne wrote to advise the president that "our new fellow Citizens are indeed involved in great ignorance, while Albert Gallatin sent along his judgment that the creoles of Louisiana "seem to be but one degree above the French West Indians, than whom a more ignorant & depraved race of civilized man did not exist: give them their slaves and let them *speak* French, for they cannot write it, & they would be satisfied." [17]

Such findings came from others than Anglo-American invaders. "A Creole told me with great naiveté one day," a visiting Frenchman remarked, "that a never failing method to make him fall asleep, was to open a book before him," and yet another ascribed the popularity of gambling in New Orleans to a lack of alternatives: "But indeed, what is there to do in the evenings? Converse? About what? Louisianians are strangers alike to art and science or even to the most ordinary items of knowledge." [18]

The obvious condescending scorn of continentals for the crudities of provincial cousins revealed in these last comments does not invalidate the substance of their observations. New Orleans at the time of the pur-

17. C. C. Robin, *Voyages dans l'intérieur de la Louisiane* (2 vols.; Paris, 1807), II, 66; Daniel Clark to James Madison, September 8, 1803, W. C. C. Claiborne to Thomas Jefferson, September 29, 1803, both in Carter, ed., *Territorial Papers of the United States*, IX (Orleans), 38, 60; Albert Gallatin to Thomas Jefferson, August 20, 1804, in Thomas Jefferson Papers, Manuscript Division, Library of Congress. Even if the absence of street signs in New Orleans stemmed from something other than public illiteracy, Robin's observation speaks to a common awareness of the problem.

18. Berquin Duvallon, *Travels in Louisiana and the Floridas in the Year, 1802, Giving a Correct Picture of Those Countries* (New York, 1806), 60; C. C. Robin, *Voyage to Louisiana* (New Orleans, 1966), 56.

chase could indeed point to few if any native doctors, lawyers, artists, editors, bankers, priests, men of letters, or merchant princes. Libraries were nonexistent and the only newspaper hardly deserved the name. Medical books and even the most fundamental legal works were practically unknown. The city had, in truth, little claim to be more than a rude village peopled by a society with remarkably scant awareness of affairs beyond its borders, stunted by the inescapable consequences of a Spanish colonial policy which for years had deliberately conspired to keep them isolated from any illuminating outside contacts, particularly with the United States. The somnolence of decades went undisturbed until the Treaty of San Lorenzo finally threw the city's port open to American commerce in 1795.[19]

By 1803 even the least imaginative of men had little trouble foreseeing that the just beginning trickle of goods down the Mississippi from the vast interior of the United States would quickly swell into the veritable flood of produce destined to make New Orleans by the mid-1830s one of the great shipping marts of the world. But at the time of the purchase the city remained a metropolis in prospect only, a compact gridiron of streets stretching no more than eleven blocks along the river and a mere six from the levee to the back limits of the town. Some spillover from this original site already inched into primitive suburbs ranged along its periphery, reaching toward Lake Pontchartrain in the rear via Bayou St. John and extending upriver from Canal Street into Faubourg Ste. Marie and downstream below the Esplanade into what would become the Faubourg Marigny. But settlement in these areas remained sparse, the entire population amounting to little more than seventy-three hundred "domiciliated residents," some 56 percent of them either slaves or free persons of color.[20]

A mere one thousand or so houses sheltered these inhabitants, almost all single-storied wooden structures, many plastered over in white or pastel colors and most topped by shingled roofs which jutted beyond the outer walls to form sheltering canopies over the *banquettes* or side-

19. John Duffy, *The Rudolph Matas History of Medicine in Louisiana* (Baton Rouge, 1958), 159; Jeremiah Brown, *A Short Letter to a Member of Congress Concerning the Territory of Orleans* (Washington, D.C., 1806), 12; Minter Wood, "Life in New Orleans in the Spanish Period," *Louisiana Historical Quarterly*, XXII (1939), 642–709.

20. Minutes of the New Orleans City Council, June 22, 1805, in New Orleans Municipal Papers, Tulane University Library; Daniel Clark to James Madison, August 17, 1803, in Territorial Papers, Orleans Series, 1794–1813, National Archives Microform T-260.

walks. Along the front streets behind the levee, some brick buildings had begun to rise by 1803 as the tempo of river trade quickened, a few of them two-tiered edifices graced with open galleries. These and the newly built cathedral, flanked by the Cabildo and Presbytere, plus some few government structures close to or abutting the central Place d'Armes, comprised the modest showpieces of a generally unimpressive urban scene. Streets, though broad, were unpaved, frequently becoming rivers of mud in the profusion of rains which proclaimed this a semitropical domain. The sidewalks banking them provided only marginally better passage, making progress through the city generally hazardous and unpleasant.[21]

Such a milieu held little possibility of promoting an elevated or highly cultivated life-style, and in truth the great majority of New Orleanians of that time possessed none of the pretentious qualities assigned them in the creole myth. Americans newly arrived in the city found a community which seemed to them pristine in its simplicity, almost childlike in its lack of ostentation and class consciousness. Neither rebuffed nor rejected, they delighted in the openness which made it possible to participate in social functions even without formal introduction, "a lady never refusing any decent stranger who asks her to dance," in keeping with a creole lack of rigidity in such matters still the custom as late as the 1830s. The dance clearly ruled as the quickening passion of the place, dominating activities at the major entertainment center, the Tivoli, in the neighborhood of Bayou St. John. Devotees flocked to its festivities, whole families driving out in ox carts or trudging there resolutely on foot. Modestly dressed in plain cloth with only an occasional flash of silk, the young women wore their hair unadorned by curls or ornaments. Admission to the hall and at most balls generally cost but half a dollar, males alone being charged, and six cents purchased the customary cup of chocolate or glass of lemonade. Unmarried women did not appear abroad with men outside their family circle, although they might frequently be seen riding forth in carriages alone, handling their own horses, or even mastering a four-mule team. No one, it seems, did anything in the line of work if it were possible to buy a slave to do it for him.[22]

21. Benjamin H. Latrobe, *The Journal of Latrobe* (New York, 1905), 209; John F. Watson, "Notitia of Incidents at New Orleans in 1804 and 1805," *American Pioneer*, II (May, 1843), 233; Berquin Duvallon, *Travels in Louisiana*, 23n.

22. Berquin Duvallon, *Travels in Louisiana*, 235; "Missions de la Louisiane," *Nouvelles de l'Association de la Propagation de la Foi* (Lyons and Paris, 1824), *passim*;

Despite the implications of indolence and inertia in this placid simplicity, the truth of which even they admitted on occasion, the creoles of New Orleans labored under no illusions as to their true self-interest, clearly aware of the certain promise of improved fortune implicit in their new status as citizens of the great republic. No matter that some were reported to have shed tears as the tricolor came down for the last time at the Place d'Armes in 1803. However strong the emotional attachment to France, it could not be allowed to stand in the way of a first enjoyment of political rights and a possibly boundless economic prosperity. In all the difficult years ahead, there was to be no real threat of creole disloyalty to the United States.[23]

But this marriage of disparate cultures quickly foundered in a sea of troubles. Nothing in their past histories had prepared the people of either Louisiana or the United States for the besetting complexities of the new relationship to which they were introduced by the Treaty of 1803. A wide consensus in both populations did indeed support the merger, but such realistic acceptance of a transformed political attachment hardly bespoke willingness by Louisianians to renounce their cultural identity or to submit passively to their new partner's unilateral interpretation of their rights under the purchase agreement. Therein lay the rub. Even such generally open-minded men as Thomas Jefferson and James Madison, carrying as they did their own cultural baggage, tended to identify "democracy," "republicanism," and "self-government" with the peculiarly Anglo-Saxon forms in which they had always known these concepts to function. They perceived English common law, language, religious tradition, and social mores as the "natural" vehicles of political freedom, and it came hard for them to accept the possibility of the fundamentals of United States constitutionalism working in any other context. Moreover, as apostles of the Enlightenment, they subscribed almost religiously to the belief that participation in self-government must rest on a firm foundation of education, literacy, and intellectual preparation. In all of these, regrettably, the citizens of Louisiana proved woefully deficient, as Jefferson came to learn from almost every source to

Watson, "Notitia of Incidents at New Orleans," 231, 234; Charles A. Murray, *Travels in North America During the Years 1834, 1835, and 1836* (2 vols.; London, 1839), 188; Robin, *Voyage to Louisiana*, 53–54.

23. *Bee*, May 22, 1833; Charles Gayarré, "The Americans in Louisiana," *De Bow's Review*, After the War Series, I (March, 1866), 256. Nowhere in the papers of the Burr trial transcripts is there a single reference to a creole conspirator. See David Robertson, ed., *Report of the Trials of Colonel Aaron Burr* (2 vols.; New York, 1875).

which he turned for information on the new members of the republican family. He was soon overwhelmed by the realization that behind his own Virginia there stretched almost two centuries of vital sharing in the routines of self-government, while behind Louisiana could be discerned not one shred of anything resembling participatory democracy. From all this it was inevitable that men of good faith on either side would find themselves at cross-purposes on almost every specific implementation of this fusion of Latin and Anglo-Saxon traditions, no matter how profound might be the commitment of each to the unprecedented experiment.[24]

As a consequence, the government imposed on the Territory of Orleans by a troubled Congress in 1804 allowed its citizens no more share in self-determination than they had known under France or Spain. Even a liberalization in 1805, providing for a popularly elected lower house of a bicameral legislature, did little to assuage the anger of men who had thought the Treaty of 1803 to guarantee them immediate admission into the Union as a full-fledged state. Already infuriated by the lopping off of the Territory of Orleans from the greater part of the old colony of Louisiana, they raged anew at a ban on the importation of slaves into their area and at the challenge by federal judges to the continuance of their familiar civil law procedures. Equally distressing, conflict almost immediately erupted within the community itself as representatives of the two variant cultures turned to the task of trying to live together. For if Latin indolence and backwardness provoked restless Americans to near fury, the newcomers for their part proved more than enough to try the patience of the most forgiving host.[25]

As a lot, they generally arrived far better equipped than the creoles to engage in a contest for supremacy, advantaged as they were by superior education, wider experience in economic and political competition, and by that dynamism and energy common to those daring enough to venture far from home to build a new life. Merchants, lawyers, doctors, teachers, stock clerks, missionaries, mechanics, carpenters, river men, editors, laborers, all saw in New Orleans an irresistible lure, whose pull kept them coming decade after decade. Some of their number, undoubtedly, were driven by motives of the highest order, physicians, perhaps, anxious to battle the notorious "wet grave" of a vulnerable city, schoolmen hoping to enlighten those still in darkness, or divines equally in-

24. Joseph G. Tregle, Jr., "Louisiana in the Age of Jackson" (Ph.D. dissertation, University of Pennsylvania, 1954), chaps. 4–5.
25. *Ibid.*, chap. 6.

spired to turn what they conceived to be a morally benighted people away from the paths of unrighteousness. But the greater mass vibrated to far crasser purpose, the consuming determination to get rich in the expected windfall of a booming New Orleans commerce. As one of them confessed, "I am going regardless of consequences, into an unhealthy climate amongst lawless and vicious men, with but one object—money getting—and this with the hope that I may be enabled to return to my native state and enjoy life." Another cheerfully admitted to a customer complaining of high prices in New Orleans, "O, Sir! We do business here to get rich—it is the object which binds us to stay!"[26]

Lust for wealth, conviction of the ignorance and backwardness of the host community, and determination to move on as soon as good fortune would allow—it was this combination of American attitudes which most quickly and persistently aroused the ire of creole New Orleanians. They took to calling the invaders "Yankee buzzards" or "birds of passage," a label General Francis Gainnié continued to affix to the entrepreneur James H. Caldwell after the latter's almost fifteen years in the community.[27]

Neither the exhilarating explosion of growth and prosperity New Orleans experienced after 1803 nor translation of Louisiana into statehood in 1812 reconciled the original inhabitants to what they increasingly felt to be the pillaging and looting of their homeland by scavengers from abroad, especially since they themselves could not resist joining in the novel scampering after wealth which the newcomers had introduced. Equally galling to them was the ill-concealed contempt displayed by Anglo-Americans toward those among whom they had come to live. By and large, those aspects of creole life identified by the eventual myth as marks of an aristocratic society struck the Americans as reflections not of good breeding or refinement but rather of an arrogance of caste, resting on servile ministrations of suppressed groups such as slaves or free persons of color, whose talents and frequently superior attainments allowed a pampered master class to indulge its taste for indolence and pleasure. The newcomers, to be sure, found nothing particularly offen-

26. *New Orleans as It Is: By a Resident* (Utica, 1849), 32; William B. Foster Journal, 1841–42, quoted in Lewis O. Saum, *The Popular Mood of Pre–Civil War America* (Westport, 1980), 171; John Mott Smith, "Journal of Adventures to California" (Photocopy of Newberry Library manuscript, Tulane University Library), unpaginated.

27. *Louisiana Gazette*, June 29, 1821, October 30, 31, 1822; *Argus*, May 27, 1833; *Louisiana Advertiser*, April 10, 1834.

sive in the exploitation of nonwhite underlings—it was creole ignorance, sloth, and resistance to change which they deplored.[28]

This American criticism of supposed inadequacies in Latin culture
embraced almost every aspect of creole life and frequently extended
even to the milieu in which it was set. The very surroundings of their
new home seemed hostile to some, who railed at "this detestable climate" and "cursed environment." "Say," wrote one to an old friend,
"did you not in your perfect simplicity and ignorance associate . . .
[this] region with bright sunshine, and gay flowers, and beautiful orange
groves and sweet singing birds, and lovely scenery, and brighter, gayer,
more beautiful, sweeter and lovelier maidens than any mere earthly ex-
cellencies? Say, did you not? Well, it is all fantasies! . . . There is not one
particular good here but is quadrupled in our Yankee home!"[29]

It was the cultural rather than the physical climate, however, that
gave them most pause. Far from being impressed by a creole "aristocracy," they saw Louisiana as a community comfortable in the stagna-
tion of its ignorance and almost willfully unprepared to function effectively in the modern world. Their upbringing had prepared them to
distrust the kind of society into which they had come, and the distinguished jurist Henry Adams Bullard delighted in telling the story of how
his old friend Bishop Warren Hay of Massachusetts had "expressed his
amazement that I could live among Catholics!" The surety that this exotic and mephitic landscape must certainly harbor at least the inclina-
tion to moral unwholesomeness proved for some impossible to put
aside, leading one young migrant to the doleful confession, "I would
not marry a girl born & brought up in New Orleans, if she was the most
beautiful thing on Earth & owned every plantation in Louisiana and
Mississippi!"[30]

Not unreasonably, creoles bristled at this set of assumptions. Even

28. Josiah Conder, ed., *The Modern Traveler* (30 vols.; London, 1830), XXIV, 214;
Tregle, "Early New Orleans Society," 28–29; Bodichon, *Diary,* 92; *La Louisiane,* September 26, October 7, 1841; Oakey Hall, *The Manhattaner in New Orleans* (New York,
1857), 23.

29. *Louisiana Gazette,* October 29, 1822, April 14, September 24, 1824; *Argus,* December 18, 22, 23, 1826; G. B. Milligan to Miss Milligan, April 3, 1827, in Milligan Family Papers, Historical Society of Delaware, Wilmington; Henry Blood to Benjamin Rotch,
March 26, May 20, 1838, in Benjamin S. Rotch Papers, Massachusetts Historical Society,
Boston.

30. Henry Adams Bullard to Amos Lawrence, March 10, 1832, in Amos Lawrence
Papers, Massachusetts Historical Society; H. C. Whittridge to Benjamin Rotch, April 3,
1838, in Rotch Papers.

acknowledging, as they frequently did, their inexperience in self-government and deficiencies in education, they especially resented the implication that these disabilities in some way stemmed from their Latin ethnicity. Much as they might sincerely wish to be good citizens of the United States, they could not see why this should require renunciation of their French heritage or affirmation of the superiority of Anglo-American mores. It was true enough that they were generally uneasy in an awareness of their own shortcomings and that much of their supposed distancing from Americans reflected an inhibiting consciousness of inferiority rather than an aristocratic aloofness. But this bound them even more doggedly to their Gallic inheritance. As one of them mused, "A country is like a beloved first mistress: you can abandon her, you may love another, but you can never forget her."[31]

And so they fumed when Americans made English the "legal language" of the state, attempted to replace civil with common law, and tried to convert historic French street names in New Orleans to others more reflective of the new order. Particularly offensive in their eyes was American attack on the traditional creole habit of celebrating the Sabbath as a day of relaxed pleasure centered in bustling cafés, bull baiting, horse racing, theatrical performances, and the beloved dance. Shocked New England puritans were forever posting signs beneath notices of Sunday balls admonishing the ungodly to "remember the Sabbath day to keep it holy!" while Protestant newspapers and ministers fulminated endlessly against a society capable of this grossly sinful rejection of established Christian morality.[32]

Such open defiance of God's law, they maintained, led ineluctably to the even more dreadful depravity found in the notorious "quadroon balls," assemblages of colored women more often than not simple prostitutes, who pandered to the concupiscence of the New Orleans male. Most pernicious sin of all, in their judgment, the institution of *plaçage* enshrined the tradition in which creole men established particularly favored mulatto girls as mistresses of their own *ménages*, giving them place as "second wives" in an arrangement unknown to the law but

31. *L'Ami des Lois*, January 4, 1823; *La Louisiane*, October 7, 1841; *La Creole*, December 24, 1837.

32. *L'Ami des Lois*, January 18, 1825; George Dargo, *Jefferson's Louisiana: Politics and the Clash of Legal Traditions* (Cambridge, Mass., 1975), chaps. 5–7; *Argus*, July 7, 1828; Timothy Flint, *Recollections of the Last Ten Years* (Boston, 1826), 307; *Louisiana Advertiser*, February 7, 1824, June 12, 1826; *Observer*, February 28, 1835.

cherished in local custom. They convinced themselves, moreover, that this indulgence of carnal appetite led to debasement of other human sensibilities as well, and when a petition came to the legislature requesting permission for a creole to marry his niece, a shaken American remarked that nothing more remained than for the state to be asked to legalize incest. In addition, shocking reports of violence visited on slaves by the infamous Madame Delphine Lalaurie, a Mrs. Lanusse, and a Mrs. Pardos, confirmed for them the existence of what Lafcadio Hearn would later call a natural Latin cruelty. In their eyes, New Orleans with its gambling dens, ballrooms, theaters, race tracks, and rampant sexual permissiveness stood condemned as the "modern Golgotha," whose history presented "the fullest measure of human woe, of moral degradation, of human suffering . . . the blackest rage of human passion, and all the dark and damning deeds that the fiends of the infernal regions could perpetrate."[33]

Understandably, creoles took this to mean that they were not only ignorant and indolent but immoral and corrupt as well. Never a particularly religious people, they nonetheless profoundly resented this attack on their established traditions, coming as it did from those whom they derided as hypocritical "saints" and "blue law tractarians." For, as they were quick to point out, while American clergy might declaim as they would against dalliance with quadroons or the frequenting of gaming halls and ballrooms, they could not make it unpopular with countless numbers of their own countrymen.[34]

As a capstone to these cultural antipathies, the full gravamen of the American charge against creole society contained yet another indictment. History and tradition, it held, made Latins incapable of understanding the mechanisms and spirit of the republican process, a failing which resulted in their placing family connections and old colonial habits of authority above promotion of the public good. What else, indeed, could one expect from a people still enthralled by Napoleon, whom they identified simply as "the Man" or "the Greatest of Mortals"? It fol-

33. *Mercantile Advertiser,* January 18, 1825; *Louisiana Advertiser,* January 27, February 10, 1826; *L'Ami des Lois,* January 18, February 4, 1823; *Bee,* April 22, 1834; Benjamin H. Latrobe, *Impressions Respecting New Orleans,* ed. Samuel Wilson, Jr. (New York, 1951), 53–54; Benjamin Lundy, *The Life, Travels and Opinions of Benjamin Lundy* (Philadelphia, 1847), 113; Elizabeth Broland, *The Life and Letters of Lafcadio Hearn* (2 vols.; Boston and New York, 1906), I, 203; *New Orleans as It Is,* 6.

34. *Argus,* January 18, 19, 1826; *Louisiana Courier,* May 28, 1827, December 1, 1830.

lowed naturally that many Americans read into this a clear mandate for their own monopoly of public offices, certainly at least until the creole population had profited from an apprenticeship sufficient finally to bring them to an appreciation of the genius of the democratic system. Some proved insensitive enough to tell the creoles bluntly "not to interfere with Government, as that is a subject peculiar to ourselves." [35]

It did not require the pride of a mythical creole to find these pretensions humiliating, demeaning, and unacceptable. Determined not to be whipped into submission like "spaniels or slaves," the *ancienne population* responded with repeated alarums designed to rouse their numbers to action. "Tremble, Louisianians!" one of their champions proclaimed. "You sleep on the brink of a precipice. One more step and these daring men will treat you as they have treated the unfortunate creoles of Missouri. They were Louisianians like you, and they have disappeared from the roll of peoples. Tremble!" The ebullient Bernard Marigny, owner of most of New Orleans below Esplanade Avenue, took to the lists threatening to "annihilate" the "very name American" in Louisiana. Galvanized by the enemy's pledge to "make all foreign and French principles crouch beneath the true American sentiments," Gallic stalwarts everywhere rose to the challenge, determined not to be outdone in any show of native patriotism. Joseph Rodriguez surpassed them all in the starkness of his vision of what lay ahead should the invader be allowed to prevail: "Such is the grand plan of the Vandals of the West, *delenda est Carthago!* And passersby, surveying with pity all this debris and ruin, will read, *hic Troja fuit! Ici exista la Nouvelle Orléans!*" [36]

But a simple flood of rhetoric could not alter the controlling fact: Louisiana creoles lagged almost hopelessly behind in education and political experience, and they could summon up no one from their ranks competent enough to assure their continued hegemony. Marigny, Jacques Villeré, Martin Duralde, Michel Fortier, Denis Prieur, and William DeBuys all ranked as men of great influence and prominence in the old population, but none of them demonstrated ability to command with authority or to generate unified support. Marigny's offensive

35. *Louisiana Courier,* November 5, 8, 1834; *Louisiana Gazette,* November 22, 1822; J. W. Windship to William Plumer, Jr., in Everett Brown, "Letters from Louisiana, 1813–1814," *Mississippi Valley Historical Review,* XI (1924), 575.

36. *Louisiana Courier,* January 17, 1824, August 22, 1825; *L'Ami des Lois,* January 24, 1823; *Louisiana Gazette,* August 13, 1822; J[oseph] Rodriguez, *Défense fulminante contre la violation des droits des peuples* (New Orleans, 1827), 35.

flaunting of wealth and crudity of manners turned many against him, while his own enormous ego was incapable of accepting creole leadership from anyone else. Most popular of them all, Duralde had the additional attraction of being Henry Clay's son-in-law, but he suffered painful insecurity and uncertainty as to his own abilities, not unaware that American associates considered him "an amiable good man, little removed from idiocy & totally incapable of performing the duties properly of the most simple office." Americans wrote off DeBuys too as a minor quantity, a favorite among his creole *compères* but crippled by talents so limited that he was reputed to be "unable to write so much as an invitation to dinner either in French or English." Villeré commanded wide affection and respect for the gentleness of his character, but this very quality made him seem weak and too much given to conciliation of the Americans, a charge the jealous Marigny constantly hurled against him. For his part, Prieur appeared in many ways the consummate professional politician, gregarious, convivial, handsome, and dapper, yet he too proved handicapped by a severely limited education, shallowness of purpose, and lack of energy. Even successive terms as mayor of New Orleans in the 1830s and 1840s failed to win him commanding position. Telling index to the pervasive weakness of creole leadership, in this community so awash in newspaper controversy no native New Orleanian filled an editorial chair until well into the 1820s.[37]

One major strength, however, permitted the creoles to hold off their rivals until at least the late 1830s. Sheer numerical superiority ensured their continued dominance in the first years after the purchase, for even with the steady flow of migrants from other states the Americans long remained in the minority. Equally important, because of their established tenure many creoles possessed assets such as real property, slaves, and horses, which placed them on the tax rolls with the right of suffrage. The preponderance of Americans, by contrast, comprised young clerks domiciled in the ubiquitous boardinghouses of the city, skilled

---

37. *L'Ami des Lois*, February 24, 1824; *Argus*, April 26, 1824; *Louisiana Gazette*, April 3, 1824; *Louisiana Courier*, February 6, May 1, 1824; Etienne Mazureau to Henry Clay, September 19, 1825, Clay to James Brown, April 17, 1830, W. C. C. Claiborne to Clay, December 14, 1834, all in Henry Clay Papers, Manuscript Division, Library of Congress; William Christy to John Tyler, April 13, 1841, Christy to William H. Harrison, February 20, 1841, in Letters of Application and Recommendation During the Administrations of William Henry Harrison and John Tyler (Christy file), National Archives Microcopy No. 687. The first creole editors were Manuel Crozat and Antoine Dupuy (*Argus*, April 19, 1824).

craftsmen whose resources went into tools and rented shops, or merchants with capital largely in fluid rather than fixed goods. Without the tax liability requisite for the franchise under the constitution of 1812, their head count, therefore, failed to translate proportionately into ballots. To make best use of this electoral advantage, creoles swallowed their pride and looked to the foreign French to add Gallic leadership to Gallic numbers. An alliance of necessity, the union would never be an easy one, for Marigny and other creoles such as Governor A. B. Roman hated this alien presence almost as much as the American, aware that its protagonists made little effort to conceal their amused contempt for the provincial inferiority of those whom they regarded for the most part as rude bumpkin innocents.[38]

The Americans quickly condemned this combination against them, assailing it as an effort by a "foreign faction" to kill republicanism in Louisiana and deliver the state into the hands of Louis XVIII and the Holy Alliance. Typically, they assigned most blame for the alleged conspiracy to the foreign French, supposing the creoles incapable of being anything more than witless pawns in a game conceived and directed by their betters. "These last have been despised by [the] foreign faction," one American observer remarked. "They do us the honor only to hate."[39]

As a result of all this, profound ethnic strife wracked New Orleans for decades, by the mid-1820s coming perilously close to armed violence. Only the irenic visit of Lafayette in 1825 and the skilled diplomacy of Governor Henry Johnson in 1826 averted what could easily have produced bloody tragedy. So disruptive and enervating had such internecine quarrels become by the late decade, and so intractably did Gallic influence seem to be set against the Americans, that the latter determined to separate those sections of the city in which they were dominant from those remaining under French-speaking control. Though still a minority, their numbers had nonetheless steadily increased over the years, so that it was now possible to mark off clear ethnic neighborhoods in the city.[40]

Over the decades a consistent pattern of migration had produced an American community drawn largely from mid-Atlantic, upper South,

38. *Daily News*, February 22, 1834; *Argus*, May 25, 26, 27, 1829; *Louisiana Advertiser*, August 27, 1823; *Bee*, May 16, 1836; *Louisiana Courier*, July 5, 1830.
39. *Louisiana Gazette*, April 28, 1824.
40. *Ibid.*, July–October, 1825; *Bee*, February 12, 1836.

and New England regions, with New York, Pennsylvania, and Virginia ranking as the three most contributory states in both 1825 and 1850. Despite tradition, no barriers blocked the earliest arrivals from settlement in closely guarded precincts of the original town, nor did lack of space within it turn them uniformly to what would eventually become known as the "American quarter." They located rather in the three- or four-block area of the present Vieux Carré just below Canal Street, establishing a dominant presence there which would persist certainly down to the Civil War. Only when that section had become heavily populated did later American arrivals gravitate primarily to the uptown Faubourg Ste. Marie or St. Mary, stretching from Canal to DeLord Street, now Howard Avenue. Even there they were interlopers, for federal census returns indicate that until well into the 1820s the French-speaking population was the majority in all sections of the city. Based on the admittedly shaky technique of deciding ethnicity on the basis of family surnames (the only method available because the census does not indicate place of birth until 1850), it appears that in 1810 a mere 9 percent of St. Mary families were American as against 75 percent French and 16 percent free colored, while in 1820 the figures are 34 percent American, 51 percent French, and 15 percent colored. By 1830, however, St. Mary Americans had risen to top rank, measuring 45 percent as opposed to the French with 35 percent and the free colored with 20. As is clear from these data, even in their imprecision, the old notion of Canal Street as a real if unofficial dividing line separating highly exclusive ethnic populations contains more fancy than fact. In 1830, for example, many of the most prominent creole citizens of New Orleans lived in Faubourg St. Mary, among them J. B. Plauché, William DeBuys, James Freret, Thomas Sloo, and Augustin Macarty, while the City, or French Quarter, housed Paul Tulane, Samuel J. Peters, John Hagen, Isaac T. Preston, John R. Grymes, John Slidell, Martin Gordon, and countless other leaders of the American colony.[41]

What really divided the city into distinctive sections was the concentration of commercial activity in the area stretching from approxi-

41. *Louisiana State Gazette,* March 13, 1826; *De Bow's Review,* XIX (September, 1855), 262–63; United States census schedules for New Orleans, 1810, 1820, and 1830 (National Archives Microcopies M-252, M-33, M-19). Delegates to the Louisiana constitutional convention of 1845 commented on the continuing "American" character of the upper reaches of the original city. See Robert J. Ker, reporter, *Proceedings and Debates of the Convention of Louisiana Which Assembled at the City of New Orleans, January 14, 1844* (New Orleans, 1845), 606, 629.

mately Rue Conti in the old quarter, up past Canal Street into the Faubourg St. Mary. Here one found the banks, insurance companies, exchanges, specialty retail stores, commodity brokers, wholesale warehouses, factors, and commission merchants, all of whom fed largely on the great piles of produce brought downriver to dock at the steamboat wharves lining the levees of the upper city. By the late 1820s American strength clearly predominated in this section, pushing even as far into the original town as perhaps St. Louis or Toulouse streets. The first five blocks of Chartres below Canal were lined in the mid-1830s with American bookshops, jewelry stores, and dry goods emporiums, for example, while even less active thoroughfares such as the upper reaches of Bourbon and Dauphine reflected a comparable major impress of the Yankee businessman.[42]

So controlling had this presence become even as early as the mid-1820s that newspapers regularly began to use the terms *commercial quarter* and *American section* almost interchangeably, generally embracing in these designations the area comprising the First, Sixth, and Seventh wards of the city, extending from Conti to the upper limits of St. Mary. It was at St. Louis Street that Bernard Marigny drew the line between the "upper" and "lower" parts of New Orleans in 1822, proclaiming that the insufferable Americans had become so entrenched in the former and had so iniquitously enriched themselves therein at the expense of the latter that justice cried out for a new direction of municipal policy. Villain of the story as Marigny told it was the foreign French mayor, Joseph Roffignac, who had in his judgment either stupidly or maliciously allowed the steamboat trade to become monopolized by the upper city, to the consequent decline and decay of the center and lower town. What everyone knew was that Marigny's fury stemmed from collapse of his once glowingly optimistic expectations for growth in his own Faubourg Marigny below Esplanade. The greater portion of the Saint Domingue refugee flood of 1809 had settled in that area, and for a while Gallic spirits soared in conviction that the future expansion of the city must surely go in the same direction. The American surge into St. Mary ended all that, and for this Marigny could find no forgiveness.[43]

42. [Joseph H. Ingraham], *The Southwest: By a Yankee* (2 vols.; New York, 1835), I, 93; United States census schedules, 1830, 1840 (National Archives Microcopy T-5).

43. [Ingraham], *The Southwest*, I, 93; *Louisiana Gazette*, January 26, 29, June 30, August 10, 1825; *Louisiana Advertiser*, August 16, 1823; *Mémoire de Bernard Marigny, Habitant de la Louisiane: Addressé à ses concitoyens* (Paris, 1822), 56; *Argus*, November 25, 1829.

As the accelerating prosperity of their rivals increasingly distressed French champions of the lower precincts, the Gallic majority in the city council responded with deliberate sabotage of the wharf system without which St. Mary could not service the steamboat traffic upon which its prosperity depended. It soon became clear as well that what some called the "bosom of the city" meant vindictively to keep from the American quarter an equitable share of street paving, gas lighting, and other major improvements, no matter how substantial its contribution to city tax revenues.[44]

Gross ineptitude and flagrant financial dereliction on the part of the council only intensified the outrage of the American section's commercial leadership at the discrimination visited upon them. Exploiting the considerable anti-French sentiment in other parts of the state, they finally, after many years' effort, managed to win legislative approval for division of the city into three municipalities in 1836, guaranteeing each of them control over its own internal financial and economic affairs but retaining a single mayor, police force, and citywide authority in such matters as regulation of drays and hacks. It proved impossible, however, to overcome the emotional resistance to any plan that would wrench the First Ward from its historic place within the original city, no matter that ethnic identification and economic characteristics tied it more closely to the Faubourg St. Mary than to the lower quarter. Thus the compromise dividing line between the First Municipality (the City) and the Second (St. Mary) was fixed at Canal Street, with Esplanade Avenue serving as the upper boundary of the Third, roughly Faubourg Marigny.[45]

This continued attachment of the area between Conti and Canal streets to the organic unity of the Vieux Carré, together with the maintenance within it of that architectural style which set the old city apart from the new, primarily accounts for the later commonplace contention that Canal became a kind of Rubicon dividing American and creole populations. It is an observation found in almost every descriptive account of New Orleans, even in the memoirs of such knowledgeable residents as S. J. Peters, but the impression, in truth, rests less on fact than on the mistaken acceptance of the municipality boundary line as a population demarcation, made particularly easy because all sections of the city below Canal Street share that ambience which even today convinces those who step into it that they have indeed entered a foreign

44. *Emporium*, December 4, 1832; *Bee*, September 10, 17, 1834.
45. *Argus*, September 26, 1826; *Union*, November 13, 1835.

world. Nonetheless, the unromantic data of the census returns for 1830 through 1860 clearly demonstrate the falsity of the traditional account. Another of its props, the seemingly plausible claim that the unique New Orleans name for a street median, "neutral ground," stems from Canal's existence as a buffer between warring creoles and Americans proves equally untenable: apparently that term originally applied to all boundaries between faubourgs, municipalities, and the original city as geographic, not ethnic, entities. What remains beyond dispute is that the 1836 division of the city changed forever the nature of the long contest between the competing populations. Bitterness and rancor would continue for many years into the future, but there was never again that anxious sense that the outcome of a great struggle was hanging in the balance. The creoles had clearly lost.[46]

Ironically, they met defeat at the very time that their first generation born after the purchase gradually came into maturity, young men such as the historian Charles Gayarré, the playwright-editor-impresario Placide Canonge, the linguist Alexander Dimitry, the physician Armand Mercier, and the priest-poet Adrien Rouquette. To a degree essentially unknown among their fathers, they embodied a highly developed literary and artistic sensibility which might seem to validate the concept of creole elitism. They represented, however, but a small minority in an overall society which by almost every measurement failed to match the standards set by the American interlopers. Creoles produced no jurist to rival Edward Livingston, no lawyers to compare with John R. Grymes or Alfred Hennen, no entrepreneurs to equal James H. Caldwell or Samuel J. Peters, no financiers to keep pace with James Robb, William C. Hewes, or Jacob Barker, no national political titans to contest with Livingston or John Slidell.

To be sure, in a major sense their failure to do so was no more real than that of the American population itself, for the latter's record of superior accomplishment belongs almost exclusively to those first-generation

---

46. George Kernion, "Samuel Jarvis Peters," *Publications of the Louisiana Historical Society*, VII (1913), 73; Cable, "New Orleans," 273. One contributor to *La Louisiane*, September 12, 1841, noted in obviously satiric vein: "For me, my country stretches from the Mississippi to the Ramparts and does not go beyond Esplanade or Canal Street . . . my Rubicon." Another contemporary, however, keeps the record clear: Henry C. Castellanos, born in the city in 1827, reports that "Canal street was not by any means, as some people suppose, the dividing line of the contending factions, inasmuch as many of the most enterprising American merchants and business men of the period, including Mr. Peters himself, had their principal establishments in the French Quarter." See his *New Orleans as It Was* (New Orleans, 1895), 253.

giants whose talents and skills had been nurtured in other climes. One might indeed argue that Latin creoles like Gayarré and Dimitry, or the later chess genius Paul Morphy, motivated perhaps by American challenge to their class and privileged with a mobility and freedom unknown to their elders, made of themselves men of cultural and intellectual attainment generally superior to that of their American second-generation counterparts. But to do so would be to distort the greater reality. In practically every measurable category, after 1836 dominance and leadership in the affairs of New Orleans gravitated ever more surely to the American party and to the section of the city identified with it.

Already in 1835 the commercial wealth of the region above Canal Street far exceeded that of the rest of the corporation, even though voter strength in the City and Faubourg Marigny outstripped that of St. Mary and the upper suburbs almost two to one. Released from the trammels of control affixed by an antagonistic opposition in the old city council, the commercial section began to move rapidly ahead of the constantly lagging lower town. In the expansive boom period just prior to the Panic of 1837, real estate speculation produced "astonishing growth" in the American quarter, while the rest of the city limped far behind. Even the remarkable building surge which finally in the mid-1840s lifted St. Mary out of years of bitter depression passed the City by, leaving it to slip slowly into tawdry and grimy disrepair.[47]

As decay deepened and spread in the old quarter, leading Oakey Hall to describe the 1840s area below Jackson Square as "the St. Giles of New Orleans . . . where poverty and vice run races with want and passion," some observers saw the blight as symbolic of a general erosion of creole society. The "immutable laws of population which will ever make the weak give room for the strong," one observer remarked, "will take everything from their hands, and leave them in the shades of oblivion. . . . Nothing hereafter will succeed unless it comes within the range of the American part of the city." To Judge E. H. Durrell, the cathedral stood between a "new" and an "old" entity, an American center of the Western world, bustling and prosperous, and a creole "decayed town of Europe," whose population was "fixed, wanting in enterprise, fearful of change, in fit unison with its own labours."[48]

47. *Louisiana Advertiser*, March 19, 1835; *Bee*, November 24, 1835; *Historical Epitome of the State of Louisiana* (New Orleans, 1840), 240; [E. H. Durrell], *New Orleans as I Found It* (New York, 1845), 21; Ferdinand de Feriet to Janica de Feriet, May 13, 1836, in Feriet Family Papers, Tulane University Library; *Picayune*, September 6, 1841.

48. Hall, *Manhattaner in New Orleans*, 102; *New Orleans as It Is*, 24, 26–27; [Durrell], *New Orleans as I Found It*, 79.

These judgments represented, true enough, opinions of members of that American faction which might be suspected of reflecting typically jaundiced criticism of an old antagonist. But the indexes of economic growth are free of ethnic bias, and what they show is a New Orleans in 1860 in which the district above Canal Street contained 63 percent of the city's total taxable property as against 37 percent for the area below, while populations balanced almost equally. If one uses St. Louis Street as the dividing line, remembering the heavy concentration of American business in the squares between it and Canal, the disparity is even more striking, 76 percent for the upper as opposed to 24 percent for the lower precinct. City directories from 1820 to 1860 reinforce this impression of a steadily aggrandizing American quarter, revealing a relentless shift of business from the older to the newer section of town. In 1822, as a single example, all six New Orleans insurance companies headquartered in the Vieux Carré; in 1850 all but one of nineteen lined Camp Street in St. Mary. Despite the claims of so many later defenders of their cause, it was not ruination attendant upon the Civil War which displaced creoles as the ruling class in the community. That fate befell them long before the dislocations of the tragic conflict.[49]

Lamentations over this decline of creole fortunes abound in the city's French-language press after 1840. There is in much of them a remarkable departure from the old bravado which had thundered in the pages of such Gallic spokesmen as *L'Ami des Lois* and *Le Courrier de la Louisiane* back in the hair-trigger days of the 1820s and 1830s. In its place a submissive acceptance of defeat prevails, a recognition that the American businessman now enjoyed a clear ascendancy. The St. Mary "speculator," one creole editor sighed, had shown himself to be "enterprising, audacious, untiring, daring," while his counterpart in the City passively watched the closing in his area of elegant establishments once "crowded with the most marvelous products of art and industry from all parts of the world" and the Third Municipality merchant drowsed sleepily in front of his door. It was a "sad spectacle" indeed, this "transition from the beautiful to the ugly."[50]

Nor could creoles find consolation in a comforting conviction that American supremacy sprang from a vulgar materialism unacceptable to

49. "Tabular Statement Showing Assessed Value of Taxable Property . . . in the Year 1860," *Journals and Debates of the General Assembly of Louisiana, 1864* (New Orleans, 1864), insert; *Paxton's New Orleans Directory and Register* (New Orleans, 1822); *Cohen's New Orleans and Lafayette Directory* (New Orleans, 1849).

50. *La Revue Louisianaise*, September 6, 1846.

a more highly refined cultural and aesthetic temperament. Even more troubling than the signs of physical decay about them loomed the evidence of how they continued to lag in other respects as well. The specter of their traditional apathy in matters of education haunted them still. "The mass of the [creole] population can scarcely read," the editor of the ardently pro-French *La Louisiane* bemoaned in 1841—"newspapers rarely enter into the family circle, the greater part of [their] minds, although forceful and occasionally even sparkling, are uncultivated and, as a sad consequence, blinded by prejudice and ignorance." In typical contrast, the Second Municipality by the 1840s had brought in trained teachers from the North, recruited by Horace Mann, staffing a model school system which by the end of the decade was educating almost as many students as the First and Third municipalities combined. Some creoles indeed went off to Paris or northern schools such as Georgetown and Mount St. Mary's College in Baltimore but in numbers never more than minimal.[51]

This creole resistance to disciplined cultivation of the mind led inevitably to such consequences as a marked predominance of Americans in the city's legal and medical practices. Formal education of would-be attorneys became essentially monopolized by them, for example. Nearly 60 percent of the lawyers admitted to the bar in 1813 derived from American ranks; by 1839 Americans outnumbered all others by a ratio of three and a half to one, and no evidence of a falling off from this tendency appears in the years which followed. Despite a more vigorous participation in the provision of medical services to the city, with some among them such as Armand Mercier and Isidor Labatut having studied in Paris, creole representation in the total physician corps of the antebellum years also failed to keep pace with that of the other ethnic group. Typically, American faculty dominated medical training at the University of Louisiana, whose list of graduates during the pre–Civil War years shows an overwhelming predominance of Anglo-Saxon names.[52]

51. *La Louisiane*, November 4, 11, 1841; Isaac Baldwin to Horace Mann, August 28, 1841, E. Yorke to Mann, November 16, 1841, John A. Shaw to Mann, October 25, 1841, all in Horace Mann Papers, Massachusetts Historical Society; *La Chronique*, March 5, 1848; *Bee*, August 6, 1831.

52. Elizabeth Gaspard, "The Rise of the Louisiana Bar: The Early Period" (M.A. thesis, University of New Orleans, 1985), 2–8; Duffy, *History of Medicine in Louisiana*, 340; Standford E. Chaillé, *Historical Sketch of the Medical Department of the University of Louisiana, Its Professors and Alumni, from 1835 to 1862* (New Orleans, 1861), 12–18.

Even that most precious of the distinguishing marks of a culture, its language, appeared now to be in jeopardy. Use of French in the newspapers, in commerce, and in legislative and judicial proceedings began to diminish rapidly in the 1840s, convincing many that the beloved tongue would soon be sustained only in the domestic circle. Any vitality in the Gallic press and literary circles centered primarily in the work of European transients, but their contribution proved neither substantial nor long-lived, much of it representing values largely unappealing to creole taste. Even when used, the traditional speech impressed some as no longer reflective of a truly Gallic soul. "New Orleans has been called the American Paris," Lucretia Everett wrote back to a Boston friend in 1842, "but resembles it in nothing that meets the eye. The same language to be sure is spoken—but the spirit seems to have evaporated." The embittered Placide Canonge, himself prolific in turning out reams of plays in the French idiom, denounced the growing tendency of his fellow creoles "to apostatize and renounce the language of their fathers." No less distressing, as early as the mid-1830s *L'Abeille* regularly moaned that James Caldwell's magnificent St. Charles Theater had "killed" the old city's St. Peter, St. Philip, and Orleans playhouses, conceding in melancholy reviews that except in choral and orchestral polish the Americans had once again outstripped their Gallic rivals. In equally mournful accents, a visiting Frenchwoman noted that in the old central market in 1855 English speech seemed pervasive and that even the opera had been forced to change its all-French programs to maintain an American patronage long since indispensable to its existence.[53]

All around them creoles heard "words of denigration and satire pronounced against us by the majority of Anglo-Americans," reinforcing the observation that their kind had "been absorbed and made to submit to the fate of a conquered race." The Americans, one visiting Frenchman reported, were "effacing [creole] civilization with a rapidity and thoroughness . . . much greater than that with which the Romans transformed the people who submitted to their arms." The will to resist seemed suddenly to have collapsed, its place taken by long looks back to happier times in a younger city, as if such retreat into the past provided

53. *La Chronique*, November 26, 1848; Viatte, *Histoire litteraire de l'Amérique Française*, 242–43, 247; Lucretia Everett to Amelia Peabody, February 15 [1842], in Everett-Peabody Papers, Massachusetts Historical Society; *La Louisiane*, October 21, 1841; *Bee*, May 13, August 3, 1835; Elisée Reclus, "Fragment d'un voyage à la Nouvelle Orléans," *Le Tour du Monde* (Paris, 1860), 189.

the only remaining solace: "But then we were something, then one could not say of us, as has just been said by the *Crescent:* 'It is a race passing into the valley of shade and oblivion.'"[54]

One great blessing flowed from this at least partial surrender of creole claims to dominance. The strident appeals to ethnic loyalties, the storms which had led to near bloodshed in 1825–26, now largely abated in the twenty years preceding the Civil War, though rumblings of old passions occasionally enlivened debates on the new constitutions of 1845 and 1852 or occasioned spasms of violence in city elections dominated by the divisiveness of Native Americanism. Loss of the state capital to the American Florida parishes, adoption of popular manhood suffrage, these too eroded creole power, taking their toll on pride and self-esteem.

The relative surcease from strife introduced by the 1840s in many ways, however, only fulfilled an always present contradictory theme in the story of creole-American relations. Despite the enormous chasms dividing the two cultures, despite their bitter clashes in all the concerns described at length above, the battle had always raged in a kind of institutionalization of contending loyalties, more a conflict between formalized ethnic identities than a clash of personalities. As individuals they had gotten along remarkably well. Not even the Americans' patent assumption of superiority over their Latin neighbors or the latter's discomfiting sense of inadequacy had prevented widespread association in business partnerships, professional undertakings, and political alliances in areas such as national party matters not affected by ethnic attachments. The list of Americans married into creole families was long and distinguished, including W. C. C. Claiborne, George Eustis, John Slidell, Nathan Morse, John R. Grymes, Evan Jones, James Wilkinson, S. J. Peters, Edward Livingston, and Henry Carleton, though the wives of the last two actually came from Saint Domingue, not Louisiana.

Little as they might have believed it at first, these intimate relationships frequently produced in protagonists of each side an eventual yielding to attractions in the life-style of the other. If creoles more and more apostatized to American ways, as Canonge charged, their rivals frequently took on the "foreign" manners of their hosts. Alexander H. Everett recorded in his diary how dinner at the home of George Eustis,

54. *La Louisiane,* September 26, November 7, 1841; Xavier Eyma, *Les femmes du nouveau monde* (Paris, 1860), 49; J. J. Ampére, *Promenade en Amérique* (2 vols.; Paris, 1855), II, 154–55.

Louisiana supreme court justice, was "*A la Française*," and the French philologist J. J. Ampére judged the soiree he attended at the home of John Slidell in the 1850s the "most Parisian thing in America," even though everyone there spoke only in English. A discerning young Bostonian, for his part, remarked on what he called the striking tendency of New Orleans to "humanize" people, finding many of his resettled New England friends "divested of much of that cautious reserve which is said to belong especially to Yankees." Most famous personification of this mellowing influence of the city, the Reverend Theodore Clapp, beloved parson of the Strangers' Church, arrived in Louisiana a rigidly orthodox Calvinist, stayed to become a close and dear friend to Catholic priests, and eventually founded the Unitarian Church of New Orleans.[55]

The dynamics of the city's economy contributed its own major impulse to the mixing of the populations. The great majority of Americans who flocked there did not, of course, ever become the millionaires of their dreams, nor did the mass of creole youth at any time enjoy the choice of exclusively patrician occupations. Most of both groups had to be content with jobs as clerks, skilled craftsmen, or petty public servants, frequently finding themselves thrown together in the unavoidable intimacy of a bustling workplace. Creoles did, it must be admitted, eschew physical labor, but this proclivity bespoke no aristocratic delicacy, native-born Americans being just as inclined to avoid jobs of that character. Not surprisingly, having longer and closer ties to the community, they both simply proved more than willing to cede the most menial tasks to newly arrived immigrant hordes grateful for any kind of employment. In 1850, for example, not one nurse at the Charity Hospital was a native Louisianian; in 1860, all chambermaids at the St. Charles Hotel gave Ireland as their birthplace, and of the fifty-five waiters working at the City Hotel, none had been born in the United States.[56]

All of which points to a New Orleans ethnic reality far beyond the familiar parameters of creole-American conflict. At the very time of the most divisive and turbulent explosions of that rivalry, a new phenomenon had gathered force to bring change to New Orleans in what would

55. Alexander Everett Diary, March 5, 1841, in Massachusetts Historical Society; Ampére, *Promenade en Amerique*, II, 154–55; Benjamin Lincoln to George C. Shattuck, February 25, 1826, in Shattuck Family Papers, Massachusetts Historical Society; Theodore Clapp, *Autobiographical Sketches and Recollections During a Thirty-five Years' Residence in New Orleans* (Boston, 1857), 235–41, 254.

56. United States census schedules, 1850 and 1860 (National Archives Microcopies 432 and 653).

quickly become a transforming revolution in its ethnic composition. Great waves of Irish and German immigrants flooded into the city during the decades from 1830 to 1860, adding to the older established migrations from France, Spain, Britain, and the Caribbean. By 1850 the free population of New Orleans had jumped to 99,071, of whom 48,601, or 49 percent, were foreign-born. So dramatically did this invasion reshape the demographic patterns of the city that old descriptive designations of "American" and "creole" sections of town became meaningless except as familiar labels of geographic location.[57]

Again tradition has seriously distorted the actuality of the city's experience, generally holding that the Irish clustered in the upper reaches of St. Mary around Julia and Girod streets, eventually to stretch out into the so-called Irish Channel in the suburb of Lafayette, adjacent to New Orleans and absorbed by it in 1852. Germans reputedly concentrated in the Little Saxony areas of the Faubourg Marigny and in the riverfront regions of Lafayette and Carrollton, foreign enclaves represented as ribbons of new exoticism bordering the still dominantly "American" and "creole" quarters. In truth, the foreign tide so engulfed the city that by 1850 in the very heart of the "American section," the area between Canal and Julia streets from the river to the lake, foreign-born residents made up 51 percent of the white population as against 30 percent American-born and 19 percent Louisiana-born. When one adds to the foreigners the considerable number of children actually members of their households though listed in census returns as native Louisianians, it is clear that no part of the city could any longer legitimately be called ethnically American. The figures for the whole of the Second Municipality show even greater weight on the foreign-born side, 53 percent of the whites belonging to that category. In the area's Third Ward, the traditional stronghold of Irish settlement between Julia and Thalia streets, immigrants did indeed constitute a massive 64 percent of the residents, but this heavy concentration in no way cancels the reality that Irish and German families were the clear majority in all other neighborhoods of the municipality as well, not simply in peripheral ethnic zones. The proof is on every page of the census field reports.

Analysis of the Vieux Carré's demography in 1850 reveals an equally profound misrepresentation in those traditional accounts which identify

57. "Origin of U.S. Born New Orleanians, 1850," *De Bow's Review*, XIX (September, 1855), 362–63.

the quarter as "the domicile of the proud creoles." In the First Ward, bounded by Canal and St. Louis streets, the foreign-born in that year made up 56 percent of the white population. Adding to them the 20 percent born in the United States outside of Louisiana leaves only 24 percent of the residents as possible claimants to traditional creole status, a grossly inflated figure when it is remembered that in that number must be counted the Louisiana-born children of foreigners as well as those whose ethnic antecedents were American rather than French or Spanish. Taking these additional factors into account, the best estimate would suggest a traditional creole population in the First Ward of something less than 12 percent, slightly more than half the American total. In the combined Fourth and Sixth wards, running from St. Peter to Esplanade, the very core of the old city, the Louisiana-born accounted for only 23 percent of the white population. Subtracting from that number the children born to foreign or American fathers leaves approximately 13 percent eligible for identification as traditionally creole, slightly less than the American 15 percent of whites living in the two wards. For the Vieux Carré as a whole, the profile is even more at odds with the tradition of a creole neighborhood: only 12 percent of the white population could possibly qualify as creoles, as against 16 percent unquestionably American-born. The latter figure does not even include locally born children of American fathers or those heads of family themselves descended from American ancestry.

How, then, can we square these data with the already noted contemporary acceptance of the lower city as something approaching an exclusively creole domain? The only reasonable answer would appear to be provided by adding to the white "creole" population those other parts of the community which seemed to fuse with them into a kind of Latin solidarity, the foreign-born French and Mediterranean stock plus their children and the 2,070 free persons of color in the mix, most of them natives closely allied to white creole culture and, indeed, equally entitled to the name *creole*, although it is not of them that the tradition speaks. This produces a total "creole" presence of some 56 percent of the overall Vieux Carré free population. Narrowing the focus to the section of the old city below St. Louis Street gives a comparable "creole" reading of some 57 percent. But getting there requires an obvious stretching of the data, and we are left with the hard fact of what the unmanipulated census figures document: an 1850 free population in the Vieux Carré made up of 54 percent foreign-born, 14 percent American-born, and 32 percent Louisiana-born, with little more than a third of these last meeting the traditional test of "creole" as set down in the native, all-white, French-Spanish terms of the myth.[58]

By 1860 the surge of immigration both from abroad and from other states had begun to slacken. The free population of New Orleans in the decade of the 1850s rose from 99,071 to 155,290, showing a jump in the Louisiana-born from 34,389 to 72,527, American-born from 16,081 to only 18,142, and foreign-born from 48,601 to 64,621. Thus while free native New Orleanians were increasing by 111 percent in the decade, the American-born total had grown only 13 percent and the foreign-born 33 percent. Since most of the native increase represented births within European immigrant households, the foreign cast to the city's population had, if anything, intensified.[59]

All this suggests that as early as 1850 the ethnic composition of New Orleans makes the traditional American versus creole approach to its history not invalid, surely, but certainly in need of considerable explication. The fact of foreign immigration into the post-1830s city has long been recognized, but remarkably little attention has been given to the pervasive influence of the phenomenon in the molding of its future. Ironically, one of its profound consequences was the increased acceleration of the Americanization of the city. For unlike the Latin creole, once master in this land, fearful and resentful of those who would wrest it from him to fashion yet another Anglo-Saxon dominion, the foreigners who pushed into the Crescent City after 1830 gave little time or effort to preservation of a cherished heritage. What they saw as the opportunities of their new world they found not in the lassitude of creole society but in the kinetic restlessness of American ambition. It was with American values that they identified, enthusiastically setting about to become, in effect, themselves American. Hibernian societies and turnvereins might

58. United States census schedules, 1850. These and all subsequent population computations are based on actual head counts of each page of the field reports, not on random spot checks. In the analyses of "creole" and "American" residence patterns, I have adopted the mythic usage of "creole" rather than what I have described as the more accurate historical one. It would be pointless to challenge a tradition except in its own terms. One striking feature of the tally from the Vieux Carré's sixth ward, bounded by St. Philip Street and Esplanade Avenue, is the listing of 1,060 seamen or riverboatmen born in the United States outside of Louisiana. It is not clear if these persons were generally away from the city, which would perhaps have lessened somewhat the "American" presence in the Quarter. But in any case they remain an official part of the community's population.

59. Eighth Census, 1860: Population, 615.

remain part of their lives, but it was to the new that they were committed, not the old.[60]

The creoles sensed almost immediately this terrible danger to their already diminished importance in the community. For though the American threat remained real and profound, not even it had produced the sheer numbers which now washed over them. They quickly perceived that the ease of Irish and German assimilation into the national mold would bring vast reinforcement to the camp of their old enemy, reaffirming the American stamp on the commercial section of the city rather than effacing it. This judgment was vindicated in 1852 when American leaders, bolstered by the added strength of their new Irish and German cohorts and confident in their now expanded power, fused the three municipalities into a reunited city, substantially increasing its size by eating into Jefferson Parish to absorb the suburb of Lafayette.[61]

Alarm at the possible totality of destruction envisioned in the union of their traditional antagonist with these new hordes of pro-American foreigners soon drove some in the creole ranks to a desperate counterstroke. This time their attack concentrated on the foreigner, who posed the greatest danger, with the consequence that in the 1850s the city witnessed the bizarre spectacle of creoles such as Charles Gayarré, William DeBuys, and Charles Derbigny taking to the hustings to join old-time foes in the name of Native Americanism, denouncing new arrivals from abroad in much the same terms as those with which they themselves had been excoriated years before as supposed minions of a "foreign faction." The New Orleans *Daily Creole* portrayed the Irish as criminals and political prostitutes, the Germans as anarchists and abolitionists. Through much of the 1850s, particularly after the demise of the Whigs, such xenophobic frenzy found outlet in the Know-Nothing, or American, party, the only national competition to the Democratic organization. Despite Gayarré's exertions, creole support for this nativist faction foundered on the group's rabid anti-Catholic stance, and in relatively short time the movement slipped into virtual extinction, its agenda less and less relevant in the deepening crisis of sectional controversy.[62]

---

60. Reclus, "Fragment d'un voyage à la Nouvelle Orléans," 189; Christian Roselius to J. B. Harrison, September 10, 1839, in J. Burton Harrison Papers, Manuscript Division, Library of Congress.

61. Robert C. Reinders, *End of an Era: New Orleans, 1850–1860* (New Orleans, 1964), 51–61.

62. *Daily Creole*, July 14, 17, 23, 1856.

The coming of the Civil War provided what some saw as their last chance for revival of creole supremacy. On May 5, 1861, a new journal made its appearance in New Orleans, *La Renaissance Louisianaise: Organe des Populations Franco-Américaines du Sud.* Launched by Emile Hiriart, it listed among its patrons many of the most illustrious members of creole society, including Placide Canonge, Cyprien and Numa Dufour, Charles Deléry, Victor Debouchel, Charles Gayarré, Henri Vignaud, and Dominique Rouquette. It committed passionately to a double goal, absolute victory of the Southern Confederacy and creation within it of a Louisiana restored to original estate as a community whose heart, mind, and spirit were irrevocably French. "We have lost our Gods," Hiriart explained, exhorting his readers to enshrine them once again in this final opportunity to preserve the Gallic race in its rightful dominion.[63]

For the lessons of the past were clear, Hiriart insisted. It should not have been impossible heretofore, he maintained, given the religious and political toleration of the United States Constitution, to find a way to "conciliate American citizenship with Louisiana patriotism," by which he clearly meant creole dominance. But "the gigantic pretensions of the northern element so frightened our people," he complained, "that they stopped just at the moment of equilibrium between two societies, suffocated in immobility." It was here that Louisiana had sinned most grievously. "Set in her traditions, enveloped in her memories, she lived almost entirely in her past, a stranger to the progress and the spirit of her times. Nothing so pitiful as her apathy! Nothing so culpable as her indifference!" Now was the time for redemptive action, now the moment to break the shackles of decades of submission to northern cultural and political tyranny and to build a new nation which would recognize creole ascendancy in "a unity and harmony which we never knew under the government of the United States." After better than a half-century, creolism had finally produced its rebels.[64]

But this recrudescence of Gallic nationalism almost immediately yielded precedence to a passion which swept all before it, a virulent negrophobia that quickly surfaced as the dominant theme in *La Renaissance Louisianaise* columns. Most fanatical of its protagonists was Henri Vignaud, the brilliant young literary editor of the sheet, who boasted incessantly that not a drop of Anglo-Saxon blood contaminated

63. *La Renaissance Louisianaise,* May 5, 1861.
64. *Ibid.*

his veins. He ridiculed those who dared instruct Louisiana on matters of race, admonishing them, *"Gardez le silence, messieurs—les Louisianais en savant plus que vous!"* What he presumed to know was that "slavery is the normal state of the black man. . . . White and Black do not belong to the same species."[65]

Collapse of the Confederacy came therefore as a terrible blow to zealots such as these, who had looked to the Civil War as their passport to a revived Gallic society secure in its cultural rebirth and guaranteed its rightful sway over "Americans" as well as naturally inferior blacks. What they were to experience after 1862, and even more completely after 1865, was occupation by the armed might of the North, whose military legions and swarming carpetbaggers seemed to them yet another wave of that Anglo-Saxon invasion which had swept over their lives in 1803. Some found it impossible to submit, preferring to exile themselves from their homeland forever. Vignaud, for example, settled in France, eventually to win international acclaim as one of the century's great students of the career and times of Christopher Columbus. Others, like Gayarré and Canonge, would spend the rest of their lives in mordant complaint against the obtuseness of a world which had allowed all this to happen.[66]

At war's end, Louisianians, like most of their southern brethren, succumbed to the seductions of a romantic falsification of the past, as if celebration of an imagined idyllic prewar society could in some way ease the pain of an intolerable present. It became especially important in this fantasy to transfigure the former existence among them of black bondage, what the New Orleans *Daily Crescent* in 1866 called an "institution of domestic servitude very wrongfully denominated 'African slavery.'" That "mild and patriarchal system of husbandry" had now, the *Crescent* complained, "been supplanted . . . by the more active, more eager, nay more rapacious . . . white newcomers from all points of the compass," thus depriving the "sable race, so much falsely pitied . . . [of] their lost happy condition, under the protection of their indulgent masters and mistresses." Surely, it was argued, the former slaves must understand this, "for the inhabitants of Louisiana had really, in many places, petted their black families as though they were their own flesh

---

65. Charles E. Nowell, "Henry Vignaud—Louisiana Historian," *Louisiana Historical Quarterly,* XXXVII (1955), 2; *La Renaissance Louisianaise,* September 29, 1861, February 2, 1862.
66. Nowell, "Vignaud," 2.

and blood." All such remarkable effusions obviously aimed at enticing the freedman into voluntary acceptance of a continuing domination of southern life by the white man, but it became increasingly certain with every passing day that the once servile class demanded of freedom more than a simple release from chains.[67]

Southern fears for the future deepened into near panic as Radical Republican plans for the implementation of black sharing in the political life of the region began to take shape. Gayarré poured out his own gloomy forecast to J. D. B. De Bow in a letter redolent of creole hatreds of ancient vintage: "I see no hope of salvation for us save in extraordinary financial ruin at the North. But so long as they think that they will continue to prosper by oppressing us, they will keep their stinking puritan foot on our breast under the hallucination of being able to squeeze more dollars from under our ribs."[68]

The reality proved more horrendous than the prediction. In short order came the Reconstruction acts of 1867 and the Fourteenth and Fifteenth amendments, imposing military rule on the conquered South and extending suffrage and civil rights to former slaves and free men of color. President Andrew Johnson's amnesty decree of 1866 did restore full citizenship to all but a handful of ex-Confederates, but balanced against this was a Louisiana Constitution of 1868 mandating universal desegregated education and prohibiting racial discrimination in public places. Crowning humiliation for the creoles, it excluded the French language from elementary schools and forbade publication of laws and judicial proceedings in anything other than English.[69]

Now the old flames of ethnic hatred flared anew, fanned nowhere more vigorously than in the pages of Le Carillon, a flamboyant new journal which had become the chief New Orleans protagonist of the creole cause. "French," it boasted, "is the language of civilization, which will serve forever to vanquish German mysticism and Anglo-Saxon materialism." "We must love our *nationality* as our fathers loved it," the *Carillon* insisted. "We must prove by our acts that we are not hybrid creatures, that we are a united whole!"[70]

67. *Daily Crescent,* January 5, 6, 1866.

68. Charles Gayarré to J. D. B. De Bow, July 4, 1866, in J. D. B. De Bow Papers, Duke University Library, Durham, North Carolina.

69. Joe Gray Taylor, *Louisiana Reconstructed, 1863–1877* (Baton Rouge, 1974), 147–55; Alcée Fortier, *History of Louisiana* (4 vols.; New York, 1904), IV, 106.

70. *Le Carillon,* October 3, 10, 1869.

But it soon became clear that creole concern no longer centered on such traditional cultural antagonisms. Just as with its predecessor, *La Renaissance Louisianaise,* the *Carillon*'s dedication to Gallic ascendancy quickly dissipated in a consuming preoccupation with race. Its founder, Dr. J. W. Durel, a creole physician and ex-surgeon in the Confederate army, became so obsessed by fear of black power that his columns overflowed with long citations of various scientists who held with the departed Vignaud that the hated minority constituted a biologically inferior species. The series brought quick rejoinder from Charles de la Bretonne, French-born editor of *Le Sud,* who ridiculed the *Carillon*'s position, extolled Negro intelligence, and flatly dismissed the matter as nonsensical because of what he identified as creole inheritance of mixed blood from French and Spanish ancestors themselves descended from racially questionable Moors and slaves brought into Gaul by Roman legions. This exchange provoked predictable creole rage, with Alfred Roman of *L'Abeille* challenging de la Bretonne to a duel, harmlessly consummated, while the *Carillon* intensified its war upon all those identified as champions of racial equality. Durel's slashing attacks cut particularly deep, his razor-sharp prose complemented by clever cartoons allowing even the illiterate to grasp the message. A favorite target, for example, C. C. Antoine, Negro lieutenant governor of the state, appeared regularly in his sketches pictured as an "orang-outan" mouthing the "gombo" French Durel ascribed to all native black political leaders.[71]

White fear of blacks mounted at the same time that the second invasion of "Yankee buzzards" brought new hordes into the city and state with less than accurate preconceptions as to the community's always complicated racial nuances. Those earlier northern identifications of "creole" with "mixed blood" and "mulatto" now took on infinitely greater significance as newcomers repeatedly demonstrated their continuing misunderstanding of the terms, to the ever growing consternation of the older community.[72]

The supremacy of this dread of black ascendancy was brought home vividly to the visiting Edward King when he gathered material for his work *The Great South* in the early 1870s. A "prominent historian and gentleman of most honorable Creole descent," clearly Charles Gayarré,

---

71. Edward Laroque Tinker, *Bibliography of the French Newspapers and Periodicals of Louisiana* (Worcester, 1933), 26–29.

72. Taylor, *Louisiana Reconstructed,* 267–73, 289–91; George Rose, *The Great Country; or, Impressions of America* (London, 1868), 194; Hearn, "Los Criollos," 195.

told him that "he did not know a single person who would not leave the State if means were at hand." Louisianians "were in such terror of negro government," Gayarré reported, "that they would rather accept any other despotism. A military dictator would be far preferable to them; they would go anywhere to escape the ignominy to which they were at present subjected."[73]

In desperate frustration they banded together in 1874 to form the White League for reestablishment of white supremacy, with predictable consequences of violence. Groundwork for its inception had been laid by repeated *Carillon* proclamations that racial ambiguity could no longer be tolerated: "We must be either White or Black. . . . The *Carillon* flies the flag of the whites, with the profound conviction that only within its folds can Louisiana be saved." On September 14, 1874, came the bloody clash in which members of the league attempting to seize control of the state government routed forces of the federally backed Metropolitan Police at what would become known as the Battle of Liberty Place near the foot of Canal Street. Victory proved short-lived; on September 18 United States troops restored Radical Governor William Pitt Kellogg to power.[74]

But the stress of such tensions and violence, replicated in such other parts of the state as Coushatta and Colfax, so intensified racial hypersensitivity as to revolutionize traditional concepts of creole identity. In pre–Civil War New Orleans division had been along ethnic lines— Latin versus Anglo-Saxon, native-born against foreigner. The polarity against which white creole self-awareness had shaped itself was that of the American or foreign Frenchman. Color had played no role in the confrontation. Nativity was all, because its sanction of local birth as a claim upon preferential civic power had evolved in a society which knew only white men as political persons. Those not of that category were powerless to challenge the social position of the ruling class, whatever the particular circumstance of their birth. No reason had existed, therefore, to deny any native-born child classification as a creole, whether white or black, free or slave, Latin or Yankee, given the social and political emptiness of the term. Unchallengeable white supremacy, in short, had made it possible to accommodate a pan-racial creolism.

The Civil War changed all that. Victory of the Radicals and its crea-

73. Edward King, *The Great South*, ed. W. Magruder Drake and Robert R. Jones (Baton Rouge, 1972), 32–33.
74. *Le Carillon*, July 13, 1873; Taylor, *Louisiana Reconstructed*, 291–95.

tion of a flood of sable citizens loosed upon the land what whites perceived as the menace of black domination, productive of the particularly violent reaction such racial challenge engendered. In the midst of this convulsion, the creole was caught up not simply in a general southern explosion of antiblack fanaticism, but as well in a peculiar complication which once again set him apart. The American Louisianians, or indeed any other southerners anywhere, could hold to their intolerance secure in the generally acknowledged racial purity of their own group. But the creoles added to the common white man's rejection of the black this additional spur to hatred: they might be confused with blacks.

The creole sense of vulnerability was as a consequence turned upside down. Whereas once the danger confronting them had been humiliating loss of Gallic identity to a devouring Anglo-Saxon homogenization, now it was the infinitely more horrible possibility of being consigned to debased status in the "inferior" race, identified as half-brother to the black, a sort of mixed breed stripped of blood pride as well as of any claim to social or political preferment. For the creole knew the world he now lived in to be one obsessed with the no longer settled issue of racial supremacy, in which the very suspicion of "tainted blood" guaranteed a ticket to opprobrium, contempt, and ostracism. He knew it because he had helped make it so. In such manner was the cardinal tenet of the now familiar myth born: for those so threatened, henceforth to be creole was to be white.

By the 1870s, moreover, the creole had come to recognize yet another reality. He knew, despite the dreams of *La Renaissance Louisianaise* and *Le Carillon*, that his hopes for political and cultural dominance had vanished in the relentless demographic Americanization of the city. Even the old claim to preferred status on the basis of nativity could promise no advantage, creoles of French or Spanish lineage having long since fallen into the minority by this measurement as well. In a society already committed to the Lost Cause image of a romanticized Old South of happy darkies and indulgent aristocratic slavemasters, it was perhaps inevitable that from this context of similar defeat there would emerge those who would seek consolation in the creation of yet another world and another people that never were. Let the American rule. The creole would find solace in a vision of past glories, set now in a tradition proclaiming his chivalric origins, the beauties of his Gallic tongue, the purity of his race, and the exquisite refinement of his culture. That this might require denigrating the attributes of the old American foe presented no real problem, for the sharpness of comparison would be confined to the dead days of the antebellum years. What ethnic conflict remained must now be essentially rhetorical, always subordinate to absolute unity in the Caucasian community, for nothing could be allowed to open a wedge for black advancement or to jeopardize creole acceptance in the ranks of a white majority. The inevitable pain of final surrender in this struggle of decades found its amelioration in the reassurances of an imagined past, in which the building blocks for the all-white and aristocratic portions of the creole myth slowly took shape. Erection of the full structure waited on the appearance of George Washington Cable.

Old habits, of course, could not be jettisoned everywhere and at once. As late as 1874, *Jewell's Crescent City Illustrated,* with Charles Gayarré and Alexander Dimitry among its advisers, was still describing New Orleans society in this fashion: "First, and foremost, is the creole population. All who are born here, come under this designation, without reference to the birth place of their parents." A direct steal from Benjamin Moore Norman's *Norman's New Orleans and Environs* of 1845, the excerpt's brazen pirating of that pioneering and celebrated work only adds emphasis to the willingness of *Jewell's* editors to maintain the racial and ethnic universality of antebellum definitions. By 1875, however, a Dimitry piece in one of the New Orleans journals signaled the emergence of a new disposition and pointed to the future by concentrating on the "pure white" criterion for "creole," replete with explanations of how that term might be used as an adjective to describe indigenous horses, vegetables, and, of course, Negroes.[75]

This shift from an old to a new self-image might well have gradually culminated in the full-blown creole myth so familiar today as passing years slowly added to an expanding tradition. What gave it explosive propulsion was the attention focused on creole society by George Washington Cable. Cable's *The Grandissimes* appeared in 1880, hailed by Lafcadio Hearn as "the most remarkable work of fiction ever created in the South." Coming on the heels of *Old Creole Days,* the 1879 compilation of the short stories which had followed "'Sieur George" in *Scribner's Monthly,* this sprawling tale of creole life in Louisiana just after the purchase catapulted Cable into the top rank of American liter-

---

75. *Jewell's Crescent City Illustrated* (New Orleans, 1874), 15; Hearn, "Los Criollos," 198–200.

ary figures and won him praise from such luminaries as William Dean Howells and Sidney Lanier. It set off a storm of protest in creole New Orleans.[76]

Part of the problem was that Cable was New Orleans–born, and though he had no claim to French or Spanish ancestry, having descended from Virginia–New England stock, it might be presumed that he wrote with accuracy about the city of his birth. This probability infuriated the upper echelons of creole New Orleans, for they were appalled at the picture of themselves in Cable's pages. The plot of *The Grandissimes* need not concern us here—what matters is the novel's searing representation of creole society as an aberration of history, committed to a dead past long ago abandoned by enlightened and progressive communities of the world. Its obeisance is to white supremacy and meaningless family pride, while its hallmarks are indolence, ignorance, cruelty, superstition, and hypocrisy. The consequences of a racial morality which condones miscegenation yet penalizes those whom it produces find graphic portrayal in the tragic life of the mulatto brother of the creole protagonist, while the horrors of slavery seethe in the history of Bras Coupé, a black whose heroic and dignified death dishonors those responsible for it. These sweeping condemnations of their culture were made even more reprehensible in creole eyes by Cable's having them speak an English dialect which they described as utterly unintelligible and little better than gibberish, more the speech of black Virginia or South Carolina field hands than their own, closer to the "orang-outan" barbarisms made familiar in the pages of the *Carillon* than to anything heard in their parlors.[77]

Their dismay intensified with the appearance in 1884 of Cable's *The Creoles of Louisiana*, for despite the work's endorsement of the all-white definition of creole, it was shot through with implications of pervasive racial impurity among those bearing the name. Later that year came his essay on New Orleans in the ninth edition of the *Encyclopedia Britannica*, equally suggestive of something less than white purity of creole blood and inescapably direct in its tracing of creole origins back

76. *Item*, September 27, 1880; Arlin Turner, *George W. Cable* (Baton Rouge, 1966), 89–104.

77. J. C. Delavigne, "Critique du dernier ouvrage de M. Geo. W. Cable," *Comptes Rendus*, March, 1883, p. 319; J. L. Peytavin, "Refutation des erreurs de M. Geo. W. Cable au sujet des créoles," *ibid.*, July, 1886, p. 126.

to "such wives as could be gathered haphazard from the ranks of Indian allies, African slave cargoes, and the inmates of French houses of correction." Little wonder that most creoles interpreted this as malicious scandal visited upon them presumably out of Cable's lust for Yankee dollars. That he was a native son and was yet willing, as Grace King put it, "[to stab] the city in the back . . . in a dastardly way to please the Northern press" made his crime, in their eyes, unforgivable.[78]

Beneath all this, however, lay a sharper goad to creole hatreds. Cable was not, after all, the first or only critic of their manners and customs, and he was certainly not the sole challenge to their claim of racial purity. The acerbic French gadfly Dr. Charles Testut had published in 1872 Le Vieux Salomon, like his Reconstruction newspaper L'Equité a violently pro-black assault on creole society. Scribner's Monthly, Cable's publisher, had carried in 1873 a short story by Anne Porter which Lafcadio Hearn read as a faithful indictment of creole cruelty and decadence, while his own pieces for the New Orleans Item in the late 1870s frequently centered on portrayals of creole personality which resemble nothing so much as the ethnic jokes of a later day. At much the same time, a string of novels by Dr. Alfred Mercier, founder of the Athénée Louisianais, appraised creole life in such dismal accents as to make Cable seem almost complimentary. Even Cable's harshest critics, moreover, frequently shared his appreciation of creole character. Grace King, for example, once described a particularly unsatisfactory chef as being "so stupid & so creole" and on another occasion reported to her mother, "I do not think any of C[able]'s creations ever made more grammatical mistakes and mispronunciations in the course of a half-hour than de Rolades [her cousin's fiancé] did. . . . [Annie] looked about as dirty and Creolish as did the Dr."[79]

78. Encyclopedia Britannica, 9th ed. (1884), 405; Grace King, Memories of a Southern Woman of Letters (New York, 1932), 60. Whatever his motive, it is clear that Cable was less than forthright in his treatment of many aspects of the creole question. The original draft of his manuscript "Creole Slave Songs," for example, contains much more positive imputation of creole racial mixture than he allowed himself in his published work. He speaks there of "low white creoles—not milk white or lily white or even probably white, but just white enough to be ten thousand times better than a negro," a passage which is missing from the Century Magazine version of April, 1886, where one finds the softer reference to "many a creole—white as well as other tints." The manuscript is in Cable Papers.

79. Charles Testut, Le Vieux Salomon (New Orleans, 1872); Anne Porter, "Ninon," Scribner's Monthly, XVII (1878), 372–77; Brisland, Hearn, I, 203; Item, September 27, 28, October 5, November 13, 1879; George F. Reinecke, "Alfred Mercier, French Novel-

What set Cable apart from all the rest was a series of differences which made him the principal focus of creole bitterness. Most important, perhaps, his international fame gave him an audience of incalculable scope, when no more than a handful of readers outside Louisiana had likely ever heard of Testut, Mercier, or even, as yet, of Lafcadio Hearn. In creole judgment, then, Cable had not only grossly libeled creole life and exposed them to identification as "half-breeds" and cultural paupers, he had done it on a world stage, so effectively that New Orleans was frequently beset by tourists roaming its streets, one of Cable's books in hand, seeking out the haunts of their favorite characters. Maddeningly, creoles heard it said that he had "discovered" them, as if all their existence had waited on his pen to give them validation, and then, to their disgrace. Equally as galling, they suspected Cable of profiting handsomely by his villainy, at a time when most New Orleanians felt themselves still in almost unbearable economic and social distress. Not even the end of Reconstruction had much lifted their spirits or their fortunes, Gayarré in 1879 lamenting that "the curse of God is upon this benighted and rotten community." Never a man to discount his own talents, he found it both demeaning and infuriating to see Cable fawned on and enriched while he and others of his kind struggled in poverty and neglect.[80]

And, finally, there remains the distinction that creole intuition had properly perceived Cable's attack to be more than simply an incidental condemnation of a society repugnant to his personal sensibilities. Though he did not confide it to them, Cable would later confess that he had indeed "meant to make *The Grandissimes* as truly a political work as it ever has been called—not a *party* thing, but a *principle* thing."[81]

The full dimension of that determination became finally apparent with the 1885 publication of Cable's "Freedman's Case in Equity," an

---

ist of New Orleans," in *In Old New Orleans,* ed. Kenneth Holditch (Jackson, Miss., 1983), 145–76; Grace King to May King McDowell, February 17, 1895, King to Sarah Ann King, April 17, 1886, both in Grace King Papers, Louisiana State University Library, Baton Rouge.

80. Arlin Turner, introduction to George W. Cable, *Creoles and Cajuns* (New York, 1959), 1; *Critic,* VI (December 11, 1886), 297; Pennell, *Life and Letters of Joseph Pennell,* I, 54; Charles Gayarré to J. C. Delavigne, February 27, 1878, February 9, March 12, 1879, Gayarré to John Dimitry, November 14, 1881, all in John Minor Wisdom Collection, Tulane University Library.

81. George Washington Cable, "My Politics" (Manuscript notebook in Cable Papers).

impassioned defense of the black in American society and a call for acceptance of his enjoyment of public civil rights equal to those of all
other citizens. Although the protest pointedly avoided support of social
integration or racial mixture, it vigorously demanded an end to the reality "that there is scarcely one public relation of life in the South where
the [black] is not arbitrarily and unlawfully compelled to hold toward
the white man the attitude of an alien, a menial, and a probable repro-
bate, by reason of his race and color." [82]

The brief set off a storm of controversy, challenging as it did a whole
body of social conventions both North and South. Its argument struck
not only at the white man's nonsectional marmoreal conceit as to racial
superiority but even more directly at a dominant southern commitment
to a particular vision of the future. For if Cable's position had any merit,
it followed inescapably that there could be no room in southern society
for that solution of its postwar problems which many such as Gayarré
and Canonge had been propagating for years. Faced with the immov-
able presence of the Negro, they spoke for an accommodation in which
the black man would come to realize that his only true reliance lay in the
goodwill of the southern white, not the duplicitous seductions of exploi-
tative northerners. A restoration of the prewar black-white partnership
might thus be effected, with the old master class still in control and the
black man provided for in a paternalistic grant of freedom without citizenship. Cable's brief proclaimed that what Gayarré and Canonge and
others like them saw as their only deliverance from the hell of racial
equality constituted in fact a renunciation of every fundamental precept
of justice and reason. [83]

Though no overt linkage ties "The Freedman's Case in Equity" to
his fictional work, it now seemed clear that Cable in *The Grandissimes*
had used the creole experience to illustrate graphically the evils which
he held must flow inevitably from a society grounded in the abomina-
tion of racial arrogance and social injustice, with a consequent debasement of values so profound as to condemn itself to ignorance, moral
insensitivity, and cultural impoverishment. This was the message that
his "haunted heart" would give to the world, repeated now in explicit

82. George Washington Cable, "The Freedman's Case in Equity," *Century Magazine*, XXIX (January, 1885), 409–18.
83. See Gayarré's appeal for the alliance of "honest whites and blacks." *Times*, May
20, 1874. Canonge preached much the same gospel in his introduction to Hinton Rowan
Helper, *Nojoque* (New Orleans, 1867), iv–v.

appeal to the nation lest in its disregard of the freedman's rights it allow itself to decay into that morbidity he had so often discerned in creole society, though he made no specific reference to that community in the brief itself.

To many of its members, however, the implication leaped from Cable's every word and came as proof that he had deliberately used them to further what had always been his real purpose, advancement of the monstrous plan for black aggrandizement now revealed in this latest obscenity. Whereas before they had felt isolated in victimization by their tormentor, now they could expect to find allies in those millions of whites all over the country who indignantly rejected Cable's prescription for social justice. As national criticism of the "Freedman's" brief widened, the New Orleans press intensified its assault on him in terms which reminded a friend of those once used against abolitionists in pre-war days. It required little acumen to determine where to strike. Who could not be persuaded that a man capable of such vile and destructive nonsense had also been miscreant in falsifying the realities of creole life to serve these same sinister purposes? What better time to pose against Cable's calumnies the "true" picture of the creole in unsullied whiteness and aristocratic superiority of spirit and cultural richness?[84]

Hitherto strangely silent through all this tempest, Gayarré now moved quickly to the attack, his interjection into the fray precipitated by personal considerations of overwhelming intensity. As he and Alexander Dimitry had grown old together, Gayarré seemingly more and more came to see in his longtime friend the personification of the character and fate of creole society. Before him burned the constant image of this connoisseur of French civilization and culture, master of the history, language, and literature of many nations, once vigorous and central in the affairs of the state, now blind, impotent, and impoverished. When death finally touched his formerly brilliant companion in late 1882, it came with Dimitry clutching him to his breast, sightlessly running tired fingers over his forehead and whispering, "Charley, don't forget me!"[85]

Gayarré had dismissed Cable as no more than a malevolent, ignorant dwarf, until January, 1885, brought two events of shattering import. First came "The Freedman's Case in Equity," with what he saw as its disgusting negrophilia and program for destruction; then, to his as-

84. Marion Baker to Cable, March 9, 1885, in Cable Papers.
85. Gayarré to John Dimitry, November 22, 1882, in Wisdom Collection.

tonishment, a report that Cable had taken to defending himself against charges of knowing nothing at all about creoles with assertions that everything he had written about them rested on information from Alexander Dimitry. This ascription of hateful racial and cultural heresy to the archetype of creole manhood struck an appalled Gayarré as the blackest of Cable's sins, and it now seemed to him that his dying colleague's plea for constancy called not for remembrance simply of an old comrade but of all that they both had cherished in the creole past. "Well, I did not forget!" he wrote Dimitry's son, to explain why now at last he had taken up arms against Cable, the inescapable thrust being that true recollection must finally embrace far more than a single lamented friend.[86]

His efforts soon proved to be prodigious. A two-part series from his pen in the New Orleans *Times-Democrat* during January, 1885, unabashedly reaffirmed classic racist arguments against Cable's "Freedman's Case in Equity" and reminded his readers how this same supposed expert had so fallaciously and maliciously savaged creole society. A week later saw him before the Athénée Louisianais delivering an address titled "La race Latine en Louisiane," which treated his audience to dramatic recitation of the richness of their French and Spanish heritage, with a glowing appraisal of the superiorities of creole culture. A second delivery of the address received such plaudits that the old man, now eighty, decided to give over a whole evening to particular assault on Cable's work, which he did in a lecture entitled "*Les Grandissimes*," a scathing indictment of what he portrayed as the novel's inaccuracy and infelicities of style. Culmination of this tireless campaign came on April 25, 1885, with Gayarré's English-language address at Tulane University, "The Creoles of History and the Creoles of Romance," in which all those elements fundamental to a fully developed creole myth finally fall into place. Here is the meticulous account of the derivation of the term *creole* so central to the faith, with constant reaffirmation of the "pure white" blood of all those entitled to the name, the patient explanation of the use of *creole* as an adjective, the glorification of the "aristocratic" and "chivalrous" lineage of creole stock, and the recital of the unparalleled contributions of the race to Louisiana's past.[87]

86. Gayarré to John Dimitry, February 1, 1885, in Wisdom Collection.

87. There is some evidence of private recrimination of Cable by Gayarré, not surprisingly. See, for example, Marion Baker to Cable, September 17, 1884, in Cable Papers; *Times-Democrat*, January 11, 18, March 25, 1885; *Comptes Rendus*, March, 1885, pp.

Despite Gayarré's indisputable gifts as an historian, the speech abounds in reckless assessments of the role of creoles and peninsulares in the Spanish colonial empire, designed obviously to support the notion of creole nobility and accomplishment. Given the understandable determination to destroy Cable's projection of the ugliness of creole life, such exaggeration and distortion seem natural enough in the argument of a champion passionately committed to a given set of subjective values. But so intense was Gayarré's obsession that he moved far beyond these predictable prejudices, casting off all sense of historical responsibility to proclaim in a startling declaration that from colonial times forward racial mixture had been unknown in New Orleans society and that "Alpine heights . . . [had always existed] between the blacks, or colored, and the natives of France, as well as the natives of Louisiana, or creoles." He must certainly have been aware that countless members of the audience knew from their own experience that this was a lie and indeed that some were probably privy to the fact that he had himself fathered a child in 1825 by a free woman of color.[88]

The impression carried away from a reading of this speech today gives us perhaps a clue to the explanation of this otherwise unbelievable flaunting of notorious falsehood. For though Gayarré's remarks clearly aim at glorification of creole culture, their focus returns always to the bugbear of race. Every theme finds its way eventually to Cable's falsely imputed advocacy of racial fusion, suggesting that this fixation on color had now so possessed New Orleans white society that even such blatant hypocrisy as that of Gayarré's performance could be accepted as an understandable necessity of the times. Redolent more of racial fears than of ethnic pride, in such fashion did the creole myth receive its definitive promulgation.

This identification of creolism with racial purity and an implicit white supremacy so met the emotional needs of a distraught society that it defied rational examination. In a convoluted reference to the archenemy, Grace King explained her position, for example, by insisting to Richard Watson Gilder, editor of *Century Magazine*, that "Cable proclaimed his preference for colored people over white and assumed the inevitable superiority—according to his theories—of the quadroons

---

78–100; *L'Abeille*, March 24, 1885. The Tulane address was published in pamphlet form by C. E. Hopkins (New Orleans, 1885).

88. Edward M. Socola, "Charles Gayarré: A Biography" (Ph.D. dissertation, University of Pennsylvania, 1954), 320–21.

over the Creoles." Her feelings ran so deep on the race question that publication of Gayarré's reminiscences of life on an antebellum sugar plantation led to a temporary alienation from the old man because of her outrage at a passage in his account which described cruel treatment of blacks by a white master.[89]

Others of like mind banded together in 1886 to organize the Creole Association of Louisiana for the promotion of "Mutual Aid, Assistance, and Protection" of its members and to disseminate "knowledge concerning the true origin and real character . . . of the Creole race of Louisiana." Significantly, membership was limited to "white persons of age and good standing." Nowhere is the changed focus of creole identity more clearly highlighted than in the speech of Vice-President Charles Villeré to the organizational meeting of the group, reflecting as it does an attitude which old warriors such as Joseph Rodriguez and General Gainnié would have found utterly incomprehensible. In paragraph after paragraph, Villeré develops the theme of ethnic unity, heaping fulsome recognition and praise on a host of men claimed as compatriots but actually numbered among the principal architects of the Americanization of Louisiana at the expense of creole interests. The whole climaxes, to be sure, with reiteration of a cry evocative of ancient rivalries: "We are battling for our rights, and under a name scoffed at, ridiculed, blackened, tortured, deformed, caricatured. . . . This is our soil. We are in the house of our fathers!" But no one listening could doubt the identity of those against whom that house must now be defended: "On the Fourteenth of September . . . Creole boys rushed to the front and vied in heroism with veterans of many a hard fought battle. They . . . stamped that day on the seal of Time!" "The Fourteenth of September" commemorates the 1874 Battle of Liberty Place, when the White League had warred with the Metropolitan Police in the name of white supremacy.[90]

In the decades which followed, the creole cause triumphed in at least two major respects. The flights of fancy found in Gayarré's *Creoles of History and Creoles of Romance* quickly became so universally accepted as truth that they found eventual ratification even in the pages of otherwise competent professional historians, providing the substance of what has been described here as the creole myth. The last years of the nineteenth century, moreover, established precisely that order of society

89. King, *Memories*, 60; Robert Bush, "Charles Gayarré and Grace King: Letters of a Louisiana Friendship," *Southern Literary Journal*, VII (Fall, 1974), 122–27.
90. *Charter, By-Laws & Rules of the Creole Association of Louisiana* (New Orleans, 1886), 4, 14; *Times-Democrat*, June 21, 1886.

so warmly embraced by Gayarré and Canonge, largely because creole racism made up but part of a larger consensus within the whole white community. A "separate but equal" statute in 1890 gave legal sanction in Louisiana to the ever-widening exclusion of blacks from previously integrated public accommodations, the "grandfather clause" of the Constitution of 1898 initiated a series of political devices which eventually effectively stripped away their rights of suffrage, and legislative Act 87 of 1907 decreed that "concubinage between a person of the Caucasian or white race and a person of the negro or black race is hereby made a felony." A twentieth-century Louisiana State Court of Appeals in due time ruled that "when a person is called a creole this evidences an absence of any negro blood," and the Louisiana Historical Society in 1915 sealed the question by proclaiming that "the definition of 'creole' as stated by Prof. [Alcée] Fortier is the correct one," that definition, of course, being the one sanctified by Gayarré. Finally, the degree to which the memory of antebellum reality had been extinguished in the enveloping acceptance of fantasy emerges clearly in this excerpt from a New Orleans newspaper editorial of 1922: "Here in Louisiana a 'creole' has never been anything but a descendant of the original French and Spanish settlers born in Louisiana instead of in France or Spain. . . . One dictionary says that the term was once applied to negroes born here to distinguish them from negroes brought from Africa. We have never heard it used in that sense. Such usage must have died out as soon as the slave trade closed." [91]

No comparable victory sustained the faltering fortunes of creole society itself. The late nineteenth century saw a continuing dissipation of the enspiriting Gallic tone which had once been the very essence of the city, though some waged courageous battle to keep it vibrant. None did so more patiently or with more grace and charm than Dr. Alfred Mercier, founder of the Athénée Louisianais for the preservation of the city's French heritage and its guiding spirit from 1876 to his death in 1894. [92]

Neither the success of the Athénée over the years in publishing its *Comptes Rendus,* a collection of literary and scientific papers of varying merit, nor the social éclat of its annual conferring of literary awards in

91. Marc-Etienne Ficatier, "Les Louisianais français: Créoles et Acadiens," *Revue de Psychologie des Peuples* (Le Havre, 1957), 19; Henry Rightor, "The Creoles," in *Standard History of New Orleans, Louisiana,* ed. Rightor (Chicago, 1900), 184–95; *State ex. rel. Cousin* v. *Louisiana State Board of Health* (138 So. 2d 829); *Publications of the Louisiana Historical Society,* VII (1915), 54; *Item,* March 26, 1922.

92. *Comptes Rendus,* July, 1894, p. 102.

the hall of the Union Français blinded him to the reality that even if creole language and customs were to be preserved, they would never again be more than a nostalgic remnant in the midst of an American city. From the very beginning of its existence, the Athénée drew only meager support from the general creole population, which Mercier once described as a "touchy group, little used to exerting themselves in any manner in the search for perfection." Without the slightest belief in creole "aristocracy" or cultural superiority, he found satisfaction in the simple joy of keeping alive the endangered use of the French tongue. Hopes for more than that, he insisted, were delusions.[93]

Matters grew progressively worse over the years. Mercier's old friend Athanase Nicolopolus in 1888 reported that he had gone bankrupt in his French bookstore and had also been forced to close down his paper *L'Opinion* because of lack of patronage: "No one reads in Louisiana! There is here a prodigious apathy toward everything addressed to the intellect. Do you believe it? I scarcely sell one book per month!" Mercier could indeed believe it, immersed as he was in daily struggle to keep the *Comptes Rendus* in print. Attendance at Athénée meetings continued to dwindle alarmingly, by the 1890s falling generally to fewer than fifteen at the gatherings. Visitors from France at the turn of the century often expressed delight at finding in New Orleans a society which reminded them of home, but their comments revealed as well a sense of how small the circle of the "cultivated class" of creoles had become.[94]

True to his motto of "Allons Toujours!" Mercier managed to ensure the Athénée's survival despite his own failing health until death claimed him on May 12, 1894, in his seventy-eighth year. Later stalwarts such as Alcée Fortier sustained the organization in the next century, keeping it fitfully alive until its disappearance in the late 1980s. But Mercier knew, as others knew, that by the 1890s what might be called "creole society" was already an anachronism in the city where once it had been the vital present, more foreign even to the old quarter than were the swarming Sicilians now crowding into its streets and alleyways.[95]

93. Alfred Mercier Diary, April 26, 1891, in Tulane University Library.

94. *Ibid.*, July 10, November 2, 1888, October 24, 1891; *Comptes Rendus*, May, 1897, pp. 65–67; Jules Huret, *En Amerique: De New York à la Nouvelle Orléans* (Paris, 1904), 336.

95. Mercier Diary, October 24, 1891, July 23, 1893; *Comptes Rendus*, July, 1894, pp. 1–2.

In the early morning of February 11, 1895, Charles Gayarré slipped from semiconsciousness into the stillness of death, the brightest flame of creole identity extinguished forever. His devoted friend Grace King sadly joined the funeral cortege from the little house on North Prieur where he had eked out the painfully humiliating last years of life, and it seemed to her as the carriages rattled through the cold, wet, foreign-looking streets, which the judge had walked for more than half their existence, that they were "burying all the early colonial history of the state." The coffin came finally to the vestibule of the cathedral, resting there at the focus of all those monuments to the Latin heritage which he had so passionately defended. As the mournful cadences of the dead march poured forth, the great doors were thrown open to an interior ablaze with gleaming candles.

Inside, the church was empty.[96]

96. Grace King to May King McDowell, February 17, 1895, in King Papers. Robert Bush, in his biography of King, renders the quotation as "burying all the early *cultural* history of the state." Given the formidable challenge of King's handwriting, that is perhaps the proper reading, but not my own.

PART III

Franco-Africans and African-Americans

Introduction

The pattern of race relations in New Orleans generally strikes American scholars as being either an exception to or an exotic variant of behavior found elsewhere in the United States. As a result, social scientists have not discovered much relevance in it for those living in more "typical" environs. Yet if we expand our vision beyond our national borders, New Orleans may be seen not as an exceptional case to be ignored but as a significant counterpoint against which to measure the rest of a deviant North America. Almost all of the New World's slave societies, whatever the origins of their colonizers, developed three-tiered, multiracial social structures in which a class of marginal status and frequently mixed origin was inserted between blacks and whites. In its early years, New Orleans replicated that broader history while the rest of the United States (with a few notable exceptions) constructed a rigid, two-tiered structure that drew a single unyielding line between the white and nonwhite.

If New Orleans was culturally, demographically, and economically part of the French and Spanish empires during its formative years, it was legally and institutionally part of the United States during the nineteenth and twentieth centuries. Because of its association with these two worlds, the city's history has much to tell us about both. It is an intellectual hinge connecting the two interracial systems that appeared in the Western Hemisphere. The evolution of race relations in New Orleans also speaks to the timeless issues of ethnogenesis, the process of assimilation, and the development of social leadership.

Moreover, the Americanization of New Orleans was more than just a struggle between Americans and creoles. It also involved, for nearly a century, the curious coexistence of a three-tiered Caribbean racial structure alongside its two-tiered American counterpart in an ethnically divided city. Only the transformations wrought by massive European im-

189

migration and a brutal Civil War assured the disappearance of the city's traditional, if unorthodox, racial order. It was a turbulent history that left its mark on national events and continues to influence modern New Orleans.

Divided in the antebellum period by color, culture, law, occupation, and neighborhood, nonwhites in New Orleans faced the challenge of Reconstruction with a sense of their own distinctive histories, a dawning perception of shared racial concerns, and an imposed awareness of mutual interest. Whatever their background and persistent differences, their role as a single group—as one-half of New Orleans' rapidly Americanizing racial order—was inescapable.

The imposition of Jim Crow at the dawn of the twentieth century symbolized the ascendance of the new order and accelerated the submergence of ethnicity—both black and white—as a stark racial dualism held uncontested sway. The Redeemer constitution of 1879, the disfranchising constitution of 1898, and the subsequent avalanche of segregationist legislation institutionalized a rigid system of social subordination. In an age of racial totalitarianism, the rapid assimilation of white immigrants and the fierce determination of white creoles to link their identity to a biological rather than a cultural heritage sharply demonstrated how Americanized white New Orleans had become.[1]

Black New Orleanians also forged a greater sense of racial unity and

---

1. The impact of New Orleans' peculiar and evolving racial order on the assimilation of white immigrants is a large and vital topic that begs for scholarly attention. On one hand, the presence of large numbers of blacks among the "host" population meant that the immigrants assumed the identity (although not exclusively and not necessarily willingly) of whites as soon as they came ashore. The high tide of antebellum immigration coincided with rising sectional and racial tensions, creating additional pressure to take up the cudgels of racial identity to enhance the immigrants' own position and status in New Orleans society. Job competition and the growing fear of servile insurrection, for example, led to the proliferation of legal racial restrictions—especially in the 1850s—designed to secure both the peace and the economic well-being of the newcomers. Abolition of slavery and Reconstruction accelerated developments already well under way. Yet, on the other hand, the color line was not an absolute barrier. Contact between immigrants and blacks was frequent and close in New Orleans' congested neighborhoods, and a one-dimensional portrait of unrelieved tension does not do justice to the complexity of the situation— especially among particular groups, such as the Germans and Italians, or in particular locales, such as the downtown creole quarters.

For some initial exploration of the topic, see Randall M. Miller, "The Enemy Within: Some Effects of Foreign Immigration on Antebellum Southern Cities," *Southern Studies,* XXIV (1985), 30–53; Ira Berlin and Herbert Gutman, "Natives and Immigrants, Free Men and Slaves: Urban Workingmen in the Antebellum South," *American Historical Review,* LXXXVIII (1983), 1175–1200. For Reconstruction and the late nineteenth century, see Ted Tunnell, *Crucible of Reconstruction: War, Radicalism, and Race in Louisi-*

solidarity, but the process was hardly identical. Long-standing cultural differences remained well defined because, unlike the whites, there was no continuing stream of immigrants to blur the line between creole and American. Most important, the rush to establish uncompromising standards of racial "purity" and unity may have offered some privilege for whites (for those white creoles whose own heritage might have been questioned, it represented flight from the abyss), but post-Reconstruction New Orleans hardly extended the same rewards to those championing their blackness. Black leaders recognized that the architects of the color line wanted to subordinate them. Acceptance meant resignation; defiance connoted hope. In resisting the color line, black New Orleanians sought alternatives to the emerging Jim Crow order. Though seemingly inexorable, the Americanization of black New Orleans was thus a slower, more contested, and somewhat more uneven process than the one taking place on the other side of the great racial divide.

This black assertiveness and resistance may well account for the appearance of some of the harsher aspects of race relations in postbellum New Orleans. It also sets the New Orleans experience apart from those other American towns—most notably Charleston—where a three-tiered racial framework also made an appearance. The sheer novelty of such a superstructure in mainland North America, as well as the prevailing racial paradigm, however, has produced a tendency to consider all such phenomena simply a single deviation from the expected norm. The free people of color of New Orleans and Charleston are often spoken of in a single breath, their experiences merged, their status and culture undifferentiated.[2] Taken on their own terms, though, it is their differences that are most striking.

---

ana, 1862–1877 (Baton Rouge, 1984), 162–63; Peyton McCrary, *Abraham Lincoln and Reconstruction: The Louisiana Experiment* (Princeton, 1978), 56, 96, 249–50; David Paul Bennetts, "Black and White Workers: New Orleans, 1880–1900" (Ph.D. dissertation, University of Illinois at Urbana-Champaign, 1972), 313–92; George E. Cunningham, "The Italian, a Hindrance to White Solidarity in Louisiana, 1877–1898," *Journal of Negro History*, L (1965), 22–36. Louis Armstrong's autobiography, *Satchmo: My Life in New Orleans* (New York, 1954), may be the most accurate treatment of the complicated—sometimes friendly, sometimes hostile—relationship between immigrants and black New Orleanians. Two recent labor histories, Daniel Rosenberg, *New Orleans Dockworkers: Race, Labor, and Unionism, 1892–1923* (Albany, 1988) and, especially, Eric Arnesen, *Waterfront Workers of New Orleans: Race, Class, and Politics, 1863–1923* (New York, 1991), emphasize the point.

2. See, for example, Joel Williamson, *New People: Miscegenation and Mulattoes in the United States* (New York, 1980), 15, 27, 41; Eugene D. Genovese, *Roll, Jordan, Roll:*

The cities and their demographics provide the first hint of contrast. A booming commercial metropolis, antebellum New Orleans possessed a population, free and slave, that dwarfed that of South Carolina's stagnating provincial backwater. At its peak in 1860, Charleston had roughly 3,200 free people of color (divided between approximately 2,400 mulattoes and 800 blacks); yet New Orleans' free people of color numbered nearly 20,000 in 1840 (when Charleston had but 1,500), and, after two decades of precipitous decline, a community of nearly 11,000 remained in 1860. Even in that latter year, New Orleans had more mulatto slaves (3,500) and free blacks (2,700) than Charleston had free mulattoes (2,400). Charleston's free people of color also accounted, between 1800 and 1860, for no more than 5 to 8 percent of the city's total population. Although rapidly growing New Orleans fell into that range by 1860 (6 percent), free people of color represented nearly 29 percent of the Crescent City's population in 1810, 23 percent in 1820, 25 percent in 1830, and 18 percent as late as 1840. They composed a fully articulated community, with a complex class structure, that occupied far more than the fringes of society. Providing valuable services in the local economy and militia into the 1830s, they constituted a community worlds apart from that of Charleston.[3]

The World the Slaves Made (New York, 1972), 408, 409, 412, and Genovese, "The Slave States of North America," in Neither Slave nor Free: The Freedmen of African Descent in the Slave Societies of the New World, ed. David W. Cohen and Jack P. Greene (Baltimore, 1972), 269–70, 272; August Meier, "The Nineteenth-Century Southern Free Colored Elite: New Sources, New Views," Reviews in American History, XIV (June 1986), 222–25; George M. Frederickson, "Brown History," Reviews in American History, IX (December 1981), 436. Ira Berlin, Slaves Without Masters: The Free Negro in the Antebellum South (New York, 1974), 108–32, does note the exceptionalism of south Louisiana in the early nineteenth century but does not pursue the implications or continuing effects of such exceptionalism into the late antebellum era. Berlin also occasionally loses sight of that exceptionalism and displays a tendency to make generalizations about free people of color on the basis of examples taken from Charleston. See Slaves Without Masters, 58, 60, 65, 73, 214–16, 282–84.

3. On Charleston, see E. Horace Fitchett, "The Free Negro in Charleston, South Carolina" (Ph.D. dissertation, University of Chicago, 1950); Marina Wikramanyake, A World in Shadow: The Free Black in Ante-Bellum South Carolina (Columbia, S.C., 1973); and Michael P. Johnson and James L. Roark, Black Masters: A Free Family of Color in the Old South (New York, 1984). For New Orleans, see Donald E. Everett, "The Free Persons of Color in New Orleans, 1803–1865" (Ph.D. dissertation, Tulane University, 1952); David C. Rankin, "The Forgotten People: Free People of Color in New Orleans, 1850–1870" (Ph.D. dissertation, Johns Hopkins University, 1976); Anna Lee West Stahl, "The Free Negro in Ante Bellum Louisiana," Louisiana Historical Quarterly, XXV (April 1942), 301–96; and Herbert E. Sterkx, The Free Negro in Ante-Bellum Louisiana

That sense of difference was significantly reinforced by the difference in the two cities' core cultures and the persistence of New Orleans' creole and French presence throughout the antebellum era. In the more fully Americanized Charleston, the overwhelmed free people of color displayed an intense color consciousness that they institutionalized in the Brown Fellowship Society and developed pretensions that prevented the nonwhite elite from even sitting with blacks in church services. When they used the phrase *our people,* they described a free mulatto aristocracy whose members identified with one another, maintained their distance from slaves and blacks (whether free or not), and staked out a middle ground between black and white. And when Charleston's blacks organized in response to the Brown Fellowship Society, they created a Humane Brotherhood specifically for "free Dark men." [4]

It was different in New Orleans. Those Americanizing tendencies were certainly present (and destined to grow stronger in time), but the population's primary divisions were rooted in ethnocultural differences, not simply color or legal status. The Crescent City, for example, lacked an analogue for the Brown Fellowship Society. When the elite among the creoles of color wished to express a sense of institutional exclusivity, they organized on the basis of class and profession, creating the Société d'Economie. The nonelite reaction among nonwhite creoles produced only a Société des Artisans—an organization hardly defined by color and one that attracted individuals such as the well-to-do (later Parisian) poet Victor Sejour, who enjoyed satirizing the exclusive pretensions of the upper class. New Orleans' Franco-Africans, whatever the aristocratic notions of some, did not neatly categorize themselves by color; and the city's black Anglo-Americans, with their own organizational network, similarly failed to replicate the Charleston experience.

More important, there was outright resistance among New Orleans' black creoles to ascribing status on the basis of race or color. Writing at the height of the Jim Crow mania in the early twentieth century, the fair-skinned black creole Rodolphe Desdunes still referred to those debating the merits of "passing" as persons who were mesmerized by a "foolish controversy over the color of the skin." Moreover, when Desdunes referred to "our people" in his history *Nos hommes et notre histoire,* he proudly included among his pantheon of heroes the very dark-skinned

(Rutherford, N.J., 1972). See also Leonard P. Curry, *The Free Black in Urban America, 1800–1850* (Chicago, 1981).

4. Johnson and Roark, *Black Masters,* 203–27.

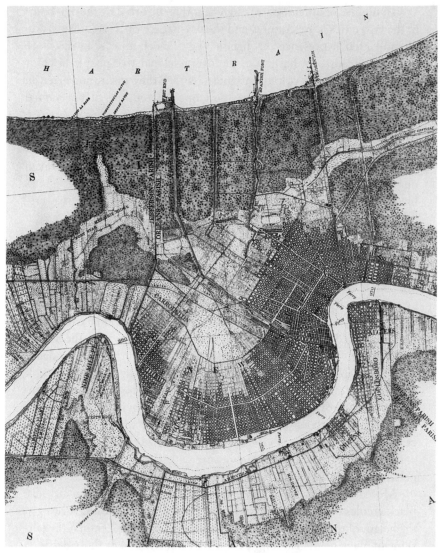

Drawn by the Mississippi River Commission in 1896, this map shows the still-restricted nature of development in New Orleans at the turn of the twentieth century. Confined by river, lake, and swamp, the city had changed very little since the Civil War, as is evident from a comparison with the 1863 map drawn for the Union army.

Courtesy Louisiana Collection, Howard-Tilton Memorial Library, Tulane University, New Orleans

musician Edmond Dédé, Civil War luminary André Cailloux (who prided himself on being the blackest man in New Orleans), and Madame Marie Couvent, "a black African woman [who] was perhaps a slave in her youth." By providing in her will for the establishment of a school for, as Desdunes put it, "our black orphans," this "noble woman" had placed the "Creole people of color" in her debt.[5]

The differences in the cities, their demographics, their cultural roots, and their enduring foreign ties meant that the free people of color in Charleston and New Orleans necessarily developed different perspectives and worldviews. If those in South Carolina never presumed to ask for the rights of whites and adopted an accommodationist survival strategy that was rooted in their small numbers, color consciousness, and tenuous hold on freedom, a good number of New Orleans' free people of color chose another path. A strain of creole radicalism, more assertive and independent, with broader horizons and self-confidence, emerged to challenge American racial conceptions and the imposition of Jim Crow. It was no accident that Homer Plessy came from New Orleans and not Charleston.

The striking character of New Orleans' black community becomes clear as Joseph Logsdon and Caryn Cossé Bell trace its ethnocultural fault line through the seismic upheaval of Civil War, Reconstruction, and Redemption. They document the persistent split between the Americans and the creoles, paying particular attention to the latter's desire to maintain their peculiar identity, their resistance to Americanization, and their ongoing French connection. The influence of the revolutions of 1789 and 1848 and the colored creoles' "un-American" views on race enabled them to help set the national agenda for Radical Reconstruction and encouraged their legacy of dissent in the wake of its collapse. Moreover, in describing the politics of Reconstruction, Logsdon and Bell chronicle the growing unity of the city's nonwhites as well as the ability of self-interested parties to exploit and exacerbate their persistent divisions. It was, ultimately, a white-black "American" alliance that eclipsed creole eminence and weakened the resistance to a policy of racial separation. In any event, whatever occurred elsewhere, the authors

5. Rodolphe Desdunes, *Our People and Our History: A Tribute to the Creole People of Color in Memory of the Great Men They Have Given Us and of the Good Works They Have Accomplished,* trans. and ed. Sister Dorothea Olga McCants (Baton Rouge, 1973; original ed. in French, 1911), 62, 85–86, 101–108, 124–25.

Children and staff of the St. John Berchmans Asylum about 1900. Operated by the Sisters of the Holy Family, the institution stood at the corner of Bourbon and Orleans and served creoles of color.
Courtesy Sisters of the Holy Family and Archives and Manuscripts Department, Earl K. Long Library, University of New Orleans

reveal the danger in assuming a close correlation between color, economic status, and political conservatism among black New Orleanians.

Arnold R. Hirsch follows the themes discerned by Logsdon and Bell through the twentieth century. The rise of Jim Crow not only imposed a system of racial subordination and separation (an outright repudiation of the values held by the radical creoles) but fostered a debilitating paternalism while exalting and rigidly defining racial identity. It was a corrosive combination that ate away at the substance and foundations of a separate black creole culture and compelled greater unity in the desperate defense of besieged "racial" interests. Indeed, Hirsch emphasizes that the appearance of myriad social clubs, civic leagues, political organizations, and citywide groups such as the local branch of the National Association for the Advancement of Colored People (NAACP) straddled the old divisions while pushing a racial agenda that united all nonwhites.

Still, the ethnocultural divide within New Orleans' black community could be detected in the second Reconstruction as well as the first. There remained an uptown versus downtown, American versus creole split that stamped an indelible mark on twentieth-century racial and political relationships. If the more assimilated descendants of the creoles of color sought status and solace by acquiescing in the American racial hierarchy and advantageously adopting its color consciousness, continued resistance to such notions remained manifest within a less accommodating creole fragment. Indeed, the last remnants of New Orleans' creole radicalism found institutional expression in the local NAACP and political vindication in the 1978 election of Ernest N. (Dutch) Morial as the city's first black mayor. Ironically, however, the racial crusades that made such achievements possible undercut the vision of a casteless society that had initially driven Jim Crow's most aggressive adversaries. In the end, the legacies of slavery and segregation held sway in the Americanized city. Strident calls for racial unity and identity and the dogged persistence of paternalistic relationships seemed organically bound to the racial dichotomy that emerged not merely intact but reinvigorated from the struggle against segregation.

As always, the city's social history was both paralleled and influenced by its physical development. If the city's geography had once forced New Orleanians into intimate association, physical changes in modern New Orleans facilitated the drive of white supremacists toward racial segregation and polarization. Well into the twentieth century, New Orleans' pattern of settlement remained as it had always been.

Residents huddled in crowded interracial neighborhoods, clinging to the natural levees that stretched along the riverfront or the ridges left by the Mississippi's ancient distributaries. It was not until the 1920s that technology offered the possibility of mastering—or at least altering—the environment to the extent that the restraining backswamp and an inhospitable lakeshore no longer thwarted growth and development.

The first real breakthrough came when A. Baldwin Wood fashioned a heavy-duty pump that was capable of lifting large volumes of debris-laden water with great speed. These pumps, which were so powerful that Dutch engineers who came to New Orleans to study Wood's designs later used their knowledge to drain the Zuyder Zee, radically altered the landscape of both New Orleans and the Netherlands. Coupled with a new system of canals that carried swamp and floodwaters to Bayou Bienvenue, Lake Borgne, and, in emergencies, Lake Pontchartrain, the pumps drained the backswamp and broke the choking hold nature had imposed on New Orleans' development for the first two hundred years of its existence. The city legislatively mandated the construction of the expensive pumping system in 1899, and within a decade much of midcity had been drained. By the 1920s, homeowners had begun to replace the black and white squatters of New Orleans' infamous backswamp.

Also in the 1920s, the Orleans Levee District pursued a plan that extended, raised, and tamed the forbidding lakeshore that formed the city's northern boundary. By building a seawall more than three thousand feet out into the lake and filling in behind it to an elevation of five to ten feet above the lake's level, the Levee District created more than two thousand acres of prime real estate that could be developed along what was no longer a threatening waterfront. The result was that New Orleans, like most other American cities, experienced a building boom in the 1920s, and its population began to roll north, away from the river and toward the lake.[6]

This activity, of course, took place during the early twentieth century, when the South was obsessed with Jim Crow, and the redistribution of New Orleans' population was hardly random. Building in the most desirable new areas was so expensive that few of the city's poor would have moved into these developments, but explicit racial prohibitions made certain that they were exclusively white. Expansion of black

6. Peirce F. Lewis, *New Orleans: The Making of an Urban Landscape* (Cambridge, Mass., 1976).

neighborhoods, however, particularly uptown, occurred along the edges of existing black enclaves that crowded the backswamp—areas that were the first to flood and the last to be pumped dry and thus never a sought-after residential location. Modern technology accelerated the growth of that black concentration and the process of residential segregation.

New Orleans had hardly begun to sample the freedom from its age-old restraints when the Great Depression and World War II brought new development to a virtual halt. The absence of transportation improvements also restricted urban sprawl. Persistent drainage problems in suburban areas and the availability of considerable vacant land within the city combined with the lack of good roads to inhibit further outward growth. Only after World War II, when Interstate 10 and a new span across the Mississippi River were built, did development revive. Between 1950 and 1975, the built-up area in New Orleans and its surrounding suburbs doubled in size.

The metropolitanization of New Orleans finally wrote into the city's spatial relationships the same uncompromising racial dualism that had conditioned political and legal rights for the past century. New Orleans came to resemble other American cities, both North and South, with an increasingly black core surrounded by a ring of white suburbs. Between 1960 and 1980 the city's white population declined by 155,627 while the nonwhite grew by 85,854. Once again, whites were a minority, representing but 42.5 percent of the city's 557,482 inhabitants. Blacks had been in the majority until 1840 and were again after 1980. In contrast, New Orleans' suburbs not only remained overwhelmingly white but became increasingly so, going from 78.7 percent in 1940 to 87 percent in 1970. The 1980 census revealed only a slight moderation of that trend as the white suburban percentage declined to 85.4. Eight out of ten blacks in the New Orleans metropolitan area live within the city proper, and seven out of ten whites reside in the growing suburbs. The outlying districts contained barely 14 percent of the area's population in 1940, but by 1980, an absolute majority, 53 percent, lived in the suburbs. This city-suburban, black-white cleavage is the most striking ecological development in the modern New Orleans metropolitan area.[7]

Metropolitanization meant more than racial polarization. The de-

7. Arnold R. Hirsch, "New Orleans: Sunbelt in the Swamp," in *Sunbelt Cities: Politics and Growth Since World War II*, ed. Richard M. Bernard and Bradley R. Rice (Austin, 1983), 103–106.

struction of the old city, the disappearance of its tightly knit, clustered, multicultural neighborhoods, also meant the disintegration of the residential base that had created, nurtured, and sustained New Orleans' unique culture. This was nothing new, of course. The process of Americanization promised such an eventuality, and it had been urged by those of a "progressive" cast of mind for at least a hundred years. The developers of Lakeside, for example, in 1907 promised to build the "New York of the South." In a fancy brochure, they pictured the decaying edifices of the French Quarter juxtaposed to the boxlike, wooden buildings of the newer developments. "The old French style of architecture," they crowed, "which is fast becoming obsolete . . . is now looked upon as a relic of antiquity." Their motto was simple and self-assured: "Tear down the old and make way for the new."[8]

True, New Orleanians have resisted some of these encroachments; in the 1960s, they defeated proposals for both a riverfront expressway in front of the French Quarter and an uptown river bridge that surely would have destroyed the heart of the city. Consequently, much of the older city remains in evidence, and New Orleans has retained one of the most vibrant urban cores in the United States, attracting some new Asian and Central American immigration that demands further examination. But as its increasing black-white polarization indicates, it seems to be rushing along the trail blazed earlier by the industrial cities of the Northeast and Midwest. The delicate cultural amalgam that gave us jazz, a unique cuisine, and a love for public festivals is beleaguered but not yet obliterated. Moreover, promoters have institutionalized much of what remains of the city's unique entertainments to serve the needs of a burgeoning tourist trade. Ultimately, it appears, New Orleans will be dragged, not kicking and screaming but dancing, into the American century.

8. New Orleans Land Company, *Crescent City: The New York of the South* (N.p., 1907?), in Special Collections, Earl K. Long Library, University of New Orleans.

5

The Americanization of Black New Orleans 1850–1900

JOSEPH LOGSDON
AND CARYN COSSÉ BELL

Several years after the collapse of Reconstruction, about fifty black and white Republican leaders of New Orleans met for dinner at Antoine's Restaurant in the French Quarter in an effort to heal some old wounds within their ranks. After their party's crushing defeats in 1876 and 1878, they were trying to recapture what one speaker at the dinner called "the fraternal feeling which characterized the early days of the party."[1]

Dr. Louis Charles Roudanez, the founder of the state's first official Republican newspaper, had not for more than a decade spoken with two of the most prominent guests at the dinner—P. B. S. Pinchback and Henry Clay Warmoth, both former Republican governors of Louisiana. Racial differences could not explain the black doctor's deep disdain for these two men; Warmoth was white and Pinchback black. Nor was the shade of skin color the crux of their confrontation, for both Roudanez and Pinchback had complexions about as light as Warmoth's.

Pinchback understood the import of this rare meeting and tried to join in its spirit. He singled out Roudanez and declared that the doctor's decision to attend the party confab "demonstrated the possibility of Republican unity." His generous toast brought the normally taciturn physician to his feet. Roudanez politely acknowledged the flattery but did not reciprocate with any comparable praise for Pinchback. Instead,

1. *Louisianian,* January 4, 1879.

he took advantage of the moment to recall at some length "his own aims and purposes in the early days of reconstruction . . . to educate and advance the interests of his down-trodden race." When Roudanez finished, he reached across the table and shook hands with Governor Warmoth.[2]

In an account of the meeting in his newspaper, Pinchback reported that these symbolic gestures showed Roudanez' "desire to let the past be forgotten." He was wrong. The old bitterness remained between these two black leaders. True, Roudanez never reentered politics to confront Pinchback, but other black friends of the doctor, such as Judge A. J. Dumont, took up the old cudgels against his nemesis. Indeed, Pinchback pointed to the new rivalry by observing that the party harmonizers had placed him and Dumont at one end of the banquet table, just as they had placed the two earlier protagonists, Roudanez and Warmoth, at the other end—"facing each other." The two new party leaders had already reopened the old Republican feud within Louisiana, and by 1882 newspaper columns emblazoned the clash of their forces as a contest of "Creoles vs Americans."[3]

This lingering fifteen-year conflict among black leaders in New Orleans involved more than ordinary political factionalism and petty personal rivalry over patronage. It reflected a fundamental cultural duality in the city's black community that stemmed from different backgrounds and leadership and was similar to the division between white creoles and Americans. But the rift in black New Orleans may have even been more fundamental and lasting because no third group of later immigrants blurred the cultural distinctions and because black creoles seemed much more determined than their white counterparts to maintain their peculiar identity in the face of the relentless process of Americanization that worked on all segments of the city's population. As a result, the cultural duality continued well into the twentieth century and, although diminished and subdued, is still evident in New Orleans.

In 1907, almost three decades after the dinner at Antoine's, Rodolphe L. Desdunes reviewed the post–Civil War era in New Orleans for a younger historian, W. E. B. Du Bois. Desdunes felt that the duality within the New Orleans black community still endured. He did not seek simplistically to define the two groups by their skin color or antebellum status. Desdunes was born in 1849, and his firsthand experiences in New Orleans undoubtedly taught him that neither group could be in-

2. *Ibid.*
3. *Ibid.*, January 4, 1879, April 15, 29, 1882.

corporated into the racial categories of "black" and "mulatto" that have appeared so important to American census takers and later academic observers. He also knew that neither group had emerged from the Civil War either all slave or all free. Instead, he chose to describe them in ethnic categories—the "Latin Negro" and the "Anglo-Saxon or American Negro."[4]

Desdunes felt that these two groups had evolved "two different schools of politics" and differed "radically . . . in aspiration and method." Keeping the "Latin Negro" as the former and the "American Negro" as the latter in his comparison, he tried to explain this unusual concept in American historiography: "One hopes, and the other doubts. Thus we often perceive that one makes every effort to acquire merits, the other to gain advantages. One aspires to equality, the other to identity. One will forget that he is a Negro in order to think that he is a man; the other will forget that he is a man to think that he is a Negro. These radical differences act on the feelings of both in direct harmony with these characteristics. One is a philosophical Negro, the other practical." Desdunes refused to indulge in any of the fashionable racialism or biological determinism of his day to explain the makeup of the two groups. He insisted that their contrasting outlooks as well as their political disagreements "arise, partly from temperament, and partly from surroundings, just as a difference in the manner and thinking will soon crystallize between the Northern Negroes and the Southern Negroes."[5]

Desdunes considered himself, as well as Roudanez and Dumont, to be Latin Negroes or creoles. They were an anomaly in the United States for both white and black Americans such as Warmoth and Pinchback. In turn, the creole Negroes regarded Americans, particularly those born outside of New Orleans, as members of a separate and sometimes hostile society. Creole blacks, particularly those like Roudanez and Desdunes, who formally learned French intellectual traditions and also carefully observed revolutionary movements in the nineteenth-century French world, staked their claim to equal status on unique political principles. English-speaking Protestants, by contrast, acculturated to

4. Rodolphe Lucien Desdunes, *A Few Words to Dr. DuBois: "With Malice Toward None"* (New Orleans, 1907), 13. For a sketch of Desdunes, see the foreword by Charles E. O'Neill in the new edition and translation of Desdunes' original history, *Nos hommes et notre histoire* (Montreal, 1911): *Our People and Our History*, ed. and trans. Dorothea Olga McCants (Baton Rouge, 1973), ix–xix.

5. Desdunes, *Few Words to DuBois*, 13. For an elaboration of Desdunes' definition of the creoles as "one community, alike in origin, language, and customs," see Desdunes, *Our People*, 3.

Anglo-American traditions, approached events with strategies derived from their own historical experience in the Anglo-American world.

In Louisiana Reconstruction politics, white Democrats as well as white Republicans often exploited the ethnic differences among black New Orleanians and made it more difficult for them to achieve political unity. Nevertheless, in crucial struggles during Reconstruction, black leaders transcended their ethnic differences and helped to forge a new identity as free men and citizens not just for themselves but for all persons of African descent in the United States. What follows is a study of their difficult but important struggle.

Black Creoles and Americans

From the beginning of the nineteenth century, race relations in New Orleans had puzzled American newcomers, particularly those who were sent to govern the city in 1803. The new rulers encountered a black majority that grew larger with the addition of French-speaking West Indian immigrants. More perhaps than its size, the nature of the city's black population—particularly those who were free—confused and frightened American officials.

The free black creoles of New Orleans had emerged from French and Spanish rule not only with unusual rights and powers but also with a peculiar assertiveness and self-confidence. Many were armed and had gained military training and experience in the official militias of Louisiana. They had also secured wealth and a firm foothold in skilled occupations normally closed to free persons of African ancestry in Anglo-America. Most may have been fair-skinned but not all; they ran the spectrum of skin color. In the urban setting of New Orleans, moreover, free black men and women intermingled with slaves, often living in the same quarters and intermarrying or cohabiting with those still in bondage. In such a racial order, "the consummate linkage of negritude and servility, the dominant feature of race relations in the American Old South, never fully emerged in colonial Louisiana."[6]

6. Thomas Marc Fiehrer, "The African Presence in Colored Louisiana: An Essay on the Continuity of Caribbean Culture," in *Louisiana's Black Heritage*, ed. Robert R. Macdonald *et al.* (New Orleans, 1979), 30. See also Ira Berlin's comparative treatment of the free people of color in the former French and Spanish colonies of the Gulf Coast, *Slaves Without Masters: The Free Negro in the Antebellum South* (New York, 1974). For two comprehensive studies of free blacks in Louisiana, see H. E. Sterkx, *The Free Negro in Ante-Bellum Louisiana* (Rutherford, N.J., 1972), and Donald E. Everett, "Free Persons of Color in New Orleans, 1803–1865" (Ph.D. dissertation, Tulane University, 1952). On

New American officials soon faced the self-confidence of free black creole leaders of the city, who felt that the Louisiana Purchase treaty had assured them of equal citizenship in the United States. Even before the transfer to the American authority, the explosive events of the revolutions in France and Haiti had raised the aspirations of black New Orleanians for equality and freedom. When they petitioned for civil rights, American leaders showed no desire to perpetuate, much less extend, the rights of black Louisianans. Instead, the new rulers tried to impose their own American racial order on New Orleans and the rest of Louisiana.[7]

In the rural Louisiana countryside, little may have distinguished the severity of the Anglo-American slave order from that of the French or the Spanish. But in New Orleans American authorities faced a severe challenge to the racial policies that they wished to establish. The new American governor, William C. C. Claiborne, made no overt move against the armed free black population. Faced with the possibilities of insurrection by either slaves or some of the non-American white inhabitants, he and his associates tried to avoid creating any additional enemies. Time and events only compounded their ambivalence. The reverberations of the slave revolts in Saint Domingue brought more French-speaking black settlers into the territory. By 1810, the free Negro population of the city rose to 4,950 from 1,566 in 1805, and the slave population rose to 5,961 from 3,105 (see Table 1). Among the West Indian newcomers were even more skilled, better-educated, and probably more assertive leaders—both free and slave—than those who had already disturbed the Americans in 1803.[8]

Pressed by fearful white creoles and Americans, the territorial government thinned the ranks of the free black militia, imposed white officers, and finally allowed the legislature to disband it. Having already

the question of phenotype among slaves and free blacks, see John W. Blassingame, *Black New Orleans, 1860–1880* (Chicago, 1973), 21.

7. Marcus B. Christian, "Demand by Men of Color for Rights in Orleans Territory," *Negro History Bulletin*, XXXVI (March, 1973), 54–57. For Jefferson's approval of the repressive policies, see his notes on the cabinet meeting, October 4, 1803, in Thomas Jefferson Papers, Library of Congress.

8. David C. Rankin, "The Tannenbaum Thesis Reconsidered: Slavery and Race Relations in Antebellum Louisiana," *Southern Studies*, XVIII (Spring, 1979), 5–31; Paul F. Lachance, "The Politics of Fear: French Louisianians and the Slave Trade, 1786–1809," *Plantation Society*, I (June, 1979), 162–96; Laura Foner, "The Free People of Color in Louisiana and St. Domingue: A Comparative Portrait of Two Three-Caste Slave Societies," *Journal of Social History*, III (1970), 421–22. For population data, see *New Orleans in 1805: A Directory and a Census* (New Orleans, 1936), 11; and *Third Census, 1810: Population*, 295.

TABLE 1. Whites, Free People of Color, and Slaves in New Orleans, 1769–1860

Population Figures

Year	Whites	Free People of Color	Slaves	Total
1769	1,803	99	1,227	3,129
1788	2,370	823	2,126	5,319
1805	3,551	1,566	3,105	8,222
1810	6,331	4,950	5,961	17,242
1820	13,584	6,237	7,355	27,176
1830	20,047	11,562	14,476	46,085
1840	50,697	15,072	18,208	83,977
1850	89,452	9,905	17,011	116,368
1860	144,601	10,939	14,484	170,024

Percentages

Year	Whites (%)	Free People of Color (%)	Slaves (%)
1769	57.6	3.2	39.2
1788	44.6	15.5	39.9
1805	43.2	19.0	37.8
1810	36.7	28.7	34.6
1820	49.9	23.0	27.1
1830	43.5	25.1	31.4
1840	60.4	18.0	21.6
1850	76.9	8.5	14.6
1860	85.0	6.4	8.5

SOURCES: Population figures and percentages for 1769 to 1820 are drawn from Paul F. Lachance, "New Orleans in the Era of Revolution: A Demographic Profile" (Paper presented at the American Society for Eighteenth-Century Studies, New Orleans, 1989). Respective figures for 1830 to 1850 are from Leonard P. Curry, *The Free Negro in Urban America, 1800–1850: The Shadow of the Dream* (Chicago, 1981). Figures for 1860 are taken from John W. Blassingame, *Black New Orleans, 1860–1880* (Chicago, 1973).

denied the creoles' petition for equal citizenship, Governor Claiborne forced their leaders to renounce any further public declarations. Slowly but surely the existing rights of the free black population were eroded. The territorial assembly's purpose was clear when it declared: "Free people of color ought never insult or strike white people, nor presume to conceive themselves equal to whites." To guard the color line, the assembly ordered that racial designation be applied to all persons of African ancestry in every public document.[9]

In a generation or two, a resolute policy along these lines might have Americanized the racial order in New Orleans, but a slave revolt in 1811 and a British invasion in 1814 persuaded the American authorities to relent in their repressive policies toward the state's free black inhabitants. For their own survival, they recommissioned white-officered black militia units and almost created a legalized, triparte racial order similar to those of the Caribbean. From 1815 to 1830, state officials did not further reduce free black rights, and the economic boom in the city enabled skilled black workers and merchants to improve their already impressive occupational status.

When a repressive mood returned in the 1830s following the revived abolitionist movement and the Nat Turner insurrection, creole white lawmakers still had enough power in the state legislature to exempt many of the free black creoles from increased restrictions by giving special status to those who were in Louisiana at some earlier date. More significant, most of the black creoles of New Orleans—both free and slave—escaped much of the renewed severity by living within the virtually autonomous creole municipal districts of New Orleans that were created in 1836, where enforcement of almost all laws was notoriously lax. As a result, free and slave black creoles continued to gather for festivities, frequent bars and dance halls, and cohabit despite the state laws designed to constrain such activity.[10]

In 1850, almost all free black creoles, and quite likely those enslaved as well, lived downriver from Canal Street in the First and Third municipalities. Their voluntary relationships across the color line were, it seems, not so much with the long-resident white creoles as with immigrants, especially those from France, who concentrated in the same

9. Berlin, *Slaves Without Masters*, 114–23; Everett, "Free Persons of Color," 55–74.

10. Berlin, *Slaves Without Masters*, 130; Foner, "Free People of Color," 424–27; Everett, "Free Persons of Color," 101–104, 123–25.

areas during the 1830s and 1840s. Because European immigrants, who flowed constantly into the booming city before the Civil War, took a while to learn the mores of the United States, the racial order remained fluid during most of the antebellum period. The large number of immigrants from France and the French-speaking West Indies also nurtured the French culture, language, and institutional loyalty that pervaded black creole society. Music teachers, Catholic priests and nuns, shopkeepers, live-in lovers, radical émigrés, and saloonkeepers helped to maintain relationships between black and white New Orleanians that were more elaborate than those in any other city in the United States.[11]

It was not accidental that the 1852 consolidation of the three separate municipalities coincided with a new serge of racial repression. For many years after the Civil War, creole black leaders recalled 1852 as the year of the breakdown of their sheltered and privileged order in New Orleans. At that point, the state legislature began an assault on their rights of manumission and began transferring enforcement of existing restrictions from local to state authorities.[12]

Almost every major black creole leader of the Civil War and Reconstruction era was chastened by the repression of the 1850s. The large number who sought refuge outside of Louisiana fled not to the American North but to France and Latin America, especially Haiti and Mexico. Dr. Roudanez was just one of many who found greater freedom in France. There he not only gained a prestigious medical degree but also took to the revolutionary barricades. Both experiences helped him gain a radical vision of an alternative racial order for his native city and nation.[13]

11. A sample study (by the authors) of the 1850 census shows that creoles constituted 76 percent of the adult free male black population in the First Municipality of the city (82 percent below St. Louis Street) and 88 percent in the Third Municipality. By contrast, Americans constituted 78 percent of the comparable population in the uptown Second Municipality. The methodology for this study was based on the work of D. L. A. Hackett, "The Social Structure of Jacksonian Louisiana," *Southern Studies*, XII (Spring, 1973), 324–53. For a similar preponderance of the 10,564 white French immigrants in the downtown wards, see Victor Hugo Treat, "Migration into Louisiana, 1834–1880" (Ph.D. dissertation, University of Texas, 1967), 328–32.

12. On the crisis of the 1850s, see Desdunes, *Our People*, 111, 134–35, and a speech by Robert B. Elliot (*Louisianian*, September 17, 1881), who learned from creole leaders that their struggle to challenge racial subordination began in 1852.

13. Jean-Charles Houzeau, *My Passage at the New Orleans "Tribune,"* ed. David C. Rankin (Baton Rouge, 1984), 25–29; Paul Trévigne, "Dr. Louis Charles Roudanez," New Orleans *Daily Crusader*, March 22, 1890.

During the decade or so before the Civil War, the divergent racial policies of France and the United States helped shape the thinking and outlook of many black creole leaders. Edicts issued by officials of the Second Republic in 1848 not only ended slavery in the French West Indies but also gave full political rights to all black inhabitants of these islands. These radical actions outside the Anglo-American experience opened new possibilities in the minds of black creoles in New Orleans. Before the Civil War, even the Garrisonian abolitionists in the United States seldom reached the vanguard racial policies of the Second Republic in France. As a result, the black creoles of New Orleans looked less to the North Star than to La Belle France.[14]

The Anglo-American assault on the anomalous world of the black creoles had some long-term results, producing among some a measure of acceptance and accommodation and among others nostalgia for the world that was lost. But far more important, the repression helped to develop a young leadership class that resisted Americanization and stood poised to create a new order based not merely on French ideas but also on recent applications of those ideas in other areas of the New World.

The French-oriented creoles were not the only black New Orleanians. The role of black migrants from the United States during the first half of the nineteenth century has too often been forgotten in the story of social and cultural change in the city. Slaves and free men and women brought a highly developed way of life that had been fashioned over many decades in other areas of the United States. Their institutions and values often differed from those of the black creoles of New Orleans, and the resulting interchange between the two communities helped shape the peculiar way of life in the city for years to come. White American officials long tried to discourage the migration of free black men and women from the American seaboard or the upper South to the Mississippi Valley. Like other white Americans who moved out to the western frontier, the migrants to Louisiana passed laws to keep free black Americans from entering their new settlements. Despite the remarkable success of white leaders in other states, however, Louisianians failed in their efforts to keep out or effectively expel free black Americans.[15]

14. Shelby T. McCloy, *The Negro in France* (Lexington, Ky., 1961), 145–59; Mc-Cloy, *The Negro in the French West Indies* (Lexington, Ky., 1966), 141–59; Lawrence C. Jennings, *French Reaction to British Emancipation* (Baton Rouge, 1988), 194–98.

15. In the 1860 census, Texas had only 355 free blacks, Mississippi had 753, and Arkansas had 114, whereas Louisiana had 18,647.

The increase in the number of free black Americans was in part a result of American slaves gaining their freedom after arriving in New Orleans under the lenient manumission laws that survived from the colonial days of the city. Surprisingly large numbers of free black Americans also came to New Orleans voluntarily. For the most part, they came to work on coasting vessels or river steamers. Ship owners, in need of compliant, cheap labor, recruited them and even helped them evade the state laws and city ordinances passed to exclude them. The lure of jobs and the city's relatively open racial order made it an island of freedom and opportunity in the Deep South.[16]

Most of the migrant workers probably returned to their home states, but some stayed in New Orleans. Few, if any, ever gained legal residency. Most had to subvert the law in order to remain, but in the labyrinth of a large seaport, evasion was often easy. In the 1850s the police, under employers' pleas for leniency, arrested fewer than ten free black residents per month for violating the exclusion laws. Only when a new city administration began enforcing a harsher law in 1859 did the monthly arrest total of almost one hundred free black aliens reveal the true level of their migration into the city.[17]

So many fugitive slaves fled into the city that their presence began to undermine distinctions between free and slave in New Orleans, but their status proved very precarious and probably led to harassment of many blacks who were legally free. Because the underpaid and undermanned police force won private bounties for recovering runaways, the fugitives had a much more difficult time avoiding apprehension than did free black aliens. During the 1850s, more than eighty-five hundred fugitives fell into the hands of the police. Most had escaped from neighboring plantations, but slaves resident in the city also made at least two thousand attempts to escape bondage during that decade. Some of the

---

16. Biographies of some manumitted black Americans appear in *Southwestern Christian Advocate*, March 27, 1879, March 22, 1888, September 10, 1896. Loren Schweninger provides a revealing autobiography of James P. Thomas, a black migratory worker, in "A Negro Sojourner in Antebellum New Orleans," *Louisiana History*, XX (1979), 306–308. For Thomas' comparative views of northern cities and their racial mores, see John Hope Franklin, *A Southern Odyssey: Travelers in the Antebellum North* (Baton Rouge, 1976), 141–44. For a similar appraisal of antebellum New Orleans by other black informants, see John Freeman Clarke, *Condition of the Free Colored People* (1859; rpr. New York, 1969), 253–54.

17. Richard R. Tansey, "Out of State Blacks in Late Antebellum New Orleans," *Louisiana History*, XXII (1981), 375–84.

latter may have managed to flee from the state, but most probably tried to disappear into the ranks of the free black community inside the city.[18]

As slaves or as free men and women, black Americans brought with them a North American culture that was much older than that of the black creoles of New Orleans. It was not only rooted in different blends of African traditions but had been subsequently entwined with the life-styles of the different European and Indian peoples whom African-Americans had encountered in North America. Central to the culture of most black men and women in Anglo-America was the Protestant church and the role of the black preacher. During the antebellum era, most religious leaders had realistically urged their followers not to revolt against the numbers and power arrayed against them in the Old South but rather to find shelter and solace in the church.[19]

The Baptists laid the earliest foundations for the black Protestant church in Louisiana. In 1799, a black Baptist preacher landed in a Spanish jail for violating the colony's ban on all religious creeds except Catholicism. As soon as American control removed that restraint, another black American minister, Joseph Willis, became the first Baptist missionary west of the Mississippi River.[20]

The first Baptist church in New Orleans, which lasted from 1818 to 1820, began like those on the rural frontier—with both black and white members and a tolerance for black preachers. The First African Baptist Church, with an all-black congregation, tried to set roots in New Orleans on October 31, 1826, but survived only until 1830, when its first pastor, Asa C. Goldsberry, died and harassment forced it to disband. In the early 1830s some Virginia slaves, led by a slave minister, Nelson D. Sanders, resuscitated it in a small house in Gentilly on the eastern outskirts of the city and sustained it there for the next decade. In 1843,

18. Richard R. Tansey, "Economic Expansion and Urban Disorder in Antebellum New Orleans" (Ph.D. dissertation, University of Texas at Austin, 1981), 124–30; Richard B. Wade, *Slavery in the Cities: The South, 1820–1860* (New York, 1964), 219.

19. John W. Blassingame, *The Slave Community: Plantation Life in the Ante-bellum South* (New York, 1972); Lawrence W. Levine, *Black Culture and Black Consciousness: Afro-American Folk Thought from Slavery to Freedom* (New York, 1977); Eugene D. Genovese, "Black Plantation Preachers in the Slave South," *Louisiana Studies,* XI (1972), 196–214.

20. William B. Posey, "The Early Baptist Church in the Lower Southwest," *Journal of Southern History,* X (1944), 161–73; William Paxton, *A History of the Baptists in Louisiana* (St. Louis, 1888), 140–48; John T. Christian, *A History of the Baptists in Louisiana* (Shreveport, 1923), 42–43, 50–51.

under Sanders' leadership, the congregation built a church on Howard Street, in the uptown American sector of the city. Although frequently troubled by arrests, they eventually gained permission to meet "two hours on Sundays from 3 to 5 p.m. under the watch of a police officer who was paid $2 per hour." Three other African Baptist churches were established before the Civil War, all in the uptown American sector. In 1859, under increasing pressure, all four placed themselves under the supervision of the white Coliseum Baptist Church and the Mississippi River Association, and the slave pastors were required to work under the direction of a white minister.[21]

It took longer for the Methodist church to gain a firm foothold in the city. The first white Methodist missionary, Elisha Bowman, met so much indifference to his efforts in 1806 that he gave up on the "ungodly city of New Orleans." Several other hardened circuit riders tried their hand during the next two decades but also gave up in despair. Benjamin Drake, who finally organized a congregation in 1824, reported that "New Orleans presents a more unyielding resistance to the evangelical gospel . . . than any other city in the South."[22]

As in the case of the Baptists, black American newcomers anchored the Methodists in New Orleans. Of the first eighty-three members of Drake's church in 1826, at least sixty were black. During the first two decades, black and white Methodists worshiped together in New Orleans, but the black members had to sit in a segregated gallery. After Southern Methodists separated from the national Methodist Episcopal church and formed their own denomination in 1845—the Methodist Episcopal Church, South—they set up separate, subsidized congregations for black Methodists in New Orleans. In this arrangement, white presiding elders supervised the black congregations, and black preachers acted as subordinates.

The black preachers were not recent converts. Each, it appears, had chosen his religious persuasion well before he came to Louisiana. The Reverend Scott Chinn, for example, had secretly learned to read by the

21. Marcus Christian, "The First African Baptist Church of New Orleans, 1817–1842" (Typescript in Marcus Christian Papers, University of New Orleans), 6–8. The quotation is from R. W. Coleman, "Church Anniversary of the First African Baptist Church," quoted in Marcus Christian, "The Negro Church in Louisiana" (Chapter in MS WPA history of the Negro in Louisiana, in Christian Papers).

22. Walter N. Vernon, *Becoming One People: A History of Louisiana Methodism* (Bossier City, La., 1987), 8, 13.

age of thirteen and had been raised by Methodist parents. He began preaching at the age of fifteen and continued to do so after he was brought to New Orleans by his owner in 1849. There he joined two other slave preachers, Henry Green and Anthony Ross, in caring for the members of the three black congregations of the Methodist Episcopal Church, South. Ordained by a Methodist Episcopal bishop "without laying of hands," he was permitted to administer sacraments only "to the negroes and such white persons as may accept them."[23]

Few free blacks, either Americans or creoles, appear to have joined the Baptist and Methodist Episcopal congregations. Some slaves who had gained their freedom while members of those churches remained as members, but most free black Americans turned to the African Methodist Episcopal (AME) church, a truly independent black institution that had its origins in eighteenth-century Pennsylvania. Although this denomination had been banned from the Deep South during the 1820s after the exposure of Denmark Vesey's 1822 slave revolt conspiracy in South Carolina, it managed to gain a foothold in New Orleans about two decades later.

In 1842, a small group of Methodists, tied together by Masonic loyalties, made contact with an AME minister, the Reverend Jordan Winston Early, who worked on a steamboat traveling between St. Louis and New Orleans. When Early advised them not to attempt to start an AME congregation unless they could get an act of incorporation from the state, one of the group, James Hunter, persuaded white friends to obtain the necessary charter from the Louisiana legislature in 1847, on the condition that the church meet only in daylight hours. Until then the group had met furtively in private houses, posting lookouts to warn them of approaching police.[24]

In 1848, the group sent a member, Charles Doughty, to Indianapolis to ask the Indiana AME conference to send a minister to set up an AME church in New Orleans. The conference agreed to seek out a likely prospect but in the meantime ordained Doughty as a deacon to take pastoral

23. *Southwestern Christian Advocate*, July 20, 1882. For information on smaller black Protestant groups, see Robert C. Reinders, "The Church and the Negro in New Orleans, 1850–1860," *Phylon*, XXII (Fall, 1961), 244–46; John F. Nau, *The Lutheran Church in Louisiana* (New Orleans, n.d. [*ca.* 1952]), 45–50; and Hodding Carter and Betty Werlein Carter, *So Great a Good: A History of the Episcopal Church in Louisiana* (Sewanee, Tenn., 1955), 169.

24. Charles Spencer Smith, *A History of the African Methodist Episcopal Church* (Philadelphia, 1922), 20, 33–36.

charge of its "Louisiana Mission," subsequently called St. James Church. In the fall of 1852, Bishop Paul Quinn sent the Reverend John Mifflin Brown to guide the affairs of the congregation, which existed near Canal Street, just inside the First Municipality. Brown had the misfortune to arrive just as the city was being consolidated and more severe restrictions were being imposed on the black community. During his five years in the city, Brown was arrested five times for not excluding slaves from the services of the church. Still he bravely continued to expand the AME operations by opening two other churches in the city, Morris Brown and Quinn chapels.[25]

As the repressive mood grew worse in the late 1850s, city officials harassed the AME members with arrests. By 1857 the church's activities had been severely curtailed, but the authorities were not satisfied and, in 1858, finally closed the church by passing an ordinance that banned any black organization or church not under the control of whites. The AME members fought back by successfully suing the city on the basis of their state charter in the District Court, but the state Supreme Court overturned the decision, noting that the "African race are strangers to our Constitution, and are subject of special and exceptional legislation."[26]

After this defeat, some of the AME members found shelter within the white Congregational church, while others went back to the secret meetings of the Prince Hall Masons, whose order had drawn heavily upon an Anglo-American heritage. From the beginning, the leadership of the AME churches was almost identical to that of the Prince Hall Masons in New Orleans. Many of the key figures had been in the state as free men before 1835. Without any state approval or charter, they had formed a secret Masonic group in the 1840s and in March, 1849, managed to obtain a charter from northern black leaders to open a Prince Hall (York Rite) unit in New Orleans. The newly sanctioned Richmond Lodge spawned two offspring before the Civil War, Stringer Lodge in 1854 and Parsons Lodge in 1857.[27]

25. *Ibid.*, 33–36.

26. City ordinance No. 3847, April 7, 1858, cited in *African Methodist Episcopal Church* v. *City of New Orleans*, 15 La. Ann. 441 #6291 (1858). The original records and testimony of this case are filed in the Louisiana Supreme Court Records, Case 6342, in the Department of Archives of the University of New Orleans. The quotation is taken from page 4 of the Supreme Court ruling.

27. *Proceedings of Eureka Grand Lodge, 1863–69* (New Orleans, 1869); and *100 Years of Legitimate and Progressive Free Masonry, Centennial Souvenir* (New Orleans,

Almost all of the Prince Hall members before the Civil War were black Americans. In the repressive climate of the late 1850s, the lodge was one of the few organizations that allowed leaders from the free black American community to consider options to remaining in the United States. Even the moderate and long-settled black American Jordan B. Noble joined the group and represented Louisiana in the Negro Emigration Convention of 1854 in Cleveland, which commissioned agents to seek a place of refuge in Africa.[28]

Like the black creoles, black Americans tried to protect their rights and dignity in face of the rising tide of racial discrimination during the 1850s. In establishing a black clergy and racially separate institutions, they expressed a desire to create a separate identity within the confines of the American racial order, and for a while they had some success. They repeatedly challenged laws prohibiting the assembly of free black men and women with those who were enslaved. Indeed, their assertiveness thoroughly alarmed white officials, who finally concluded that "such assemblages are dangerous to the institution of slavery. They create discontent among the slaves."[29]

Neither the creole nor the American black leaders could resist the relentless pressure placed on all black residents. By 1860, fear and discouragement ran deeply through the entire black community of New Orleans, as the fragile rights and freedoms of those who were free or slave, creole or American vanished in the decade before the Civil War. Many fled the city. Of those who remained, most tried to make the best of a worsening situation by either enduring the conditions or finding whatever protection they could in paternalistic relationships with white New Orleanians. Some, however, secretly organized themselves and stood poised for action. In the late 1850s, few black New Orleanians could have predicted that the deteriorating racial climate in their city and other places in the Deep South would have led to emancipation and black suffrage, but they soon learned that liberation often comes to the oppressed when they least expect it.

---

ca. 1963), both in George Longe Collection, Amistad Research Center, Tulane University, New Orleans.

28. Howard H. Bell, ed., *Search for a Place: Black Separatism and Africa* (Ann Arbor, 1969), 38; *Louisianian*, February 11, 1882. Noble's interest in immigration to Liberia is documented in "Letters to the American Colonization Society," *Journal of Negro History*, X (April, 1925), 271–72, 275.

29. *African Methodist Episcopal Church* v. *City of New Orleans*, 15 La. Ann. 441 #6291 (1858).

Union Occupation and Black Troops

In the spring of 1862, the sight of the Union military forces was an occasion for rejoicing by almost all black New Orleanians. Union sailors recalled them thronging on the levees as their ships approached the city. The Lincoln administration had not yet dedicated itself to a policy of emancipation, but the slaves did not wait. Thousands poured into the city from the surrounding plantations, and many bade farewell to their former masters in the city.

How the new white American rulers from the North would react to the aspirations of black New Orleanians remained to be tested. The story of that relationship is the most complex in the Reconstruction saga. Nowhere did Reconstruction begin so early or advance so far in its legal changes as in New Orleans. And probably nowhere were black leaders so demanding or, on occasion, so divided in their response to the new American leadership.

In most areas of the South, particularly in the cities, the reaction to emancipation and Reconstruction may have differed among those who were already free and those who were slaves. Antebellum status and skin color may have led to differing outlooks and ideology, an inevitable result in a color-conscious society. But in most localities these differences did not produce anything like the lasting legal and political distinctions that arose in the postemancipation societies of the West Indies.

Still, some leaders tried to make color distinctions a basis for their programs. Such racialist appeals, for example, continued to sputter forth well into the late nineteenth century from the black and white leaders of the American Colonization Society, which tried to revive its antebellum program of sending black Americans to Africa. When one of the society's white officials blamed the organization's meager accomplishment in seventy-five years on the contempt in which light-skinned black leaders held Africa, a black New Orleans newspaper editor, A. E. P. Albert, responded with some interesting insights about the nature of the black community in his city. As a bilingual former slave of creole ancestry and a convert to Methodism, Albert understood the peculiar situation in New Orleans.[30]

Albert did not deny the reality of color prejudice among Negroes in

---

30. *Southwestern Christian Advocate*, January 28, 1886, August 22, 1889, February 13, 1890, August 13, 1891, March 17, 1892.

the United States, but he ridiculed the official's comparison of this antipathy to the once deadly clash of blacks and mulattoes in Haiti. He insisted that the occasional antagonisms that the official noticed in the American South were the "outgrowth of conditions and not of blood." Albert also observed that, because white southerners had indiscriminately classed "free people of color" with the freedmen, black southerners had "almost everywhere fused into one homogeneous people." He thought that Louisiana provided a "notable exception" but explained that the divisiveness there resulted "not so much from the perpetuation of antebellum lines of division as from difference in language and religion" because most of the free people had largely been "French and Roman Catholics" and most freedmen held to "English and Protestant religion."[31]

Despite his own fervent anti-Catholicism, Albert admired the creole radicals of New Orleans and worked so closely with them that their shared assertiveness eventually jeopardized his career as a Methodist church official. His knowledge of French and his militant racial views enabled him to bridge the two ethnic communities and to discern their cultural and occasional political differences.

From the fall of the Confederates in New Orleans in 1862 until well into the twentieth century, black creole leaders remained in the forefront of thinking and planning about the destiny of black people in the city. But these leaders never gained the full adherence of their own ethnic group because some creoles were ambivalent about the dramatic changes the Civil War brought to the city's social and racial order. A sizable number had joined the Confederate army during the first months of the war. Some felt pressured to do so, but their motivations differed. A few were probably enthusiastic Confederates, but such sentiment was rare, even among those who did not at first enthusiastically welcome the Union army.[32]

31. *Ibid.*, August 2, 1888. On color consciousness among black Americans, see Joel Williamson, *New People: Miscegenation and Mulattoes in the United States* (New York, 1984).

32. The discussion of the Native Guards by Rodolphe Desdunes may be the most balanced appraisal. Errors in the recent translation of his history of the black creoles unfortunately reversed his original meaning and led some scholars to use his work to prove widespread pro-Confederate views among the Native Guards. Compare Desdunes, *Our People and Our History*, 120, with Desdunes, *Nos hommes et notre histoire*, 161. See also the judicious work by Mary F. Berry, "Negro Troops in Blue and Gray: The Louisiana Native Guards, 1861–1863," *Louisiana History*, XIV (Winter, 1973), 21–39.

When the Union army first occupied the city, for instance, Armand Lanusse, director of the Catholic Institute for Indigent Orphans, ignored General Benjamin F. Butler's order to hoist the American flag over the school. But his hesitance did not proceed from pro-Confederate feeling. The Civil War had tormented him. He served as an officer in the Native Guards, as he later explained in a letter to a black newspaper, to contribute to the defense of "his native land." His devotion to his native soil transcended his contempt for racial injustice in Louisiana. Despite his own reluctance to take up arms and possibly kill antebellum friends who had joined the Confederacy, he supported those black New Orleanians who joined the Union army. But the skeptical Lanusse refused to throw his loyalties quickly to any group of white Americans. In another letter, he elaborated on his reluctance to embrace the Union cause in the spring of 1861: "Many men thought that the prejudice of caste was going to disappear with the arrival of federal troops in this city. They wanted to forget that in every free state of the Union, this prejudice is twice as strong as it was here before and during the rebellion."[33]

Other attitudes heightened the complexity of reactions within the black creole community to the changes wrought by the war. Some black creoles had been slaveholders for the same reasons that whites were slaveholders and may have wished to perpetuate the peculiar institution. Others wished to protect their antebellum privileges that had set them apart from the degraded lives of most slaves. Some added a racial justification for their distinctiveness and tried to perpetuate their light skin color among their descendants. Still others wished to pass to a white identity. But such individual reactions cannot define the general attitudes of the overwhelming bulk of the black creole community and its leaders during the last half of the nineteenth century.

During the Civil War, a new generation of black creole leaders emerged, who condemned such castelike attitudes and quickly came to guide and dominate the political views expressed by their community. Indeed, for the rest of the century, the most radical and consistent position on almost every subject came from creole leaders and the small number of American black spokesmen who regularly allied with them. Whatever may have been the case in other areas of the South, no one has found any correlation of political conservatism, wealth, and light skin

33. Desdunes, *Our People and Our History*, 22–23; *L'Union*, October 18, 1862, July 12, 1864.

color among the black political leaders of New Orleans during the Civil War and Reconstruction.[34]

If there was any hesitancy about the Union cause among the black creole leaders, it resulted, as with Lanusse, from the apparent conservatism of the Yankee leadership. Benjamin Butler, Lincoln's choice to govern occupied New Orleans, did not come to liberate or to enfranchise black Louisianians. His goals were not much different from those of Governor William C. C. Claiborne, whom Jefferson had sent to govern the area in 1803. Butler came to pacify the city and adapt its future to the purposes and outlook of federal authorities. He, too, feared slave insurrection and found it difficult to understand the free black creole leaders. Little in his American experience had prepared him for their status or requests.

When Butler sought to disarm the civilian population of the city, a group of free creole black leaders who had joined the Confederate Native Guards sent a four-man delegation to check on his intentions. To protect their interests and safety, they had hidden their meager store of weapons in three different locations. At least one circle of the free black militia had become organized into a vigilance committee (Comité de Vigilance) as early as the spring of 1861 and met in the hall of the oldest black organization in the city, the Economy Society (Société d'Economie et d'Assistance Mutuelle). A sizable number of the inner circle of this group also appeared to be tied together in the late antebellum period in a radical spiritualist society.[35]

Butler evidently admired the educated and dignified demeanor of the

34. For a different view, see the work of David Rankin, "The Impact of the Civil War on the Free Colored Community of New Orleans," *Perspectives in American History*, XI (1977–78), 379–416; and Rankin, "The Politics of Caste: Free Colored Leadership in New Orleans During the Civil War," in *Louisiana's Black Heritage*, ed. Macdonald *et al.*, 107–46. Rankin's sample of Reconstruction leaders, in Howard N. Rabinowitz, *Southern Black Leaders of the Reconstruction Era* (Urbana, 1982), 181–88, shows both the youthfulness and the small number of slaveholders among the younger black creole leaders. Of the two hundred identified leaders, only twenty-three were identified as slaveholders. Of that number, about eighteen were clearly creoles, but none except Francis Dumas and V. E. Macarty were closely identified with the radical *Tribune* faction. The circumstances that had led Dumas and probably others to owning slaves undercuts the idea that a large number of the Reconstruction leaders had either bought slaves or held them for profit or social prestige.

35. Howard Westwood, "Benjamin Butler's Enlistment of Black Troops in New Orleans in 1862," *Louisiana History*, XXVI (1985), 14–15. See minutes of Economy Hall Native Guards for June 11, 15, 1861, in the back of the 1864 seance register, in René Grandjean Collection, Department of Archives, University of New Orleans.

delegation. Like most northern observers, he was also fascinated by the near-white complexion of many of the free black creoles. But in these first meetings, he showed no willingness to accept their offers to transfer their armed support to his occupation army. He was not ready to transform the war into a campaign of racial liberation.[36]

Meanwhile, some other creole black leaders had already gathered around the bolder initiatives of General John W. Phelps, a Vermont abolitionist, whose forces guarded the river road above New Orleans from Confederate army counterattacks. Because his outpost, Camp Parapet, became a haven for fugitive slaves, Phelps decided to drill the young black men in military fashion and eventually requested standard equipment for them. His actions shocked and frightened Butler, but they pleased and attracted free creole black leaders, who met with him to encourage his efforts to arm black troops.[37]

Such activities by the creole leaders forced the issue of black troops upon Butler and the national administration. At first, Butler tried to stop black recruitment by forcing Phelps to retire; but when President Abraham Lincoln shortly thereafter supported the idea of black soldiers, the ambitious Butler quickly got the message. He called back the leaders of the Native Guards and urged them to raise the first black regiment for the Union. Within a few weeks, the black activists filled the ranks of one regiment with free black volunteers and began to raise two more with recruits who were both free and enslaved, creoles and Americans. Their call for bilingual black officers demonstrated their desire to cross old ethnic and status lines for the purposes of defeating the Confederates and ending slavery.

Few, if any, incidents of antagonism based on ethnicity or color emerged within the black military units, demonstrating how a common agenda of liberation could bind their ranks. Captain Henry L. Rey celebrated the triumph in a letter to a compatriot: "Come visit our camp. . . . In parade, you will see a thousand white bayonets gleaming in the sun, held by black, yellow or white hands. Be informed that we have no prejudice; that we receive everyone into the camp; but that the sight of salesmen of human flesh makes us sick; but, since we know how to be-

36. Desdunes, *Our People and Our History*, 118–20.
37. J. W. Phelps to Benjamin Butler, August 2, 1862, in *Freedom: A Documentary History of Emancipation, 1861–1867*, ed. Ira Berlin (Cambridge, Eng., 1982), II, 63–64. For memoirs of two black leaders who offered help to Phelps—Emile Detiège and Robert Isabelle—see the *Louisianian*, February 20, 1875, and the *Anglo-African*, June 13, 1862.

have, though Negroes, we receive them, completely concealing from them the violent internal struggle that their prejudice forces us to wage within ourselves." [38]

Military service allowed antebellum free black men such as Rey to become active agents of liberation. Perhaps the most famous example was the dramatic service of Francis E. Dumas, a young, wealthy free black creole. Although Dumas may have inherited slaves from his family, he had grown up in France, where he "imbibed his Republicanism and principles of the equality of men." After the Union capture of the city, he returned to the state just in time to hear Butler's call for black troops. He served as a captain in the first black regiment but then obtained the rank of major to begin enrolling the second regiment. Disregarding the restriction against slave recruits, he not only enlisted slaves but also equipped them with his own funds after white officers refused to accept his authority as a major. What is more, he led them successfully in battle. [39]

Demands for Equal Citizenship and Suffrage

The struggle to become voting citizens of Louisiana paralleled the difficult effort to become fighting soldiers and officers in the Union army. Once again the radical creole leaders set the pace and helped to fashion a coalition with black Americans and white radicals to assert claims for black suffrage that soon set the entire national agenda. They may well have discussed their concerns with Butler in the fall of 1862 and received some encouragement from him to form Union clubs and to begin a newspaper that would establish their claims to equal citizenship. Whatever the precise genesis of the campaign, on September 27, 1862—just a few weeks after Butler's call for black troops—Paul Trévigne, a highly respected figure in the antebellum creole black community, began editing *L'Union*, a biweekly French-language newspaper.

With amazing bravado, Trévigne set forth the objectives of the cre-

38. *L'Union*, October 18, 1862.
39. Manoj K. Joshi and Joseph P. Reidy, "'To Come Forward and Aid in Putting Down This UnHoly Rebellion': The Officers of Louisiana's Free Black Native Guard During the Civil War Era," *Southern Studies*, XXI (1982), 330, 336. For conflicting versions of Dumas' slaveholding, see George Washington Williams, *A History of the Negro Troops in the Rebellion, 1861–1865* (1888; rpr. New York, 1969), 214–23; Joseph T. Wilson, *Black Phalanx* (1888; rpr. New York, 1968), 207–11; New Orleans *Tribune*, July 2, 1867; and *Crusader*, July 19, 1890.

ole radicals: "We inaugurate today a new era in the South. We proclaim the Declaration of Independence as the basis of our platform. . . . You who aspire to establish true republicanism, democracy without shackles, gather around us." Trévigne had taught French history and literature and could draw upon more resources than the unfulfilled promises of the American Revolution. A few weeks later, he wrote of "a new sun, similar to that of 1789 . . . on our horizon."[40]

French-speaking radicals like Trévigne had carefully noted that when France emancipated all remaining slaves in her possessions in 1848, authorities had also granted universal male suffrage, which enabled black Antillians to take political control of Guadeloupe and Martinique. Almost immediately after L'Union appeared in New Orleans, Trévigne used the experience in the French Antilles as a model for the United States. Writers in the paper could spin off the names of "Pory-Papy, Mazaline, Charles Dain, Louisy Mathieu, Périnon, and other celebrated blacks and mulattoes," who represented their native land in the French Chamber of Deputies after 1848. One exclaimed: "Ah, la France, in proclaiming liberty for blacks, did not try to expatriate them or colonize them in Chiriqui: she wanted to make them men and honored citizens. . . . Nations of America! . . . model your fundamental principles on those of France, and like her, reach the heights of civilization."[41]

L'Union, in the vanguard of almost all radical opinion in the United States, moved quickly during the revolutionary events of the war. Trévigne's self-assurance stemmed not only from the recent experience of blacks in French-controlled areas but also from the rich history of the black creoles of New Orleans. He reached back to those traditions to find legal support for his claims for black suffrage, recalling the demands of his ancestors for equal citizenship that they felt was promised to all free men in the Louisiana Purchase Treaty. This claim became par-

40. L'Union, September 27, October 18, 1862, as translated in James McPherson, The Negro's Civil War (New York, 1969), 276, 61. The paper expanded to a triweekly on December 23, 1862, and to a bilingual edition on July 6, 1863 (Desdunes, Our People and Our History, 66–68; Pelican, September 10, 1887; Picayune, September 1, 1907).

41. L'Union, October 18, 1862. A recent comparative study of emancipation by Eric Foner failed to note the French action of 1848, claiming that emancipation in the United States was "distinctive" because "uniquely in postemancipation societies, the former slaves during Reconstruction enjoyed universal manhood suffrage and a real measure of political power" (Nothing but Freedom: Emancipation and Its Legacy [Baton Rouge, 1983], 3). The French emancipation of 1848 shocked white creoles in New Orleans but equally impressed the black creoles, who eventually began an annual celebration of the radical French decrees. See Guillaume de Berthier de Sauvigny, La Révolution parisienne de 1848 vue par les américains (Paris, 1984), 112, 139–41.

ticularly pertinent after Lincoln's attorney general, Edward Bates, challenged the *Dred Scott* decision and declared in November, 1862, that native free black people were to be regarded as citizens of the United States.[42]

Trévigne's objective of achieving the full rights of citizenship for African-Americans in the United States seemed almost as visionary in 1862 as it had been for the free black creoles in 1803. It became even more unlikely when Butler left his command in December, 1862, and was replaced by the more racially conservative General Nathaniel P. Banks. The new military ruler and former governor of Massachusetts tried to assuage the conservative white Unionists of the city as well as racist elements within his army who had become disturbed by the "arrogance and intolerable self-assertion of black officers." By insult, humiliation, and dogged persistence, Banks began to drum almost every black commissioned officer out of the occupation army and refused to consider suffrage rights for anyone in the city's black community.[43]

In reaction to Banks's reversal of gains won under Butler, free black leaders—both creole and American—began to coalesce as never before behind the political struggle launched by *L'Union.* Central to this coalition were the Prince Hall Masonic lodges that had been forced underground during the late 1850s. Even before the Civil War, creole and American leaders had begun to transcend barriers of language and culture. Oscar J. Dunn, a free black New Orleanian of American parentage, recruited free black creoles into his unit, the Richmond lodge, and by 1864, when Dunn became grand master of all the Prince Hall units in the city, this Masonic group provided an important nucleus for political activism. Together with other creole activists, they joined with a small group of white radicals led by Thomas J. Durant, whose Union Association made *L'Union* its official French organ on June 5, 1863. Within a month, the French newspaper became a triweekly and extended its reach in both the white and black English-speaking communities by publishing a bilingual edition.[44]

42. Recognizing the importance of the policy decision, the publishers of the paper reprinted Bates's opinion, first in the newspaper and then in a separate pamphlet, *Opinion de l'Avocat-Général Bates sur le droit de citoyenneté* (New Orleans, 1863). Trévigne felt, as he stated in the pamphlet's preface, that the "truly remarkable" opinion should get into the hands of "those most directly affected by it."

43. The quotation on black officers comes from Richard B. Irwin, adjutant to Banks, as cited in Joshi and Reidy, "'To Come Forward,'" 331.

44. *Louisianian,* November 26, 1871. See also *100 Years of Legitimate and Progressive Freemasonry: Centennial Souvenir* (New Orleans, ca. 1963) in the George Longe

For these free black activists, cooperation with white allies never meant subordination. When they met for the first time in an interracial rally in November, 1863, to consider equal suffrage, a conservative white Unionist urged them "not to ask for political rights" because racial prejudice among whites would not permit anything beyond emancipation. Led by P. B. S. Pinchback, an American newcomer, and François Boisdoré, a creole resident, black leaders protested sharply and pushed their reluctant white associates into support of voting rights for all black men who had been free before the war.[45]

This initial demand did not exclude the possibility of extending suffrage to slaves. At this point, the radicals tried to shape their short-term strategy to fit the Bates decision that declared as citizens only those African-Americans who were legally free. Because Louisiana slaves had not yet been freed either by Lincoln's decrees or by any state action, they tried to convince Banks to include at least the black men who had been free before the war in the voting scheduled for February, 1864, to select a new Louisiana constitutional convention. When Banks ignored their requests for voting rights, they vowed to "go to President Lincoln." But before they could organize their efforts, Lincoln also disappointed them when, on December 8, 1863, he announced general guidelines for Reconstruction that excluded all black voters.[46]

Despite these severe setbacks, the black leaders pressed forward. They bolstered their case for free black suffrage by drafting a petition on January 5 that was signed by a thousand free black property owners in the city, as well as twenty-seven black veterans of the War of 1812 and twenty-two white radicals. Simultaneously, they raised funds to send two delegates to bring the petition not only to Lincoln but also to Republican leaders in Congress. In mid-February, the two delegates— E. Arnold Bertonneau, a wine merchant, and Jean Baptiste Roudanez, a mechanical engineer—set off on their revolutionary mission.

The assertive position of these Franco-Africans on black suffrage

---

Papers at the Amistad Research Center, Tulane University. The membership rolls of the Prince Hall Masons of New Orleans can also be found in the Longe Papers.

45. Peyton McCrary, *Abraham Lincoln and Reconstruction: The Louisiana Experiment* (Princeton, 1978), 183–84; *L'Union*, December 1, 1863. Pinchback's migration to New Orleans as a steamboat worker followed the pattern of many American free blacks who settled in New Orleans. See James Haskins, *Pinckney Benton Stewart Pinchback* (New York, 1973), 11–27.

46. New Orleans *Times*, November 6, 1863; Charles Vincent, *Black Legislators in Louisiana During Reconstruction* (Baton Rouge, 1976), 19.

placed them in the political vanguard of the entire nation because even the most radical Republicans feared the political risks among their northern constituents of turning black Americans into voters. Indeed, almost all northern states still limited suffrage to white males, and virtually no one in the country had yet taken up the question of black suffrage in the South. Congress had already buried one bill introduced by James Ashley, the ultra-radical Republican congressman from Ohio, and Lincoln as well as the radical members of his cabinet were treating the issue in the most cautious manner, afraid to speak out publicly. Even the radical wing of the abolitionists, including William Lloyd Garrison, continued to view suffrage as impractical as long as emancipation still required their attention. True, a few stalwarts, like Wendell Phillips and Frederick Douglass, had begun to call for black suffrage about the same time as the free black radicals of New Orleans; but when this small band of northerners pressed the issue during the winter of 1863–1864, they caused a major rift in the abolitionist movement that led to a bitter feud between Phillips and Garrison.[47]

When Bertonneau and Roudanez arrived in New York during this clash, they knew none of the Garrisonians or free black leaders in the North such as Frederick Douglass, Henry Garnet, and John Mercer Langston. Indeed, black northerners apparently first learned of the political demands of the New Orleanians only after their petition was noted in the New York *Evening Post*. After they arrived in Washington, however, Bertonneau and Roudanez quickly discovered that Lincoln and Banks did not represent the most advanced thinking in the Republican party.

A conference with the Massachusetts senator Charles Sumner and Representative William D. Kelly of Pennsylvania showed these creoles a new brand of American opinion. Together, on March 10, they produced an addendum to the petition of the New Orleanians in the form of a memorial signed by Bertonneau and Roudanez, which clarified that the principles behind their petition for free black voting "require also the extension of this privilege to those born slaves, with such qualifications as shall affect equally the white and colored citizen; and that this is required not only by justice, but also by expediency, which demands that full effect should be given to all the Union feeling in the rebel States, in

---

47. For the petition see *Liberator*, April 17, February 5, 1864; Herman Belz, "Origins of Negro Suffrage," *Southern Studies*, XVII (1978), 115; James M. McPherson, *The Struggle for Equality* (Princeton, 1964), 238–46.

order to secure the permanence of the free institutions and loyal governments now organized therein."[48]

When Lincoln met the black New Orleanians on March 12, he was obviously impressed by their demands and demeanor. For the first time, the president received a firsthand account of Louisiana events from black leaders. Reportedly, Lincoln listened to them attentively and "sympathized" with their objectives but concluded that he would not act on moral grounds but only on grounds of military necessity. On the very next day, unbeknownst to the visitors, Lincoln wrote to the newly elected governor of Louisiana, Michael Hahn, urging him to make voters of "some of the colored people . . . as, for instance, the very intelligent, and especially those who have fought gallantly in our ranks." But these cautious, confidential suggestions had little effect because the Banks-dominated convention of 1864 made no provision for black suffrage except to allow the legislature to grant limited voting rights if it so wished.[49]

Bertonneau and Roudanez did not return to New Orleans discouraged. Before they set off for home, the instant celebrities accepted various invitations to meet with white and black northerners. At first, northern black leaders reacted negatively to the two strangers from New Orleans. Indeed, Robert Hamilton, the influential New York editor of the weekly *Anglo-African,* denounced them at public meetings because their petition, as reported in the daily press, seemed intended to limit suffrage to free black men and to create legal castes among African-Americans. For that reason, the black editor praised Lincoln for rejecting their petition. Until this time, most northern black leaders, like Hamilton, had paid little attention to suffrage questions and postwar reconstruction of the South. Many of younger leaders, moreover, had also rejected the integrationist leadership of Frederick Douglass and directed their energies to emigration schemes in West Africa and Haiti. The dramatic actions of the New Orleans delegation now compelled them to reconsider their own objectives.

When Hamilton finally met the New Orleanians in New York fol-

48. *Liberator,* April 17, 1864.

49. *Ibid.,* April 15, 1864. For some additional speculation about this meeting with Lincoln, see LaWanda Cox, *Lincoln and Black Freedom* (Columbia, S.C., 1981), 94–95. Although Lincoln and Hahn showed the letter to several people, the black leaders in New Orleans did not learn its contents until after Lincoln's death (New Orleans *Tribune,* July 7, 1865).

lowing their meeting with Lincoln, he publicly confessed that he had totally misjudged them. The editor learned that they had originally insisted "that the right to vote must be asked for all, and not for those
only who have all their lives been free." They also explained to him in
detail the strategy of their white allies that was embodied in the petition
and noted that they had accepted it only "after much persuasion and
long deliberation." After this meeting, Hamilton pulled all stops in
praise of their revolutionary campaign: "We say all hail, faithful Louisiana! This act shall decorate the brow of her dusky children with a
crown of glory that shall be coequal with civilization itself." Within
weeks, the editor came out in solid support of the New Orleanians and
made their civil rights drive the basis of a call for a national convention
of black Americans.[50]

Bertonneau and Roudanez drew similar reactions from white abolitionists and Radical Republicans. Accepting an invitation to go to
Boston, they attended a dinner meeting in their honor that included
William Lloyd Garrison, Wendell Phillips, Frederick Douglass, and the
incumbent Republican governor of Massachusetts, John A. Andrew.
Seated on either side of the governor at the head of the table, the two
creoles elaborated upon their unusual outlook and vision of a new society in the Americas.

Roudanez reported on the meeting with Lincoln and noted that
their petition and memorial had also been laid before both houses of
Congress. Bertonneau, a former captain of black Union troops, got
more readily to the point. He described how his compatriots had given
"imagination full scope and play" after Butler encouraged them to think
of themselves as "men and citizens." He explained that their immediate
objectives were that "the right to vote shall not depend upon the color
of the citizen, that the colored citizens shall have and enjoy every civil,
political and religious right that white citizens enjoy; in a word, that
every man shall stand equal before the law." Their ultimate goal, he
said, was to change "the character of the whole people" by sending their
children to schools "to learn the great truth that God 'created of one
blood all nations of men to dwell on the face of the earth'—so will
caste, founded on prejudice against color, disappear." Bertonneau then
turned to Garrison, president of the Massachusetts Anti-Slavery Society,
and to prolonged applause vowed that he would urge his compatriots in

50. *Anglo-African*, April 2, 16, 23, July 23, 1864.

New Orleans to fight for the same integration of public accommodations and schools that the Garrisonians had helped to inaugurate in Massachusetts. Clearly moved by the cheers, Garrison stood up and praised the visitors for "their self-respect, their dignity, and the noble regard which they feel for their oppressed brothers." Although he noticeably failed to applaud their suffrage cause, his comments still managed to bring the gathering to a loud rendition of the "John Brown Song." Before the gathering ended, however, the seasoned activist Frederick Douglass warned the New Orleanians that "the prospect was not so sanguine."[51]

Black Creoles and White Yankees

Douglass was right. Bertonneau and Roudanez returned to a state where white conservative Unionists, with General Banks's sanction, were still meeting in a convention that steadfastly refused to grant suffrage to any black Louisianians, free or slave. Even before their return, *L'Union* had already shown its true colors by coming out for extending the suffrage to all freedmen and calling for "harmony among all the descendants of the African race." The editor, Trévigne, urged that voting qualifications be based on "the rightful capacity of all native and free born Americans, by virtue of their nativity in the country, irrespective of national descent, wealth or intelligence—and that all not free, within the state, be immediately enfranchised by the abolition of slavery in the state forever, and by a statute or constitutional provision declaring the absolute equality of all free men as to their governmental rights." The newspaper also praised the emissaries and heralded the new support and publicity that they had gained in the North for the enlarged cause of universal male suffrage. At the same time, Trévigne warned his readers how Napoleon had divided black Haitians and undermined the freedom and citizenship granted by the French Revolution of 1789. He therefore urged "all those of our race" to remember that "United, we stand! Divided, we fall!"[52]

Banks resented the creole black leaders' successful recruitment of support from important northern Republicans.[53] He had wanted to succeed Lincoln based on his accomplishments in Louisiana both as a mili-

51. Boston *Daily Advertiser*, April 13, 1864, as quoted in the *Liberator*, April 15, 1864.
52. *L'Union*, April 9, 14, May 26, 1864.
53. *Liberator*, March 11, April 8, 1864.

tary leader and as the political maestro of Reconstruction. When the widened campaign of the black creole leaders complicated his efforts, Banks and his cohorts went on a counterattack. At first, they made a frontal assault against the oracle of the criticism, *L'Union*. Thomas A. Conway, a Baptist chaplain, who had been assigned by Banks to clean up the general's scandal-ridden labor program, cut off the subsidy the black newspaper had received from the army for printing public notices.

The tactics almost worked. The collapse of the economy in New Orleans had placed terrible burdens on every inhabitant, including those in the free black community. Without the army's support, sustaining the triweekly paper—indeed, even subscribing to it—required not only financial sacrifice but also great courage. Nonetheless, the free black creole community stuck to its guns when Paul Trévigne announced that his desperate financial situation was forcing him to fold the only organ "which the oppressed class of the State ever had." Within a few days, Dr. Louis Charles Roudanez, the brother of J. B. Roudanez and a participant in the Paris revolution of 1848, came forward to finance another paper, the New Orleans *Tribune*, and gave its editor, Paul Trévigne, a more secure forum.[54]

To herald the new paper's first issue and to bolster racial solidarity, a key group of American black leaders founded a new organization, the National Union Brotherhood Association, which publicly endorsed the *Tribune*'s political program.[55] Each rebuff by Banks only seemed to increase the radicalism and confidence of the assertive black leaders. By fall, the new surge of community support enabled the *Tribune* to become the first daily black newspaper in the history of the United States. Its new, regular correspondents in Boston, Washington, and Paris also kept black New Orleanians in touch with those major centers of political and ideological influence.

To meet the new, enlarged challenge of the *Tribune*, another Banks associate struck from a different front. Major B. Rush Plumly, an abolitionist soldier from Pennsylvania, who had switched sides in Louisiana from the radical camp to the Banks group in early 1864, took up Banks's defense among his fellow abolitionists in the North by questioning the motives and attitudes of the free black creoles. Aware that Garrison had broken with Wendell Phillips and the majority of the New England abo-

54. *L'Union*, July 19, 1864.
55. *Anglo-African*, August 27, September 24, October 1, 1864.

litionists over their demand for universal suffrage in Louisiana, Plumly shrewdly nurtured the deeply hurt editor of the *Liberator*. Plumly's task was made easier when the *Tribune* fiercely attacked Garrison for not endorsing their demands for suffrage. Plumly bolstered the Bostonian's resentment by noting that many of "the free colored men have not yet forgotten that they were slaveholders" and had "not attained to all the grace and wisdom of freedom." In an open letter to the *Liberator,* Plumly pleaded with the abolitionists to realize that the *Tribune* was the mouthpiece of an "aristocratic" and "exclusive" caste that still remained loyal to the Confederacy and was "bitterly hostile to the black, except as a slave." [56]

Plumly blatantly lied. From the beginning the *Tribune* had endorsed suffrage for the freedmen. Indeed, at the very moment that Plumly was making his wild charges, the *Tribune* was leading a campaign against the Smith bill then pending in the new state legislature. Designed by Banks, the bill proposed to enfranchise those free black men who were quadroons or lighter in complexion by legally defining them as white men. The *Tribune* condemned such a racist approach and ridiculed Plumly's general knowledge of all but a handful of free black creoles. [57] Deeply angered, the *Tribune* editors renewed their fierce attack on those Yankees who denied their demands for universal male suffrage and equal citizenship: "The Garrisonians do not often forget that they belong to the white race, and seem to say to the Negro: 'now that you are free, you will go no further.' . . . It is in rising up against an arrogant and vindictive race that we sometimes run afoul of the feelings of those who play the part of defenders of the principles of the Declaration of Independence, and who dare not throw off their irrational and absurd prejudices." [58]

Once Plumly and Conway realized that their attacks on the creole leaders had backfired, they tried to make amends by calling a meeting with the creole leaders to plead for their support for the Banks program. [59] But this time, the Banks surrogates had fatally injured themselves. Like so many American power brokers, Conway and Plumly had

56. New Orleans *Tribune,* August 4, October 12, 1864.
57. Donald E. Everett, "Demands of the Free Colored Population for Political Equality, 1862–1865," *Louisiana Historical Quarterly,* XXXVIII (1955), 56; New Orleans *Tribune,* December 7, 1864.
58. New Orleans *Tribune,* October 11, 1864.
59. *Ibid.*

a difficult time fathoming the radical politics of the Franco-Africans in New Orleans who sought no mere political favor from their agitation but rather an entirely new social and racial order.

The *Tribune* editors tried to explain their rejection of the overtures to negotiate their differences: "We do not fight for a material advantage that we can peddle between the two parties: we defend a principle. We can compromise with interests, but we cannot compromise with principles. Assured of the sound basis of our rights, we proclaim them, we uphold them fully and completely, and we will hear nothing of sacrificing them. . . . This is why we do not accept the proposition of the Major [Plumly] of supporting the new Constitution of Louisiana. . . . The revolution moves forward; we await our hour; it will come, and we will enter into the temple not dressed in the garb of the catechumen, led to the altar by a godfather and a godmother, but in the dress of Uncle Sam's men in arms." [60]

The *Tribune* leaders would not retreat; they had gone too far in their struggle to win universal male suffrage. They had cemented a political coalition among black New Orleanians by drawing upon key allies within the American black community, particularly Oscar J. Dunn and James Ingraham. The former was the grand master of the Prince Hall Masons and the latter a Freemason and an AME church member as well as a hero for leading the first black combat troops of the war at Port Hudson.

As an officer of the city's National Union Brotherhood Association, Ingraham did more than draw together black Americans and creoles in New Orleans. He also linked the political efforts of the New Orleans radicals to a national organization of black Americans, the National Equal Rights League. In early October, 1864, at Syracuse, New York, that new group had come into existence during a reassembling of the prewar Negro Convention called by Henry Garnet and the editors of the *Anglo-African*. At this meeting, black delegates from all parts of the country met under the direction of Frederick Douglass to consider their role in a postwar society. They demanded unequivocal abolition of slavery and universal male suffrage. To help establish those demands, they formed the National Equal Rights League as a permanent civil rights federation. [61]

60. *Ibid.*, November 16, 1864.
61. *Proceedings of the National Convention of Colored Men Held in the City of*

After Ingraham captured the limelight at the Syracuse convention by waving his regiment's battle standard and pledging the largest amount of money to the new federation, he rushed back home to create a state chapter of the newly christened league at a state convention of black leaders in January, 1865.[62] The gathering endorsed the resolutions of the Syracuse convention, formed the first state chapter of the league, and voted for Ingraham as its president and the *Tribune* as its official organ. These steps only reinforced the determination of the black radical leaders to defeat Lincoln's Reconstruction plans for Louisiana just then before Congress and to urge Republicans to impose black citizenship and universal male suffrage over the entire South.

Creole-American Division

The strategy of the radical faction in New Orleans pushed the Banks "oligarchy" into taking desperate measures that exploited lingering divisions within the black community of New Orleans. Having failed to isolate the New Orleans leaders from Northern abolitionists, Plumly and Conway now tried to open a wedge within the city's black community by recruiting black American Protestants to help them in their struggle against the creole-dominated opposition. As northern Protestants, Plumly (a Quaker) and Conway (a Baptist minister) appealed to religious and cultural prejudice to divide the black political opposition and seek support for their more moderate plans.

By 1865, the demography of the black population in New Orleans had changed dramatically. The percentage of black creoles in the city declined when almost fifteen thousand slaves fled into the city from the countryside, badly in need of housing, employment, medical care, education, and spiritual support. Most of the freedmen and women were English-speaking Protestants of American heritage. The freedom to build community organizations took up most of the energies of both black creoles and Americans. Unlike the political movements for emancipation and suffrage, this activity, however, often bolstered ethnic autonomy among both the creoles and the Americans.

Syracuse New York, October 4, 5, 6, and 7, 1864 (Boston, 1864), 13, 36–43, as found in *Proceedings of the National Negro Conventions, 1830–1864*, ed. Howard Bell (New York, 1969).

62. *Anglo-African*, October 8, 15, 1864.

With greater resources and freedom in the antebellum period, black creoles had already fashioned a considerable number of organizations, but emancipation brought several important changes. First, without the prewar legal restrictions, they could more easily cross the old barriers between those who had been free and those who had been slaves. Many slave residents in the antebellum city as well as postwar refugees from southern Louisiana who were French-speaking Catholic creoles became part of a working black creole community in New Orleans.[63]

Black Catholic benevolent organizations rapidly expanded after Union occupation, particularly under the forceful leadership of a radical French-born Catholic priest, Father Claude Pascal Maistre, who in early 1863 began a radical congregation that prayed for Union victory, celebrated emancipation, and memorialized John Brown. After he was suspended by the city's archbishop, he continued to hold the allegiance of many black Catholics within his schismatic church. In July, 1863, his role first became notable in the city newspapers when he organized over thirty-seven black societies, primarily creole groups, to follow in the funeral procession of Captain André Callioux, the black hero of Port Hudson.[64]

The presence of this famous priest symbolized the troubled relationship that had developed between the Catholic church and the city's black community. Since its founding in the city, the Catholic church had remained in the hands of foreign-born, French-speaking prelates and clergy. Indeed, as late as 1869, only one priest in New Orleans was American-born, and all of the bishops and archbishops of the church since its formal organization in 1793 had been ordained in Europe by French-speaking orders. The non-American origins of the clergy and the

---

63. For the complicated relationships of free and slave status within a single black creole family, see Document 295 in *Freedom*, ed. Berlin, II, 684–85. Two very prominent black creole leaders in postwar Louisiana had been slaves until the war began: Basile Barrès, the musician, and Theophile T. Allain, a state senator.

64. Ted Tunnell, *Crucible of Reconstruction: War, Radicalism, and Race in Louisiana, 1862–1877* (Baton Rouge, 1984), 71–73; New Orleans *Bee*, January 13, 1859. For a list of some of these organizations, see Roger Baudier, *Centennial: St. Rose of Lima Parish* (New Orleans, 1957), 21. For a good analysis of Maistre, see Geraldine M. McTigue, "Forms of Racial Interaction in Louisiana, 1860–1880" (Ph.D. dissertation, Yale University, 1975), 37–41. *L'Union*, January 26, 1864; New Orleans *Tribune*, June 13, July 31, November 30, December 27, 1867, January 9, 1869; Baudier, *Centennial*, 20–24; Roger Baudier, *The Catholic Church in Louisiana* (New Orleans, 1939), 393–413.

nuns probably help to explain why the Catholic church in southern Louisiana offered various services for its black members and long resisted the complete racial segregation of its congregations.[65]

Integrated churches, however, had not brought much semblance of racial equality in Catholic circles. Well before the Civil War, the diocese had forbidden racial intermarriage, denied the entrance of black men into the priesthood, and implemented segregation in its schools, cemeteries, and lay societies. In some churches, particularly uptown churches that catered to pugnacious Irish immigrants, black members had to use segregated pews and special entrances. In addition, the church prelates sanctioned slavery and gave enthusiastic support to the Confederacy.[66]

The attitudes of Catholic church leaders led many black creoles to seek other forms of organization to meet their spiritual and communal needs. Some left the Catholic church for Protestant churches, but the most defiant leaders turned to traditional French, anticlerical outlets—spiritualist societies and Masonic lodges. In the North, American spiritualism had spread rapidly during the 1850s, deriving strength from the conversion of leading politicians, activists, and journalists. A similar surge of spiritualism occurred in New Orleans about the same time, but it proceeded from distinctly French origins and remained confined during the antebellum period to a limited group within the French-speaking population. It was to this tradition that key black creole leaders, such as Joanni Questy, Nelson Desbrosses, Henry and Octave Rey, Charles Vêque, Aristide Mary, Antoine Dubuclet, and Rodolphe Desdunes, turned for inspiration and direction.

An even larger and perhaps more important organization in the black creole community was the Scottish Rite Masonic order, under the jurisdiction of the grand master of France. Unlike the leaders of the Catholic church, the well-established French-speaking Masons made a bold and radical departure from the city's antebellum racial order.

65. John T. Gillard, *The Catholic Church and the American Negro* (Baltimore, 1929), 38–42, 72–73. Also see a later, expanded work by the same author, *Colored Catholics in the United States* (Baltimore, 1941), 122–23. For a critical appraisal of segregation in the Catholic churches in New Orleans, see Charles B. Rousséve, *The Negro in Louisiana: Aspects of His History and His Literature* (New Orleans, 1937), 139–41.

66. *L'Union* and the *Tribune* often criticized the Catholic church for its conservatism. See *L'Union*, November 15, December 6, 1862, May 31, 1864; New Orleans *Tribune*, November 6, 1864, May 11, 1865, December 1, 1867. Paul Trévigne, however, also noted the strong attachment of black Catholics to the Catholic church, despite the political conservatism of its clergy. See *L'Union*, May 31, 1864.

Shortly after the Civil War, they responded favorably to orders from French superiors to open their lodges to black members.[67] When the local leader, Eugène Chassaignac, invited black New Orleanians to join his group, they responded enthusiastically. Within newly formed lodges, many prominent black creole men found not only spiritual but also political support from the colony of radical white French émigrés in New Orleans.[68]

By 1867, the organizational structure of black creole society was largely intact. Antebellum groups such as the Economy Society, the Veterans of 1812, and the Society of Artisans openly flourished, and their members overlapped into anticlerical organizations such as the Masons and spiritualists. At one time or another, all of these groups endorsed the New Orleans *Tribune* or made it their official organ.

Community building was much more difficult for black New Orleanians of American heritage, particularly the freedmen who fled into the city during the war. From the beginning, the Federal army had tried to disperse these rural refugees back into agricultural labor on Union-controlled plantations, but the forced evacuations had created a national uproar. By early 1864, Banks—in response to his critics—permitted greater freedom of movement and began to provide for some of the educational and health needs of the freedmen. Various northern Protestant church groups had also sent missionary teachers and ministers to help in this monumental effort. After considerable political infighting among Federal officials and the religious missionaries, Plumly had emerged in charge of the freedmen schools and Conway had gained control of the labor program.[69]

These positions gave Plumly and Conway a perfect opportunity to try to use the freedmen against the army's political adversaries, the

67. New Orleans *Tribune*, October 7, 1865. The French Masonic leader, Felix Vogeli of Lyons, appealed to French Masons in the United States: "Let us be the first to combat on this land of Liberty . . . prejudices of all kinds; let us furnish the example of their irrationality."

68. *Ibid.*, June 18, 23, July 25, 26, November 6, 8, 1867. In late 1868, the integrated Scottish Rite lodges gave Chassaignac a gold medal "as a Token of esteem for his courageous action in the cause of humanity in opening the Masonic temples to all men without distinction of color" (*ibid.*, January 5, 1869).

69. William F. Messner, *Freedmen and the Ideology of Free Labor: Louisiana, 1862–1865* (Lafayette, La., 1978), 99–105, 171–72. For a discussion of the rivalry among Protestant leaders, see Jacquelyn S. Haywood, "The American Missionary Association in Louisiana During Reconstruction" (Ph.D. dissertation, University of California at Los Angeles, 1974), 67–75, 129–37.

creole-dominated radicals. Because most of the refugee freedmen and women in New Orleans were Americans with ties to the Baptists and Methodists, the Banks group worked closely with those churches. Since most of the black Baptists as well as the black members of the Methodist Episcopal Church, South, had already been dependent on white southern churchmen and benefactors, their new relationship with the white army personnel represented only a slight departure from their earlier dependency.

Even if there had been no political disagreements, black Protestant ministers and their white northern co-workers would probably have run into conflicts with the black creoles of New Orleans. Both black and white Protestants abhorred the Catholic faith that predominated among black creoles. Evangelistic fervor also led some of the preachers into believing that the black creole communities offered a major potential for conversions. One black Methodist minister exhibited this outlook when he boasted that many black Catholics had already thrown away "the rosaries or beads and come to Jesus. . . . In their religious delight they declared that they like our American God." [70]

Protestant ministers disliked more than just the creoles' Catholicism. They also scorned the city's deeply rooted Afro-Latin way of life that offended their Anglo-Protestant sensibilities. The ministers condemned dancing, desecration of the Sabbath, gambling, drinking, lavish entertainment, and the open sensual pleasures that infused Mardi Gras and other public festivals in New Orleans. When, for example, black creoles tried to raise funds for orphanages or schools by holding raffles, the clerics denounced them as gamblers and urged their fellow Protestants not to cooperate. In one case, they even removed Protestant children from a nondenominational creole orphanage to keep them free of such Catholic influence. [71]

A fundamental difference about race relations also caused friction between the two groups. Creole leaders resented racial separation even in private institutions and constantly nagged black as well as white recalcitrants about any adherence to the color line. Most of the Protestant

70. Methodist Episcopal Church, *Proceedings of the Second Session of the Mississippi Mission Conference* [1866], 8.

71. *Louisianian,* May 18, 1871; Methodist Episcopal Church, *Journal of Louisiana Conference* [1876], 20–22; *Southwestern Christian Advocate,* November 6, 1873, February 26, 1874, May 9, 1876, June 22, September 14, 1882, March 15, 1883, April 3, 1884. For a discussion of the orphanage quarrel, see New Orleans *Tribune,* October 25, November 23, December 5, 1865, June 14, November 24, 1866, May 21, 1867.

leaders, however, had responded to racial discrimination in Anglo-America by forming their own all-black institutions where they could find solace and support. The reluctance of most black creoles to adopt Victorian behavior or to accept the norms of the American color line struck some black Americans as a denial of racial solidarity.

The leaders of the *Tribune* tried to surmount the rivalries. In addition to printing their newspapers in English as well as French, they opened special columns for news of Protestant churches and fraternal organizations. They also hired a black American assistant editor, Moses Avery, who was the secretary of the National Union Brotherhood Association in New Orleans. In the midst of the intrablack power struggle, Dr. Roudanez made another important change by recruiting an outsider, Jean-Charles Houzeau, to edit the paper's English columns.[72]

Houzeau, a radical Belgian émigré who had fled from Texas because of his abolitionist views, concentrated on healing the divisiveness stimulated by the Banks cohorts. He quickly recognized that the primary obstacle to greater unity stemmed from the "spirit of independence" among the "Franco-Africans." Their stubborn pride and assertiveness led them to resent the white Yankees who dominated Unionist politics in Louisiana. Houzeau never seemed to understand the depth of the antagonism that the racially conservative white Unionists had created among the black creoles before he arrived in November, 1864, but he realized that most black Louisianians of Anglo-American heritage rejected the creole leaders' hostility to the white northerners who were doing so much to help the Protestant freedmen.[73]

When Houzeau reached New Orleans, the two-year-long battle between the *Tribune* leaders and the Banks forces was well under way; by early 1865, it had reached a critical stage. At that point, the creoles and their black American allies in the National Equal Rights League of Louisiana joined forces with Radical Republicans in Congress to defeat a bill backed by Lincoln's administration to restore Louisiana to the Union. Because the Radicals had insisted upon universal black male suffrage throughout the South, they felt that Louisiana's restoration without any black suffrage would jeopardize their larger goals.

The editors of the *Tribune* continued to direct their Gallic rage

72. New Orleans *Tribune*, June 18, 1867, January 21, February 5, May 7, 1865. See also Houzeau, *My Passage at the New Orleans "Tribune,"* 48–49, 82–84.

73. See the letters of Houzeau to his parents, March 2, April 2, 1868, in the Houzeau Collection at the Bibliothèque Royale in Brussels, Belgium.

against all of their critics inside and outside of Louisiana. When, for example, William Lloyd Garrison justified his public endorsement of Lincoln's Reconstruction bill for Louisiana by noting that the British had not enfranchised the slaves they emancipated in the West Indies, the editors lashed out against him. They urged the abolitionists to broaden their vision to areas beyond the English-speaking world, where universal male suffrage had never been tried. They proclaimed that their own demands for equality came from the experiment in French territories, where "at the moment that liberty was proclaimed, legal equality was immediately a fact." They wanted America to follow that example and put into its Constitution what the French had done in theirs by declaring "all Frenchmen without distinction of class or color . . . equal before the law." The *Tribune* wondered why the "proud Anglo-Saxon" hesitated "to fulfill an act of justice." [74]

To counter this resolute opposition in New Orleans, Conway and Plumly reached out to black American leaders, particularly the Baptist and Methodist Episcopal preachers. The two officials tried to placate some of the black opposition by circulating a petition to the Louisiana legislature in support of limited black suffrage. In part, their strategy worked. Conway and Plumly also gained enough support among black Protestant leaders to force a reconvening of the National Equal Rights League chapter in the city, but after several votes failed to reverse the group's earlier stand against the petition for limited suffrage, the Banks forces devised another stratagem to offset the *Tribune*'s effective attack on their halfway measures. [75]

In April, 1865, they launched the *Black Republican* under the apparent leadership of two Baptist ministers and several other leaders in the black American community. To Banks, who was directing the administration's efforts in Washington, Conway exaggerated his little conspiracy, claiming that "the American negroes are indignant" about the attacks of "the rich colored men" and were starting the paper "to more fully represent the cause of the black man." Plumly joined in the distortion by writing to Lincoln that "the American colored people here, disgusted with the 'N. O. Tribune'—the French Jesuit (color'd) paper, that under Durant and a few colored Creoles, has always been against us— are just starting another paper. . . . It will be out in a few days. I have

74. New Orleans *Tribune,* January 28, 1865.
75. *Ibid.,* January 14, February 4, 5, 1865.

been requested, by the Association to send the first copy to you, with the renewed expression of the undying gratitude and confidence of the People of Color." [76]

The columns of the *Black Republican* nurtured the potential ethnic antagonisms within the black community of New Orleans. The paper repeated Plumly's old innuendos about wealthy, free black creoles and their non-American sentiments. It praised Banks and his labor program and found excuses for his failure to implement black suffrage in Louisiana. On the key issue of suffrage, the *Black Republican* meekly noted: "It would be an anomaly in the history of politics to change in a short season the usages of a State like this to such as to confer upon the colored race rights and privileges heretofore not enjoyed by them in any other state of the Union save one." [77]

The Banks cohorts also turned to black American leaders who had come to New Orleans after the Union occupation. Some, like the Baptist minister S. W. Rogers, had come to establish new Protestant churches; some, like Edmonia Highgate, to teach in the freedmen schools; and still others, like P. B. Randolph, to take advantage of the new promising field for their political ambitions.

Randolph was an extraordinary man who had already traveled to Europe, Asia, and Africa. He was well-known in black communities of Boston and New York and had played a key role in the Syracuse convention of October, 1864. He came to New Orleans with the intention of "bringing my Southern brethren up to the highest standard of [the] men of Boston." Such presumptuousness, however, did not sit well with the proud creoles. They needed no one to lecture them about the world or their aspirations. When Randolph arrived, he met an "icy" reception and quickly learned that he had no understanding of New Orleans. He could compare the vast mixture of races, nationalities, and cultures only to "Beyrout, Syria." Because he was curious and fluent in French and English, he eventually discerned the "two totally distinct and widely divergent classes" of people within black New Orleans, which he perceptively labeled "Creole and American." Creoles, he also discerned, were "not as many suppose . . . the miscegens or mixed bloods, but . . . natives of the city." He noticed, too, that "the lines between the separate

76. Cox, *Lincoln and Black Freedom,* 128. Before he set up the black rival paper, Conway apparently tried to get the army to shut down the *Tribune.* See Henry A. White, *The Freedmen's Bureau in Louisiana* (Baton Rouge, 1970), 18–19.

77. *Black Republican,* April 15, 22, 29, 1865.

sections of colored Society here, are distinctly marked. Very few French live above Canal St., very few Americans below it, and save politically, they seldom affiliate."[78]

Randolph, who arrived in the midst of the contest between the creole-led *Tribune* faction and the Banks forces, picked his sides. After he and his cousin from Boston, Frank Potter, gained jobs in the army schools under Plumly, the newcomers joined the fray against the creoles. In the New York *Anglo-African,* Randolph insisted that the National Equal Rights League of Louisiana had been packed by black creoles and did not represent the view of most black Louisianians. "My entire sympathy," he declared, "is with the freedmen and the American people, for the reason that they do the fighting; but I see no French soldiers—not one. . . . There may be . . . but we outnumber them ten hundred to a single one, and therefore if any interest predominates, it ought to be ours, not theirs. Vive l'Amerique touts les jours!" Randolph ended his letter by complimenting General Banks, praising Conway as "the noble heart," and insisting that Plumly's "glorious acts in our favor deserve to be written in the same constellation."[79]

The black creole leaders in New Orleans did not flinch. When they learned of Randolph's letter, they reprinted it openly in New Orleans and dared Randolph to prove his charges. They also declared him no "true representative of the North" and "unworthy of a place in our community." Thoroughly ostracized, he lost his job as a regular columnist of the *Anglo-African* and quietly disappeared from the political scene. He had more than met his match in New Orleans.[80]

Despite their unscrupulous and damaging plots to divide the New Orleans black community, Banks and his cohorts failed to undermine the radical program for racial change in Louisiana. For the next three years the *Tribune* evoked the political demands of the New Orleans black community without any significant dissent. And no black leader appeared to take a more radical position than the *Tribune.*

The only notable division came during the terrible riots of 1866,

78. *Anglo-African,* October 1, 1864, January 21, 28, 1865.
79. *Ibid.,* February 25, 1865; New Orleans *Tribune,* March 10, 11, June 30, July 17, 1865.
80. Although initially an outspoken proponent of black racialism, Randolph (1825–1874) ended his career as a bizarre apostle of spiritualism and free love and even denied his African ancestry. See Pascal Beverly Randolph, *P. B. Randolph: His Curious Life, Works, and Career* (Boston, 1872).

when the last antebellum mayor of the city, John T. Monroe, returned to power and unleashed full police power against a pro-black suffrage convention in July, 1866. The repression caused Methodist Episcopal leaders to urge their black members to pull back from the political arena. Another black emigrationist leader, John Willis Menard, who came to the city from Illinois, via British Honduras and Jamaica, where he had seen a similar backlash in 1865, also recommended a retreat in a pamphlet entitled *Black and White*. He thought that the "African race" should turn inward and "help itself." The *Tribune* editors could sympathize with his racial pride, but they refused to accept Menard's view that universal suffrage had been demanded "too soon or too harshly" and should be abandoned in favor of "suffrage on the basis of intelligence" to encourage "the friendship of the dominant class" and to gain "security of life, liberty, and property." Instead, the *Tribune* editors bemoaned that the enactment of universal suffrage had not come before the end of the war and that its delay had only encouraged violent opposition. The right to vote, they insisted, had to remain "an attribute of citizenship." [81]

The *Tribune* agenda held the day, despite some of the worst racial violence in the South. Black Louisianians not only gained universal male suffrage but also went beyond almost all other southern states in their attempts to end racial segregation. Indeed, the paper's Belgian editor played a major role in 1866 in winning support for universal male suffrage by continuing the paper during the height of the violence and broadcasting news about it, which helped turn the political tide against Andrew Johnson and pass the Fourteenth Amendment and the Reconstruction acts. In their constitution of 1868 and in subsequent legislation, the Louisiana radicals mandated the integration of all government facilities, including public schools, and also all private businesses licensed by the state to serve the public. In quest of these ends, black leaders remained united behind the agenda set by the *Tribune* leaders—at least for a time.

81. Methodist Episcopal Church, *Proceedings of the Second Session of the Mississippi Mission Conference,* 20–21. At this conference, Methodist officials urged their Louisiana flock to "command better relations with conservatives"; "to banish all erroneous and strange notions, instilled in them by impractical men, concerning their own destiny"; and "to counsel obedience to law and patient endurance for righteousness sake." See also New Orleans *Tribune,* October 31, November 6, 1866; J. Willis Menard, *Black and White* (New Orleans, 1866), 4.

Cultural Transfers in Black New Orleans

More than a common political agenda in the early years of Reconstruction helped to diminish ethnic differences and unify the black community of New Orleans. Educational needs, particularly in the creole sectors, led many of the Catholic French-speakers into closer association with Protestant English-speakers. True, free black Catholics had reached relatively high levels of literacy before the Civil War, but only the wealthiest families could send their children outside the city for schooling beyond the elementary grades. A few orders of Catholic nuns offered elementary education in their antebellum parochial schools, but none opened their doors to black boys. And until after World War II, the Jesuits, Christian Brothers, and diocesan clergy limited the use of their schools and academies in New Orleans to white males.[82]

Although the number of Catholic schools expanded rapidly after the Civil War from about ten elementary schools and three high schools to about sixty schools and academies by 1885, only five of them accepted a total of about three hundred black students out of the approximately ten thousand children in the entire Catholic system in the city.[83] Most black creoles had to turn to public and Protestant schools for an education. Because Benjamin Butler ended the use of French as a teaching language when he consolidated the city's three separate public school districts in 1862, those institutions became a powerful instrument of Americanization for many French-speaking white and black creoles in the postwar era. To be sure, a few private tutors tried to keep alive the French language, history, and literature, but not many black creole families could afford to pay their fees.

For secondary or higher education, most black creoles also had to turn to Protestant colleges that opened during Reconstruction: Leland College (Baptist), New Orleans University (Methodist), and Straight University (Congregational). Straight University proved the most popular for black Catholics during the nineteenth century both because it was closer to their downtown neighborhoods and because it apparently

82. *Catholic Directory*, 1858–1900; Gillard, *Colored Catholics*, 203; Carolo E. Nolan, *Bayou Carmel: The Sisters of Mount Carmel of Louisiana* (Kenner, La., 1977), 17–23. Among the ten elementary schools and three secondary academies in 1860, there was only one elementary school for black girls and none for boys (Edward D. Reynolds, *Jesuits for the Negro* [New York, 1949], see the foreword and pp. 162–66, 174–75).

83. *Catholic Directory*, 1885. See also Mary Di Martino, "Education in New Orleans During Reconstruction" (M.A. thesis, Tulane University, 1935), 172–81.

made less effort to proselytize its student body. Some creole leaders tried to avoid this dilemma by founding a nondenominational, public land-grant college, the Agricultural and Mechanical College, but its duration as a desegregated college was too short to have much effect. During Reconstruction, all of the public high schools in the city enrolled black students, but between 1879 and 1917 no city-run high school was available for black students in New Orleans. For secondary education they had only the preparatory schools of the Protestant-dominated colleges or the meager facilities of the segregated, state-sponsored Southern University.[84]

American black leaders also set the pace in establishing organizations that linked black New Orleanians to other black people in the United States. Drawing on national associations elsewhere, they duplicated local units in New Orleans after the Civil War. These included the Odd Fellows in 1866, the Knights Templar in the 1870s, the Knights of Pythias in 1881, and the Eastern Star, a women's auxiliary of the Prince Hall Masons. Because many of these benevolent organizations were nonsectarian, both Catholic and Protestant blacks in New Orleans could join in association. The Odd Fellows made a special point of downplaying religious views and concentrating on the sheer joy of camaraderie. The penchant for forming branches of national groups became such a craze by the 1880s that one newspaper found them "so numerous . . . that they can scarcely be enumerated." So it must have seemed, for by the early twentieth century, more than 280 clubs and organizations were meeting regularly in New Orleans.[85]

In addition to their commingling in schools and benevolent societies, black Americans and creoles also transcended ethnic boundaries in their social life and entertainment. Black newspapers during the 1870s and 1880s regularly noted this interaction. The well-established creole life-style of good food, dance, music, gambling halls, ritualized festivals, and marching bands quickly caught the attention of the Protestant newcomers. One Protestant reporter who covered a sumptuous creole ball for the *Louisianian* confessed that he did not dance but still admired

---

84. Blassingame, *Black New Orleans*, 107–30.

85. *Louisianian*, February 1, August 9, 1879, September 24, 1881; *Southwestern Christian Advocate*, December 6, 1883. See also Dorothy Rose Eagleson, "Some Aspects of the Social Life of the New Orleans Negro in the 1880s" (M.A. thesis, Tulane University, 1961), 77–80. For a list of the many black groups in New Orleans, see *Woods Directory: A Classified Colored Business, Professional and Trade Directory of New Orleans* (New Orleans, 1912).

creole frolicking: "We love music and dancing, and chatting with the Belles." Although some creole societies showed religious exclusivity by beginning their parades and outdoor dances with a mass at the cathedral, uptown Protestants quickly copied the creole customs of "music, dancing, feasting, and romps" in their own neighborhoods. By the 1880s their own marching bands were stopping at Protestant churches to have their banners "blessed." [86]

The pace of this creolization frightened some of the Protestant leaders. The *Louisianian* warned: "Whilst patronizing liberally balls and parades, our young men should not forget the revivals at St. James [AME] and Central [Congregational] churches. Remember the hereafter." The ministers were less restrained. The Methodist newspaper was particularly scornful of the regular frivolity in the city and noted that the lures of "the dance, the card table, and the theater" were leading the young people away from the church. The editor called for a revival of religion to "shut up theaters, dancing houses, and rum holes." [87]

When one of the white Methodist Episcopal bishops, John F. Hurst, came from the North, he could hardly believe the city's scandalous behavior. He noted that "there is certainly no place in the country where it is more difficult . . . for a Christian to preserve his religious fervor, than in New Orleans." But at the same time he had to recognize that "there is a cheerful air throughout the city. In the French or English part, it makes no difference—all is bright, cheery, hopeful. . . . There is less anxiety in the face and speech than one generally finds among Americans." By 1894, even the more disciplined black Methodist preachers of this bishop's church were "sprinkling" banners, regalia, dolls, and other paraphernalia and holding festivals on Saturday night that extended "far into the Sabbath." Drawing from this peculiar creole-American cultural interchange, black New Orleanians added many new features

86. *Louisianian*, February 26, 1871, February 12, 1881. For examples of social activities at which newspaper reporters noted creole and American commingling, see *ibid.*, February 16, May 14, 21, September 28, October 1, November 30, 1871. A decade later the interchange still drew notice: *ibid.*, December 25, 1880, June 25, July 30, August 27, 1881, February 18, 25, 1882. In a careful review of the social columns and editorials of New Orleans black newspapers, we found no mention of any society formed on the basis of light or dark skin color as happened in Charleston, South Carolina. Another historian recently came to the same conclusion: Virginia R. Dominguez, *White by Definition: Social Classification in Creole Louisiana* (New Brunswick, N.J., 1986), 164.

87. *Louisianian*, January 8, 1881; *Southwestern Christian Advocate*, June 22, September 14, 1882, March 15, 1883.

to the city's vibrant folk culture—none more famous than the new musical forms of jazz.[88]

Despite all these examples of erosion in the ethnic boundaries of their communities, black creoles and Americans continued to concentrate in different neighborhoods and often formed separate social and cultural institutions. And if they worked together in the early years of Reconstruction to win impressive political and civil rights, their leaders never fully surmounted the rivalries that reflected their different values, goals, and aspirations. Throughout the late nineteenth century, the major division among black politicians still ran along the creole-American rift that had been exacerbated by the Banks leaders in 1865. New black and white leaders may have entered the political scene, but, like earlier leaders, some still continued to stir the ethnic divisions.[89]

Henry C. Warmoth and the Creoles

After 1867, the radical creole leaders who had so brilliantly maintained their agenda of revolutionary demands found it more difficult to exert the same dominance in the more normal electoral politics initiated by the Reconstruction acts of 1867. They did not shrink away from the new political arena, but they found it difficult to win elective office, proving to be better agitators than pragmatic politicians. By 1868, they lost control of the Republican party to a coalition of white carpetbaggers and American black leaders.

The nature of the electoral districts in New Orleans helps to explain the meager number of black creoles in the Reconstruction legislatures. Since less than 30 percent of the city's population was black from 1860 to 1900, no creole electoral district had a black majority to provide a secure voting base for their candidates. In their racially mixed neighborhoods, only Algiers on the west bank of the river contained even a substantial black voting plurality, and it was from this ward that a key black

88. *Southwestern Christian Advocate*, March 15, 1883, May 17, 31, 1894; Alan Lomax, *Mister Jelly Roll: The Fortunes of Jelly Roll Morton, New Orleans Creole and "Inventor of Jazz"* (1950; rpr. Berkeley, 1973), ix–xvii.

89. In 1912, all of the black Baptist churches were on the upriver side of Canal Street, as were the overwhelming number of black Methodist churches. Of thirty-seven black Protestant churches in 1912, thirty were uptown. When the Catholic church, by 1945, established ten so-called "national" churches for black Catholics, all but two small churches were downriver from Canal Street. See *Woods Directory* (unpaginated). See also *Catholic Directory*, 1925, and *Claverite*, XXV (October, 1945), 5.

creole politician, A. J. Dumont, found the base for his leadership position in the local Republican party during the 1870s and early 1880s.[90]

The large mass of black voters in Louisiana lived outside of New Orleans. After the war, several black creoles left the city to seek office in black rural districts, such as Jacques Gla in Carroll Parish and Louis Martinet and Emile Detiège in St. Martin Parish. Particularly in the south Louisiana sugar parishes, where French-speaking Catholic slaves had been concentrated, a few New Orleans creoles managed to find an electoral base, but not many, it seems, wished to uproot themselves from their urban homes and life-styles to seek office in the isolated countryside. Besides, resident black leaders in those areas had their own ambitions.[91]

Some black creole leaders from New Orleans managed to win major statewide positions. In addition, they vied to retain control of the Louisiana Republican party and sought the governorship for a black candidate more energetically than any comparable group of black leaders elsewhere in the South. But they lost those two power struggles in Louisiana, largely because of the ethnic division within the black population both in the city and the state.[92]

By 1867, Henry C. Warmoth, a brilliant young politician, fell heir to the Banks forces after Andrew Johnson dismissed the Massachusetts general and restored Confederate leaders to power in Louisiana. During the summer of 1865, in the face of Johnson's obdurate and reactionary policies, Warmoth brought about a fusion of the Banks moderate forces and the *Tribune* radicals to create the Republican party of Louisiana and then shrewdly used it to push his own candidacy for governor. Anticipating opposition, he not only stacked the nominating convention of 1867, but he also carefully nurtured the rivals of the black creoles in the black American community.

As a member of the Ames Methodist Episcopal Church pastored by the Reverend John P. Newman, Warmoth formed an important alliance with that key white leader among the black Methodists. Only several months before the nominating convention, Newman had reopened the old ethnic feud among black New Orleanians when he condemned the

90. For information on the racial composition of electoral districts in New Orleans see Londa L. Davis, "After Reconstruction: Black Politics in New Orleans, 1876–1900" (M.A. thesis, University of New Orleans, 1981), 222–25.

91. *Louisianian*, February 20, 1875; Vincent, *Black Legislators in Louisiana*, 226–38.

92. Tunnell, *Crucible of Reconstruction*, 135, 145.

Tribune's call for a black mayor in New Orleans. In his weekly newspaper, the New Orleans *Advocate,* Newman rhetorically asked, "Shall white men or black men rule this city?" He answered by warning his largely black Methodist readership against "certain men of color in New Orleans who now claim the exclusive right to rule this city." When Newman threatened to encourage Protestant freedmen to revolt against the black creole radicals, the *Tribune* editors flew into a rage against the northern "philanthropists" who wished to divide black New Orleanians "in politics, in religion, in social relations." They countered the Methodist editor with charges of their own: "We understand fully, Mr. Advocate, why you do not like us. It is because when you came here, you expected to find a servile population, and you have found MEN."[93]

The *Tribune* insisted that "the idea of having the freedmen cut away from the creoles will not work." The paper admitted that the two groups differed "somewhat in religious matters" but confidently declared that "the interests and the blood of both classes will keep them as a unit." In making this prediction, the *Tribune* editors drew confidence, no doubt, from their earlier victories over the Banks forces, but this time they clearly underestimated the political abilities of Warmoth as well as the new divisions that had been developing between themselves and some key black American leaders.[94]

The conflict with Newman involved much more than a black or white mayor. The *Tribune* had been pressing for a new state constitution that would bring not just universal male suffrage but also desegregated schools and public accommodations. The paper's vision of a new society threatened many conservative and moderate white Louisianians: "We want to inaugurate a state of things in which the law and authorities will know but citizens, and in no case discriminate, be it at the school door, between any class of these citizens. . . . Our society should be one—formed of one people instead of two—keeping only as immaterial varieties, unknown to the law and its officers, the differences of origin, color, fortune, education, language, religion and physical strength. . . . None is a true Republican who says 'it is too soon.'"[95]

93. New Orleans *Tribune,* May 19, 1867.
94. *Ibid.,* May 21, 1867. The quarrel between Newman and the editors of the *Tribune* continued through 1867. Indeed, it went on for years and finally resulted in his removal from New Orleans by Methodist Episcopal bishops because of the antagonism he had engendered within the black community of New Orleans. See *ibid.,* May 26, June 12, July 2, 1867, January 6, 1869.
95. *Ibid.,* October 23, 1867.

To counter this concept of a color-blind civil order, many white Republicans excoriated "Africanization" and "social equality" with almost as much ease as their Democratic opponents. Few white Republicans endorsed the black radicals' vision of civic fraternity. Indeed, Henry C. Warmoth mobilized his conservative faction of white Republicans around opposition to the *Tribune*'s call for the integration of public schools.[96]

Just when the *Tribune* leaders were quarreling with Warmoth and Newman, several of the paper's staff engaged in another, more damaging conflict with their most important black American ally, Oscar J. Dunn. When the white French Masons opened their Scottish Rite lodges to black New Orleanians, many of those who accepted the invitation were French-speaking creoles who had earlier joined the Prince Hall (York Rite) lodges headed by Dunn. As leading creoles, including *Tribune* editor Paul Trévigne, formed rival lodges, both sides engaged in rancorous accusations that produced lasting bitterness between the competitive Masonic organizations. The wrangling also exposed a serious difference over racial values among black New Orleanians.[97]

Dunn had long supported the radical demands of the black creole leaders to remove all color bars from public life, but he did not feel that the logic of integration extended to the voluntary societies that blacks had fostered within their communities. He also accused the white French-speaking Masons of avoiding the challenge of true integration by forming all-black units within their grand lodge. He was wrong in this charge, but such accusations demonstrated how severely the creole desertions had antagonized some of their key American allies. The mutiny in Prince Hall ranks coincided, moreover, with Dunn's personal defeat as a delegate to the constitutional convention from a ward with numerous black creole voters. Both losses made Dunn ready to seek political revenge.[98]

Carefully nurturing these divisions, Warmoth gained critical sup-

96. Roger Fischer, *The Segregation Struggle in Louisiana, 1862–77* (Urbana, 1974), 47–48.

97. New Orleans *Tribune*, June 18, 23, July 25, 26, 1867.

98. In his report, as grand master, to the Eureka Grand Lodge in December, 1867, Dunn excoriated the defection and admitted that "our Temple has been shaken to its foundation" when many of the members "became demoralized and unruly, and were consequently lopped off from our jurisdiction." See the "Proceedings of the Most Worshipful Grand Lodge of Louisiana, 1863–1869," 48, in the George Longe Collection at the Amistad Research Center.

port from black delegates when he sought the Republican nomination for governor of Louisiana. When the creole radicals could not get their trusted white ally, Thomas J. Durant, to accept the nomination and instead turned to a black candidate, Major Francis Dumas, Warmoth's friends raised the fear of black rule among whites and, at the same time, portrayed Dumas among black Americans as a conservative former slaveholder. Relying primarily on a rising black American leader, P. B. S. Pinchback, to convince black delegates that it was not time to elect a black governor, Warmoth won the nomination by just one vote and then named Oscar J. Dunn as his nominee for lieutenant governor.[99]

In their most serious mistake of the entire Reconstruction era, the owners of the *Tribune*—forcefully led by Dr. Louis Charles Roudanez—refused to support the Warmoth-Dunn ticket. They rejected the advice of their Belgian associate, Jean-Charles Houzeau, to wait for another chance to win control of the party. Instead, they discouraged Dumas from accepting the lieutenant governorship proffered by the Warmoth wing and set up an alternative ticket headed by a white Republican, James G. Taliaferro, with Dumas running for lieutenant governor. It was a terrible blunder born of anger and stubbornness. True, Taliaffero had been a remarkably defiant Unionist, but he also had been a slaveholding planter. Even some of the *Tribune*'s most loyal creole supporters, such as the Rey brothers and Emile Detiège, refused to join the bolt by Roudanez from the regular Republican ticket, and the mass of Louisiana's black voters, particularly the freedmen outside of the city, · remained loyal to the party of Abraham Lincoln.[100]

After Warmoth's victory, black creole leaders never recovered their dominant leadership role in black political circles. When the national Republican party cut off its subsidies to the *Tribune,* the discouraged Belgian managing editor decided to quit, and a more conservative, white newspaper, the New Orleans *Republican,* replaced it as the official organ of the party in Louisiana. Although the *Tribune* continued sporadically as an independent Republican weekly until 1870, it never regained its former stature as the daily oracle of the black community in New Orleans. The sudden turn of political events made many of those who had sacrificed so much to keep it going for three years as a daily

99. Tunnell, *Crucible of Reconstruction,* 135, 145.
100. Well after this election, black leaders recalled Roudanez' decision a serious political error but honored him as a man of independence and integrity. See *Southwestern Christian Advocate,* March 19, 1885.

newspaper reconsider their careers. Both the primary owner, Dr. Roudanez, and the managing editor, Jean-Charles Houzeau, felt that their political work had reached a fitting conclusion with the passage of the national Reconstruction acts and the new Louisiana constitution. The Belgian radical returned to Europe, and the black doctor virtually abandoned politics.[101]

It was inevitable, moreover, that black American leaders such as Dunn and Pinchback would assume greater influence and visibility among the overwhelming numbers of black voters in the city and especially the state who shared their Anglo-American cultural background rather than the Franco-African traditions of the New Orleans creoles. The alliance between Pinchback and Warmoth also appeared to lay a more practical base for the new era of electoral politics. Pragmatic and gifted, Pinchback extracted major rewards and benefits from the Warmoth administration for himself and a growing circle of his political associates, who like their boss had honed their skills elsewhere in the United States and only recently migrated to New Orleans.[102]

The dominance of American leadership did not, however, mean that the creoles abandoned politics in a fit of disillusionment and despair. Quite the contrary: in 1869, they staged a comeback of sorts after Warmoth vetoed various measures to enforce the integration of public schools and public accommodations that had been mandated in the constitution of 1868. By mending their quarrels with Oscar J. Dunn, black creole leaders also temporarily restored their old radical, biethnic coalition, first to pass measures in the legislature to enforce desegregation and then, in the face of continued opposition from Warmoth, to help make Dunn the state's governor by impeaching Warmoth. And they almost succeeded despite Pinchback's backing of Warmoth. But Dunn's sudden death in 1871, under mysterious circumstances, ended the campaign and allowed Warmoth to use his influence in the state senate to elevate Pinchback to Dunn's old position as lieutenant governor.[103]

The creole leaders continued the struggle after Dunn's death. Joining

101. Houzeau, *My Passage at the New Orleans "Tribune,"* 47–57, 149–53.
102. Tunnell, *Crucible of Reconstruction,* 77. Pinchback kept up his contacts in the North, particularly in Ohio, by leaving New Orleans almost every summer. On the staff of his newspaper, the *Louisianian,* he gathered a coterie of political lieutenants who had come from northern states: J. Henri Burch (New York), William G. Brown (New Jersey), James Kennedy (Washington, D.C.), and several others.
103. Fischer, *Segregation Struggle in Louisiana,* 66–69; Marcus B. Christian, "The Theory of the Poisoning of Oscar J. Dunn," *Phylon,* VI (Fall, 1945), 4–10.

with an anti-Warmoth faction of white Republicans led by William P. Kellogg, they helped remove Warmoth from office in 1872. Scornful of the temporary governor, Pinchback, they tried to nominate another black creole, Aristide Mary, as the Republican candidate for governor in 1872. When that effort failed, the creole leaders helped elect Kellogg as governor and C. C. Antoine, a bilingual black Methodist from northern Louisiana, as lieutenant governor. For the next decade, the black creoles warily backed Kellogg's customshouse faction, which controlled the Republican party in Louisiana. But this loose alliance was powerless either to advance the radical cause of the creoles or to stop the violence that, after 1874, engulfed the northern part of the state and kept black voters there from participating freely in local and state elections. When the Grant administration refused to intervene any longer in the South to ward off such violence, the white Democrats gained control of Louisiana in the disputed election of 1876 and proceeded to undermine almost every gain that black Louisianians had made during Reconstruction.

The ethnic division within the New Orleans black community may help to explain some of the factionalism among black New Orleans leaders, but it cannot explain the collapse of Reconstruction in Louisiana. If anything, black Louisianians, despite their divisions, held off the relentless force of white violence longer than black southerners did in other states. Warmoth rightly recalled the black creoles in his history of Louisiana Reconstruction as the ultra-radicals, even if he distorted their objectives as an attempt to "Africanize" the state.[104]

Creoles, Americans, and the Redeemers

For black New Orleanians, the collapse of Reconstruction ended neither political involvement nor their old ethnic and personal antagonisms. The latter survived the restoration of white conservative control, not only because the black creoles never forgave Warmoth and Pinchback for undermining their plans during Reconstruction, but also because their political rivalry continued after the Democrats returned to power under Governor Francis T. Nicholls. When Pinchback's conciliatory gestures about the Compromise of 1877 won political patronage from both President Rutherford B. Hayes and Nicholls, creole leaders accused him of party and racial treason. The conflict reached a zenith,

104. Henry C. Warmoth, *War, Politics and Reconstruction: Stormy Days in Louisiana* (New York, 1930), 51–54; Tunnell, *Crucible of Reconstruction*, 164–72.

however, when Pinchback extended his cozy relationship by supporting the Redeemers' new constitution of 1879 in exchange for the black college, Southern University.

Pinchback defended his actions as realistic in face of the abandonment of southern blacks by the national Republican party. He declared: "I have learned to look at things as they are and not as I would have them . . . this country, at least so far as the South is concerned, is a white man's country. . . . What I wish to impress upon my people, is that no change is likely to take place in our day and generation that will reverse this order of things." [105]

The creole leaders rejected such talk and never forgave his apostasy. Their chief political spokesman after 1876, Judge A. J. Dumont, maintained a running battle with Pinchback for control of the Republican party. Despite the apparent futility, Dumont and other creoles in New Orleans also opposed the Constitution of 1879 because it sanctioned segregated public schools and public accommodations. Many years later, in 1893, at the funeral of Aristide Mary, Rodolphe Desdunes expressed the bitterness that still lingered among his fellow creoles for Pinchback's betrayal.

In his memorial, Desdunes contrasted Pinchback with Aristide Mary in much the same way that he later, in remarks addressed to W. E. B. Du Bois, tried to contrast the political viewpoints of "Latin Negroes" and "Anglo-Saxon Negroes." Desdunes made Pinchback's outlook a symbol of "American reasoning" in which "the first principle was to succeed." Mary, he felt, operated on "entirely French ideas" in insisting on principles and self-respect. He extended the parallel by portraying Mary as the principal architect of the state's radical constitution of 1868 and Pinchback as the apologist of the reactionary Redeemers' constitution of 1879.

To explain Mary, a dark mulatto, Desdunes made no reference to skin color but instead referred to an episode in which Mary refused to give up his candidacy for governor in 1872 in exchange for the lieutenant governorship. Desdunes explained: "Mary understood that equality could not take up its residence within the domain of subordination, and that compromises which resulted in this political anomaly, only postponed the solution which we envisioned with the abolition of slavery." The real test of contrasting political outlooks, however, came over the

105. *Louisianian*, June 14, 1879.

constitution of 1879, when Pinchback publicly acceded to the segregation of the public schools in return for the creation of the all-black Southern University. Desdunes recalled how Mary "thundered with indignation against the scheming of men of color who took part in the Convention of 1879." Because Mary saw Pinchback as the leader of the group who accepted a segregated black college, the creole radical "never spoke a word to Pinchback from that time until his death" because of his "contempt for the man who had said that 'this government is a government of whites,' in order to justify his conduct on this occasion." Mary's stance, Desdunes claimed, had "the support and sympathy of the population called creole." [106]

Although something of a hyperbole, Desdunes' polarization of political outlooks rings true. Creole leaders such as Mary and Desdunes refused to accommodate to the new color line in Louisiana or the rest of America. Despite their obvious abandonment by the national Republican party, they undertook various forms of resistance to Jim Crow laws and other denials of civil rights. When Democrats resegregated the city schools and public accommodations in 1877, they sued under the state constitution of 1868. When the Bourbons passed the state constitution of 1879, which sanctioned such segregation, they turned to the federal courts for relief. [107]

Although many prominent black Americans joined with the creole leadership in these battles, increasing numbers of black American leaders in the South followed the path of Pinchback in seeking some form of racial accommodation with the more moderate southern white Democrats. After 1876, black and white Methodist Episcopal leaders in the region, for example, began to articulate such ideas. When the more assertive black Methodists in Louisiana under the leadership of the white radical presiding elder, Joseph C. Hartzell, resisted the general Methodist tendency, national church leaders tried to halt the carping dissent in Louisiana by removing Hartzell from the editorship of the *Southwestern Christian Advocate*. His replacement, Marshall Taylor, was a black minister from Kentucky, who proved more acceptable to the national leaders. [108]

---

106. Rodolphe Lucien Desdunes, *Hommage rendu à la mémoire de Alexandre Aristide Mary* . . . (New Orleans, 1893), 5–9.
107. Fischer, *Segregation Struggle in Louisiana*, 143–46; *Louisianian*, February 22, March 8, 1879.
108. *Southwestern Christian Advocate*, June 5, 1884.

Within a few months, the newspaper took a new line. It defended the development of racially exclusive Methodist districts in the South, condemned interracial marriages, and urged its black readers to turn inward and away from politics and the white community. Taylor, who had been free in antebellum Kentucky and Ohio, acknowledged that "deeds of violence here and there now occur" but insisted that the post-Reconstruction South offered black residents opportunities to find "a life of wealth and power." He therefore urged "less of politics and more acres for awhile." Still later he suggested that his readers "let politics alone and attend strictly to getting money, land, education, sound morals and religion." [109]

To be sure, many creole families also turned inward toward their own communities and kinship networks to escape the wave of racial oppression and humiliation that was overtaking the South, but their organized leadership in New Orleans seldom, if ever, took the conservative and racialist stand of Marshall Taylor and other leaders who were assuming greater authority in the black American communities of the city and the state. Instead, the creole leaders used what few weapons they had to resist the reactionary movement of the southern Bourbons.

Rodolphe Desdunes and the *Crusader*

The primary strategist of creole resistance was the remarkable young intellectual and activist Rodolphe Desdunes. He not only saw himself as a leader following in the traditions of the Civil War radicals but was their protégé, since he had not only studied French literature and history as their student but also modeled his life after their examples. He wrote in both French and English, but most elegantly in French. And throughout his life he turned to the radical ideals of France in 1848 "because all Frenchmen were equal before the law." [110]

Although too young to play a major role in the events of the 1860s in New Orleans, Desdunes emerged in the public eye during the mid-1870s because of his refusal to surrender to the violent counterrevolution in Louisiana. He felt certain that the virtual lack of organized protest and resistance among blacks only encouraged the growing number of lynchings of rural blacks in the northern part of the state. He also

109. *Ibid.*, March 25, 1886, January 27, 1887.
110. *Daily Crusader*, undated clipping from 1892 signed by Desdunes, in *Crusader* Scrapbook, 7, Xavier University of Louisiana, New Orleans.

came forward to challenge the corruption and conservatism that had infiltrated the Republican party in Louisiana. In 1878, to instill renewed militancy and idealism among younger black leaders, he helped organize a key group of creoles and Americans into the Young Men's Progressive Association. "If we are citizens of this great and free country," they declared, "we demand our rights as such." Desdunes openly labeled himself a "radical" and allied with the creole-dominated faction of the party against the cautious approach of Pinchback's largely American faction.[111]

While attending the integrated law school of Straight University, from which he gained a law degree in 1882, Desdunes became convinced that the federal courts offered black southerners the best opportunity to reverse their declining status. By 1881, he began to agitate for an "Association of Equal Rights" to support a counterattack in the courts to protect black voting rights. "It is time," he wrote, "that some of these 'unregenerates' should know that we mean to test their legal right to humiliate us. . . . It is the duty of colored men to fight for an equal chance in the race of life and not depend upon the generosity of others to do so for them."[112]

Desdunes increasingly reached back into his French and creole heritage for a radical ideology and militant tradition. Not only did he draw on his knowledge of French history and literature, but he also nurtured his outlook inside several organized groups of like-minded French-speaking radicals in the city, particularly a black spiritualist society and an integrated Masonic lodge. Discouraged by the methods of other black leaders in the South, Desdunes urged his fellow black creoles to return to the methods that had worked during Reconstruction. Without the centrality of a black Protestant church or the leadership of black clergymen in the creole communities, he knew that they needed an ideological organization and a newspaper—their own bold, militant newspaper—to unify and lead them. In 1887, he helped form the organization L'Union Louisianaise and circulated its prospectus for a revolutionary paper with French columns: "Our efforts to create here a republican organ in the language that is still spoken with pride by a class of men who have drawn their republicanism from reading the great philosophes of the 18th century. . . . Those to whom it [L'Union Louisianaise] has

111. *Louisianian*, October 30, December 4, 1875, December 28, 1878.
112. *Ibid.*, July 2, 9, 16, 23, 30, August 6, 13, 1881, May 6, 1882.

entrusted the editing will put all their efforts . . . into continuing its progressive work. They will endeavor to graft, so to speak, the truth onto the side of error, in order to produce a result, which . . . assures to each the plenitude of his civil and political rights." [113]

The call eventually resulted in a community corporation to support the New Orleans *Crusader*. Printed in both French and English, it was an aggressive vehicle for racial protest in New Orleans. The managing editor, Louis A. Martinet, had once been an ally of Pinchback and had even joined him in support of the constitution of 1879, which overturned many of the key features of the 1868 Reconstruction constitution, but Martinet later abandoned the narrow patronage politics of his former mentor and closed ranks with his fellow creoles. The newspaper obviously struck a chord in the black community and helped encourage a new assertive spirit in the city as its founders had hoped. By 1894, the editors received enough support from black New Orleanians that the *Crusader* became the only black daily newspaper in the United States during the 1890s.

That the *Crusader* resounded with the same spirit of the earlier *Union* and *Tribune* from the Reconstruction era was not accidental, because one of its regular contributors, Paul Trévigne, then an old man, helped in its founding and reminded its readers how he and an earlier generation had originally won the rights that the *Crusader* now proposed to regain three decades later. The new paper rallied the community to protest an upsurge of political violence in the sugar parishes of southern Louisiana and condemned police brutality in New Orleans. Calling itself a "Labor and Republican" paper, it also supported labor unions, including the Knights of Labor, and any other movement in the South such as the early Populist party that seemed to offer protection for the rights of black citizens. [114]

But above all, the *Crusader* served as the organ of an assertive civil rights effort in the courts that Desdunes had envisioned at the beginning of the 1880s. The editor, Louis Martinet, who had also graduated from the Straight University Law School, agreed with Desdunes that well-chosen legal suits offered more hope than the fraudulent politics of the state to recapture basic constitutional rights under the Fourteenth and Fifteenth amendments. In early 1890, the editors helped to gather other

113. Editorial Committee, *Prospectus*, (September 15, 1887), in Charles Roussève Papers, Amistad Research Center, Tulane University.
114. *Crusader*, March 29, 1890, in Roussève Papers.

leaders throughout the South at Washington, D.C., to form a new national civil rights group, the American Citizens Equal Rights Association (ACERA). The *Crusader* purposely insisted upon a name that would open the group to all sympathizers irrespective of race, setting it at odds with all those—black or white—who sought racial isolation. Within a few weeks of the group's formation, a cause emerged for the Louisiana branch of the association: the state legislature passed laws forbidding interracial marriage and mandating segregation of blacks on all railroads operating within Louisiana.

Initially both American and creole leaders participated in the campaign to protest these new laws. Some American leaders joined the board of the *Crusader,* and even Pinchback helped at the beginning. But before too long, black creoles had to maintain the burden of the struggle as other leaders, particularly the black Protestant ministers, backed away from the dangerous challenge to the white supremacists. A few were forced out. At the outset, the Reverend A. E. P. Albert, the first president of the state branch of the American Citizens Equal Rights Association, aligned his Methodist newspaper with the *Crusader;* but when he gathered support for the campaign and called upon Methodist churches to pledge opposition to the state laws, national church officials removed him from the editorship of the *Southwestern Christian Advocate* and left him without any comparable base of leadership in Louisiana.[115]

Before long, black creoles stood virtually alone. They provided almost all of the financial support as well as the plaintiffs for the test cases. Daniel F. Desdunes, the son of Rodolphe Desdunes, served as the plaintiff in their first case, and Homer Plessy, another creole activist, served in the second and more famous suit. After the national organization of the ACERA also collapsed, the black creole leaders, under Desdunes' leadership, formed a Citizens Committee with financial help from the old Reconstruction radical Aristide Mary to support the expensive court suits.[116] The New Orleanians also cooperated with another civil rights group, headed by the white activist Albion Tourgée, for national assistance and publicity.[117]

115. *Southwestern Christian Advocate,* March 3, 1892.

116. Desdunes, *Hommage rendu à la mémoire de Alexandre Aristide Mary,* 3.

117. Martinet to Tourgée, October 5, 1891, as quoted in Otto H. Olsen, *The Thin Disguise: Turning Point in Negro History, "Plessy v. Ferguson": A Documentary Presentation, 1864–1896* (New York, 1967), 55–61.

Jubilation greeted their impressive victory in the first case, which dismissed Louisiana's efforts to segregate trains that crossed state borders. Desdunes and his compatriots confidently pronounced Jim Crow "dead as a door nail." Desdunes, a regular columnist for the *Crusader*, hammered away at the white supremacists while the lawyers continued the long process of legal maneuvers and appeals that brought their second, more significant suit based on the Thirteenth and Fourteenth amendments to the Supreme Court of the United States. "No theory of white supremacy," Desdunes reminded the fainthearted, "no method of lynching, no class legislation, no undue disqualification of citizenship, no system of enforced ignorance, no privileged classes at the expense of others can be tolerated, and, much less, openly encouraged by any citizen who loves justice, law and right."[118]

The group did not organize simply to attack segregated railroads. They pursued several other legal cases, especially one against the denial of the right of black citizens to sit on criminal juries. Between 1892 and 1896, Desdunes also tried to rally opposition against the efforts of southern legislatures to disfranchise black voters by literacy and property requirements. In 1895, after the *Crusader* became the only daily black newspaper in the nation, he assumed the role of associate editor and brought a greater class appeal to the paper: "This question of qualified suffrage," he warned, "is one in which all the common people, whether colored or white, are vitally interested." He rued the day "when once the wealthy classes get the laws as they want them. The elect of creation, as they believe themselves to be, aim to kill the right [of universal suffrage] as a short cut to assured and permanent ascendancy."[119]

In 1896, however, the paper's bravado ended when the Supreme Court of the United States ruled against Plessy and explicitly sanctioned segregation. It must have seemed that the total weight of American power suddenly arrayed itself against the long struggle of the black New Orleans leaders. Even most of the stalwarts who helped pursue the case were too discouraged or fearful to continue any further protests. With the numbing efficiency of undertakers, they dismantled the Citizens Committee and distributed a published accounting of their fund-raising before they called a large public meeting to announce their formal disbandment. Desdunes later recalled that pessimism and fear had finally

118. R. L. Desdunes, "Judge Ferguson and Allies," *Crusader*, n.d. [1893], in *Crusader* Scrapbook, 19.
119. *Crusader*, June 12, 1895, in *Crusader* Scrapbook, 53.

taken their toll. Most of the leaders, he said, "believed that the continuation of the *Crusader* would not only be fruitless but decidedly dangerous." They believed that "it was better to suffer in silence than to attract attention to their misfortune and weakness." [120]

The end to organized resistance did not lessen the violent determination of the white supremacists to subordinate black Louisianians. Within the next few years, black New Orleanians lost the right to vote and were slowly deprived of almost all access to public education. Even the leaders of the Catholic church in the New Orleans diocese finally imposed the color line. For a while the storm of black creole protest in 1895 led by Desdunes and Martinet in the *Crusader* had confined the creation of exclusively black "national" parishes to two small churches. In that battle, Desdunes had urged the church to maintain its universal principles and to uphold "justice, equality and fraternity" within its ranks. He repeated his constant refrain: "Whether we be citizens or Christians, we never cease to be the children of God and the brothers of other men." But here, too, he could only delay the inevitable. By the end of World War I, the prelates of the city segregated all of the city's Catholic churches. [121]

Church leaders praised these and other developments as part of the Americanization of their church. As in other private organizations in the city, almost all of the foreign white leaders, particularly the foreign French, had died off by the early twentieth century, and few new French immigrants took their place. Other integrated institutions, like the Scottish Rite Masonic lodges, either became all black as older white members died or, like the French Opera House, disappeared from the city. Even from afar, colonialist France itself must have lost much of its glow as a beacon of liberation for black New Orleanians. Most of the younger creoles also lost the ability to speak French or to read French literature and history. Increasingly, New Orleans became, in its race relations, very similar to other American cities in the South.

From the perspective of the early twentieth century, the promise that Radical Republicans and abolitionists once held out for black New Or-

120. Desdunes, *Our People and Our History*, 147; Citizens Committee, *Report of the Proceedings for the Annulment of Act 111 of 1890* (New Orleans, [ca. 1897]). This publication and an earlier one, L. A. Martinet, ed., *The Violation of a Constitutional Right* (New Orleans, 1893), demonstrate the large following that the committee gathered at various meetings to protest discrimination and to support various legal cases.

121. See Dolores Egger Labbé, *Jim Crow Comes to Church: The Establishment of Segregated Parishes in South Louisiana* (Lafayette, La., 1971).

leanians of freedom, opportunity, and equal citizenship had turned into a nightmare of peonage, segregation, and disfranchisement. In the face of such reality, even the black creoles of the city turned inward. By 1915, a new generation of their leaders greeted Booker T. Washington with almost the same enthusiasm as did other black southerners. If creoles and Americans still maintained their own distinctive churches and benevolent societies in different neighborhoods, both groups apparently had conformed to the American color line.[122]

The unusual nineteenth-century resistance led by the black creoles to the Americanization of the city's race relations had not been a prolonged fool's errand. The complex traditions that had produced their peculiar militant resistance had left a proud legacy not only for themselves but for the whole nation because they played a major role in embedding a policy of racial justice into the Reconstruction amendments to the U.S. Constitution. Indeed, even the *Plessy* case had not been a total failure, for it generated a powerful dissent that would be used to rescue those amendments in later Supreme Court decisions.[123]

And, finally, the peculiar traditions of black New Orleanians survived within their own communities, for they have preserved their own memories and written history. Even after the defeat of the *Plessy* suit, not all the leaders accommodated to the new racial order. Many maintained a militant interracial labor organization in the city; hundreds boycotted segregated streetcars; and before the end of the 1920s, black leaders returned to the federal courts to reopen their old battles. None of these recalcitrants was more defiant than Rodolphe Desdunes. He decried any accommodation to the prevailing American racial order. From the beginning of the struggle against the state laws that segregated railroad cars, Desdunes recognized that he was fighting against all odds in resisting racial oppression in the American South.

Early in that battle, when a subscriber complained to the *Crusader* that Desdunes was calling the black community to a "battle which is forlorn," Desdunes refused to be shaken from his faith that "liberty is won by continued resistance to tyranny." What is more, he would not succumb to the obvious burden of the federal judiciary's opinion that "colored men ought to be satisfied with the enjoyment of the three first

122. New Orleans *States*, February 29, 1915; New Orleans *Times-Picayune*, April 13, 14, 1915.

123. Charles A. Lofgren, *The Plessy Case: A Legal-Historical Interpretation* (New York, 1987), 204–207.

natural rights" of the Declaration of Independence. He insisted that there must be more than life, liberty, and the pursuit of happiness. He argued that equal rights could not be divided among groups of humanity living within the same society. Fraternity and equal rights were inseparable. His reading of history told him that "forlorn hopes like utopias have been the cause or beginnings of all the great principles which now bless . . . the free and progressive nations of the earth." In his mind a "forlorn hope" should not be "a disconcerting element to a true lover of the good and the just, and . . . his devotion to principle must be above perturbation from the most threatening prospects of temporary disappointment." In this response, Desdunes frankly warned his compatriots that they should be prepared to "show a noble despair" and be ready to "face any disappointment that might await them at the bar of American justice." He seemed to know that he was fighting not just for them but for a generation yet unborn. He proudly admitted on a later occasion that he fought in the tradition of Victor Hugo, Alphonse de Lamartine, and John Brown as a "champion of impossible doctrines, or as a debater of dreams, just fallen from the skies."[124] It was in this spirit that he responded to W. E. B. Du Bois' remarks when that younger leader seemed to be at wit's end after the terrible Atlanta race riot of 1906.

Before an accident blinded him about 1910, Desdunes completed a history in French of his people so that their achievements and struggles would be remembered and used by its readers to continue the fight against racial prejudice in America. He wanted the accomplishments of the creoles to be absorbed by all blacks, whether American or creole. But above all, Desdunes wanted any reader to learn from the story of the creole radicals that "it is more noble and dignified to fight, no matter what, than to show a passive attitude of resignation. Absolute submission augments the oppressor's power and creates doubt about the feelings of the oppressed."[125]

---

124. *Crusader*, August 15, 1891, in Rousseve Papers, and May 14, 1895, in *Crusader* Scrapbook, 45.
125. Desdunes, *Our People and Our History*, 147.

6

Simply a Matter of Black and White: The Transformation of Race and Politics in Twentieth-Century New Orleans

ARNOLD R. HIRSCH

Each spring New Orleans' children gathered to pay homage to John McDonogh, the nineteenth-century benefactor who left much of his fortune to the city's public schools. In 1954, however, in the weeks preceding the Supreme Court's landmark *Brown* decision, New Orleans' blacks protested what had become a galling civic ritual. In years past, white students paraded by the McDonogh monument, were greeted by the mayor, and listened to their bands while black children stood by in Lafayette Square, enduring both a brutally oppressive sun and a stifling racial hierarchy. The year of *Brown*, though, was different. Only thirty-four of the roughly thirty-two thousand black public school students participated in the ceremony that spring, and the black dignitaries who had regularly attended the proceedings were conspicuously absent.

Calls for the boycott came from a variety of black groups and leaders. Black parent-teacher associations took the lead and received ready support from Arthur J. Chapital, Sr., creole president of the New Orleans branch of the NAACP; from labor attorney Revius Ortique, a "Ninth Ward Methodist" (whose father's family had been Catholic); and from uptown Baptist minister A. L. Davis, president of the Interdenominational Ministerial Alliance (IMA), among others. Ortique argued that "youngsters ought not be encouraged to witness a public demonstration of racial supremacy." He found it "particularly revolting that this practice is not merely condoned but sponsored by our school system." The Orleans Parish School Board remained unmoved, however, and provoked (in the eyes of the black-owned *Louisiana Weekly*) a remarkable display of black unity as parents "kept their youngsters away from the shameful spectacle."[1]

The exhilaration and nearly palpable pain caused by the successful demonstration and its deplorable necessity were almost immediately overwhelmed by news of the Supreme Court's action in the school desegregation cases. Indeed, the judicial overthrow of the "separate but equal" doctrine restored the *Weekly*'s "hope and faith in democracy."[2]

But the U.S. Supreme Court's overturning of *Plessy* v. *Ferguson* was—as local black historian Marcus Christian observed—"strangely ironic." Christian noted that New Orleanian Homer Plessy, who remained symbolically "the legal embodiment of Negro inferiority," was not "a full-blooded Negro, but . . . a man who . . . seemed to be wholly white."[3] And that was precisely the point. For more than a half-century, an uncompromising philosophy had placed all perceived or acknowledged African-Americans behind a racial barrier that obscured previous distinctions based on shadings of color, class, or culture. Such divisions among New Orleans' nonwhites certainly did not disappear, but they were subordinated to an overarching system of discrimination that paid them no heed. The fundamental distinction between black and white had always served as a powerful assimilative agent incorporating European immigrants into the latter category, and the rise of segregation did not protect that identity (it had earlier been openly breached and would continue to be surreptitiously so) as much as it completed the process of forging a black one. The McDonogh Day protest was its tangible expression.

The Burdens of Jim Crow and the New Paternalism

The very nature of segregation structured interracial contacts within an uncompromising paternalistic framework. More than a legacy of the slave era, the paternalism of Jim Crow flourished because of renewed black needs for white patrons within a system built on the denial of black power.

1. *Louisiana Weekly*, May 1, 8, 15, 1954; Kim Lacy Rogers, "Humanity and Desire: Civil Rights Leaders and the Desegregation of New Orleans, 1954–1966" (Ph.D. dissertation, University of Minnesota, 1982), 95–99.

2. *Louisiana Weekly*, May 29, 1954.

3. *Ibid.*, December 8, 1956.

The political career of Walter Cohen, black New Orleans' preeminent spokesman between the turn of the century and the Great Depression, illustrates the dominant themes of the era. A successful businessman and civic leader, Cohen organized the People's Industrial Life Insurance Company in 1910 and had been a Republican activist for years before that. Appointed registrar of lands under the McKinley administration, he was nominated by Warren G. Harding to be comptroller of customs and, after a long and bitter fight against southern opposition, won confirmation in 1924. Controlling the major source of federal patronage in New Orleans, Cohen dominated the state's "black-and-tan" Republican organization from his position as secretary. Careful not to seize the party's top state job, Cohen "always had a white national committeeman." If he eschewed symbolic titles and the prestige of chairing meetings, however, Cohen placed himself at the center of the party's day-to-day operations. Eventually he earned a reputation as the black community's primary contact with white elites.

Though Cohen never developed an assertive style, black civil rights attorney A. P. Tureaud deflected later charges of "Uncle Tomism" and claimed that Cohen was "just as aggressive as the times permitted." But his political efforts were confined to warding off intraparty challenges by Louisiana's "lily-white" Republicans and pressing successive national administrations for more patronage. It was a brand of politics that emphasized patron-client relationships both in Cohen's connection to the outside world and in his dominance within the black community. It was an accommodationist style that sought only to maximize concessions made within the existing system.[4]

Other black civic and business leaders operated in much the same fashion. Dr. Joseph Hardin, Dr. Rivers Frederick, James Lewis, Jr., Emile and George Labat, and Dr. George Lucas, among others, tried to exert influence among powerful whites on issues of concern to the black community. According to Tureaud, "people like Hardin and Jimmy Lewis . . . appealed personally to the white power structure in individual cases. . . . In these cases someone on the board of the NAACP knew

4. Donald Devore, "The Rise from the Nadir: Black New Orleans Between the Wars, 1920–1940" (M.A. thesis, University of New Orleans, 1983), 18–34; interview with A. P. Tureaud by Joseph Logsdon, Tape 10 (Logsdon conducted a series of undated interviews with A. P. Tureaud in the late 1960s; the consecutively numbered transcripts of those interviews are in his possession, and he generously made them available for this study); *Civic Leader*, I (September, 1929), 12, in A. P. Tureaud Papers, Amistad Research Center, Tulane University, New Orleans.

someone who was an authority or had influence. Sometimes it was the editor of the *Times-Picayune*. Through these personal interventions our grievances would be made known." Even Tureaud himself, aware of the limits of white goodwill, had to acknowledge the force of the systemic push toward paternalistic relations. Returning to New Orleans from Howard University Law School in the mid-1920s, he declined to assist in the prosecution of police brutality cases. "Being new in the community and not having anyone I could turn to who was an authority," Tureaud believed that his prominence in such cases would inevitably make him or his prospective clients targets for police abuse.[5]

The uncertainty, danger, and fundamental unpleasantness of interracial contact in the age of segregation led many blacks to turn inward, to seek solace and security within their own number. The tendency among some New Orleans creoles to wrap themselves in their downtown neighborhoods, sheltered within their unique history, language, and religion, perpetuated a sense of distinctiveness. Their concerns for respectability, family values, and even—for some—a pronounced color consciousness provided coherence, stability, and certain rewards. Feeling the same pressures as the white creoles, who were simultaneously denying their past while self-consciously applying Americanized standards of racial identity, many black creoles similarly turned to biology and genealogy in the search for status. Divergent tendencies among the Franco-Africans subsequently became more distinct, separating those who acquiesced in or advantageously seized upon American racial values from a recalcitrant unassimilated fragment that still rejected the application of any color line. Indeed, with a stinging dissent that was as significant as the phenomenon it acknowledged, the black creole Rodolphe Desdunes deplored the existence of the "amalgamated Negro" who was "a fool in his own house" and who "esteem[ed] nothing so much as the fairness of his skin, and the souple [*sic*] strains of his hair."[6]

But such inner flights from Jim Crow were hardly unique to the creoles. The multitude of black Baptist and Methodist congregations that flourished in New Orleans served as communal bases and autonomous,

5. Nida Harris Vital, "Dr. Rivers Frederick and the History of Black Medicine in New Orleans" (M.A. thesis, University of New Orleans, 1978); interview with Tureaud, Tape 7.

6. Arthe Agnes Anthony, "The Negro Creole Community in New Orleans, 1880–1920s: An Oral History" (Ph.D. dissertation, University of California, Irvine, 1978); R. L. Desdunes, *A Few Words to Dr. DuBois: With Malice Toward None* (New Orleans, 1907), 10.

insulating institutions. Black ministers consequently assumed key roles connecting the black and white communities, both representing their flocks and serving as buffers for them. The pursuit of bourgeois success and respectability was similarly not confined to the creoles by the 1920s. If the creation of fledgling institutions such as the *Louisiana Weekly* (founded in 1925 by the Dejoie family) symbolized creole eminence, a growing number of ministers, doctors, teachers, insurance executives, and others reflected the black "Americans'" willingness to seize the opportunities presented by their urban concentration. Such tendencies even appeared among the working class, some three thousand of whom joined the local chapter of Marcus Garvey's Universal Negro Improvement Association, which stressed self-help and bourgeois values while permitting expressions of racial pride and protest.[7] Black creoles and Americans shared more than racial proscription.

Most striking, however, were the myriad social clubs that were woven into the fabric of New Orleans' black society. These organizations were neighborhood affairs that took on the characteristics of their locales. A. P. Tureaud, who served as the president of the Autocrat Club in the 1930s, recalled that it was situated in the "heart" of the downtown creole community and that it "naturally" embodied that constituency, although not exclusively so. The Autocrats, he remembered, were "a little more heterogeneous" than the San Jacintos. The uptown Bulls Club was "typically American."[8]

But more than reflecting persistent intrablack differences, the clubs served as secular bridges over them. Many were active in racial affairs and served as neutral meeting places for those leery of attending gatherings in churches not their own. They occupied, according to Tureaud, "a unique position in the community" and "served as the vehicle for getting people concerned and interested." After 1920, they worked continuously to improve black schools and other public facilities. Perhaps most important, they provided the resources and leadership that sustained the black civic leagues of that era.[9]

The first of the black New Orleans civic leagues emerged in the downtown, largely creole Seventh Ward. Retired postman Alexander Mollay and Dr. Joseph Hardin responded to "lily-white" Republican attempts to purge black party leaders by creating an organization "through

---

7. Judith Stein, *The World of Marcus Garvey: Race and Class in Modern Society* (Baton Rouge, 1986), 171–85.

8. Devore, "Rise from the Nadir," 38–39; interview with Tureaud, Tape 9.

9. Interview with Tureaud, Tape 9.

which civic-minded members of the group would be able to express themselves." The Seventh Ward Civic League subsequently arose from a meeting held in the Autocrat Club in November, 1927. Finding the political environment hostile, the league focused on improving civic pride and welfare, encouraging education, supporting black business, and promoting "intelligent interracial cooperation." Within a year, other wards followed the example of the Seventh, and a federation of ward organizations drew together. The federation's organ, the *Civic Leader*, editorialized on the need for unity. "When every good-thinking Negro begins to feel," it announced, "that he has been mistreated because another Negro suffered unjust treatment of some kind . . . [we will be] bound together more closely." [10]

The Federation of Civic Leagues' support for the New Orleans branch of the NAACP (each ward organization paid a $10 fee for NAACP membership) revealed yet another secular bridge with a citywide orientation that drew together disparate black elements. Established in 1915, the local branch became a focal point for proto-political activity for those virtually excluded from the larger political system. Physicians such as Rivers Frederick, a descendant of Louisiana creoles and antebellum free people of color; Joseph Hardin, a Mississippi native who relocated in New Orleans' creole Seventh Ward; and George Lucas, a large, exuberant man, who was "very dark in complexion" and a lay leader in the Baptist church, served as the initial links between the NAACP and the network of social clubs that served the local black elite. The interlocking directorates make it difficult to discern where the initiative originated, but the NAACP clearly encouraged and the clubs supervised the payment of poll taxes, the solicitation of NAACP memberships, the signing of petitions, and the raising of funds. Between the world wars, the local NAACP engaged in intermittent protests while serving as a source of prestige and status within the black community. There was a tension inherent in these roles in the age of Jim Crow, and if the local branch pioneered new approaches to federal authority during the 1920s and 1930s, it did so by treading cautiously, always aware of the limits that circumscribed its actions. [11]

Looking back on that era, A. P. Tureaud acknowledged that "we were not looking for anything that much. We were asking for separate

10. T. J. Dejoie, "The Origins, Development and Achievements of the N.O. Federation of Civic Leagues" (Typescript in Tureaud Papers), unpaginated; *Civic Leader*, I (January, 1930), 5, in Tureaud Papers.

11. Harris, "Dr. Rivers Frederick," *passim;* interviews with Tureaud, Tapes 6, 7.

schools or enough of them to house the children." They attacked tru-
ancy, overcrowding, and physically dilapidated structures and raised the
issue of police brutality because those problems "did not generate a
whole lot of hostility." As Tureaud noted, "Whatever benefits we got,
we got . . . by supplication rather than by demanding." [12]

Occasionally, however, more compelling challenges arose. In 1924,
the Louisiana legislature passed permissive legislation that granted cities
with a population of twenty-five thousand or more the power to mandate residential segregation. With strong editorial support from the
Times-Picayune, the New Orleans city council took exactly one week to
pass unanimously a segregation ordinance. City attorney (later mayor)
T. Semmes Walmsley appointed a special attorney to prosecute cases
arising under the new law, and a wave of house bombings emphasized
the hostile white mood. Local black leaders protested, and the NAACP
moved even more forcefully to have the legislation declared unconstitu-
tional. In 1927, the U.S. Supreme Court handed them, as the *Louisiana
Weekly* declared, a "signal victory." [13]

The New Orleans branch of the NAACP, however, was unable to
follow up its achievement. Appeals for new members generated little
enthusiasm. Large numbers of blacks lacked resources and justifiably
feared the consequences of a direct confrontation with a militant white
community. But as community organizations pushed their members to
pay their poll taxes and prodded them to pursue the daunting registration process, it became clear that political powerlessness remained a primary concern. "Without the ballot," black undertaker and community
leader George Labat wrote in 1929, "our race will always be . . . segregated and deprived of our rights and privileges." At the time Labat
spoke, the white Democratic primary (instituted in 1906) supplemented
the poll tax and literacy restrictions that had been adopted earlier, and
the infamous "understanding clause" (adopted in 1921) that allowed
white registrars to challenge potential black registrants had replaced the
outlawed "grandfather clause." Such twentieth-century innovations, the
creole Labat knew, "were enacted solely to disfranchise our race and to
eliminate us from politics." [14]

In 1931, the NAACP challenged Louisiana's discriminatory registration procedures in court. Under George Labat's leadership, the six-

12. Devore, "Rise from the Nadir," *passim;* interview with Tureaud, Tape 10.
13. Devore, "Rise from the Nadir," 60–73.
14. George Labat to New Orleans Branch, NAACP, George W. Lucas, President, September 13, 1929, in *Civic Leader,* I (October–November, 1929), 4, in Tureaud Papers.

hundred-member San Jacinto Club pledged $1,200 in support and the Autocrat Club—in the person of businessman and president Antoine Trudeau—provided a plaintiff. The NAACP planned a series of fund-raisers throughout the city. Although the courts ruled against the plaintiffs in *Trudeau* v. *Barnes,* the *Louisiana Weekly* reflected later that the effort addressed "the problem of awakening or instilling race pride in Negroes themselves." In the interwar period, it was necessary to open the eyes of those who still "depended on their 'good white folks',," according to the *Weekly,* as well as those "who were 'doing it for themselves' and . . . adopted a 'don't rock the boat' attitude." [15]

The failure in the *Trudeau* case highlighted the divisions among those willing to protest. If Labat appreciated the significance of politics and the singularity of race, his conduct infuriated A. P. Tureaud. One of a handful of local black attorneys, Tureaud resented that "the NAACP fought for three years over which white lawyer would handle the case." He recalled that even among black leaders "there was a disbelief in the ability of a Negro lawyer to even practice in the courts." Tureaud most bitterly denounced the "inferiority complexes" that poisoned the minds of some prominent black leaders and was brought to near distraction when "the cause of [the] colored attorneys was defeated by a packed [NAACP] executive committee." Tureaud, who was fair enough to infiltrate the meetings of white segregationists, staunchly resisted all assertions of inferiority but displayed a finely honed racial consciousness and no small degree of militance. It is significant that he did all that without succumbing to an embittered racial chauvinism. His demands were advanced not in the name of securing black patronage but on the grounds of equality, the assertion of his own competence, and the refusal to acquiesce in invidious racial distinctions.[16]

The incident moved Tureaud to appeal to the national NAACP office to invalidate George Labat's somewhat irregular elevation to local branch president or, failing that, to approve the creation of a second New Orleans chapter. Labat's social pretensions and his contention that running the NAACP was a "small job" compared with the presidency of the San Jacinto Club proved too much for Tureaud. "There are many of us," Tureaud wrote Robert Bagnall, the NAACP's director of branches,

15. *Ibid.;* interview with Tureaud, Tape 9; *Civic Leader,* I (January, 1930), 5, in Tureaud Papers; *Louisiana Weekly,* March 7, 1970; Devore, "Rise from the Nadir," 38–39.

16. A. P. Tureaud to Walter White, October 2, 1931, and A. P. Tureaud to Robert W. Bagnall, October 24, 1931, both in Tureaud Papers; interviews with Tureaud, Tapes 7, 9.

"who just can't stomach his brand of administration with its French . . . flavor." Tureaud, who spoke French, could not resist informing Bagnall that "the 'never-de-less' and 'in-divid-ual' president may serve his constituents down at the San Jacinto Club quite well, but there are many of us, particularly of the younger group, that feel more inclined to work with the National Office. . . . Unfortunately, the older men about these parts seek honor and glory for themselves first, and the organization's progress afterwards." [17]

The national office did not encourage Tureaud's insurgency, and, following the deaths of Walter Cohen and George Lucas, the fragmentation of black leadership, the defeat in the *Trudeau* case, and the onset of the Great Depression, local reform efforts declined. It was not until the late 1930s that the NAACP filed—and lost—a suit to desegregate the Municipal Auditorium; apparently an inexperienced white attorney mishandled the case. This stunning defeat, according to Tureaud, "brought on . . . [a] crisis in the NAACP." We decided "that the time had come to replace this leadership with younger people . . . [and] with more aggressive ideas," he recalled. Key leaders such as Donald and Victor Jones, Daniel Byrd, John Rousseau, Octave Lilly, Winston Moore, Arthur J. Chapital, Sr., and Tureaud established a newspaper, the *Sentinel*, to advance their efforts to take over the organization. [18]

Though the insurgents were unable to sustain the *Sentinel* financially, by the early 1940s Dan Byrd assumed the presidency of the local branch and its membership swelled into the thousands. Most important, they contacted Thurgood Marshall and the national office with the notion of pursuing school equalization cases similar to those being filed elsewhere. Marshall's insistence on working through a local black attorney and Tureaud's success in winning a 1942 suit that equalized the salaries of black and white teachers (*McKelpin* v. *Orleans Parish School Board*) established both his credibility as a civil rights lawyer and the prestige of the new leadership. "We made quite a hit with the community," Tureaud remembered, "because there were 1,200 Negro teachers" who won substantial pay increases when the Orleans Parish School Board unified its wage scale. [19] The post–World War II era promised great changes.

17. Tureaud to Bagnall, October 24, 1931, and George Labat to Members, New Orleans Branch, NAACP, November 12, 1931, in Tureaud Papers.
18. Interviews with Tureaud, Tapes 8, 11.
19. *Ibid.*, Tape 8. For *McKelpin* v. *Orleans Parish School Board*, see Raphael Cassimere, Jr., "Equalizing Teachers' Pay in Louisiana," *Integrateducation*, XV (July–August,

A. P. Tureaud and the Legacy of Creole Radicalism

It was hardly surprising that Tureaud was conspicuous among those urging the local NAACP to assume a more aggressive posture. He was born and raised in the Seventh Ward, a descendant of antebellum free people of color, and the legatee of a proud creole protest tradition. Although not all creoles were "radicals," and not all such dissidents were creole, there is no doubt that the Seventh Ward historically served as a base for those pursuing the most radical racial goals. And the tradition included not only a peculiarly "un-American" vision of a multiracial society without slavery in the immediate postbellum age but survived to Tureaud's day when Rodolphe Desdunes and Louis Martinet organized their famous Citizens Committee to protest, through Homer Plessy, Louisiana's march toward segregation. It was a living tradition that demonstrated not only institutional antecedents but communal and individual connections that bound the first and second Reconstructions together.

Tureaud displayed a deep historical consciousness. His grandfather was a member of the Corps d'Afrique in the Civil War, and he remembered listening to the tales related by another corps veteran during his childhood. Later on, Tureaud loaned copies of Desdunes' *Nos hommes et notre histoire* to acquaintances and promoted efforts to translate and republish *Les cenelles*, the literary legacy of New Orleans' free people of color. And when he organized the city's black attorneys, he called the group the Martinet Society after the distinguished Straight University Law School graduate who had edited the *Crusader* during its assault on Jim Crow.[20] Even though Tureaud's education and travels took him to Chicago, New York, and Washington, D.C., before his return to New Orleans in 1927, his roots remained in that downtown creole community. It was in the Seventh Ward, in the Autocrat Club, and with the words of the *Tribune*, the *Crusader*, and the *Sentinel* that he felt most at home.

That background provided Tureaud with the inner resources to resist

---

1977), 3–8; Mark V. Tushnet, *The NAACP's Legal Strategy Against Segregated Education, 1925–1950* (Chapel Hill, 1987), 97–99; Barbara Ann Worthy, "The Travail and Triumph of a Southern Black Civil Rights Lawyer: The Legal Career of Alexander Pierre Tureaud, 1899–1972" (Ph.D. dissertation, Tulane University, 1984), 25–56.

20. Red to Alex, August 1, 1935, E. M. Coleman to Alex, April 4, 1944, Alexander P. Tureaud to Red, October 18, 1945, all in Tureaud Papers; interview with Tureaud, Tape 4.

the most debilitating influences of the Jim Crow era. He complained, for example, that James Lewis, president of the Fourth Ward Civic League, reached into his own pocket to pay the fifteen-cent monthly dues for his followers. Tureaud found paternalistic relationships just as abhorrent in intraracial as in interracial contacts. Indeed, one of the purposes of the league, as he saw it, was to encourage participation and an awareness of shared responsibility—results vitiated by Lewis' conduct. Indeed, Tureaud regarded Lewis as an "ultra-conservative" who believed he "could accomplish anything through the intervention of his white friends." It was a mode of thought that Tureaud rejected. As a lawyer, Tureaud resisted the temptation to associate with a white attorney who could serve as a "front." "I wouldn't have a white lawyer hanging around . . . for anything," he asserted. "I wouldn't want that image to get out." Tureaud, in fact, sometimes extended his interrogation of witnesses in court just to get the message across that a black man could, indeed, practice law in New Orleans. "We may as well stop fooling ourselves," Tureaud said in the late 1920s, "if we are ever to enjoy full citizenship as a race, we will have to unite our forces and fight for it." [21]

Through leaders such as Tureaud, the Seventh Ward continued to exert disproportionate influence into the modern era. It remained the center of black-and-tan Republicanism in Walter Cohen's day as it had been during Reconstruction. Moreover, its most prominent citizens ventured forth almost as missionaries, often providing the impetus for organization elsewhere in the city. Dr. Joseph Hardin and Alexander Mollay started the civic league movement there. They and others such as Antoine Trudeau, Albert Chapital, and Tureaud addressed gatherings in other neighborhoods and ultimately stimulated the founding of eleven such organizations in the city's seventeen wards. Tureaud remained a Seventh Ward resident but organized and served as president of the Eighth Ward Civic League. He also served as counsel to the Federation of Civic Leagues (as he did for the NAACP) and was among the hosts when the citywide group held its regular meetings at the Autocrat Club. [22]

Nor was this pattern of activity restricted to the civic leagues. In the summer of 1944 the Seventh Ward Republican Club protested most vigorously the party's selection of all white district leaders, "thereby giving no recognition to faithful workers and leaders among the Negro Repub-

21. Interview with Tureaud, Tape 7.
22. Typed notes of the Eighth Ward Civic League meeting, n.d., in Tureaud Papers; interview with Tureaud, Tape 9.

licans, and especially the Negro leaders of the 7th ward who have for many years carried on and gave life to the Republican party in this city and state." And when growing numbers of blacks became convinced that the Democrats represented a real alternative, the Pelican State Democratic Club organized itself and held its regular meetings in the Autocrat Club. A hotbed of political activity for both parties, the downtown creole heartland consistently explored every avenue of racial advance.[23]

The Reemergence of Black Politics: The Morrison Years

The black community's push for access to the political system in the 1940s coincided with the reappearance of deep divisions among whites. Although very much a part of the solidly Democratic South, Louisiana's one-party system was split along the fault line driven through it by Huey Long during the Great Depression. By the late 1940s, more than a decade after an assassin had ended Huey's personal march to power, the Long organization still polarized state politics.

Earl Long followed in his brother's footsteps, deemphasizing race as a political issue and pursuing black support. He denounced Louisiana's crudest racists as "grass-eaters" and "race nuts" and proclaimed that "if those colored people helped build this country, if they could fight in the Army, then I'm for giving them the vote." A. P. Tureaud's 1942 victory in *Hall* v. *Nagel* loosened Louisiana registration procedures somewhat, and the subsequent outlawing of white primaries across the South made it possible for a governor such as Earl Long (who appointed local registrars) to have some influence. Indeed, whereas only four hundred black New Orleanians were registered voters in 1940, more than twenty-eight thousand could be counted by 1952. As Tureaud recognized, however, the enrollment of enough black voters to be of assistance to besieged white politicians, but not enough to wield independent power, was an act of self-preservation, not altruism. But it was a start.[24]

To mobilize that vote, Long, operating within the paternalistic frame-

---

23. Ernest Bayard, Sr., to Dear Friend and Fellow Democrat, October 5, 1940, Ernest Bayard to Joseph Cawthorn, November 16, 1940, Alexander P. Tureaud to Dr. Channing Tobias, October 4, 1944, A. P. Tureaud to Dr. Virgil Jackson, August 17, 1944, all in Tureaud Papers.
24. Numan V. Bartley and Hugh D. Graham, *Southern Politics and the Second Re-*

work, needed a mediator who could tie the black community's interests to his own. Ernest Wright, born in neighboring Jefferson Parish and educated at New Orleans' Gilbert Academy and Xavier University before acquiring a master's degree in public welfare administration at the University of Michigan, served as that link. Wright recalled later that "Earl Long had latched onto me for his 1948 campaign for governor." Wright had earlier attracted attention by berating the Housing Authority of New Orleans for its refusal to hire black officials for the recently completed Magnolia project. His harangues, a combination of "constitutional rights, Biblical quotations, and black pride," succeeded in moving five thousand blacks to pledge that they would not move into the uptown development. A successful labor organizer, Wright also orchestrated a "Don't spend where you can't work" campaign and in 1941 created the People's Defense League as a forum from which Wright pushed for greater black voter registration and political awareness. He was a natural choice for Long.[25]

Long's maneuvers in New Orleans did not go uncontested. His chief rival was DeLesseps S. ("Chep") Morrison, a young army veteran who returned to upset incumbent Robert Maestri and the Regular Democratic Organization (RDO) in the 1946 mayoralty. Morrison's antagonism toward the Long organization antedated the war and was further fueled by Earl Long's support for the Old Regulars. The young mayor's firmest backing came from uptown New Orleans, the city's economic and social "establishment," and particularly from a small group of financial supporters known as the Cold Water Committee. Such "silkstocking" sources provided ready cash and policy direction while Morrison attracted dissident RDO elements with the lure of patronage and blacks as well. In light of the historic antagonisms between the machine politicians and uptown "reformers" on one hand, and the RDO and blacks on the other (the Regulars were instrumental in disfranchising blacks in 1898), Morrison's handiwork in creating his machinelike Crescent City Democratic Association (CCDA) was remarkable indeed.[26]

construction (Baltimore, 1975), 59; A. J. Liebling, The Earl of Louisiana: The Liberal Long (Baton Rouge, 1970), 30, 195, 251.

25. Daniel C. Thompson, The Negro Leadership Class (Englewood Cliffs, N.J., 1963), 114; interview with Tureaud, Tape 15; New Orleans Times-Picayune, September 26, 1976; Louisiana Weekly, July 6, 1946, November 10, 1979.

26. For Morrison's career, see Edward F. Haas, DeLesseps S. Morrison and the Image of Reform, 1946–1961 (Baton Rouge, 1974), and Joseph B. Parker, The Morrison Era: Reform Politics in New Orleans (Gretna, La., 1974).

Like Earl Long, Morrison had to establish a personal connection to mobilize the black community on his behalf. He found what he was looking for in the Reverend A. (Abraham) L. (Lincoln) Davis and the Orleans Parish Progressive Voters' League (OPPVL). Davis was born in Bayou Goula, Louisiana, a small village just south of Baton Rouge, in 1914. His father was a Baptist preacher whom Davis, at the tender age of twenty, emulated by taking over the New Zion Baptist Church in New Orleans. It remained his base for the next forty-three years. Davis was instrumental in creating the Interdenominational Ministerial Alliance and assumed its presidency in 1941. The IMA joined some two hundred of the most active black ministers in the metropolitan area and represented a constituency in the tens of thousands. He also served as president of the Ideal Missionary and Educational Baptist Association, whose uptown offices on Jackson Avenue served as the OPPVL's birthplace in March, 1949.[27]

OPPVL board members A. L. Davis, Jackson Acox, Dave Dennis, Avery Alexander, C. C. Dejoie, and A. P. Tureaud represented a cross section of black New Orleans. Reflecting the increasing ease with which intraracial divisions were being bridged in the age of Jim Crow, the founders included Protestant ministers, longshoremen, businessmen, and creoles. Within months, A. L. Davis became its president, and his influence gave it a distinctly uptown flavor. If a growing tradition of city-wide civic and political cooperation made it difficult to identify such organizations as strictly "American" or "creole," their geographical bases and leadership cadres still imparted distinctive cultural styles. Davis' commanding presence atop a network of social, religious, and political groups proved an irresistible lure to Chep Morrison, and association with Morrison further enhanced Davis' stature. The combination was effective enough to cause Earl Long to sputter that the mayor had "a Baptist preacher that didn't preach nothing but Morrison."[28]

Davis' exhortations on Morrison's behalf were especially useful at election time, but neither Davis nor any other black was a member of the CCDA—that remained a white man's club. The OPPVL and other black groups served as auxiliaries that were tied to Morrison personally and aided by him financially during campaigns. When Dave Dennis, a Baptist minister who also served as president of the International Long-

27. Rogers, "Humanity and Desire," 61–63.
28. Haas, *DeLesseps S. Morrison*, 251; Parker, *Morrison Era*, 87.

shoreman's Association local 1419, broke away from the OPPVL and created the Crescent City Independent Voters League (CCIVL), he and his successor, Clarence ("Chink") Henry, dealt with Morrison in much the same manner. Personal connections also characterized Morrison's relations with Avery Alexander's Consumers League and Ellis Hull's United Voters League. Indeed, after Morrison's reelection in 1958, he sent telegrams to Alexander, Hull, Chink Henry, A. L. Davis, and other key black leaders assuring them that they had "a real friend at City Hall."[29]

Morrison's appeal to black voters carried beyond his rapport with selected black leaders. His nose-counting pragmatism and the push provided by a group of largely Jewish uptown supporters led Morrison to make both important symbolic gestures and tangible overtures to the black community. Whether giving Louis Armstrong the key to the city, entertaining Ethiopia's emperor Haile Selassie, or announcing Negro Advancement Week, Morrison gave substance to his assurances that he was mayor of "all the people." More concretely, he improved housekeeping services in black neighborhoods, made new facilities available to blacks through the New Orleans Recreation Department, and assisted in the removal of long-standing racial barriers in the hiring of police officers and staff in the public libraries. Finally, his willingness to appeal directly to black audiences and his winning personality (he was always "apologetic" about being unable to do more, according to Tureaud) were strong political assets. Indeed, when asked, most black ministers in New Orleans expressed the belief that Morrison had "improved their lot . . . and had earned the right to be called 'their friend'."[30]

But there were limits. A native of Louisiana's plantation country, Morrison absorbed the racial values of his milieu, referred to blacks as "darkies" in private conversations, and sought improvement only within the framework of segregation. At best, his upgrading of services for blacks only partially fulfilled the agenda set by the black civic leagues in the 1920s. Working always to "preserve [the] traditions and habits of our city," Morrison's administration offered no challenge to

29. Haas, DeLesseps S. Morrison, 286; DeLesseps S. Morrison to Scott Wilson, March 6, 1954, telegram sent to Avery Alexander, Ellis Hull, A. L. Davis, Earl Amedee, and others, February 5, 1958, both in Scott Wilson Papers, Howard-Tilton Library, Tulane University, New Orleans.

30. Haas, DeLesseps S. Morrison, 67–71, 271; David William Frederichs, "The Role of the Negro Minister in Politics in New Orleans" (Ph.D. dissertation, Tulane University, 1967), 37.

Jim Crow. And if the "grass-eaters" were offended by the public services he made available to black communities, it was still true that blacks did not enjoy access equal to that of whites. His stance was ambiguous enough that Morrison could use his record to appeal to blacks and segregationists alike.[31]

Even more striking, however, than Morrison's pirouettes along the color line was the dogged persistence of paternalism. There was a difference between dispensing favors and sharing power—and Morrison never confused the two. His black "friends" could appeal to his generous nature, but granting them influence on policy matters or allowing them to engage in the rough-and-tumble of politics among equals was something else.

Shortly after his first election, Morrison created a citizens' advisory committee to aid his administration in shaping civic policy. But he brushed aside all requests for direct black participation even though blacks comprised about one-third of the city's population at the time and set up an all-white agency under the chairmanship of Dillard University benefactor Edgar B. Stern. For the mayor, Stern was the ideal choice because he had "been very conspicuous in the movement for the Advancement of Colored People."[32]

There is no question that the group's select composition influenced its deliberations. When the advisory committee considered the integration of the New Orleans Police Department and the city's parks, it entertained the former prospect merely as a "short-cut preventative of wider measures." In the end, two blacks were hired, assigned to the juvenile bureau, dressed in plain clothes, and placed in neighborhoods where they were invisible to the white community. As for the parks, the committee recommended the development of a "sizable" facility for blacks but, in the words of Morrison's biographer, "apparently never considered integrating the existing facilities."[33]

Ultimately, Morrison did appear to consult blacks directly in racial

31. Haas, *DeLesseps S. Morrison*, 71–73; DeLesseps S. Morrison to Joyce Folse, September 3, 1959, Morrison to George V. Haralson, January 21, 1950, in DeLesseps S. Morrison Papers, Howard-Tilton Library, Tulane University, New Orleans.

32. DeLesseps S. Morrison to Daniel E. Byrd, March 14, 1946, in New Orleans Branch NAACP Papers (hereafter NAACP Papers), Earl K. Long Library, University of New Orleans.

33. Haas, *DeLesseps S. Morrison*, 74, 76–78; DeLesseps S. Morrison to Edgar B. Stern, May 31, 1949, Scott Wilson to Dave McGuire, May 28, 1949, both in Wilson Papers; DeLesseps S. Morrison to Daniel E. Byrd, March 14, 1946, in NAACP Papers.

matters by setting up an all-black advisory body that the *Louisiana Weekly* denounced as a "Jim Crow Committee" and mere "window dressing." In a bitterly ironic move, one Morrison adviser suggested that the mayor might deflect such charges by allowing blacks to select "a name for the athletic field to be built in Pontchartrain Park." Indeed, the suggestion as well as the Pontchartrain Park development itself measured the limits of Morrison's approach to racial affairs.

The development of the Pontchartrain Park subdivision for middle-class blacks was financed by Rosa and Charles Keller and Edgar and Edith Stern and was staunchly supported by the New Orleans Urban League. The initiative emerged from a dinner party hosted by the Sterns at which the inability of an aide's servant to locate decent housing became the topic of conversation. The Sterns and the Kellers then decided to underwrite the Pontchartrain Park project in the Seabrook area of the upper Ninth Ward. From their perspective, such a development would both meet a real need and undermine prevailing racial stereotypes. Morrison, pressed at the time by A. P. Tureaud and the NAACP to desegregate the City Park golf course and other park facilities, saw it as an opportunity to pursue his separate but equal strategy by providing such services as part of the larger project.[34]

The NAACP "insurgents" and their largely creole leaders articulated serious misgivings. A. J. Chapital opposed the project because it reinforced the existing pattern of segregation and because he gauged the mayor's backing as an attempt to subvert any move toward integration. Tureaud also opposed a new segregated development, and several others objected to the obvious paternalism.[35]

Both the proposal and its critics revealed the persistent divergent undercurrents in the Crescent City's black community. A. L. Davis' protest efforts, though notable, were circumscribed by his political relationship to Morrison. Aside from the galvanizing and polarizing issues relating to school desegregation, his and other uptown ministers' protest activities seemed confined to areas in which Morrison invited challenge. Unwilling to initiate desegregation, the mayor sometimes found it convenient to respond to court orders, as when Davis filed a "friendly" suit to desegregate public transportation in New Orleans in the aftermath of

34. Haas, *DeLesseps S. Morrison,* 249–50; Rogers, "Humanity and Desire," 40–42.
35. Rogers, "Humanity and Desire," 42–43.

Martin Luther King, Jr.'s, boycott in Montgomery, Alabama. Both the mayor and the preacher were able to play to their constituencies. Davis rallied churchgoers in the name of "freedom and human dignity," and Morrison, in his near-obsessive quest for the governor's mansion, appealed to whites as the NAACP's leading legal adversary.

But if not really harassed by his uptown ministerial allies, Morrison found himself truly pressed on racial matters by the downtown creoles. A. P. Tureaud believed, for example, that Morrison "didn't do a whole lot for Negroes" other than to "stimulate their desire to participate in politics." Realist that he was, Tureaud still served as Morrison's black leader in the Seventh Ward and even occasionally slowed the progress of court cases at the mayor's request when elections were pending. As Tureaud noted, Morrison's relative moderation stood in stark contrast to the atavistic racial views of other white politicians. But Tureaud's support was neither reflexive nor unconditional, and, as the Pontchartrain Park controversy indicated, he reserved the right to dissent.[36]

Not only did Tureaud and the NAACP bring the string of lawsuits that began to lift the veil of racial proscription (whether invited by Morrison or not), but they repeatedly confronted the mayor on a host of issues. When Morrison suggested that Edgar Stern could represent black interests on his advisory committee, the NAACP, through Dan Byrd, told the mayor that "it [was] an impossibility for Mr. Stern to know the heart beat of our people." Byrd, an Arkansas-born, Chicago-raised former Harlem Globetrotter, could be unusually blunt. When Morrison endorsed an individual who publicly glorified the exploits of Louisiana's Reconstruction-era White League for the position of United States district attorney, Byrd informed the mayor that the appointment was "impossible for Negroes to accept."[37]

NAACP jabbing continued throughout Morrison's administration and was especially persistent during the deepest racial crisis of the Morrison years—the bitterly resisted desegregation of New Orleans public schools in 1960–1961. If Morrison's pursuit of racial "moderation" was limited by his personal views and the inherent paternalism of New Orleans' social and political relations, it was also held hostage by his burning ambition to become governor and his three unsuccessful gubernatorial races in 1955, 1959, and 1963. Faced with a wave of reaction that swept Louisiana in the wake of the *Brown* decision, Morrison was first paralyzed and then emasculated by the race issue. When the NAACP and Tureaud successfully pursued *Bush* v. *Orleans Parish School Board* and confronted the city with the necessity of desegregation, the abdication of leadership on the part of the mayor and the city's social and business elite set the stage for the riotous disturbances that virtually immobilized New Orleans. Fearful of the political consequences of supporting even court-ordered school desegregation, Morrison ran for cover and permitted arch-racists such as Willie Rainach and Leander Perez to seize the initiative. He also denied the NAACP's Thurgood Marshall use of the Municipal Auditorium, claiming that his appearance "was not in the interest of the people of New Orleans."[38]

In explaining himself to the New Orleans branch NAACP's Arthur J. Chapital and Ernest N. ("Dutch") Morial, Morrison suggested that the "leadership of the Negro Community has a responsibility to do everything possible to maintain the cause of good race relations." He lectured them further that the "NAACP is doing a disservice to the community in general and to the well being of the Negro population in particular when it sponsors meetings and speeches that may have the effect of emotionally arousing members of both races."[39]

Responding to Morrison's "personal observations" on the "merit and service of the NAACP," Chapital and Morial stressed the importance of getting the mayor "to appreciate the dissatisfaction of the Negro citizens of New Orleans." In a terse history lesson they noted that, at the time of the NAACP's founding, "the Negro's status as a citizen was nil. He was disfranchised, he was bereft of education to an appalling degree, he was given only menial jobs as a wage earner, he was treated with paternal indulgence and when he raised his voice in protest of inhuman treatment he was lynched. These nefarious conditions made the found-

38. Haas, *DeLesseps S. Morrison*, 252–82; Morton Inger, *Politics and Reality in an American City* (New York, 1969); Edward L. Pinney and Robert S. Friedman, *Political Leadership and the School Desegregation Crisis in New Orleans* (New York, 1963); Louisiana State Advisory Committee, *The New Orleans School Crisis: Report to the United States Commission on Civil Rights* (New Orleans, 1961); Mary Lee Muller, "The Orleans Parish School Board and Negro Education, 1940–1960" (M.A. thesis, University of New Orleans, 1975) and "New Orleans Public School Desegregation," *Louisiana History*, XVII (1976), 69–88.

39. DeLesseps S. Morrison to Arthur J. Chapital, Sr., and Ernest N. Morial, April 18, 1960, in NAACP Papers.

ing the NAACP a necessity. . . . With heavy heart we observe that there is no sound basis, some fifty-one years later, to argue that the NAACP is doing a disservice in New Orleans."[40]

Such differences finally led the local NAACP to oppose Morrison's appointment as ambassador to the Organization of American States when he decided to leave city hall in 1961. The mayor tried to mollify the opposition by turning to the uptown ministry and appointing A. L. Davis as a "race relations officer." It was a move that, in the NAACP's eyes, reinforced segregation and made Davis "a messenger boy, who will fulcrum a see-saw between the city government and the Negro citizens of New Orleans."[41]

The NAACP's resistance made it a special target. The 1950s, particularly, witnessed an intense antisubversive crusade, the emergence of the White Citizens' Councils (New Orleans provided over half the state's total membership), and the bitter fight over school desegregation that shook the Jim Crow system to its foundations. Politically, the reactionary mood manifested itself most strikingly in a wave of legislative enactments. In 1956, thirteen separate pieces of "hate" legislation poured out of Baton Rouge and led the *Louisiana Weekly* to conclude that "Louisiana has sunk lower than . . . Mississippi in the seemingly popular contest of who can do the most to degrade, oppress, and thwart the Negro's aspirations for dignity and respect." And that was but a prelude to the ninety-two measures passed five years later when the Louisiana legislature tried to prevent the desegregation of New Orleans' public schools.[42]

As the source for much of white Louisiana's discomfort, the NAACP became the segregationists' *bête noire*. Years of repeated verbal onslaughts led A. L. Davis to conclude that there were forces "trying to make us afraid of using the name NAACP." Indeed, that appeared to be literally the case when in April, 1956, the Louisiana Supreme Court prohibited the state's NAACP branches from holding meetings or conducting regular business. The state legislature had applied a 1924 law designed to reveal the identities of members of the Ku Klux Klan when, in an act of intimidation, it asked the NAACP to surrender its member-

40. Arthur J. Chapital, Sr., and Ernest N. Morial to DeLesseps S. Morrison, April 22, 1960, *ibid.*

41. Arthur J. Chapital to Gentlemen, June 20, 1951, June 27, 1961, *ibid.*

42. Neil R. McMillen, *The Citizens' Council: Organized Resistance to the Reconstruction, 1954–1964* (Urbana, 1971), 64–70, 267; *Louisiana Weekly*, July 28, 1956.

ship list. The New Orleans police even went so far as to raid NAACP offices "to 'muzzle' any possible discussions by leaders of the civil rights organization." NAACP secretary Roy Wilkins subsequently suspended operations in Louisiana, and normal activity did not resume until the early 1960s, when the federal courts—under A. P. Tureaud's prodding—overturned the legislative directives.[43]

A. L. Davis' praise and defense of the NAACP—even as that organization warily viewed his rise in the Morrison administration—symbolized the unity of race, the persistent divisiveness of ethnicity, and the complex legacies of the Jim Crow era. The common consciousness and interest among New Orleans' blacks were demonstrated by the McDonogh Day protest and the white reaction to school desegregation. And though in citywide groups such as the OPPVL and the NAACP blacks of all backgrounds joined in seeking political gain and advances in civil rights, each maintained its own base and style. The former, rooted uptown and most firmly among the members and followers of the Interdenominational Ministerial Alliance, tied its interests to a white political sponsor in a curious blend of expanding democratic possibilities and lingering paternalistic inhibitions. The latter, its leadership and demeanor emerging from its downtown creole quarters, mobilized its black base, maintained its independence, and earned the enmity of its adversaries. Two things remained clear. First, the fear provoked by the NAACP enhanced its stature throughout the black community. Second, if the different approaches embodied in the rising black public presence had the utility of combining pressure with cooperation, they also contained the seeds of dissension and remained fault lines barely hidden beneath the crust of racial solidarity.

The legacy of the Morrison era was also mixed politically. His characteristic evasiveness and studied ambiguity on racial matters ultimately rendered him suspect to all parties concerned. There was no safe middle ground in the midst of one of the great social upheavals in American history.

Political forces within the black community remained fragmented, fighting for favors dispensed by their respective white patrons. Not only was the Long-Morrison feud mirrored among black groups, but even within the Morrison camp the mayor's selected, largely uptown leaders jockeyed individually for position. They were little more than shards of

43. Rogers, "Humanity and Desire," 124–26; Arthur J. Chapital, "President's Report" (Mimeo, November 11, 1957, in NAACP Papers); *Louisiana Weekly*, December 22, 1956, January 5, 26, 1957, November 6, 1971.

black support, enlisted as cutting edges in various white causes. If the NAACP kept its distance from the partisan wrangling, it still served as a mobilizing political force, pursuing—in conjunction with the OPPVL, black unions, and others—voter registration crusades in the attempt to transform the black vote into something more than a useful adjunct to white campaigns. As in much else, the Morrison years provided a start.

The Civil Rights Era and the Citizens' Committee

Councilman-at-large Vic Schiro succeeded Morrison as mayor in the summer of 1961. Appointed by the city council after Morrison's resignation, the Italian Schiro had the virtue of lacking Morrison's burning ambition, and consequently, he moved quickly to suppress the disorders surrounding the desegregation of New Orleans' public schools. His tenure (1961–1970), however, was less notable for such forthright attention to racial problems than it was for cynical manipulation of them. Moreover, Schiro presided over the disintegration of Morrison's political empire while confronting the realities of the civil rights revolution. With Morrison no longer in city hall, the center of New Orleans' politics did not hold, and the constituent elements of the city's political landscape flew apart.

Schiro's 1962 campaign for election in his own right illustrated the process. Representing a single faction in Morrison's Crescent City Democratic Association, Schiro faced opposition from the RDO's James Comiskey, as well as from another Morrison protégé, Paul Burke, and the Cold Water Committee's Adrian Duplantier. In a fight for his political life, Schiro tapped the latent animosities he had capped in the school crisis.

In the runoff, Schiro attacked Duplantier for being "soft" on integration and accepted the support of the South Louisiana Citizens' Council after affirming his attachment to the city's "traditional customs and mores." His supporters, including the traditionally antiblack RDO, followed his lead and employed racially inflammatory tactics that the *Times-Picayune* found "disgraceful." In the absence of Morrison's cohesive presence, the tattered remnants of the New Orleans "machine" and their traditional uptown adversaries went after one another with renewed vigor.[44]

44. Parker, *Morrison Era*, 129–30; New Orleans *Times-Picayune*, March 1, 1962; New York *Times*, February 26, 1962.

Blacks were stunned by Schiro's publicly expressed disinterest in winning their votes after he had spent most of his career "begging for them." Moreover, Schiro's repeated verbal assaults on the NAACP placed him in the mainstream of Louisiana racial demagoguery, and he used his position to deny Avery Alexander's Consumers League access to the Municipal Auditorium. As Morrison had before him, he slammed the door on civil rights forces—this time Martin Luther King, Jr., was to be the speaker—but presented no such obstacles to the Citizens' Council. The mayor's electoral effort was, in the eyes of the black press, "one of the most vicious race-baiting political campaigns in history." It also demonstrated black New Orleans' isolation and fundamental weakness. Without a "friend" in city hall, it remained vulnerable before hostile and malevolent forces.[45]

Schiro's election presented both a dilemma and an opportunity. Although he clearly could not assume Morrison's tarnished mantle as the guardian of black interests, the Cold Water Committee's support of Duplantier's more moderate candidacy, the beating suffered by the business community during the chaotic months of school disorders, and a powerful legacy of paternalistic relationships drew uptown white leaders into direct negotiations with blacks on a variety of issues. Seeking peace and an aura of "progress"—and able to trade off interests not vitally their own—an extraordinary collection of white economic and social elites effectively "privatized" the political give-and-take that previously existed in the public arena. Bereft of Chep Morrison's soothing mediation, black and white community leaders came into closer and more direct contact.

The vehicle for negotiation on behalf of New Orleans' blacks was the newly created and significantly named Citizens Committee. The memory of the original Comité des Citoyens and its pursuit of justice in Homer Plessy's name remained alive during the civil rights era. Indeed, as late as 1957, Marcus Christian lamented persistent white resistance to desegregation and wondered aloud when a "new Citizens' Committee [would] come forward to wipe out the long, stinging defeat suffered in the case of *Plessy* v. *Ferguson*." Inspired by Aristide Mary (who wished "to give a dignified appearance to the resistance" to Jim Crow), founded by Louis Martinet, given voice by the *Crusader,* and served by officers such as Arthur Esteves, C. C. Antoine, Firmin Christophe,

45. *Louisiana Weekly,* January 13, 20, February 17, March 3, 1962.

Rodolphe Desdunes, and Paul Bonseigneur, the original Comité des Citoyens embodied, in the 1890s, the remnants of the still vital black creole determination to fight the white community's "exaggerated fanaticism about caste." Marcus Christian's call for a resurrection was answered in the social and political wreckage that followed New Orleans' school desegregation crisis.[46]

The new Citizens Committee had a broader base in the black community than its antecedent even if, according to attorney and organizer Lolis Elie, it remained a "tenuous" coalition. Fused by history, Catholic creoles such as Leonard Burns, Norman Francis, and Dutch Morial worked with uptown Protestant ministers such as A. L. Davis and Avery Alexander. Institutionally, older groups such as the Interdenominational Ministerial Alliance, the NAACP, and the Urban League made common cause with the new progeny of civil rights protest such as the Congress of Racial Equality (CORE). In the half-decade between the reactionary chaos of the school crisis and the empowering passage of the Voting Rights Act of 1965, the Citizens Committee and its elite counterparts in the white community tried to make New Orleans' civil rights "revolution" a bloodless one.[47]

CORE was a significant new element in that revolution. Inspired by the 1960 sit-ins conducted by Southern University students in Baton Rouge and associated with the boycotts conducted in the uptown Dryades Street shopping district by Avery Alexander's Consumers League, Xavier University student Rudy Lombard, Oretha Castle, and a nucleus of black activists assumed positions in the vanguard of New Orleans' CORE. Members of CORE brought direct action out of the neighborhoods and onto Canal Street, the city's main business artery, in September, 1960. Coordinating their activities with the NAACP Youth Council, they provoked arrests, campaigned to desegregate both service and jobs, and sparked private negotiations between black and white leaders. Such discussions provided the background for the creation of the Citizens Committee and defined the issues on its agenda.[48]

46. *Ibid.*, January 26, 1957; Charles Barthelemy Roussève, *The Negro in Louisiana* (New Orleans, 1937), 129, 157; Rodolphe Lucien Desdunes, *Our People and Our History*, trans. and ed. Sister Dorothea Olga McCants (Baton Rouge, 1973), 140–48; C. Vann Woodward, *American Counterpoint: Slavery and Racism in the North-South Dialogue* (New York, 1983), 214–22.

47. Rogers, "Humanity and Desire," 307–20.

48. *Ibid.*, 180–85, 261–63; August Meier and Elliott Rudwick, *CORE: A Study in the Civil Rights Movement, 1942–1968* (Urbana, 1975), 112–16.

The mercurial appearance of New Orleans' CORE chapter, however, was matched by its rapid eclipse. It was a crucial precipitating agent in the early 1960s and the entrée into civil rights activity for black attorneys Lolis Elie, Nils Douglas, and Robert Collins, but the chapter went into a steep decline when key leaders left the city and factionalism went unchecked. Its ranks were augmented by returning white college students in late 1961, and the black leadership responded to complaints about interracial dating and socializing by expelling its white members in 1962. Remaining members increasingly emphasized "pride in their blackness and African origins," ironically rejecting "white values" while stressing the criterion of color and denouncing "light-skinned" blacks active in the older civil rights groups as "bourgeois conservatives."[49] It was doubly ironic, of course, that those posing as radicals adopted so thoroughly the prevailing American racial dualism and included among the "conservatives" many who remained true to the original Comité's abhorrence of the "fanaticism of caste." Still, CORE's inversion of the existing racial order did not immediately split it irrevocably from those who might have taken issue with the application of color-based standards of acceptability. All were united in the Citizens Committee in a common crusade against the status quo.

The committee did enjoy some success. In the summer of 1962, working through Harry Kelleher, Harry McCall, and other members of Chep Morrison's old Cold Water Committee, it was able to bring enough pressure to bear on Canal Street merchants to desegregate their lunch counters. The next year the Citizens Committee and its white allies concluded a negotiation in which the city agreed to amend its hiring practices and remove the humiliating signs restricting black access to certain public facilities, and the Canal Street merchants agreed to open a significant number of jobs to blacks. By mid-1963, a *Louisiana Weekly* columnist commented that "numerous breakthroughs have been made in the wall of segregation" and the changes "have been implemented with such ease . . . that [they] . . . have been accepted by the general public without protest."[50]

But there were still problems. The Citizens Committee may have been able to get the leaders who dined at the exclusive Boston Club to open the lunch counter at McCrory's, but its very existence and the pro-

49. Meier and Rudwick, *CORE,* 169, 206; Rogers, "Humanity and Desire," 278–84.
50. Rogers, "Humanity and Desire," 307–22; *Louisiana Weekly,* July 27, 1963.

cess of extracting concessions from white benefactors merely institutionalized arrangements between black and white elites that had been delineated by A. P. Tureaud a half-century before. The heavy hand of paternalism still lay at the root of this relationship, no matter how demanding the black negotiators became. The tone of the negotiations might have shifted over the years, but not the substance. If black attorney and Urban League representative Revius Ortique felt that he could "call upon . . . the top people in this community . . . and make strong suggestions to them," he was still disguising rights as favors and reinforcing both the power and the cast of mind of those with whom he was dealing.[51]

The blacks' relative lack of power meant that they had to rely on the good faith of those promising change. The Canal Street merchants proved painfully slow in delivering the coveted jobs, and when the NAACP Youth Council resumed picketing in 1963, the papered-over cracks in the wall of black unity reappeared. CORE, already in disarray, failed to pursue enforcement of the agreement its initial demonstrations had made possible. Blacks on the Citizens Committee who offered peace for progress were embarrassed about negotiating while picketing continued and focused their displeasure on the protestors. It remained for the NAACP and its independent Youth Council to push for implementation.

Four of its executive board members were on the Citizens Committee, and the NAACP did not at first publicly support the Youth Council's actions, although it privately endorsed them. According to Raphael Cassimere, Jr., president of the NAACP Youth Council, Dutch Morial, the new president of the local NAACP, informed him of the terms of the Canal Street agreement and asked him "to check them out." The lack of compliance revealed by a subsequent Youth Council survey triggered the renewed round of picketing. Moreover, three weeks before the picketing began, Morial informed Mayor Vic Schiro that the "Negro citizens of New Orleans will no longer tolerate the spoon feeding of their rights. We want all our rights now." Morial continued: "This city is not immune to the new temper and tensions that are being manifested everywhere. Perhaps demonstrations against racial inequality in this community would be the spark to free this city of its inertia and complacency in the area of human relations."[52] In rejecting Morial's call for the

---

51. Rogers, "Humanity and Desire," 320.
52. *Louisiana Weekly*, July 6, August 3, 10, 1963.

appointment of a biracial committee on human relations, Schiro high-lighted blacks' lack of leverage in the political system.

Indeed, Schiro not only failed to countenance Morial's call for a biracial committee, but the city refused to deliver on its earlier prom-ises. In the face of court action ordering the desegregation of the city's swimming pools, Schiro, claiming financial exigencies, had the pools closed. City jobs—certainly those in government itself—were not forth-coming, and the use of many public facilities remained anything but open. Blacks responded with a massive march on city hall in September, 1963, a march approved by the white elite, who believed it to be "an intelligent safety valve" and a means of releasing "emotional heat." Little changed. A month after demonstration leaders delivered their peti-tion calling for the desegregation of New Orleans, Avery Alexander was refused service in the city hall cafeteria and dragged bodily from that building; A. L. Davis and others were similarly arrested when they tried to meet with the mayor in his office.[53] New Orleans' blacks obviously needed more than the assistance of gracious white intermediaries.

The Voting Rights Act and the Evolution of Black Politics

The Voting Rights Act of 1965 gravely altered the political landscape and was felt far beyond the political arena. In 1964, 63 percent of the city's eligible white population was registered to vote, but only 28 per-cent of the blacks could make that claim; the latter represented but 17.5 percent of the registered electorate. By the summer of 1966, 42 percent of the black eligibles had signed up (the comparable white figure re-mained at 63 percent) and blacks constituted 25.2 percent of the city's registered voters. With New Orleans only belatedly feeling the tug of white flight, the potential for future demographic—and political—shifts seemed enormous.[54]

Equally striking, however, were the ways in which the Voting Rights Act served as a social force. Blacks could exert political influence only through discipline, organization, and a high degree of racial solidarity. Those who mobilized voters made increasingly explicit racial appeals,

53. Rogers, "Humanity and Desire," 329–32; *Louisiana Weekly*, November 9, 1963.

54. Allen Rosenzweig, "The Influence of Class and Race on Political Behavior in New Orleans, 1960–1967" (M.A. thesis, University of Oklahoma, 1967), 16–17.

reinforced the prevailing racial dualism, obfuscated all other sources of identification, and accelerated an ongoing process now generations old. The heat of repeated political battles, fought out increasingly along racial lines as color came to replace party as an organizing principle on the local level, served as a forge, purging elements that failed to line up on one side or the other of the great racial divide. If racial interests were not always clear—or perhaps subject to manipulation—there was no doubt that they moved more frequently to center stage.

The 1965 mayoralty showed the transforming power of the Voting Rights Act as well as the dogged persistence of powerful local traditions. Jimmy Fitzmorris, a Chep Morrison protégé and Vic Schiro's major opponent, found every chink in the mayor's racial armor, promising to hire without regard to race, end discrimination in city hall, reopen the city's swimming pools, and appoint a biracial human relations committee. Schiro, who had picked up the race issue as a matter of convenience, now took out ads in the *Louisiana Weekly* and cut deals with the old black auxiliaries in the Morrison manner.[55]

Despite his recent record, the incumbent had enough success to ensure victory. A. L. Davis had been fired and arrested by Schiro but supported him along with the rest of the OPPVL; so did A. P. Tureaud and Avery Alexander. Fitzmorris' ties to labor won him the endorsement of Chink Henry and the CCIVL, and he added to that the backing of the *Louisiana Weekly* and those who were not impressed by the mayor's "grandstanding." It was not enough. The important point, however, was that this first post–Voting Rights Act campaign was carried out, according to the *Louisiana Weekly*, in the "absence of the hobgoblins of race hate." It was also notable that the black vote remained fragmented. It was neither sufficient nor independent enough to strike out on its own.[56]

The Voting Rights Act also stimulated the opportunistic creation of a new range of black organizations. The two most important groups were the Community Organization for Urban Politics (COUP) and the Southern Organization for Unified Leadership (SOUL). If, as the *Louisiana Weekly* claimed, blacks found themselves "plunged into a sea of political maneuver," COUP and SOUL were two quickly fashioned vessels carved from different, long-standing tendencies within the larger black

55. *Louisiana Weekly*, October 9, 30, 1965.
56. *Ibid.*

community. Designed to capitalize instantaneously on New Orleans' radically altered political opportunities, both groups were narrowly and conventionally political. Literally born out of the need to corral black voters in particular legislative races, they eschewed systemic change in favor of the more immediate rewards the system now had to offer. They thus differed not only from the NAACP but even from the older political groups, which, although they had sought tangible advantage, also maintained some sense of pushing a communal agenda. Setting themselves up as intermediaries to broker the black vote, the new groups became convenient channels for white politicians who were still isolated from a black community they could no longer ignore.

SOUL, as its acronym clearly implied, embodied the heightened racial consciousness and militance of the civil rights era. Its links to that movement were explicit because the organization itself was the political offshoot of New Orleans' CORE. CORE attorney Nils Douglas originally ran for the state legislature from the downtown Ninth Ward in 1963, but it was his next stab at that seat, initiated a year after the passage of the Voting Rights Act, that served as the impetus for SOUL's creation. Though unsuccessful, Douglas became the first black candidate to lead the pack in a first primary since Reconstruction; and SOUL, which survived the election, became an important downtown black political organization.[57] Fully accepting, indeed championing, America's duochromatic social framework, SOUL stressed racial identity and mobilization as the best way to squeeze concessions out of the "system."

Similarly, COUP coalesced around Charles Elloie's unsuccessful Seventh Ward race for state representative. Led initially by CORE-affiliated attorney Robert Collins, COUP brought together young black professionals who represented the "assimilationist" and conservative tendencies found in that downtown creole stronghold. Its key leaders such as Henry Braden IV and Sidney Barthelemy had not been conspicuous in the civil rights movement, and indeed, as their Urban League orientation demonstrated, they were more adept at cultivating white contacts. If SOUL tried to capture the new racial assertiveness, COUP traveled the more well-worn path of accommodation and relied heavily on white familiarity and support.[58]

57. Furnell Chatman, "Black Politics: A Concept in Search of a Definition," *New Orleans*, V (August, 1971), 29ff.; Tom Dent, "New Orleans Versus Atlanta," *Southern Exposure*, VII (Spring, 1979), 64–68.

58. Thompson, *Negro Leadership Class*, 36–37.

Most notably, however, the first real breakthrough made possible by the Voting Rights Act resulted not from these institutional initiatives but rather from the intersection of the new opportunity structure and the most deeply rooted independent black force in New Orleans—the "unassimilated" creole leadership of the NAACP. Victory came with Dutch Morial's election to the Louisiana legislature in 1967. Always a man in a hurry, Morial became the first black elected to the Louisiana House of Representatives in the modern era as well as the first black graduate of the Louisiana State University Law School (in 1954) and the first black assistant United States attorney in New Orleans. He would later append to these accomplishments a veritable string of other firsts: first black to serve as Juvenile Court judge, first on the Fourth Circuit Court of Appeals, and, ultimately, the first black mayor of New Orleans. Dutch Morial was himself a civil rights revolution.

Morial's initial forays into electoral politics came well before the Voting Rights Act. He campaigned in 1959 for a seat on the Democratic State Central Committee and did so again in 1963 from the downtown Ninth Ward. Intended both to stimulate and benefit from augmented black voter registration (the NAACP conducted a registration drive in the lower Ninth Ward in late 1962), Morial's second race coincided with the failure of another black candidate to make the runoff for the Louisiana legislature by a single vote in the uptown Twentieth District (Wards 1 and 2). By the end of 1964, Morial had established a legal residence in that district at 1242 Magazine Street, and by mid-1967 the NAACP Youth Council was conducting a voter registration campaign headquartered at 1242 Magazine that included Wards 1 and 2. Morial won his election in the first primary by a majority of 107 votes and then won the suit brought by a disgruntled white opponent who challenged his residential qualifications. A Seventh Ward creole, an unsuccessful Ninth Ward candidate, Morial found his first safe electoral haven in uptown New Orleans. The *Louisiana Weekly* concluded that he provided "new direction and a new political freedom to Negro voters . . . throughout the entire city." [59]

In his background, his vision, and his willingness to challenge racial barriers—his determination to confront the "fanaticism of caste"— Morial remained the most prominent legatee of the creole protest tradi-

59. Untitled handwritten report, November, 1962, in NAACP Papers; *Louisiana Weekly,* June 10, November 11, 1967; New Orleans *Times-Picayune,* November 6, 1967.

tion. Born in 1929, he represented a new generation, one yet another step removed from the pitched battles of Reconstruction and the embittered resistance to the imposition of Jim Crow, but nonetheless with a clear connection to that legacy. His link, mentor, and law partner was none other than A. P. Tureaud, and if, like Tureaud, he was fair-complexioned enough to have "passed," there is no doubt that he "identified black." If anything, the passage of time blurred the distinctions that might have tempered that identification. The last of six children, Morial was the only one in his family who spoke no French. And he had no memory of his family's antebellum status. But as John Higham has noted of European ethnic groups, "it has been possible to shed the outward marks of foreign origin without undergoing total assimilation. Some differences of attitude or world view linger after the group itself has ceased to figure largely in a person's consciousness." So it was with Morial.[60]

Morial's identification with and service to New Orleans' black community was reciprocated with deeply felt pride and admiration. Morial moved freely through black New Orleans during the civil rights era, recruiting plaintiffs with the assistance of the Interdenominational Ministerial Alliance, raising funds in churches of all faiths, and mobilizing marchers for the demonstrations of the early 1960s. The civil rights movement was thus an ethnic crucible melding black New Orleans into a single whole to a greater extent than it had been since the colonial era. As the local attorney, along with Tureaud, most closely identified with the dismantling of Jim Crow in New Orleans, and the president of the NAACP (1963–1965), he remained in the forefront of black protest, and his entry into the political arena was, as he put it, merely the "logical extension" of his earlier career. He consequently enjoyed "a degree of acceptance" in the community even as that community took greater pride in its "blackness." For Morial, however, the goal of the struggle against invidious racial distinctions remained the obliteration of caste or color privilege, not the mere manipulation of the existing racial order. His fight became, in his own words, "more of a moral and human rights thing that affects all people." It was a vision that owed more to his cultural antecedents than it did to the emerging racial consciousness of the 1960s.[61]

The full implications of the Voting Rights Act rose into sharp relief

60. John Higham, *Send These to Me: Jews and Other Immigrants in Urban America* (New York, 1975), 12; interview with Dutch Morial by Arnold R. Hirsch, April 24, 1987.
61. Interview with Morial, April 24, 1987.

with the city elections of 1969–1970. Because of the chief executive's two-term charter limitation, the race for city hall was wide open. Ultimately, councilman-at-large Moon Landrieu won that campaign by garnering over 90 percent of the black vote and only a minority of the white vote in a rare general election in which a surprisingly strong Republican showing resulted from explicit white concerns over rising black political strength. Landrieu's success in solidifying the black vote while endorsed by the new black political organizations also seemingly overturned a tradition of endemic fractiousness and permitted the perception that the new groups were, indeed, major players. Finally, that same election witnessed Dutch Morial's citywide race for councilman-at-large, a seemingly premature effort inasmuch as blacks constituted no more than 30 percent of the electorate, yet one that came surprisingly close, failing by only about 5,000 votes out of 160,000. These developments were important not for their individual significance but for their interrelationship and consequences for black empowerment and independence.

In running for mayor, Moon Landrieu seemed to be a natural choice for the black community. As a freshman legislator in Baton Rouge during the school crisis of 1960–1961, Landrieu opposed the segregationists, denying them the unanimity they ardently sought. As a leader in the city council (1965–1969) he responded sensitively to black needs, facilitating the removal of the Confederate flag from council chambers and pushing through the ordinance establishing a biracial human relations committee near the end of Vic Schiro's second term. And as a candidate for mayor he promised passage of a public accommodations ordinance that would enhance the protection offered by existing federal law and the appointment of blacks to key positions in government. Landrieu, moreover, actively sought to run on a citywide ticket with an at-large black candidate for the city council; and when Dutch Morial's candidacy preempted the field, Landrieu offered Morial his endorsement. Supported by SOUL, COUP, and much of the newer black political leadership, Landrieu positioned himself well in the black community.[62]

But in a crowded first primary field of twelve, Landrieu drew no more than 39 percent of the black vote, sharing it with Judge David Gertler, Billy Guste, councilman John Petre, and runoff opponent Jimmy Fitzmorris. Gertler and Guste had connections among New Orleans' blacks, and the traditional political fragmentation of that community clearly persisted in the 1969 mayoralty. It was only in the runoff—

62. Interviews with Moon Landrieu by Arnold R. Hirsch, May 8, 13, 1987; *Louisiana Weekly*, November 8, December 6, 13, 20, 1969.

after Fitzmorris calculatedly rejected Landrieu's guarantees on public accommodations and appointments and failed to endorse Dutch Morial—that the black community rose as a unit to defeat a contender who was clearly running as the "white candidate." That solidarity only increased when Republican Ben Toledano pursued Landrieu in the general election, his candidacy fueled by white anxiety over the decisive leverage black voters demonstrated in the Democratic primary.[63]

The belated consolidation of the black vote, however, belied its earlier diffusion and Landrieu's apparent efforts to wrap it up early in the campaign. Despite later denials, Landrieu had close ties to a new uptown group, the Black Organization for Leadership Development (BOLD), that sponsored a "Black Primary" in the hopes of eliminating intrablack competition while mobilizing for the upcoming mayoralty. On the surface, the September 27, 1969, Black Primary seemed little different from earlier efforts to stimulate racial and political solidarity. It targeted the overlapping uptown councilmanic District B and Fourth District assessor's races where, given New Orleans' relatively mixed neighborhoods, intrablack divisions meant continued white victories. In calling for a privately held Black Primary, BOLD wished to encourage black interest and unity and also certainly hoped to improve the chances of one of its own leaders, Jim Singleton, in the District B race.

But there were other motives as well. Black candidate and onetime NAACP president Bennett Ross attacked the Black Primary and tied it to Moon Landrieu. "What the Black Primary sponsors are really interested in is having two candidates, one in the assessor's race and one in the councilmanic race, who will carry the banner of a particular mayoralty candidate. . . . The sponsors of the Black Primary, BOLD, the vehicle of SOUL, T[otal] C[ommunity] A[ction], and the Urban League [desire only] . . . to . . . garner a few votes for their man for mayor." In linking BOLD to SOUL, he noted the irony that many of the primary's organizers were not registered to vote in the district and came from the Eighth and Ninth wards, where they "all enjoy[ed] healthy helpings at the white man's feeding trough."[64]

SOUL, TCA, and the Urban League all had strong ties to Landrieu. The Urban League, particularly, provided much of his moderate-to-liberal business support and connected him to a particular segment of

63. New Orleans *Times-Picayune*, October 16, November 9, 1969, April 8, 1970; New Orleans *States-Item*, December 15, 1969.

64. *Louisiana Weekly*, August 19, November 18, 1967, September 13, 27, 1969; Chatman, "Black Politics," 29ff.

the emerging black leadership; he would turn to that link time and again in selecting young black professionals to serve in his administration. And though SOUL's support of Landrieu was never in doubt, its deep involvement in the Black Primary became evident when organizer Don Hubbard left his downtown bailiwick to assist in SOUL's unsuccessful effort, as the *Louisiana Weekly* put it, "to extend its political influence uptown via the Black Primary."[65]

Ironically, the Black Primary turned out fewer than 15 percent of the area's sixteen thousand black voters, stirring less interest and unity than did the subsequent galvanizing negative candidacies of Jimmy Fitzmorris and Republican Ben Toledano. Landrieu's solid black support materialized only in the second primary and the general election. It was also stark testimony to the overwhelming significance of the Voting Rights Act. Capturing roughly 90 percent of a 75 percent black turnout against Fitzmorris and nearly 99 percent of a 77 percent black turnout against Toledano, Landrieu received more black votes than white in each instance.[66]

There is no question that Morial's nearly successful citywide race for the city council greatly aided Landrieu by bolstering black registration and turnout. Morial did not endorse Landrieu in the first primary, but he did in the second, and the two campaigned from then on as a "ticket." Landrieu contended that he "did everything [he] could" to get Morial elected. But Morial—obviously feeling the sting of a narrow defeat—remembered that they appeared together only in black neighborhoods and believed that he lent considerably more to Landrieu's campaign than vice versa. Reflecting on the event years later, Landrieu admitted that Morial "may be right." In his postelection statement, though, Dutch Morial captured the significance of the 1969 campaign. "Our people have exerted an influence in the recent election," he declared, "that will not soon be forgotten."[67]

The Landrieu Years

Moon Landrieu, like so many other postwar New Orleans political figures, was a Chep Morrison protégé. He nonetheless differed from Mor-

65. *Louisiana Weekly,* September 13, October 4, 11, 1969.
66. New Orleans *Times-Picayune,* December 14, 1969; *Louisiana Weekly,* April 18, 1970.
67. Interview with Landrieu, May 13, 1987; interview with Dutch Morial by Arnold R. Hirsch, June 20, 1987; *Louisiana Weekly,* January 10, 1970.

rison in significant ways. First, there was the simple question of timing. Morrison governed at the beginning of the civil rights era whereas Landrieu did not assume office until the 1960s were a receding—if still vivid—memory. There is no question that Landrieu's vision was sharpened by the struggles he witnessed in the turbulent decades preceding his election as mayor, and as a consequence he did not suffer the political paralysis that doomed Morrison when he found himself whipsawed by the winds of change and gales of reaction. Despite continuing bitter resistance, Landrieu saw and brought the future to New Orleans. Second, if Landrieu's political calculus proved unerring, his actions on racial matters could not be dismissed as merely self-serving. He displayed political courage and a moral vision that were alien to Morrison, for example, in confronting the rabidly segregationist Louisiana legislature during the school crisis.

There is no question that Landrieu saw the necessity of breaking with tradition on race. Indeed, where Morrison extolled the "customs and mores" of the South, Landrieu believed that his "single greatest accomplishment" was the "significant progress" made in opening up opportunities for blacks "through the political process." There was much to substantiate the claim. At the beginning of 1970, blacks occupied only 19.4 percent (1,833 out of 8,219) of the positions in the city's classified civil service; eight years later they claimed 43 percent (4,304 out of 10,009). Landrieu also kept his promise to name black department heads—director of property management Andrew Sanchez and twenty-nine-year-old welfare director Sidney Barthelemy were the first—and he went even further by naming Robert Tucker an executive assistant and ultimately appointing Terrence Duvernay as chief administrative officer.[68] And if the new black presence in government was unprecedented, Landrieu also did not hesitate to use his political leverage to create opportunities in the private sector as well.

Such unprecedented actions contributed greatly to Landrieu's standing and popularity in New Orleans and enabled him to run for reelection in 1973 without serious opposition. He won the first Democratic primary with about 75 percent of the vote and discouraged Republicans from contesting the general election. When he left office in 1978, he re-

68. New Orleans *Times-Picayune*, October 2, 1977, March 12, April 19, 1978, July 31, 1979; *Louisiana Weekly*, May 9, 16, July 11, 1970, October 16, 1971, February 26, 1972, March 3, 1973, August 28, 1976; James Gillis, "No Race Wall at City Hall," *Dixie Magazine*, New Orleans *Times-Picayune*, June 4, 1972, 44ff.

ceived a nearly unanimous chorus of accolades from the local press.[69]

The real key to Landrieu's popularity, though, was not simply his perceptive shattering of obsolete customs but his skillful maintenance of those that were still useful. If, in the post–civil rights age, racial relationships had to be restructured, it was Landrieu's ability to work within existing political traditions and within the fully Americanized racial dichotomy that fostered change without pain. Landrieu was able to offer new opportunities to blacks without grievously antagonizing whites because he was cutting large new slices off an expanding economic pie. Landrieu's exceptional skill in obtaining significant federal revenues provided a new source of funding that he directed into black channels with great political dexterity. And on the state level, especially after black votes helped elect Governor Edwin W. Edwards in 1971, additional largesse came from Baton Rouge. One of the largest plums of the Landrieu years—the Louisiana Superdome—was a state project that conveniently fell into his lap. The result was that Landrieu did not have to take anything away from existing interests to reward new friends. And in specifically providing new opportunities for blacks, Landrieu did not have to face the more daunting and politically dangerous task of providing opportunity generically across the board. White interests could be protected in their traditional bailiwicks, and even those initially hostile to Landrieu's precedent-shattering initiatives could ultimately be recruited as allies.

Landrieu's adroit political maneuvering led at least one journalistic critic to swim against the tide of praise bestowed on the outgoing mayor in 1978 by referring to him as the "major domo of New Orleans sleaze." Bill Rushton's unflattering portrayal focused not on Landrieu's racial breakthroughs but on a "series of urban policies whose sole beneficiaries were his major campaign contributors."[70] In dealing with black New Orleans, the practice of traditional politics meant the creation of a patronage network in which rewards were doled out in the established manner—the servings were larger and more regular, but the ladle remained in white hands.

Landrieu felt that he was merely engaging in individualistic, tangible, and pragmatic politics—the essence of American urban governance. He provided opportunity on a nondiscriminatory basis—he

69. *Figaro*, March 15, 1978.

70. Bill Rushton, "New Orleans Elects a Black Mayor," *Southern Exposure*, VI (1978), 5–7.

"opened up" the system. But that was precisely the point. By providing access, he muted the call for systemic change. Black Louisiana politicians could behave as white Louisiana politicians did; indeed, those who adapted most quickly to the existing political ethos would most assuredly reap the largest prizes. New Orleans' reified system of ethnic patronage politics remained—as elsewhere—essentially conservative and incapable of fundamentally altering conditions for the city's poor masses.

The initial conduit for federal poverty program money in New Orleans was Total Community Action, Inc. It was created in 1965 as an agency outside city hall because Vic Schiro wanted no part of the controversial program and did not see its possibilities. The vacuum at the top enabled councilman-at-large Landrieu, according to *Times-Picayune* reporter James Gillis, to "exercise considerable influence . . . in connection with the Great Society programs." Ostensibly nonpolitical, TCA created a multi-million-dollar string of neighborhood centers, child development centers, and job and recreational programs; but as columnist Iris Kelso noted, its payroll quickly became "the backbone of many black political organizations." Key black Landrieu allies such as Edwin Lombard, Sidney Barthelemy, and Jim Singleton were, at one time or another, TCA board members; others, such as Sherman Copelin, Don Hubbard, Dorothy Mae Taylor, Robert Tucker, and Terrence Duvernay, were employees; and board member Barthelemy held four different positions with TCA between 1967 and 1969. TCA was, as reporter Gillis asserted and Black Primary critic Ross contended, a "political haven for a large number of Landrieu's black supporters." Similarly, Singleton, Copelin, Duvernay, and Lombard found occasional sustenance through the Model Cities program. And during the Landrieu years, Henry Braden IV directed the federally funded "New Orleans Plan" through the local Urban League. Barthelemy, Braden, and Tucker were all founders of COUP and central Urban League figures; Singleton and Taylor represented BOLD; and Copelin, Hubbard, Lombard, and department head Sanchez carried SOUL's banner. Only the tip of the proverbial iceberg, these agencies, programs, and jobs altered the character of black politics in New Orleans.[71]

Consciously cultivating a newer, young generation of black leaders, Landrieu made them the most direct beneficiaries of the civil rights struggles even as their success diverted their energies into narrower,

71. Gillis, "No Race Wall at City Hall"; *Figaro*, May 17, August 9, 30, 1978, December 10, 1979; New Orleans *Times-Picayune*, November 4, 1975, August 21, 1979.

shallower political channels. SOUL, the political progeny of CORE, showed the nature of the transformation. After his first election, Landrieu recalled that veteran civil rights leaders Lolis Elie, Robert Collins, and Nils Douglas "didn't want anything and didn't know what to ask for" from the new mayor; they were concerned about appearing "co-opted." Elie never did take anything, and Landrieu steered the others away from symbolic prizes toward less visible but potentially more remunerative positions.[72] The older SOUL leadership, however, was soon supplanted by former CORE activist Don Hubbard and Dillard University graduate Sherman Copelin, who completed the transformation of a civil rights initiative into a conventional political organization. SOUL's new guiding spirits would never be at a loss in suggesting just rewards for services rendered. The frequent and calculated use of the rhetoric of racial militance proved insurance enough against charges of co-optation.

COUP had an even shorter road to travel. Its leaders, for the most part, had not been active participants in the pitched battles for civil rights, had already established close ties to the white community, and, indeed, entered Landrieu's office with a bill of particulars. Landrieu recalled exchanging words with Sidney Barthelemy over some specific demands before reaching an accommodation. COUP's directorate, in short, echoed the sentiments of the *Louisiana Weekly* when it extolled, rather than condemned, the "spoils system." "We must 'play the game' just as others have played it," the *Weekly* declared. "We know that in order to rise within the system you must use the system to your advantage."[73]

The *Louisiana Weekly*'s euphoria over the strategic placement of a new generation of black leaders at the beginning of Landrieu's administration gave way to questions at its close. By 1978, it noted COUP's success in getting Sidney Barthelemy elected state senator and then councilman-at-large, in Henry Braden's elevation to Barthelemy's vacated senate seat, and in Robert Collins' appointment as the first black federal judge in "the Deep South Eastern District." "The important question now," the *Weekly* asserted, "is . . . will COUP measure up and be able . . . to create long standing economic opportunities not only for its immediate supporters, but for the black community at large?" The obvious answer, of course, was that COUP's agenda was already on the table. Indeed, Rodolphe Desdunes' castigation of early twentieth-century black political operatives seemed prophetic and applicable to

72. Interview with Landrieu, May 13, 1987.
73. *Ibid.; Louisiana Weekly*, March 4, 1972.

the current crop of "political leaders who worked on the principle that personal recognition is race elevation, and that the race is never so well represented as when he holds a sinecure as a 'representative Negro.'" COUP's domination of the city's CETA program (funded under the federal Comprehensive Employment and Training Act) epitomized their approach. Injecting heavy doses of nepotism and favoritism into the hiring process, they provided more immediate support for their college-educated, middle-class associates than for the hard-core unemployed.[74]

SOUL's leadership proved even more adept at blending race and politics for profit. In a curious mix of newfangled militance and old-style politics, its directorate allegedly stimulated charges of "genocide" to threaten the publicly funded Family Health Foundation's (FHF) family planning mission while issuing "demands" for patronage. Nils Douglas and Don Hubbard, among others, eventually found slots on the FHF payroll, and Model Cities director Sherman Copelin reportedly received over $50,000 in payoffs designed to overcome community suspicions and facilitate the construction of FHF clinics in Model Cities neighborhoods. Such financial arrangements coincided with the cessation of intimidating demonstrations and ultimately resulted in the indictment and conviction of FHF executives who engaged in creative bookkeeping to cover their costs. "Unindicted co-conspirators" Copelin and Hubbard earned immunity for their testimony and rallied the black community on their behalf by attacking the "antagonistic reporting" of the white media.[75]

In many ways, however, it was the creation of Superdome Services, Inc. (SSI), that was the literal and symbolic capstone to the transformation of black politics in the Landrieu era. A freshly minted corporation whose initial ownership was more than three-quarters black, SSI received the contract to provide security, janitorial, and ticket services for the Superdome. James Gillis subsequently reported that "the formation of SSI was initiated from the office of Mayor Landrieu and the task of putting it together was assigned to Dan McClung, one of Landrieu's executive assistants." He created a corporate umbrella under which virtually all the mayor's black allies gathered and through which they used their political leverage to economic advantage. Within its first year of

74. Desdunes, A Few Words to Dr. DuBois, 8, 13; Louisiana Weekly, June 10, 1978; New Orleans States-Item, August 17, 1978.

75. Martha Ward, Poor Women, Powerful Men: America's Great Experiment in Family Planning (Boulder, Colo., 1986), 93–96, 122–25; Louisiana Weekly, March 29, 1975.

operation, SSI had nearly 250 permanent employees and tapped a pool of hundreds more. Directed by Sherman Copelin and Don Hubbard, it constituted a small patronage army.[76]

Almost from the beginning, there were complaints about the inflated costs of SSI's negotiated "cost-plus" contract and its after-the-fact ratification by a state legislature dominated by Edwin Edwards. Charges of inefficiency and incompetence also dogged SSI during its early months. As the calls for investigation began to mount, Copelin's and Hubbard's involvement in the FHF scandals came to light.

Edwards' and Landrieu's political adversaries, as well as the local press—particularly the *Times-Picayune*—made the most of the charges. But both Landrieu and Copelin ably defended SSI from accusers they believed to be politically and racially motivated. The mayor pointedly noted that "it was perfectly acceptable" to enter negotiated contracts with established white interests that had the proper "social connections" and that the furor over such routine procedures erupted only when blacks became the beneficiaries. Responding to charges of SSI's inefficiencies, Copelin similarly raised questions about "sweetheart deals" with favored Dome users that did not provide enough revenue to service events. In sum, neither side entered the dispute with clean hands and each provided the other with ample ammunition.[77]

The political legacy of the Landrieu years, then, was—echoing Chep Morrison's experience—a mixed one. In granting access to government and dispensing the traditional, tangible rewards of politics, Landrieu had no parallel. But the black political community remained fragmented, held together only by the centripetal pull of its major white benefactor. Large numbers of black interests came together only in their support of Landrieu and in SSI—a profit-seeking venture that "was an in-house City Hall operation involving Mayor Landrieu's political subordinates."[78]

Moreover, it was ironic that black identification with scandals in TCA, FHF, CETA, and SSI did so much to undermine Landrieu's truly constructive efforts at overturning traditional white racial attitudes. The indictments and convictions that marked the various scams uncovered

76. New Orleans *Times-Picayune*, October 31, November 14, 1975, January 11, 1976; *Louisiana Weekly*, March 2, 1974.

77. *Louisiana Weekly*, April 6, 1974, April 5, October 10, 1975; New Orleans *Times-Picayune*, September 26, 30, October 23, November 6, 12, 14, 1975; New Orleans *States-Item*, November 20, 21, 1975.

78. Garry Boulard, "Power Brokers: Black Political Organizations," *New Orleans*, XX (October, 1985), 46ff.; New Orleans *Times-Picayune*, April 25, 1976.

at TCA and FHF and the political exploitation of the CETA program and SSI burdened black politics with the image of corruption, reinforcing old prejudices.[79]

Even more significant, though, was the price paid by the black community in its loss of independence. To the degree that black political advances were tied to Landrieu's efforts and success, that administration's interests took precedence over all others. And there is no question that at least in the conventional political organizations, Landrieu's presence dominated.

The electoral breakthroughs of the Landrieu years were virtually all tied to the mayor's exertions. Israel Augustine's successful citywide judicial race in 1970 was notable for the biracial support it received because of Landrieu's strong backing and the campaign orchestrated by Landrieu's law partner Pascal Calogero. Similarly, in 1973, SOUL's Edwin Lombard (a "relatively unknown 27-year old attorney," according to the *Louisiana Weekly*) became the second black parochial (parishwide) official since Reconstruction when Landrieu appeared on television to boost his campaign for clerk of the Criminal District Court—a move welcomed by Landrieu's executive assistant Dan McClung, who was guiding Lombard's effort. And lest anyone confuse such success with the black organizations' independent ability to churn out the vote, eleven other black candidates running for parochial offices suffered stunning first primary defeats. The 1973 campaign, as the *Louisiana Weekly* regretfully acknowledged, demonstrated black political weakness rather than strength. Finally, Sidney Barthelemy became the first black Louisiana state senator in nearly a century when Governor Edwards appointed the incumbent to the judiciary. In a district evenly split between white and black voters, Barthelemy ran successfully against three white opponents with Landrieu's backing in a 1974 special election and was unopposed in the following year's regular contest.[80]

None of this, of course, inspired black independence. Indeed, even the "militant" SOUL's ties to Landrieu were so close (as when it backed Pascal Calogero in his 1972 race for the state supreme court against black attorney Revius Ortique) that in some quarters its members were called "Moon's Coons." It was not surprising, then, that when black

79. *Louisiana Weekly*, October 18, 1975; New Orleans *States-Item*, December 27, 1975.
80. Louisiana *Weekly*, August 22, 1970; November 3, 17, December 22, 1973; March 9, 16, 1974; New Orleans *Times-Picayune*, April 21, May 1, 1974.

community groups marched to protest police brutality and the Landrieu administration's inattention to that problem in 1977, civil rights forces such as the NAACP and Southern Christian Leadership Conference strode in front, while the conventional political organizations such as BOLD, SOUL, COUP, and OPPVL—and the Urban League (derisively called the "Bourbon League" by some of the NAACP's creole leaders)— were conspicuously absent.[81]

Even the appearance of A. L. Davis on the New Orleans city council in 1975 resulted from white discretion rather than the mobilization of black political strength. A vacancy on the council resulted when a member assumed a seat on the Municipal Court. With the reapportionment of the council in litigation—its 1973 elections were canceled and the case was not resolved for another three years—the six remaining white councilmen selected Davis to represent the majority black district. And when special council elections were finally held in 1976, Mayor Landrieu supported the status quo even to the point, it was rumored, of short-circuiting challenges by SOUL-backed candidates not only uptown but also in SOUL's own backyard, where a white incumbent had to face a new constituency that was nearly 50 percent black.[82]

Nothing else rendered the patron-client relationship so clear, and nothing threatened it until the two-term limitation forced the black political organizations to look to the future. Both COUP and SOUL acted entirely in character. COUP was clearly grooming Sidney Barthelemy to be the city's first black mayor and opted for the traditional route that had served both Vic Schiro and Landrieu. First he would make a race for councilman-at-large and later pursue the big prize. Never having strolled through a political door that had not been safely held open for him, Barthelemy chose a cautious path—he would wait.

SOUL, despite its militant posturing, took a different route. It set out to anoint and make itself indispensable to the next white mayor. It found a ready ally in state senator Nat Kiefer, a fellow downtowner, who was a floor leader for Edwin Edwards and chairman of the investigative committee probing improprieties at the Superdome. Eagerly pursuing the mayoralty, Kiefer was obviously in a position to help—or hurt—SSI and SOUL and had, in the process, made a bitter enemy of Moon Landrieu. As Sherman Copelin and Don Hubbard read the future

81. *Louisiana Weekly,* September 27, 1975, March 26, 1977.
82. *Ibid.,* September 4, 1976.

and moved into Kiefer's orbit, Landrieu used his still considerable influence to cultivate his own loyal faction within SOUL and precipitated a struggle for dominance. The bitter infighting led to litigation that eventually confirmed Copelin's and Hubbard's control of the organization. The fratricidal warfare for SOUL's soul on the eve of the 1977 mayoralty indicated the depths to which white leaders were implicated even in the group's internal politics.[83]

Dutch Morial and the Survival of Creole Protest

Unlike the leaders of COUP and SOUL, Dutch Morial was neither disposed to wait until the white electorate seemed ready for a black mayor nor willing merely to accept largesse from white sponsors in need of black support. Throughout the Landrieu administration, Morial had maintained a low political profile. He returned to his legislative seat following his defeat in the 1969 city council race and remained there until the end of the 1970 legislative session, when Governor John McKeithen elevated him to the Orleans Parish Juvenile Court. Following a successful race for the Fourth Circuit Court of Appeals in 1972, Morial spent the Landrieu years literally and figuratively on the bench, insulated from the day-to-day political maelstrom that swirled about city hall. He seemed, for example, to be the only major black political figure not involved with SSI or some other Landrieu-affiliated project. When he announced his candidacy for mayor in 1977, he literally seemed to have come from nowhere and quickly became a wild card that disrupted the professionals' carefully laid plans. For those unfamiliar with the history of New Orleans' black community—a community that now constituted about 43 percent of the total electorate—his candidacy seemed quixotic at best.[84]

Certainly COUP and SOUL knew about Morial. Moon Landrieu recalled a 1969 campaign meeting when it became clear to him that Morial "never played with these guys" and that there was no "personal affection" between them. Trying to solidify support for his at-large council race, Morial had launched into what Landrieu considered an "astounding talk." Morial told them that he would not give them a penny and that they should be raising money for him rather than vice

83. *Ibid.*, November 13, 20, 27, 1976, January 8, March 5, 12, September 10, 17, 1977.
84. *Figaro*, March 9, 1977.

versa. As far as Landrieu could see, Morial "threw down the gauntlet" before those groups for "no reason"; and as far as he could tell, Morial did not get the effort out of the black organizations a "different approach" might have achieved. How valuable a more devoted effort would have proven is arguable. What was clear was that Morial still refused to "play with these guys." Landrieu did. Each had his reasons.[85]

The difference between Morial, on one hand, and Copelin, Hubbard, Braden, and Barthelemy, on the other, was best described by Rodolphe Desdunes seventy years earlier when he elaborated on the "two distinct schools of politics" that characterized the "Latin Negro" and the "Anglo Saxon." Differing in "aspiration and . . . method," the former made "every effort to acquire merits" while the latter tried "to gain advantages." Raising the ghosts of an earlier generation of Latin-creole leaders, Desdunes also spoke of the "moral Negro" who fought to "have the Negro *respected* rather than *protected*." Such leaders, in his mind, contrasted most favorably with the more "practical," self-serving political leadership he saw emerging at the end of Reconstruction.[86] Similarly, in his perceptions, values, and, ultimately, goals, Morial *was* different from the professional black politicians. Consequently, despite the apparent unity of race, the leaders of COUP and SOUL found it easier to work with Moon Landrieu than Dutch Morial; they understood one another and shared the same assumptions. Morial, as Landrieu recalled that 1969 meeting, seemed to have his "own agenda." Indeed, he did. And it is no wonder, then, that Morial's performance should seem so incomprehensible to Landrieu, who was primarily concerned about winning an election. Morial was, too—but in his own way, on his own terms, and for his own reasons. When he offered his black counterparts nothing more than a chance to fulfill their "sense of duty" in supporting his candidacy, Landrieu considered it a needless provocation.

There was also a particular racial vision that survived in the creole radicalism embodied by Morial that remained at odds with the prevailing American social order. Although Morial and others like him displayed fierce pride in their racial heritage, they wanted to create a society free of what Desdunes called the "dissensions of caste." Indeed, it was an article of faith for Desdunes that "Negroes, in treating of essential principles, should cease to be Negroes, in order to live, think, feel

85. Interview with Landrieu, May 13, 1987.
86. Desdunes, *A Few Words to Dr. DuBois*, 7, 8, 13.

and act as true Americans, just as Brown, Garrison, Lovejoy, Phillips, Lincoln and Long[fellow], ceased to be whites, that they might become the instruments of loving humanity. The white man's history is the black man's study." [87] Morial's struggle was to transcend racial barriers and to make such distinctions meaningless. Displaying a finely tuned racial consciousness and more genuine militance than most in confronting a society that adhered to invidious racial distinctions, Morial pursued neither black separatism nor chauvinism but a single society, open to all on the basis of merit, free of the chains of race prejudice.

In contrast, the very existence and success of COUP and SOUL depended on the persistence of a racially divided and highly race-conscious environment. COUP set itself up to mediate between black and white, occupying a middle ground as "black" leaders who enjoyed— and were enamored with—"white" support. The bridge between two societies, these brokers seemingly had no purpose beyond securing their own favored position and that of their sponsors. Any serious effort to redistribute society's resources would effectively end their role as mediators, as would the emergence of a unified society in which race was irrelevant. Their stake was in the status quo. Race for SOUL's leaders was a lever to be used to pry concessions from whites in the post–civil rights era. For them, too, it was therefore absolutely essential that society remain racially segmented and highly race conscious. A society that operated on the basis of racial difference and distinction was not, for them, abhorrent—it provided their living. They were amply rewarded for accepting the American racial dualism and for working within its framework. If, to whites, COUP and SOUL represented cooperation and confrontation, respectively, neither challenged the fundamental structure of the prevailing political order.

With Morial out of the political limelight for much of the 1970s, the articulation of that vision—as well as evidence of its tenacious persistence—came from the institutional incarnation of creole radicalism in New Orleans, the local branch of the NAACP. Although Morial was not visibly active in its deliberations, the NAACP took stands on desegregation in higher education and on reapportionment with which its former president had "no quarrel" and that set Morial and the NAACP apart from those more comfortably ensconced in a fully Americanized racial order.

87. *Ibid.*, 5.

In the early 1970s, the NAACP reopened the issue of maintaining a dual system of higher education nearly a century after P. B. S. Pinchback offered his support for the Redeemers' state constitution in exchange for the creation of Southern University. In proposing the creation of a unitary system, the NAACP was well aware that in the years following Pinchback's accommodation strong black interests had arisen that "were adamant in their opposition to any action that would eliminate separate black schools or alter their identity." But though it urged the maintenance and expansion of private black institutions, the NAACP did not believe that black colleges "should . . . [get] significant support from public funds" because such support placed these schools under white control. Its conclusion that blacks would receive equity only when "state authorities cannot single out black people in separate facilities" led to an inescapable recommendation for merging the black and white schools despite the acknowledged "difficulties and sacrifices." In making that choice, the NAACP approvingly quoted W. E. B. Du Bois' comment that the *Brown* decision presented blacks with a "cruel dilemma." "They must eventually surrender race solidarity and the idea of American Negro culture," Du Bois asserted, "to the concept of world humanity, above race and nation." [88]

Similarly, the reapportionment controversy that wracked the city council in the 1970s led the NAACP to articulate a vision that was rejected by the more Americanized segments of the community, both black and white. When, following the 1970 census, the all-white New Orleans city council proposed a reapportionment plan that was an obvious racial gerrymander, it triggered four years of litigation. Suggested compromises included the expansion of the seven-member council to nine, or even eleven, in efforts to satisfy sitting councilmen and guarantee a certain number of new "black" seats. Both the *Louisiana Weekly* and the black political organizations championed expansion as the best "method of getting two or three blacks on the City Council," but the NAACP rejected that course. Allison Chapital voiced the association's determination not to "support any plan merely to have one or two hand-picked machine politician blacks placed on the Council." The NAACP proposed instead the retention of the existing system that

88. "Report of the Louisiana NAACP Special Committee on Desegregation of Public-Supported Higher Education in Louisiana" (Mimeo, November 12, 1972, in author's possession).

elected five councilmen from districts and two at large and outlined what it perceived to be an equitable redrawing of the district boundaries. Under the NAACP proposal there would be one district with a black voting majority, the possibility of two others (if blacks worked at registration—here was an opportunity, not a guarantee), and the need, in any case, to build multiracial coalitions in a small number of large districts. It never had a chance. Councilman Jimmy Moreau adopted the format of the NAACP plan, altered its substance to minimize black influence, and successfully urged its acceptance on his colleagues. The Moreau Plan was eventually upheld by the U.S. Supreme Court in 1976.[89]

Given their differences, it was not surprising that the black political organizations greeted Morial's announced 1977 candidacy with less than overwhelming enthusiasm. And they certainly must have been taken aback by his willingness to risk a citywide race so soon after two other blacks—Robert Tucker and Sidney Cates—suffered crushing defeats in their races for the at-large seats in the special city council elections of 1976. For the political professionals and conventional thinkers, the time was not right and Morial was not their man. Still, he persisted, and in charting that course he presented the black organizations with a "cruel dilemma" of their own.

For SOUL, the decision was easy because it had already been made. In backing Nat Kiefer in his 1975 race for the state senate, SOUL had made one of its rare breaks with Moon Landrieu, evidently deciding that the waning influence of a lame-duck mayor presented fewer possibilities than did support for the heir apparent. SOUL also saw the advantage in having a white mayor. Landrieu, despite his record, still felt dependent on the black organizations to mobilize their communities on his behalf. He could not appeal over them or work around them the way Dutch Morial could. The result was that even though Landrieu was determined "not to replace white incompetents with black incompetents," his power to discipline his black allies—as was evident in the SSI case— was sharply circumscribed by their political leverage. He needed them— as, presumably, any white mayor would. SOUL's leaders, moreover, had learned valuable (and lucrative) lessons in provoking white anxiety and intimidating the leaders of the Family Health Foundation. Facing a black mayor—particularly one who refused to guarantee patronage as a

89. *Louisiana Weekly,* February 19, 26, March 18, September 16, October 21, 1972, March 17, April 28, 1973.

matter of principle—was another matter. Although some sense of ethnic difference still persisted (Sherman Copelin joked about needing a visa to get into the Seventh Ward), Morial represented, more than anything else, a threat to SOUL's interests. Indeed, in one of the rare instances of agreement between Morial and media critic Iris Kelso, both perceived that a Morial victory would mean that "there won't be any more black political leaders who can mau-mau the Mayor, claim to represent blacks, and walk off with all the rewards."[90]

COUP had additional considerations. There were long-standing personal rivalries, particularly between Morial and the Bradens, that grew out of their shared communal base, the old creole Seventh Ward. But their common base also made it difficult for COUP to oppose a "favorite son" who promised to become the city's first black mayor. Still, Sidney Barthelemy's ambitions and the fear that COUP's support for two blacks at the top of the ticket (Morial for mayor, Barthelemy for councilman-at-large) might appear to be an attempted black takeover (they were still worried about alienating whites) made Morial's endorsement anything but automatic. Finally, after debating three hours and taking five ballots, COUP issued a lukewarm endorsement for Morial. Patron-client ties were still very much in evidence as Nat Kiefer's allies, as well as those tied to the candidacy of Chep Morrison's son Toni, tried unsuccessfully to win approval for their sponsors. COUP president Monk Dupre sounded almost apologetic when it was all over: "We didn't want to be considered racist . . . and we wouldn't have endorsed Dutch just because he is black. But he is qualified."[91]

The jockeying for the black vote was completed when Moon Landrieu furnished campaign assistance and an endorsement for Toni Morrison. Once a member of the Young CCDA, Landrieu was now in a position to give Chep's son a boost. As the fourth major mayoral candidate, Joe DiRosa, made little pretense about pursuing black voters, Morial, Kiefer, and Morrison were left dueling over that turf.

Interestingly, Kiefer had not only pocketed SOUL's support but had that of the CCIVL, BOLD's Dorothy Mae Taylor and Jim Singleton, and, remarkably, the *Louisiana Weekly*. He had done his homework. Toni Morrison, moreover, had Landrieu's help in picking up A. L. Davis

90. *Figaro*, March 9, October 12, December 7, 1977.
91. Interview with Henry Braden III by Arnold R. Hirsch, June 29, 1987; *Figaro*, September 7, 1977.

and the OPPVL. And though Morial had COUP's less-than-ringing endorsement, it was clear to columnist Iris Kelso that "COUP doesn't really want Dutch Morial to be elected mayor." Despite running without the substantive or (with one exception) even the nominal support of the major black political interests, Morial led the field and picked up 58 percent of the black vote. The primary tally was all the more remarkable given the real fear that Morial might be unelectable in the runoff. Blacks still represented only a minority of registered voters, and many of those given to shrewd calculation undoubtedly tried to pick a white winner in preference to going down with a black loser. Morial surprised them all. His long years of service, his identification with the cause of civil rights, and his independence stood him in good stead. His unshakable black base emasculated the Kiefer and Morrison campaigns and pushed him into the runoff with Joe DiRosa.[92]

Even after his strong showing, Morial's candidacy hardly became a racial crusade for the professionals. COUP's reticence remained evident, and SOUL's Hubbard displayed his "pragmatism" by asserting that "politics is the art of the possible. I'm interested in backing somebody who can win." That political leaders who made a career out of promoting racial causes and the city's only black newspaper (the *Louisiana Weekly* issued no endorsement in the runoff) could still distance themselves from Morial's campaign against an opponent who railed at "junglebunnies" when given black voter registration figures was grave testimony to their differences and the tortured calculation of self-interest. But the elimination of Kiefer and Morrison also left those whites who were appalled at DiRosa's antiestablishment rhetoric (one columnist labled him the "bête blanc") and less than comfortable with his own ethnic heritage nowhere to go but to Morial—the candidate whose manners, polish, erudition, and intellectual attainments made him appear the "aristocrat" in this race. When it was over, Morial had piled up 97 percent of a 78 percent black turnout and nearly 20 percent of a 75 percent white turnout. It was enough to produce a 6,000-vote victory (out of 175,000 cast)—a tally similar to DiRosa's margin of victory over Morial in 1969.[93]

Morial's electoral strength had immediate ramifications for the major black political organizations. SOUL's close identification with

92. *Figaro*, October 5, 1977.
93. *Ibid.*, March 9, August 3, October 5, 19, November 9, 1977; *Louisiana Weekly*, November 19, 1977.

Kiefer left it particularly exposed. As the campaign heated up, SSI had finally proven enough of an embarrassment to Governor Edwards that he called a meeting of interested black leaders to declare "all political accounts at the Dome paid in full." He brought in the Hyatt Management Corporation to handle Dome affairs in the summer before the mayoral balloting and SSI maintained its presence only by reducing operating costs by $1 million and cutting its staff of two hundred in half. The Hyatt canceled the SSI contract within days of Kiefer's defeat. The timing suggests that it was the loss of SSI's patron that freed Hyatt from any remaining political constraints and rendered SSI vulnerable. The housecleaning began even before the runoff election.[94]

COUP was hit in an even more spectacular fashion. Less than six months after Morial took office, police conducted a raid on the New Orleans Regional Service Center, eventually rounding up some forty-three CETA employees, almost all of whom were COUP members or supporters. COUP officials Henry Braden, Sidney Barthelemy, and George ("Nick") Connor (who had some relatives picked up in the sweep) denounced the raid as politically motivated and part of a personal vendetta that revealed the new mayor's taste for revenge. Whatever private pleasure Morial derived from COUP's discomfiture, the attempt to write off the raid as evidence simply of personal pique was more self-serving than the raid itself.[95]

Morial and his new police chief, Jim Parsons, claimed that the raid was triggered by a series in the *States-Item* that illustrated how the CETA program had been "marked by nepotism" and abused by "bureaucratic and political mercenaries . . . [who] rip[ped]-off much of the funds for their own personal gain, and [left] the poor and unemployed worse off than before." For Morial (who was characterized as "rigidly honest" in an FBI report before his 1965 appointment as an assistant U.S. attorney) such freebooting was anathema, and he had already told his own staff that they had "better keep their hands clean." While his new director of manpower, Sandra Gunner, "laid down the law to the agencies that got jobs under the CETA . . . program," Parsons set up a special Integrity Unit to investigate white-collar crime and corruption in government. COUP was less the victim of a personal vendetta than of the loss of its former political protection and its own practices. Within a

94. *Louisiana Weekly,* June 25, October 15, 22, 1977.
95. New Orleans *Times-Picayune,* October 20, 1978; New Orleans *States-Item,* October 20, 1978; *Louisiana Weekly,* October 28, 1978.

year, the U.S. Conference of Mayors selected Morial's Office of Manpower and Economic Development as a national model because of its oversight of CETA operations. It was named the "most improved" and "best in the state" by the Department of Labor's regional Dallas office.[96]

This opening round of sparring led to eight years of virtual political war between Morial and COUP. More than occasionally manifested in bickering between the mayor and councilman Sidney Barthelemy, it was most spectacularly evident in COUP's outright opposition to Morial's reelection in 1982 and the mayor's subsequent successful effort to defeat Henry Braden and Nick Connor in their state legislative races the following year. Both sets of contests demonstrated Morial's appeal to the black electorate and the bankruptcy of a political organization whose influence, seemingly, did not reach beyond its shrinking patronage rolls. In the first instance, COUP backed a black challenger, state senator William Jefferson, who garnered 7 percent of the vote and actually received more support from whites than blacks. In the runoff, COUP endorsed Morial's white opponent, Ron Faucheux, and stood helplessly by as Morial swept black precincts. The success of Morial's retaliatory purge simply emphasized the point. Black voters indicated decisively where they stood in the Morial-COUP dispute.[97]

If SOUL's relations with the mayor lacked the personal rancor that fueled the Braden-Morial feud, there were still enough serious differences to lead SOUL to support William Jefferson's 1982 challenge. Jefferson's anemic standing in the polls, however, led the pragmatists in SOUL to bail out before election day and slink back to the Morial fold. Other than that abortive effort, SOUL devoted most of its energies during the Morial years to finding a safe electoral haven for Sherman Copelin. Indeed, SOUL's move back to Morial was a desperate effort to salvage Copelin's candidacy as a councilman. Still tainted by his connection to the FHF scandal, Copelin could not overcome an opponent who carried—and quoted—his damaging grand jury testimony. In the end, the outraged voters of District E elected a white who later would be driven from office under his own legal cloud in preference to a black who received immunity for his indiscretions.[98]

96. New Orleans *States-Item*, August 17, 18, 1978; *Figaro*, May 31, August 30, 1978; *Louisiana Weekly*, August 18, 1979.

97. *Gambit*, February 20, 1982; *Louisiana Weekly*, February 20, 27, March 6, 1982, October 29, November 19, 26, 1983.

98. *Gambit*, January 30, March 6, 1982.

It was Copelin's appointment as interim assessor for the Third Municipal District (Wards 7, 8, and 9) in 1984, however, and his race for election to that seat in his own right in early 1985 that highlighted his differences with Morial and demonstrated the cynicism with which the race issue could be raised. Copelin was appointed to the vacancy by the sitting Board of Assessors after a vigorous lobbying effort by Governor Edwards. He received Edwards' backing after "knifing" black challenger Israel Augustine in his race against Congresswoman Lindy Boggs, and that of assessor Connie Comiskey after promising SOUL's support in her own race against BOLD's Ken Carter. It was enough to overcome Morial's efforts on behalf of his chief administrative officer, Errol Williams, a "squeaky clean" candidate, who, according to political columnist Clancy DuBos, had professional credentials that were unmatched. When a Morial-endorsed Williams proceeded to challenge Copelin in the March, 1985, election, Copelin—conveniently forgetting how he had won that seat in the first place—attacked the mayor and his opponent for threatening "black unity." Haunted by his own past, and, perhaps, damaged by Edwards' indictment during the campaign, Copelin failed to make the runoff against the ultimately victorious Williams.[99]

Theoretically, a mayor who waged daily battle with the traditional black political organizations, cleaned up scandalous and wasteful public programs, and promoted professional excellence as opposed to sustaining politically connected incompetence should have received a warm welcome in the white community—particularly in the historically reform-oriented uptown neighborhoods. There was much else to recommend Morial to whites as well. He was a fiscal conservative who preached the gospel of self-reliance both to the city as he tried to cut its dependence on federal revenues and to young blacks out on the street looking for work. Indeed, after he had broken a police strike in his first year in office and joined with the more progressive elements of the business community to promote economic growth in the private sector, the *Wall Street Journal* referred to him as a "black Calvin Coolidge."[100]

But it was particularly his views on race and his philosophical predisposition to emphasize merit and competence over color that should have put the white community's fears of a black mayor to rest. In a speech before the Metropolitan Area Committee shortly after his election, Morial clearly articulated a twentieth-century variant of the old

99. *Ibid.*, October 6, 1984, January 12, March 16, 23, April 6, May 11, 1985.
100. *Wall Street Journal*, May 1, 1979.

radical creole abhorrence of caste. "I have no intention of politicalizing the incoming administration," he assured his listeners, "on the narrow grounds of reverse prejudice. It does not serve this city, or the cause of black people, to tolerate prejudice or discrimination in any form. It is the daily struggle of minorities. We will never be its exponent. We will always be its enemy." Once in office, he acted on that premise. It was, in fact, his firing of the black organizations' political appointees and their replacement by blacks and whites from management, the professions, and academia that caught the eye of the *Wall Street Journal*.[101]

Morial's racial views, however, had a corollary that the white community found more difficult to accept. If blacks could not expect a free ride in his administration, the new mayor had even less tolerance for entrenched bastions of white privilege and power. An equitable, "color-blind" society had to be truly "opened up," and whites would have to grant access, not to the back of the patronage bus, where blacks could be collectively gathered in a handful of designated "black" enterprises, but to everything, across the board. Morial was not turning down the racial "heat" by stressing merit; he was turning it up by asking whites to deliver on their professed convictions. Could they "cease to be white" as Garrison, Phillips, and Lincoln did in Desdunes' forgotten memory? The answer came in the deadly drone of election data. Morial received a respectable 20 percent of the white vote in 1977 but slipped to perhaps 13 or 14 percent in his successful 1982 reelection campaign, and that total was cut in half again when he failed to change the city charter to permit more than two terms. By the end of his administration the mayor was almost totally estranged from all but a relative handful of white New Orleanians.

The mayor's unparalleled popularity among blacks, his declining standing among whites, and the subsequent racial polarization of New Orleans' electorate stemmed not simply from Morial's demands for an open city. First, whereas Moon Landrieu was able to carve new "black" opportunities out of greatly expanded federal and state assistance, Morial sought to open *every* door to potential black access in a time of budgetary stringency. Virtually coinciding with the "Reagan revolution," Morial's administration tried to do more with less. Considering the political heat turned on a popular Landrieu when he tried to toss some new "plums" (such as the SSI contract) to black supporters, it was inevi-

101. *Ibid.*; *Figaro*, January 25, 1978.

table that Morial's attempts to cut into existing white business even as local budgets were being slashed would produce cries of outrage.

Second, there was the matter of style. It was not just what Morial did but the way he did it that infuriated many whites and captivated blacks. Morial's own distinctive history, achievements, and competence provided him with a confidence and assertiveness that, in the context of race relations in New Orleans, whites often read as arrogance. It was a label hung on the mayor during the campaign, and it dogged him throughout his administration. His constitutionally short fuse and absolute refusal to be either awed or intimidated by the pillars of the white community when he became engaged in unseemly controversies made him vulnerable to the charges of political adversaries who found it more convenient to point to personality than self-interest as the fundamental cause of confrontation.

An incident that occurred in the 1977 campaign is illustrative. At a joint appearance with Toni Morrison in Corpus Christi Church, the spiritual center of the Seventh Ward, Morial savaged his opponent after the memory of Chep Morrison was invoked to appeal to black voters. According to one reporter, Morial "completely [blew] his cool and [took] off after Toni Morrison with a vengeance," excoriating "his Daddy's record" and turning on a black Morrison supporter with the epithet "Uncle Tom." Morrison responded calmly by talking about how his father taught proper "manners." The reporter, obviously stunned by Morial's outburst, left the meeting concluding that "this is one audience . . . Morrison wooed and won." Yet the returns from the Seventh Ward told another story. Morial obviously knew his audience far better than did either Morrison or the press. He gave voice to a community that was heartened, not appalled, by his actions.[102]

Finally, Morial's concept of an "open" New Orleans included a redefinition of the mayor's role that was sharply at odds with practices that had been traditional for at least a century. In asserting a primary role in urban governance for the city's democratically elected chief executive, Morial's race—or at least the public's fascination with it— obscured the real dynamics of a fundamental political challenge to the social and economic oligarchy that dominated public affairs not from any elected posts but from perches of social privilege and seats on the "independent" agencies and commissions, such as the Sewerage and

102. *Figaro*, October 5, 1977.

Water Board, Dock Board, and Board of Liquidation, City Debt, that controlled key city functions. Indeed, in his speech before the Metropolitan Area Committee, Morial told what was coming. He made pointed reference to Tulane University political scientist Charles Chai's 1971 study "Who Rules New Orleans?" and informed the committee that he was "astounded" that the mayor was not included among the list of "influentials" compiled after discussions with community leaders. It was inconceivable to him that "a majority of the people [consulted] failed to even mention the mayor as a man essential to the communal equation." He added diplomatically that he "would like to think that this perception has changed." What he meant, of course, was that it would be changed. No longer of that class, nor willing to serve its narrow ends, a democratically responsive, independent chief executive represented a real threat to the traditional elite's interests; it was a challenge that would have provoked a political firestorm for any mayor—black or white—who dared to stake out such a position.[103]

Ultimately, those blacks and whites who were alienated by the mayor tried to pigeonhole him by invoking America's racial dualism in ways that revealed little besides their own race-bound predilections. Black critic Tom Dent, for example, denounced Morial's "isolation" from black political organizations, attacked "Creoles" generically as those who "suffered from confusions and indecision about racial identity" (this was undoubtedly a reference to the fully acculturated creoles who, enamored with standards of color, extolled their "whiteness" in the age of Jim Crow and often rushed to "blackness" in the civil rights era—in either case, it was Dent who was confused in trying to attach that tendency, however indirectly, to Morial), and asserted that Morial's "prime distinction" was that he was a black mayor who did "not act like a black man." Others echoed the charge, claiming that he adhered to a "Superblack" theory that rewarded only overqualified blacks and that he retained too many white advisers and appointees.[104]

Such criticism highlighted the historical "trick bag" that enveloped Morial. If his battle was to transcend racial barriers, his political success rode the crest of an unprecedented wave of racial consciousness and solidarity. As a pragmatic politician, Morial exploited racial issues with considerable skill, wringing every ounce of electoral advantage that

103. Charles Y. W. Chai, "Who Rules New Orleans?" *Louisiana Business Survey*, II (October, 1971), 2–7; *Figaro*, January 25, 1978.
104. Dent, "New Orleans Versus Atlanta"; *Figaro*, November 16, 1977.

could be had from them and producing a certain incongruity between ends and means. Morial's very success was dependent on a historical phenomenon that denied and undercut his vision; having ridden a racial surge into office, he could not move the city beyond such confining conceptualizations—he was its prisoner as well as its beneficiary. Not all in the black community shared his vision, and their differences became more apparent once the candidate became the mayor. Some who accepted and inverted the American racial order displayed a sense of betrayal when they applied their own color-based standards of achievement to the Morial administration. If the mayor personally retained the overwhelming loyalty of the vast majority of black voters, that dissonance may still explain why no larger movement appeared to sustain the ideals he brought to city hall. The notion of a caste-free society succumbed to the overpowering presence of a segmented, highly race-conscious social order. Creole radicalism had no place in the American city.

White columnist Iris Kelso similarly displayed her own acceptance of the prevailing racial dualism when she asserted that "Dutch Morial's problem is that he's too white for the blacks, and too black for the whites." Her analysis was couched in stark racial terms, and she clearly had no idea how Morial fit such a scheme. Unable to shake her color-bound mind-set, she had no way to take the measure of a man who could not be held simply to racially based standards of appearance or political conduct. Nor could she conceive of any other paradigm.[105]

The mayor's good friend and president of Xavier University, Norman Francis, also noted Morial's racial marginality, but did understand him. "He's been white in a black man's world and black in a white man's world," according to Francis. To be recognized for his abilities, he has had to "constantly . . . break through the color barrier." Indeed, it was the desire to obliterate, not merely manipulate, that barrier that drove Morial. And it was his longing for acceptance on the basis of his abilities alone that led him to express anguish at his declining white support despite his best efforts to be mayor for "all the people."[106]

The struggle to succeed Dutch Morial was an intrablack affair that saw COUP's Sidney Barthelemy defeat William Jefferson, a Protestant north Louisianian. Campaigning as the candidate who could unite the city and overcome the "divisiveness" of the Morial years, Barthelemy

105. *Figaro*, March 9, 1977.
106. New York *Times*, November 14, 1977.

offered peace and a smile. He became New Orleans' second black mayor, but he was catapulted to office on the back of a nearly monolithic white voting bloc. Carrying barely more than a quarter of the black vote, Barthelemy swept 85 percent of the whites. He had turned the biracial coalition of Moon Landrieu and Dutch Morial inside out. Where the previous mayors combined a liberal white fragment with overwhelming black backing, joining the most progressive elements of both races, Barthelemy blended the most conservative segments of each, grafting a slender layer of black support onto a massive white base. White New Orleans had found itself a black mayor.

A final irony occurred after Sherman Copelin, stymied in his efforts to become a councilman and an assessor, found the lower Ninth Ward's 90 percent black Ninety-ninth Legislative District congenial enough to send him to the state House of Representatives in 1986. Within a year, *Times-Picayune* columnist Allan Katz praised Copelin as "one of the most effective members of the legislature" and noted that "key elements of the white establishment that once scorned him now value Copelin and speak of how useful he is in Baton Rouge." It was a remarkable turnaround. In an earlier, troubled time, SOUL colleague Don Hubbard had reveled in the fevered opposition he and Copelin aroused in the *Times-Picayune.* "The black community knows who the *Times-Picayune* is; they know what that paper represents," Hubbard boasted. "When they start to pat us on the back, then our people will know we've sold out to the establishment." Indeed. It was no accident that the white community found itself propping up the weakest and most venal black leaders. They offered no threat to the status quo.[107]

What white New Orleanians could not tolerate was the "divisive," "abrasive," and independent Dutch Morial. Seemingly before it began, black politics in New Orleans had met its Thermidor; but by 1986 any allusion to the French Revolution would have seemed out of place. In the end, Morial's significance was not simply that he was New Orleans' first black mayor but that he was probably the last of the radical creoles.

The Americanization of New Orleans, including the imposition of an unwavering racial dualism, was now virtually complete. If the white creoles, overwhelmed by demography and history, fiercely seized their "whiteness" at the dawn of the Jim Crow era, the struggle to lift that veil nearly one hundred years later did much to submerge what remained of

107. New Orleans *Times-Picayune,* August 23, 1987; Boulard, "Power Brokers," 51.

a stubbornly persistent sense of ethnic difference in the black community and compelled abandonment of even unconscious patterns of thought and behavior that had been nourished under different circumstances. The ultimate irony was that the defeat of segregation was accomplished only by an explicitly racial counterattack, an onslaught that killed Jim Crow but, when the dust had settled, left only "blacks" and "whites" facing each other across a daunting racial divide. The peculiar history of the creoles may have made them key agents in that struggle, but it also rendered them anachronistic. By the late 1980s, there were few willing to question—much less challenge—the "fanaticism of caste."

Contributors

CARYN COSSÉ BELL is completing a study of the antebellum Franco-African protest tradition in New Orleans for her Ph.D. dissertation at Tulane University.

GWENDOLYN MIDLO HALL is a native of New Orleans who was active in the civil rights movement there between 1945 and 1949. She has published numerous articles about the contemporary African-American movement in the United States and two books: *Social Control in Slave Plantation Societies: A Comparison of St. Domingue and Cuba* and *Africans in Colonial Louisiana: The Development of Afro-Creole Culture in the Eighteenth Century*. She is consulting professor of history at the University of New Orleans and associate professor of history at Rutgers University.

ARNOLD R. HIRSCH is professor of history and urban affairs at the University of New Orleans. He is the author of *Making the Second Ghetto: Race and Housing in Chicago, 1940–1960* as well as several articles on race and politics in urban America.

JERAH JOHNSON, professor of history at the University of New Orleans, has brought his training in early modern European history to bear on the Old World colonial experience in the Americas. His works include *The Age of Recovery* in the Cornell Series, *Africa and the West* in the Berkshire Series, and several articles on colonial Louisiana.

PAUL F. LACHANCE is associate professor of history at the University of Ottawa. Among other articles, he has published the prize-winning essay "The 1809 Immigration of Saint Domingue Refugees to New Orleans: Reception, Integration, and Impact," *Louisiana History,* XXIX (1988), 109–41.

JOSEPH LOGSDON is professor of history and urban affairs at the University of New Orleans and the author of several books. He has written *Horace White: Nineteenth Century Liberal,* coedited the narrative of Solomon Northup, *Twelve Years a Slave,* and coauthored *Crescent City Schools: Public Education in New Orleans, 1841–1991.*

JOSEPH G. TREGLE, JR., professor of history emeritus at the University of New Orleans, is the recognized expert on Louisiana during the Age of Jackson. Of his many contributions, the best known is his 1952 *Journal of Southern History* article "Early New Orleans Society: A Reappraisal."

Index